Routledge Revivals

Orangeism in Ireland and Britain

The Orange Lodges, originally a powerful agency for the defence of loyalist and protestant interest in Ireland, have flourished as fraternal societies in the British Army in nearly every part of the English-speaking world. Although founded by Irish protestant peasants, they soon attracted sections of the upper and middle classes who, at times, found Orangemen useful politically, but embarrassing and difficult to control. This study, originally published in 1966, deals with the founding of the movement in County Armagh just prior to the rebellion of 1798, and traces its history through the first forty years of its existence.

Orangeism in Ireland and Britain
1795-1836

Hereward Senior

First published in 1966 by Routledge & Kegan Paul Ltd.

This edition first published in 2024 by Routledge
4 Park Square, Milton Park, Abingdon, Oxon, OX14 4RN
and by Routledge
605 Third Avenue, New York, NY 10158.

Routledge is an imprint of the Taylor & Francis Group, an informa business

© 1966 Hereward Senior

The right of Hereward Senior to be identified as the author of this work has been asserted by him in accordance with sections 77 and 78 of the Copyright, Designs and Patents Act 1988.

All rights reserved. No part of this book may be reprinted or reproduced or utilised in any form or by any electronic, mechanical, or other means, now known or hereafter invented, including photocopying and recording, or in any information storage or retrieval system, without permission in writing from the publishers.

ISBN 13: 978-1-032-87094-6 (hbk)
ISBN 13: 978-1-003-53093-0 (ebk)
ISBN 13: 978-1-032-87101-1 (pbk)
Book DOI 10.4324/9781003530930

ORANGEISM IN IRELAND AND BRITAIN
1795–1836

by

HEREWARD SENIOR

LONDON: Routledge & Kegan Paul

1966

*First published 1966
in Great Britain by
Routledge and Kegan Paul Ltd
and in Canada by
The Ryerson Press*

*Printed in Great Britain by
Hazell Watson & Viney Ltd
Aylesbury, Bucks*

© *Hereward Senior 1966*

*No part of this book may be reproduced
in any form without permission from
the publisher, except for the quotation
of brief passages in criticism*

PREFACE

THE FIRST FORTY YEARS of the Orange movement form a convenient unit of study because of the dissolution of the grand lodge in 1836. The history of Orangeism during this period is of interest from three points of view: as a study in counter-revolution, involving the relations of a loyalist movement to the government it supported; as an episode in catholic-protestant relations in Ireland; and as a study of the Irish and British background of a movement which was to establish firm roots in Australia and Canada and spread to every part of the English-speaking world.

Much of Orange history is too obscure to be investigated by historians whose primary object is to consider other aspects of Irish or British history. The Orangemen are often mentioned, but seldom explained. Published studies directly concerned with Orangeism are, as a rule, the work of Orange sympathizers or their enemies. Although much useful material has been presented by such writers, their immediate concern with controversy leads them to devote most of their attention to the assertion or denial of charges against the movement, rather than to an examination of its nature and influence.

This study was prepared originally as a thesis for McGill University, and the sources upon which it is based are discussed in the introduction to the bibliography. I wish to acknowledge the assistance and encouragement given me by my tutor, Professor W. Stanford Reid of McGill University, and to thank Mr Brian MacGiolla Choille and the staff of the Public Record Office, Dublin, Miss M. Johnston and her assistants at the Belfast Public Record Office, Mr George Paterson of the Armagh Museum, and Mr J. W. Vitty of the Linen Hall Library,

Preface

Belfast, for all the assistance they have given me. I would also like to thank Mr James Jackson of Loughall, the owner of the building in which the Orange lodges were founded in 1795, who gave me useful information concerning the early history of Orangeism. I am also indebted to members of the library staff of Memorial University of Newfoundland and to Mrs Mary Campbell of the Royal Roads Library staff. To Professor T. W. Moody, of Trinity College, Dublin, I am deeply indebted for his reading and criticism of the manuscript, and to Professor J. C. Beckett, of Queen's University, Belfast, I wish to acknowledge my gratitude for his valuable comments. This work has been published with the help of a grant from the Social Science Research Council, using funds provided by the Canada Council. I wish to express my appreciation to both councils for their generous aid. Above all, I wish to acknowledge my indebtedness to my wife.

HEREWARD SENIOR

McGill University

CONTENTS

PREFACE	page v
ABBREVIATIONS	ix
I THE BACKGROUND AND ORIGIN OF THE ORANGE LODGES	1
II THE GROWTH OF ORANGEISM AMONGST THE PEASANTRY, 1795–6	22
1. The Castle and its enemies	22
2. The Armagh outrages	29
3. The Dungannon plan	41
4. The United Irish movement spreads to the south	47
III GENTRY SUPPORT OF ORANGEISM, 1796–7	51
1. United Irish military strength	51
2. Crown forces	53
3. The raising of the yeomanry, 1796–7	58
4. The disarming of Ulster, 1797	64
5. Military incidents	71
6. Dublin lodge supported by protestant party	76
IV THE REBELLION OF 1798	81
1. The Orange bogey	81
2. The appointment of Abercromby	84
3. Grand lodge efforts to control the Orangemen	90
4. The suppression of the rebellion	95
5. The Cornwallis administration	108

Contents

V UNION WITH GREAT BRITAIN, 1799–1801   page 118

VI THE CONSOLIDATION OF THE ORANGE MOVEMENT, 1800–3   138

VII BRITISH ORANGE LODGES, 1798–1822   151

VIII ORANGEISM IN IRELAND, 1803–25   177
    1. The war years   177
    2. The ebb-tide of Orangeism   194
    3. The Wellesley administration   197
    4. O'Connell and the Catholic Association   204

IX ORANGE RESISTANCE TO CATHOLIC EMANCIPATION, 1825–9   216

X REPEAL, PARLIAMENTARY REFORM, AND THE TITHE WAR, 1830–4   235

XI ORANGE CONSPIRACY, 1831–6   254

XII IN RETROSPECT   274

BIBLIOGRAPHY   285

APPENDICES
   A Rules of the Orange Society, 1798   298
   B Army regiments holding Orange warrants in 1830   302
   C Orange districts and membership in Great Britain in 1830   304

INDEX   306

ABBREVIATIONS

A.G.	*Armagh Guardian.*
A.M.	Armagh Museum.
B.M., Add. MSS	British Museum, Additional Manuscripts.
B.N.L.	*Belfast News-Letter.*
Cobbett	*Cobbett's parliamentary debates.*
D.E.P.	*Dublin Evening Post.*
D.N.B.	*Dictionary of national biography.*
F.D.J.	*Faulkner's Dublin Journal.*
F.J.	*Freeman's Journal.*
Hansard	*Hansard's parliamentary debates.*
Hansard 2	*Hansard's parliamentary debates,* new series.
Hansard 3	*Hansard's parliamentary debates,* third series.
H.O.	Home Office.
N.D.	No date.
N.L.I.	National Library of Ireland.
N.S.	*Northern Star.*
Orange Conspiracy	'Orange Conspiracy' in *London and Westminster Review,* iii–xxv (Jan.–Apr. 1836).
P.R.	*The parliamentary register or the history of the proceedings and debates of the house of commons of Ireland.*
P.R.O.	Public Record Office of England.
P.R.O.I.	Public Record Office of Ireland.
P.R.O.N.I.	Public Record Office of Northern Ireland.

Abbreviations

Rep. on Orange lodges I, H.C. 1835 [377], xv	Report from the select committee appointed to enquire into the nature, character, extent and tendency of Orange lodges, associations or societies in Ireland, H.C. 1835 [377], xv.
Rep. on Orange lodges II, H.C. 1835 [475], xvi	Second report from the select committee appointed to enquire into the nature, character, extent and tendency of Orange lodges, associations or societies in Ireland, H.C. 1835 [475], xvi.
Rep. on Orange lodges III, H.C. 1835 [476], xvi	Third report from the select committee appointed to enquire into the nature, character, extent and tendency of Orange lodges, associations or societies in Ireland, H.C. 1835 [476], xvi.
Rep. on Orange lodges IV, H.C. 1835 [605], xvii	Fourth report from the select committee appointed to enquire into the origin, nature, extent and tendency of the Orange institutions in Great Britain and the colonies, H.C. 1835 [605], xvii.
R.I.A.	Royal Irish Academy.
T.C.D.	Trinity College, Dublin.
W.O.	War Office.

I

THE BACKGROUND AND ORIGIN OF THE ORANGE LODGES

THE FOUNDING OF THE ORANGE ORDER in 1795[1] marked a revival of a tradition which had all but died in the 'enlightened' atmosphere of the eighteenth century. To many Irish contemporaries it appeared as a movement of backward peasants against the spirit of the times and hence doomed. Its early vitality and subsequent growth surprised and puzzled radicals, liberals and moderate conservatives, who, at times, sought to explain the movement as a conspiracy organized by reaction-

[1] For various accounts of the founding of the Orange Order see Cooke to ——, 21 Sept. 1795, Dalrymple to ——, 23 Sept. 1795, and Dalrymple to Pelham, 24 Sept. 1795 (B.M., Add. MS 33101); Jephson to Charlemont, 9 Oct. 1795 (*Charlemont MSS*, ii. 265–6); *B.N.L.*, 25 Sept. 1795; *N.S.*, 24 Sept. 1795; *F.J.*, 29 Sept. 1795; *D.E.P.*, 29 Sept. 1795; A.M., Blacker MS i. 220–36; *Rep. on Orange lodges III*, H.C. 1835 [476], xvi. 213–14; O.R. Gowan, *Orangeism: its origin and history*, pp. 137–9; William Verner, *The battle of the Diamond*, pp. 5–8; M.P., *History of Orangeism*, pp. 18–20; R.I.A., Stowe MS, pp. 38–9; Richard Musgrave, *Memoirs of the different rebellions in Ireland*, pp. 79–82; Francis Plowden, *History of Ireland from its invasion under Henry II; to its union with Great Britain*, ii. 539; W. J. MacNeven, *Pieces of Irish history*, pp. 114–15; M. de Latocnaye, *A Frenchman's walk through Ireland 1796–7*, pp. 258–68; W. E. H. Lecky, *History of Ireland in the eighteenth century*, iii. 421–6; R. M. Sibbett, *Orangeism in Ireland and throughout the empire*, i. 230–4; H. W. Cleary, *History of the Orange society*, p. 21.

aries in high places. Orangeism was less a puzzle to those familiar with the protestant peasantry of the border counties of Ulster where long-standing feuds and economic rivalries had kept denominational strife alive among the lower classes and consequently made the poorer protestants sensitive to any rise in the status of catholics. The Orange tradition, which gave a kind of moral sanction to the subjugation of catholics, had, therefore, a special attraction to the protestant peasantry in this part of Ulster.

This tradition had its origin in the campaign of 1690 when the forces of William of Orange defeated King James's troops and secured protestant supremacy in Ireland. The colour orange was adopted as a symbol of Irish protestant patriotism that became associated with memories not only of King William's victories but also with the earlier struggles of the 'protestant colony', particularly during the catholic rising of 1641. Throughout the generation following the campaign of 1690, the Orange tradition took root among Irish protestants. The anniversary of the battle of the Boyne, 12 July (1 July old style), was celebrated each year, and a number of clubs were founded to keep alive a spirit of militant protestantism.

As a rule these early Orange clubs bore names suggesting some incident in the 1690 campaign. There were the Apprentice Boys, the Boyne Men, the Glorious Order of the Boyne, the Aldermen of Skinner's Alley, and the Royal Boyne Society. The latter was, at the outset, open only to the protestant gentry, but usually these societies tended to mix all classes of protestants. In one of them at least, according to Sir Jonah Barrington, 'generals and wig-makers, king's counsel and hackney clerks, all mingled without distinction'.[2] The charter oath of the Aldermen of Skinner's Alley indicates the spirit of these early Orange clubs. It ran:

> To the glorious, pious, and immortal memory of the great and good King William, not forgetting Oliver Cromwell, who assisted in redeeming us from popery, slavery, arbitrary power, brass-money, and wooden shoes. May we never want a Williamite to kick the ... of a Jacobite! and a ... for the Bishop of Cork! And he that won't drink this, whether he be priest, bishop, deacon, bellows-blower, grave-digger, or any other of the fraternity of the

[2] Jonah Barrington, *Personal sketches of his own times*, p. 156.

clergy; may a north wind blow him to the south, and a west wind to the east! May he have a dark night, a lee shore, a rank storm, and a leaky vessel, to carry him over the river Styx! May the dog Cerberus make a meal of his r... p, and Pluto a snuff-box of his skull, and may the devil jump down his throat with a red hot harrow, with every pin tear out a gut, and blow him with a clean carcase to hell! Amen.[3]

Similar societies existed among officers of the British army, tolerated possibly as a counter-weight to Jacobite influence. One of these, The Loyal Order of the Orange and Blew,[4] was formed in the Fourth Regiment of Foot, sometimes known as King William's Regiment. It existed as an exclusive officers' club unconnected with Irish affairs until well into the nineteenth century.[5] Prince William Henry was made superior of the order in 1787 and the prince of Wales and duke of York became members the following year, but this nominal membership had no significance in Irish politics. Indeed, Orange historians have not claimed that this exclusive officers' club was associated with the founding of their order in 1795.[6] The two organizations were easily confused, however, and the existence of the Orange and Blew lent plausibility to the charge that the Irish Orange Order was founded by men in high places. Confusion also arose from the fact that many members of the early Orange societies were masons. One Belfast masonic lodge further complicated matters by adopting the name Orange Lodge,[7] but before 1795 the word Orange was the general property of Irish protestants and indicated only a formal protestant patriotism. Irish masons were found in all political factions but were, in general, inclined to be critical of the penal code imposed on catholics and were not enthusiastic Orange patriots.

The Orange tradition was associated closely with the main-

[3] Ibid., pp. 157-8.

[4] J. H. Leslie, 'The Loyal and Friendly Society of the Orange and the Blew', in *Journal of the Society of Army Historical Research*, vi. 199-214 (Oct. 1927).

[5] *Hansard 3*, xxx. 288; Duke of Cumberland to J. W. Patten, 5 Aug. 1835 (*Rep. on Orange lodges III*, H.C. 1835 [475], xvi. 4).

[6] Gowan, *Orangeism*, pp. 44-53, 152-53; Sibbett, *Orangeism*, ii. 114, 136-39; Edward Rogers, *The revolution of 1688 and a history of the Orange Association of England and Ireland*, p.6.

[7] C. L. Falkiner, *Studies in Irish history and biography*, p. 2; see also *B.N.L.*, 17 July 1797.

tenance of what was called the 'protestant ascendancy'. In its extreme interpretation this meant the full enforcement of the penal code imposed on catholics in the years that followed their defeat in 1690. The code excluded them from political office, the liberal professions, and the more profitable economic activities, as well as prohibiting their possession of firearms. In its moderate interpretation, catholics would merely be excluded from parliament and high political and military office. By the last quarter of the eighteenth century most upper and middle class protestants had come to take the subordination of catholics for granted, and were inclined toward the more moderate view of the ascendancy. Adherence to the Orange tradition continued, but observance of its holidays became a formality, and the early Orange societies, where they survived, evolved into social clubs. Yet this growing indifference to the catholic question could hardly be shared by the 'lower orders' of protestants who, as a result of the penal code, had become a kind of plebeian aristocracy. Latent fears of catholic domination could be aroused easily among them in any part of Ulster, but in the border districts animosities were kept alive by a more or less continuous series of petty incidents.

At the root of these animosities was the fact that nearly everywhere in Ireland the population on the land was greater than the existing system of agriculture could support. This chronic land hunger was aggravated by a form of land-holding that discouraged improvement. The land was often rented by a middle-man from an absentee landlord; then sublet periodically, in small holdings, to the highest bidder without consideration for the former occupants. The only means the peasantry had of fighting this system was the oath-bound secret society. Such societies, once organized, could normally neutralize the power of the landlord-magistrates by intimidating witnesses and juries, and could penalize unpopular landlords by houghing and slashing their cattle in nightly raids. The earlier agrarian secret societies were usually regional and non-political in character.

Two such movements flourished in the sixties, the Oakboys or Hearts of Oak in Ulster[8] and the Whiteboys in Munster. The

[8] For various accounts of the Oakboys see *Charlemont MSS*, i. 137–43; Groves documents, in P.R.O.N.I., T 808/15264(8), no. 668, bundle 76; *F.D.J.*, 2 Aug. 1763; *Rep. on Orange lodges I*, H.C. 1835 [377], xv. 32.

latter, Edmund Burke maintained, was organized by a disaffected protestant attorney called Fant, and at first included poor protestant farmers in its ranks.[9] In spite of accusations by local landlords, there is no evidence the Whiteboys were influenced by papal, Jacobite or French agents.[10] They were actively opposed by catholic landlords and denounced by catholic clergy. At least one Whiteboy appeal suggested their aims were purely economic. It read, 'Ye will give me leave to inform ye that I declare myself as true and faithful a subject as any in Ireland, both to king and government ... In England, when the tenant's lease is expired no man will dare cant him or his children off their farm'.[11] In Ireland, however, quarrels, no matter what their origin, tended to divide along religious lines. The sight of large numbers of armed Whiteboys alarmed all classes of protestants. Moreover, when landlords raised bands to subdue the Whiteboys, they normally armed their protestant retainers, thus giving the measures taken against the Whiteboys something of the character of a religious war.

In Ulster the protestant Oakboys and their successors, the Hearts of Steel, although directed primarily against landlords,[12] were potential agencies of denominational strife. A Steelboy petition in the seventies read, 'We are all Protestants and Protestant Dissenters [Church of Ireland and Presbyterians] and bear unfeigned loyalty to his present majesty and the Hanoverian succession.....; we, who are all groaning under oppression, and have no other possible way of redress, are forced to join ourselves together to resist.....; some of us, refusing to pay the extravagant rent demanded by our landlords have been turned out, and our lands given to Papists, who will promise to pay any rent'.[13]

It is evident that any movement in or near Ulster which armed and organized catholic peasants would arouse against it this Steelboy element. Catholic and protestant agrarian rebels were likely to work at cross purposes and the obvious place

[9] Edmund Burke, *Correspondence*, i. 45.
[10] Arthur Young, *Tour in Ireland*, i. 81–2; *Charlemont MSS*, i. 20.
[11] Lecky, *Ire.*, ii. 28.
[12] For various accounts of the Steelboys see Macartney Letters, in P.R.O.N.I., DOD 572/2/53,96, 572/3/152, 572/7/19; Groves documents, in P.R.O.N.I., T 808/14910(19–21), nos 43, 331.
[13] J. A. Froude, *The English in Ireland*, ii. 121–2.

for them to clash was on the border of Ulster. Such a clash might have been delayed indefinitely or avoided had not the volunteer movement disturbed the balance of forces in eighteenth century Ireland. The volunteers were, in a sense, the progenitor of both the United Irishmen and the Orange movement. They were raised in 1778 by the gentry and various vested interests, and their services pressed upon a reluctant viceregal administration[14] as defence against the apparent threat of French invasion. By 1779 some 40,000 volunteers were under arms as uniformed and drilled part-time soldiers.[15] The volunteers, by lending support to the Irish parliamentary 'patriot party', which had found a brilliant leader in Grattan, effected what has been called the 'revolution of 1782'. The pressure of the volunteers during 1779–82 removed disabilities against Irish dissenters, freed Ireland from commercial restrictions, repealed legislation that subordinated the Irish parliament to Britain, but left the Irish executive under the control of Westminster and the status of catholics virtually unchanged.

After the volunteers failed to push through a second 'revolution'[16] which would have reformed the borough franchise in Ireland, most of the corps were dissolved. However, a minority of the volunteers, best personified by the radical Dublin shopkeeper Napper Tandy, decided to take up the cause of the catholics. Although a few catholics had been admitted to volunteer ranks,[17] the various corps remained armed protestants who often marched to Orange tunes and displayed Orange symbols. A proposal favourable to catholics had been rejected by the last volunteer convention in 1783,[18] and only in Dublin and Belfast was the radical minority influential.

The radicals kept their corps together as military-political clubs; they broke openly with the Orange tradition, and invited catholics to acquire military training within their ranks. The Belfast corps paraded to St Mary's Chapel Lane, then the only catholic church in the city,[19] and celebrated the 12 July 1784 by

[14] Buckingham to Weymouth, 24 May 1779 (Henry Grattan, *Memoirs*, i. 347–8).
[15] Thomas Macnevin, *History of the volunteers of 1782*, pp. 220–2.
[16] Pelham to Portland, 30 Nov. 1783 (B.M., Add. MS 33100); Westmorland to Pitt, 14 Jan. 1792 (P.R.O.I., Westmorland papers, Fane MSS 45).
[17] W. Drennan to W. Bruce, 24 June 1784 (P.R.O.N.I., DOD 553/29).
[18] *Charlemont MSS*, i. 124–5.   [19] A. Benn, *History of Belfast*, i. 634.

presenting Lord Charlemont, the titular head of the volunteers and governor of county Armagh, with an address favouring greater equality for catholics.[20] The volunteer invitation to take military training attracted some lower class catholics[21] and the urban poor generally. This was particularly alarming to protestants in the border areas who were already worried about the way in which catholics were acquiring the arms of disbanded volunteers. Moreover, vague hopes of some impending emancipation had been aroused among the catholics by a combination of factors including the work of the conservative Catholic Committee and the unrest that accompanied the volunteer episode. These hopes often reached the poorer protestants in the form of threats shouted in taverns and at cockfights, and added to their general uneasiness.

The large quantities of arms distributed among the population and interest in things military resulting from the volunteer movement gave an exaggerated importance to normally insignificant brawls. Fights between individuals easily led to the formation of bands and the presence of armed catholics in such bands was regarded by former Oakboys and Steelboys as a provocation. It was still illegal for catholics to acquire firearms, but there was no government agency interested or able to enforce this aspect of the penal code. As early as 1784 there were reports of efforts by protestants called Peep O'Day Boys at unofficial enforcement of the code by daybreak raids on the homes of catholics to search for arms.[22] The occasion for large scale outbreaks of such raids was the intervention of a catholic in a fight between two presbyterians at Markethill, county Armagh,[23] shortly before the Belfast volunteers presented their July 12 address to Lord Charlemont in 1784. The defeated presbyterian blamed the catholic for his defeat; he raised a band among Steelboy elements which took the name Nappach Fleet, and began raids of a Peep O'Day Boy type.

Meanwhile Charlemont replied to the volunteer address by

[20] Grattan, *Memoirs*, iii. 228.
[21] Drennan-Bruce letters in P.R.O.N.I., DOD 553/29.
[22] Evidence of W. Verner, *Rep. on Orange lodges I*, H.C. 1835 [377], xv. 6; Evidence of M. O'Sullivan, ibid., p. 34.
[23] Musgrave, *Memoirs*, p. 61; R.I.A., Stowe MS, p. 21; J. Bryne, *An impartial account of the late disturbances in county Armagh 1784-1791*, in *A.G.*, 8 Jan. 1926.

declaring his personal freedom from prejudice, but insisted that raising the catholic question would divide the ranks of the reformers.[24] He stated further that he did not approve the recruiting of catholics or anyone without suitable property qualifications, declaring such men to be 'strangers to moderation'.[25] Copies of his address were circulated by Peep O'Day Boys who attempted to interpret it as a sanction for their own actions.[26]

To protect catholics from the Nappach Fleet, a band, first headed by a dissenting minister, was organized and given the name Defenders.[27] This name was soon taken up by various catholic groups resisting Peep O'Day raids, and the Defenders were ultimately to evolve into a federated society from which the Ancient Order of Hibernians claims descent. The first Defenders were formed with the evident object of preventing the growth of denominational bands. They managed to impose an initial defeat on the Nappach Fleet and persuaded it to dismiss its Steelboy captains and to accept a catholic leader. However, this attempt to prevent subsequent clashes from involving the population at large in denominational warfare had little chance of success. The presence of armed catholics in bands, no matter what their leadership, asserted the right of catholics to carry firearms. This was unacceptable to the protestant peasantry and the Peep O'Day Boy elements were prepared to oppose it by force.

Underlying the fear of the catholic peasantry acquiring arms was the economic motive suggested in the Steelboy petition,[28] as the catholics, by bidding against the protestants for leases, threatened protestant living standards. Searches for arms soon became a pretext which disguised a terrorism designed to drive catholics out of Ulster. Raids were made the occasion for smashing furniture and cutting the webs of the looms of catholic weavers. A series of attacks on unarmed catholics at

[24] Grattan, *Memoirs*, iii. 229.
[25] R.I.A., Stowe MS, p. 18; Charlemont to Maxwell, 22 Feb. 1785, Charlemont to Haliday, 14 Mar. 1785 (*Charlemont MSS*, ii. 17–8).
[26] R.I.A., Stowe MS, p. 22.
[27] For various accounts of the rise of Defenderism see, Byrne, An impartial account, in *A.G.*, 8 Jan. 1926; Lecky, *Ire.*, iii. 212–21; Musgrave, *Memoirs*, pp. 61–78; Plowden, *Hist. Ire. to 1800*, iii. 185, 254.
[28] See above p. 5.

The Background and Origin of the Orange Lodges

Willis Grange, near Loughgall, seems to have been carried on for purely economic motives.[29] There, as elsewhere, the catholics responded by raising a Defender company. Under the pressure of such raids, the Defender organization grew in numbers and became more purely catholic in character.

Contemporaries assigned much of the responsibility for the growth of these disorders to the failure of the landlord-magistrates to take vigorous action.[30] Such a charge ignores the previous failure of the magistrates in the face of Whiteboys, Oakboys and Steelboys. The magistrate system was designed to deal with the occasional breach of the peace but was powerless against systematically organized violence. Yet the magistrates followed no consistent policy. A few, at least, shared the protestant peasant's view of the penal code, and, as they were unable to enforce it themselves, were inclined to tolerate Peep O'Day Boy raids. Others undertook to shield their tenants from justice even to the point of securing the remittance of sentence for convicted raiders,[31] and still others armed their catholic tenants for self-defence.[32] Such practices led raiders to gamble on the benevolent neutrality of the law, and convinced catholics they would secure no effective protection.

By late 1787 the lord lieutenant was sufficiently alarmed to send two troops of horse to Armagh to assist in restoring order in the areas most seriously affected—Nappach, Hamilton-Bawn, Portadown, Tanderagee, Newtown-Hamilton and Keady.[33] Numerous arrests were made but landlord influence and Defender pressure on witnesses and juries limited punishment to a few token convictions of Peep O'Day Boys and Defenders. Matters were further complicated the following year by a Defender boycott of protestants which the latter reciprocated.[34] The failure of the courts, the disruption of normal economic life, and the parades of large armed bands about the country drove many of the clergy and magistrates to the conclusion that the county should be declared in a state of riot.

[29] Byrne, *An impartial account*, p. 20.
[30] Campbell to Charlemont, 9 Feb. 1788, Haliday to Charlemont, 2 Apr. 1788 (*Charlemont MSS*, ii. 69, 74).
[31] Byrne, *An impartial account*, pp. 6–11, R.I.A., Stowe MS pp. 22–7.
[32] R.I.A., Stowe MS p. 26.
[33] *Charlemont MSS*, ii. 69; Byrne, *An impartial account*, pp. 29–33.
[34] Musgrave, *Memoirs*, p. 64; R.I.A., Stowe MS pp. 28–30.

The Background and Origin of the Orange Lodges

It was, perhaps, to forestall action along these lines that Charlemont decided to raise new volunteers to carry out police work.[35] Known Peep O'Day Boys were to be excluded, and recruits to be drawn from the steadier elements of the protestant population who could be counted on to act against all disturbers of the peace. Later Orangemen insisted that the Peep O'Day Boys were entirely presbyterian,[36] and it is certain that presbyterians were associated in the Nappach Fleet when the first clashes took place.[37] However, the raids were the work of informal gatherings of men whose religious affiliations were probably nominal.[38] As both churchmen and presbyterians had associated in the Hearts of Steel a generation before,[39] it seems likely they also co-operated in Peep O'Day raids.[40]

Charlemont's new volunteers were close to the established church, but presbyterians may have served in their ranks and it is difficult to see how Peep O'Day Boys could have been completely excluded.[41] Yet Charlemont's volunteers appear to have represented the more law-abiding elements among the protestants[42] who had little desire to be lured into denominational war by their own extremists. They were, however, strongly attached to the Orange tradition, and in undertaking to preserve law and order they were also maintaining an ascendancy of armed protestants. They insisted on parading with Orange insignia and to Orange tunes like the 'Boyne

---

[35] Musgrave, *Memoirs*, p. 64; Byrne, An impartial account, in *A.G.*, 8 Jan. 1926.

[36] Evidence of W. Verner, *Rep. on Orange lodges I*, H.C. 1835 [377], xv. 5–6; Evidence of M. O'Sullivan, ibid., p. 34; Musgrave, *Memoirs*, p. 62; Gowan, *Orangeism*, p. 135; Rogers, *Revolution of 1688*, p. 19.

[37] Byrne, An impartial account, in *A.G.*, 8 Jan. 1926.

[38] See advertisement of the presbyterian congregation of Drumbanagher, county Armagh, in *N.S.*, 18 Feb. 1796; see handbill of protestants of Loughgall and its vicinity, in *N.S.*, 4 Feb. 1796; *N.S.*, 31 Dec. 1795.

[39] See above p. 5.

[40] See handbill of protestant inhabitants of Manor Acton, county Armagh, in *Hibernian Journal*, Dublin, 30 Oct. 1795; Member of Catholic Committee to ——, 26 July 1792 (P.R.O.I., Rebellion papers 620/19/91); Letter addressed to the protestants of Great Britain and Ireland, 9 July 1795 (P.R.O.I., Rebellion papers 630/39/10); Campbell to Charlemont, 9 Feb. 1788 (*Charlemont MSS*, ii. 69); R.I.A., Stowe MS, p. 30.

[41] R.I.A., Stowe MS, p. 30.

[42] Byrne, An impartial account, in *A.G.*, 8 Jan. 1926.

Water' through catholic districts where the Defender spirit was strong. In so doing the volunteers claimed they were merely continuing the customs of the county, and the gentry could hardly suppress such parades lest they be considered enemies of the Orange tradition.

From the outset catholics accused the volunteers of being Peep O'Day Boys. An incident at Benburb involving volunteers resulted in the death of a catholic whose funeral became the occasion for a demonstration.[43] It was followed by a challenge sent by the Drumbee volunteers to the Defenders.[44] Charlemont tried to bring matters under control by publishing a manifesto against catholics assembling in arms and against all attempts to disarm them without legal authority.[45] A number of ugly incidents followed. In July 1789 Edward Hudson, a clergyman of the established church, wrote to Charlemont, 'Every opportunity of revenge is eagerly seized upon, and to what lengths it may at last be carried I tremble to think'.[46] Volunteers attacked a catholic procession in the spring of that year taking a garland from them and firing several shots.[47] Regulars were responsible for the destruction of the chalice and vestments of a parish priest at Newtown-Hamilton on Christmas day of 1791.[48]

The failure of the Defenders to secure legal redress for the last mentioned incident appears to have been one of the causes for the savage mutilation of a protestant schoolmaster named Barclay and his family in nearby Forkhill.[49] Barclay ran a school established under the will of a local landowner named Jackson who died in 1787. The will provided for the establishment of four schools for children of all denominations and also for the founding of a protestant colony on the wasteland of the Jackson estate. It was administered by Charlemont's corres-

[43] Campbell to Charlemont, 26 Nov. 1788, Prentice to Charlemont, 28 Nov. 1788 (*Charlemont MSS*, ii. 79).
[44] R.I.A., Stowe MS, p. 32.   [45] Ibid., p. 30.
[46] Hudson to Charlemont, 11 July 1789 (*Charlemont MSS*, ii. 103).
[47] Ibid.
[48] Byrne, An impartial account, in *A.G.*, 5 Feb. 1926; R.I.A., Stowe MS, p. 35.
[49] For various accounts of the Forkhill mutilation see, A.M., Blacker MSS, i. 223; Musgrave, *Memoirs*, pp. 68–73; Byrne, An impartial account, in *A.G.*, 5 Feb. 1926; R.I.A., Stowe MS, p. 37.

pondent, Hudson, who was active against Defenders.[50] The Forkhill catholics interpreted the will as a scheme to drive them from their lands, and after an unsuccessful attempt to kill Hudson, they drove out a few protestant settlers and attacked Barclay and his family. The Forkhill affair alarmed nearly all elements of the protestant population and presented a serious obstacle to those anxious to effect a reconciliation between the denominations. An incident at Lisnagade, where Defenders tried to ambush a volunteer parade on 12 July 1791,[51] appears to have ended the cycle of unrest which began in 1784. This established, in effect, an ascendancy of the protestant volunteers and made the founding of protestant secret societies to combat local Defenderism superfluous.[52]

The marching about the countryside of large bands of Peep O'Day Boys, volunteers and Defenders, which characterized this period, had about it something of the holiday spirit. Parties usually met by mutual agreement, and exchanged shots and insults outside of effective range until the magistrates arrived. The real evil was the nightly raids and acts of vengeance. Charlemont's new volunteers satisfied for the moment the needs of the protestants, but drove the catholics to extend and perfect their organization. In imitation of the masonic system, the Defenders formed a federated society with county grand masters, signs, rituals and passwords.[53] Like some of the Whiteboy groups, they included in their secret oath a declaration of loyalty to the king, no doubt as a means of protecting themselves against charges of treason. Yet it also reflected their non-ideological character and their hope that some impending measure of emancipation would put the law on their side. At least eighteen lodges of Defenders existed by 1789, and a year later Defenders extended as far south as Dublin county, with their main centres of strength in Tyrone, Armagh, Down, Monaghan, Cavan, Louth, and Meath. In counties where catholics were in the majority, the Defenders assumed the role of

[50] Memorial of Justice of Peace Norman Steele to Lord Lieutenant, n.d. (P.R.O.I., Rebellion papers 620/22/58).

[51] A.M., Blacker MSS, i. 220–1.

[52] Magistrate Richard Abbott to govt. 17 June 1795 (P.R.O.I., Rebellion papers 620/22/9).

[53] Report of secret committee, H.C., to enquire into causes of disorders, Feb. and June 1793 (P.R.O.I., Westmorland papers, Fane MSS, 87–8).

Peep O'Day Boys and began disarming poor protestants. However, in the more southern counties like Meath there was little point in denominational warfare, and the Defenders, in the manner of the Whiteboys, directed their attacks against landlords and clergy of the established church. By 1792 terrorism forced down rents in Meath and Cavan, and the tithe became increasingly difficult to collect.[54] This alarming growth of Defender activity in 1792[55] provoked strong reaction the following year. County committees were organized—in some cases including catholic gentry—to discover and punish offenders, while protestant landlords began to collect bands of retainers[56] similar to those used against the Whiteboys. These bands were to become Orangemen by 1797.

Matters were further complicated in 1793 by the outbreak of war with France. Under pressure from Pitt, the Irish government reluctantly extended the franchise to catholics and raised a largely catholic Irish militia. At the same time the remaining volunteer corps were dissolved. These measures, it was hoped, would remove the grievances of the lower classes of catholics and provide a loyal militia for the maintenance of order and defence. The results were disappointing and the militia, which was raised after some difficulty, soon had Defender cells planted in its ranks. The emancipation act proved a stimulus to Defender activity which between 1793 and 1795 grew to the proportion of a national problem.

These measures dealt a heavy blow to the position of the poorer protestants. Their volunteers were gone, the extension of the vote to the catholics made the protestants less valuable to the landlords, and finally, the militia with Defenders in its ranks seemed to deprive them of the protection of the state. Thus the poorer protestants were thrown back on their own resources to meet the ever bolder and better organized Defenders. Nearly all sections of the protestant peasantry were alarmed by the new power of the Defenders. The first steps towards giving protestant

---

[54] Westmorland to Dundas, 7 Jan., 18 Nov. 1792 (P.R.O.I., Westmorland papes, Fane MSS 41, 69).

[55] P.R.O.N.I., Downshire MSS 422, 426; P.R.O.I., Rebellion papers 620/19/91; P.R.O.I., Westmorland papers, Fane MSS 66, 68.

[56] Member of Catholic Committee to govt., 26 July 1792 (P.R.O.I., Rebellion papers 620/19/91).

bands a regular organization appear to have been taken by presbyterians. The tradition of the established church was opposed to independent action, and its poorer members perhaps hesitated to create a formal organization without the sanction of the gentry. The peasantry of the established church, however, were well armed and many had volunteer training. They were known to one another and could, therefore, assemble at short notice to act independently of or co-operate with the presbyterian bands.

The effectiveness of the Defender organization suggested the creation of a similar league of protestants. Such a protestant league would naturally appeal to the Orange tradition as the best means of uniting all branches of protestants and, like the Defenders, would imitate the masonic system of organization. As early as 1793 efforts to create such a league were made by James Wilson,[57] a substantial presbyterian farmer of Dian, county Tyrone. Wilson first appears to have urged the Benburb masons to take measures against the Defenders, but without success. He then founded a small band whose members used signs and passwords and took an oath to defend protestantism and the constitution. It is hardly surprising that they adopted the name Orange Boys.

The number of formally organized protestant bands in existence after 1793 is difficult to estimate and is less important than the fact that most of the protestant peasantry was armed, self-confident and prepared for a clash with the Defenders. On their part, the Defenders could use their federated organization to concentrate their forces in any district where such a clash occurred. Serious trouble began again in the spring of 1795 when a Defender was beaten by a Peep O'Day Boy during a cockfight at Dan Winter's inn at the Diamond, a crossroads near Loughgall in county Armagh.[58] Bands were quickly assembled, and a fortnight later shots were exchanged between a Defender party returning from a wake and a protestant party on their way home from a dance.[59]

---

[57] W. Banks, *The Orange Institution of Ireland*, p. 34; Sibbett, *Orangeism*, i. 216–7.

[58] Magistrate R. Abbott to govt. 17 June 1795 (P.R.O.I., Rebellion papers 620/22/9); *B.N.L.*, 26 June 1795.

[59] Ibid., see also *F.D.J.*, 23 June 1795.

To halt further trouble, McCann,[60] the sovereign of Armagh, accompanied by a magistrate and four companies of militia, seized a quantity of arms and arrested about fifty Defenders and two Peep O'Day Boys.[61] McCann advised the immediate disarming of the lower classes[62] while another magistrate, Richard Abbott, reported that the 'partiality of certain magistrates' gave the Defenders occasion to allege that justice was not to be had and they must redress themselves.[63] He further advised the government to revoke Winter's licence. Winter's inn was now marked as a Peep O'Day Boy centre by the Defenders and was to be the object of their attack in September 1795. McCann's prompt action prevented an immediate clash and was followed by meetings of the inhabitants of Kilmore and Ruddock's Grange who optimistically passed a number of resolutions denying the fights to be of a denominational origin and announcing their determination to suppress all disturbers of the peace.[64] No substantial measures were taken to disarm the population, and the catholics were left with the feeling that they were the injured party to whom the law had given no redress. More important, perhaps, was their feeling that they were strong enough to secure redress through the agency of the Defenders.

In the early summer of 1795, however, the unrest in Armagh was only one aspect of the larger problem of the Defenders. In Connaught, where they had paralyzed local law enforcement agencies, Lord Carhampton, the commander-in-chief, intervened personally.[65] There, by the arbitrary but effective means of sending suspected Defenders to serve in the fleet, he brought the movement under control. In Meath and Kildare, the Defenders were active in July[66] and an illegal

[60] Sometimes spelled MaCan.
[61] *F.D.J.*, 23 June 1795; *D.E.P.*, 25 June 1795.
[62] MaCan to S. Hamilton, 26 June 1795 (P.R.O.I., Rebellion papers 620/22/11).
[63] P.R.O.I., Rebellion papers 620/22/9.
[64] Ibid.; see also *B.N.L.*, 26 June 1795; *D.E.P.*, 25 June 1795. Both newspapers claimed the fight had religious overtones.
[65] Camden to Portland, 28 May 1795, reporting on disturbances in Connaught before and after Carhampton's appointment (P.R.O.I., Rebellion papers 620/22/8); *F.D.J.*, 9 May 1795; *F.J.*, 12, 21, 26 May 1795.
[66] *F.J.*, 16 July 1795; *F.D.J.*, 16, 18, 25, 30 July 1795; *D.E.P.*, 30 July 1795; P.R.O.I., Rebellion papers 620/22/19.

assembly of 300 catholics was reported in county Tyrone.[67] Only the August harvest seemed to halt these activities. Even then, Dublin Castle received disquieting reports about Defender influence in the armed forces.[68] On August 27 Edward Cooke, the under-secretary, received a report that a massacre of protestants was planned in the north after the harvest.[69] He commented that the Defenders were taking up arms and 'there was no disposition to resist' on the part of the protestants. Cooke could not, of course, devote full time to the study of the special conditions in Armagh and was more worried about Defenderism in the Dublin area.[70] The attitude of thirteen Defender apprentices hanged in Dublin provoked him to comment on September 12, 'Defenderism puzzles me more and more—there is an enthusiasm defying punishment'.[71]

The clash in the north came on September 21 in the form of an attack on Winter's inn at the Diamond. On that day Cooke wrote, 'I broke off in a hurry on Saturday. Yesterday accounts came from the county of Armagh that Defenders and Protestants were in arms against each other near Loughgall'.[72] This clash, known as the 'battle of the Diamond', provided the occasion for the founding of the Orange order. In spite of numerous and extensive preparations by the Defenders, both factions perhaps expected this engagement to follow the course of previous encounters—a mutual defiance and exchange of shots at long range until the magistrates and military arrived to put an end to the affair. Its more sanguinary character resulted from the increased efficiency of the Defender's mobilization and the fears which that inspired in the protestants, as well as a large measure of accident.

The Defenders first assembled September 14 in the parish of Tentaraghan, county Armagh, and during the next few days

[67] Isaac Ashe to Pelham, 27 July 1795 (P.R.O.I., Rebellion papers 620/22/20).
[68] Camden to Pelham, 24, 30 Aug. 1795, S. Hamilton to ——, 25 Aug. 1795 (B.M., Add. MS 33101).
[69] P.R.O.I., Rebellion papers 620/22/35-7.
[70] *D.E.P.*, 30 July 1795; *F.D.J.*, 28, 30 July, 6, 13 Aug. 1795; Camden to Pelham, 19 Aug. 1795, S. Hamilton to ——, 25 Aug. 1795 (B.M., Add. MS 33101).
[71] Cooke to ——, 12 Sept. 1795 (B.M., Add. MS 33101).
[72] Cooke to ——, 21 Sept. 1795 (B.M., Add. MS 33101).

looted protestant farms in that area.[73] Protestant bands soon assembled and attacked the houses of some Defenders.[74] By September 18 the hostile parties faced one another on opposite hills looking across the Diamond and exchanged shots at very long range. At this point three catholic priests, Fathers Trainor, Taggart and McParland, and two magistrates, Archibald Cope and Joseph Atkinson, intervened. Articles of reconciliation were drawn up whereby each party put up £500 as a guarantee of peace.[75]

Meanwhile, more distant contingents of Defenders were still on their way to the 'battle'. Large numbers of Tyrone Defenders, who had begun to cross the Blackwater, were checked by James Verner of Churchill, father of the future Orange grand master, Thomas Verner. James Verner was returning from Loughgall after the truce with a party of North Mayo militia when he heard of the Defender gathering.[76] He mounted four militiamen on carriage horses and rode to the Blackwater river where the Defenders fled on his approach. To prevent further crossing of the river, he gathered up all the boats.[77] Other Defender reinforcements, however, arrived at the Diamond from Newtown-Hamilton and Keady. As they did not feel bound by the truce,[78] and were reluctant to return home without a fight, they forced local Defenders to join them in an attack on Dan Winter's inn. The total number of Defenders who turned out, including those sent back by Verner, may have numbered several thousands[79] of whom perhaps 400[80] took part in the 'battle'.

At five o'clock on the morning of Monday, September 21, they opened fire on Winter's inn which was occupied by a small

[73] Ibid.; see also A.M., Blacker MSS i. 223; M.P., *History of Orangeism*, p. 19; Gowan, *Orangeism*, 44-53, 137-8.
[74] M.P., *History of Orangeism*, pp. 18-9.
[75] Verner, *Battle of the Diamond*, p. 6; A.M., Blacker MSS i. 225; *D.E.P.*, 29 Sept. 1795.
[76] *F.D.J.*, 24 Sept. 1795.
[77] *F.J.*, 29 Sept. 1795; Jephson to Charlemont, 9 Oct. 1795 (*Charlemont MSS*, ii. 265-6).
[78] Cooke to ——, 21 Sept. 1795 (B.M., Add. MS 33101).
[79] Magistrate Atkinson to Blacker, n.d., cited in Verner, *Battle of the Diamond*, p. 6.
[80] Verner, *Battle of the Diamond*, p. 7; *Charlemont MSS*, ii. 265-6; R.I.A., Stowe MS pp. 38-9.

but well-armed band of protestants. Many protestants returning home after the truce heard the firing and began to retrace their steps. The main event of the 'battle' was an assault on the inn, possibly undertaken to decide the issue before protestant forces could be re-assembled. Figures ranging from sixteen to forty-eight have been given as the number of Defenders killed in the assault,[81] but as they carried their dead and wounded from the field, the total is uncertain. An eye-witness estimated the Defender dead at thirty.[82]

The protestant victory at the Diamond provided the setting for the formal organization of a protestant society modelled after the Defenders. The impressive Defender mobilization had not only alarmed the protestant peasantry but caused uneasiness amongst the gentry. Moreover, the broken truce put legality momentarily on the side of the protestants and made it difficult for magistrates like Atkinson, Cope, and Verner to insist that they could guarantee protestant security.

There seems to have been general agreement among those who fought at the Diamond that a league should be founded but some difference as to what form it should take. It is likely that men such as Wilson of the Dian conceived of a militant organization along Peep O'Day lines which would accept little gentry control and have no association with the established church. This view may have been favoured by presbyterians generally and the departure of Wilson from the Diamond without joining the new movement[83] suggests that it was rejected along with Wilson's possible bid for leadership. The more respectable faction which drew up the rules of the society were apparently members of the established church who wanted the gentry to take formal leadership of the movement and were prepared to accept a considerable measure of gentry control. Orangemen later insisted that no Peep O'Day Boys had joined their movement and there are several statements that the first Orangemen were all members of the established church.[84] The

---

[81] *Charlemont MSS*, ii. 266; *N.S.*, 24 Sept. 1795; Verner, *Battle of the Diamond*, p. 7; Gowan, *Orangeism*, p. 139.

[82] A.M., Blacker MSS i. 225. [83] Banks, *Orange Institution of Ireland*, p. 34.

[84] Evidence of Lord Gosford, *Rep. on Orange lodges I*, H.C. 1835 [377], xv. 258; Evidence of Rev. M. O'Sullivan, ibid., pp. 36, 46; Evidence of W. Verner, ibid., p. 18; Musgrave, *Memoirs*, p. 83; Letter addressed to protestants of Great Britain and Ireland, 9 July 1798 (P.R.O.I., Rebellion papers 630/39/10).

latter claim may have been true as the protestants in the Loughgall area were mainly episcopalian.[85] However, Peep O'Day Boys must have fought at the Diamond and excluding them would have been extremely difficult.[86]

The titular head of the new movement was James Sloan, the innkeeper at Loughgall whose role is difficult to estimate. As his establishment was used for Orange meetings, he profited materially from his position and, as secretary of the new federation, he acquired a fame which soon spread beyond the boundaries of Loughgall and even county Armagh. An innkeeper near Loughgall was needed to provide a centre for the movement and Dan Winter was unacceptable because of his past Peep O'Day Boy association. Sloan was more respectable and may even have been recommended by members of the local gentry who included at least some members of the Cope, Atkinson and Verner families and possibly others. The gentry in contact with the movement appear to have looked on it with mixed feelings. Some were reconciled to its existence and hoped at best to keep it from falling under Peep O'Day Boy influence. Others perhaps thought it might prove useful politically and hoped to make it sufficiently respectable to enable them to collaborate with it.

Two weeks after the founding of the movement, Richard Jephson wrote to Lord Charlemont, 'It is impossible for the protestant gentry to keep up the farce of impartiality between the parties, or to disavow the absolute necessity of giving a considerable degree of support to the protestant party, who,

[85] Loughgall's population in 1766 was 588 protestants, of whom 464 were episcopalians, 110 dissenters and 14 quakers, while the catholics numbered 469; see Groves documents, in P.R.O.N.I., T/808/15264(1). For two centuries Loughgall was the property of the Cope family, whose ancestor built a stone and lime bawn and settled fourteen English families nearby. On the estate, Cope located six freeholders, thirty-four lessees and seven cottagers, all Britons and able to muster eighty armed men. This was the origin of the protestant colony of Drumilly and Loughgall; see James Stuart, *Historical memoirs of the city of Armagh*, appendix xxi. 637.

[86] For various statements in which the protestants who fought at the Diamond are identified as Peep O'Day Boys and Orangemen, see Lindsay to govt., 30 Sept. 1795 (P.R.O.I., Rebellion papers 620/22/43); *D.E.P.*, 29 Mar. 1796; *F.J.*, 29 Sept., 28 Dec. 1795; *B.N.L.*, 21 Sept. 1795; Lane to Downshire, 29 Sept. 1795 (P.R.O.N.I., Downshire MSS); Dalrymple to Pelham, 24 Sept. 1795 (B.M., Add. MS 33101); Jephson to Charlemont, 9 Oct. 1795 (*Charlemont MSS*, ii. 265–6); Grattan, *Memoirs*, iv. 232.

from the activities of the two Copes, have got the name of "Orange Boys"'. Jephson went on to say, 'I do not believe that the designs of either party have at present any deeper foundation than private enmity, or are in any degree directed against the government'.[87]

Blacker, a young student from Trinity who saw the 'battle' and joined the lodges just before returning to college, wrote two generations later, 'Very few of the resident gentry joined us in the first instance. Of those few were my old friend, Joseph Atkinson, the Rev. George Marshall of Dromore, ... Captain Clarke of Summerisland, and soon after the young Verner of Churchill. Old Mr Verner never joined us as an affiliated member though he took a great interest in the proceedings of the association'.[88] Blacker mentioned Viscount Northland of Dungannon and Brownlow of Lurgan as patrons of the 'infant institution'. The men named as joining in the first instance were certainly among the first gentry to join, but apart from Blacker's testimony, it cannot be established that they joined in September 1795. Whatever the attitude of this portion of the gentry was toward the new movement, they left matters largely in the hands of Sloan and his associates. Warrants issued in Sloan's name authorized individuals to found local lodges. These were written on slips of paper with the name of the bearer of the warrant, its number, the district, date and place of issue, and were signed by James Sloan. The first ten or so warrants were drawn by lots and number one fell to the Dian, county Tyrone.[89] They are said to have cost £1 2s. 6d.[90] which was high enough, perhaps, to exclude Peep O'Day Boys seeking admission.

The early meetings were secret with initiations and oaths administered on hilltops and behind hedges in the manner of any other agrarian secret society. Blacker described the first meetings of his lodge held in the frame wall of a partially constructed house at the crossroads of Tanderagee and Lurgan near the gate of Carrick. 'An assemblage of men, young and old, collected upon these occasions as far as could be seen by the light of a few candles—some seated on heaps of sods or rude

[87] *Charlemont MSS*, ii. 265-6.   [88] A.M., Blacker MSS i. 240.
[89] Ibid., i. 236; Verner, *Battle of the Diamond*, p. 8.
[90] Rogers, *Revolution of 1688*, p. 19.

The Background and Origin of the Orange Lodges

blocks of wood; most of them armed with guns of every age and calibre... There was a stern solemnity in the reading of the scripture and administering the oath to the newly admitted brethren which was calculated to produce a deep impression and did so.'[91] The original oath ran, 'I,... do solemnly swear that I will, to the utmost of my power, support and defend the king and his heirs as long as he or they support the protestant ascendancy'.[92]

Orangeism as it stood in September 1795, was a reaction against Defenderism which, itself, had its origin in resistance to Peep O'Day Boy raids. By 1795 Defenderism had become a national movement which in the southern counties was directed against the landlords, but in Armagh opposed protestant peasants. The Orange movement, as it was organized after the battle of the Diamond, was probably an adequate means of upholding the dominant position of the protestant peasantry in Ulster. However, Ulster and Ireland were subject in 1795 to a number of external influences which were to absorb purely local quarrels into a wider conflict involving an uprising and a foreign war.

The French revolution had altered the pattern of revolt everywhere and modified the British government's attitude toward the catholics and toward Ireland. The question of protestant or catholic supremacy in Armagh was to be decided, not by rival skirmishes of factions, but by the success or failure of a republican revolution which grew out of the radical wing of the reform movement in Belfast. The Defenders, with their limited programme and outlook were, in 1795, already an anachronism, and were shortly to merge their fortunes with the Jacobin-inspired United Irishmen. But to understand this development, it is necessary to consider the impact of the French revolution on Ireland.

[91] A.M., Blacker MSS i. 237.
[92] Evidence of W. Blacker, *Rep. on Orange lodges III*, H.C. 1835 [476], xvi. 214.

II

THE GROWTH OF ORANGEISM AMONGST THE PEASANTRY 1795–6

~~~~~~~~~~~~~~~~

1. The Castle and its Enemies

THE GROWTH OF THE ORANGE MOVEMENT from its obscure beginning to a position of major influence in Irish politics took less than three years. But these were years when the emergence of the catholic peasantry as a revolutionary force under the leadership of United Irishmen awakened latent fear among protestants of catholic domination. The importance of the Orange lodges lay in that they provided an agency by which diverse protestant elements could combine, as well as a means by which the government could collaborate with the only substantial loyalist section of the population. The history of this period of Orangeism is, therefore, interwoven with the rise of the United Irishmen and the disintegration of the system by which Irish affairs were managed in the eighteenth century.

Under this system Englishmen always filled the office of viceroy and normally those of chief secretary and undersecretary, while the other executive posts were held by Irishmen in the confidence of Westminster. Among the latter by far the most forceful was John Fitzgibbon who became attorney-general in 1783, chancellor in 1789 and was made Earl of Clare in 1795. Fitzgibbon believed the protestants in Ireland could not sustain themselves without the English connection,[1] and that opposition which weakened it, like that of the volunteers of 1782, was short-sighted and irresponsible. Concessions to catholics would not, in his view, secure their loyalty. The cause of agrarian disturbances, such as those of the Whiteboys and Defenders, was, he believed, economic,[2] and thus could not be removed by reform of the franchise or repeal of the anti-catholic laws.

Fitzgibbon and those immediately associated with him were often referred to as the 'Castle clique'. Like the Orangemen, they were upholders of the ascendency, but Fitzgibbon distrusted all popular movements, while the British members of government were inclined to look upon any form of organized loyalism as a new version of the 'volunteers'. There were, however, many in the government who were prepared to encourage strong protestant feeling as far as their positions as office-holders would permit. Prominent among these were the speaker, John Foster, and the advocate-general, Patrick Duigenan. Foster accepted the necessity of removing restrictions on the personal liberties of catholics, but absolutely opposed granting them the franchise. Duigenan, who had been baptised a catholic but brought up and sent to Trinty college by a protestant clergyman, favoured the full penal code. He had devoted a good deal of his considerable talent to the acquisition of antiquarian learning, on which he drew liberally to support his ultra protestant sentiments.[3]

Associated in some degree with the views of Foster and Duigenan were about a hundred members of parliament, including a host of 'placemen', many of whom were connected with the great family interests of the Beresfords. Outstanding among these were George Ogle, the member for Wexford who was to become an Orange grand master, and David LaTouche of Huguenot descent, who exercised great influence because of his commercial connections and personal integrity. These men, together representing a mixture of sentiment and interest, feared the acquisition of the franchise and political office by catholics with the same intensity that Armagh protestant peasants feared catholic acquisition of firearms. Like the peasants, they were heirs of

[1] *P.R.*, 17 Mar. 1793, xiii. 421.
[2] *P.R.*, 13 Mar. 1787, vii. 343; Falkiner, *Studies*, pp. 101-54.
[3] *P.R.*, 27 Feb. 1793, xiii. 327.

the Orange tradition and, like them, found it convenient to associate under its symbols. They were, however, too sensitive to pressure from the Castle to initiate a popular movement.

The parliamentary 'protestants' were first drawn together in opposition to the catholic relief bill in 1792, a measure introduced under pressure from Westminster. It was resisted by the entire Irish administration on grounds that such a measure would be intolerable to Irish protestants. The viceroy himself wrote to Pitt, 'The Catholics may at times be useful to frighten the aristocracy, but in my honest opinion, they are an engine too dangerous for speculation . . . it is hardly necessary I should add that the attempt of franchise and the abolition of distinctions is impracticable, and ruinous in the attempt. The Protestant mind is so united for resistance, that I see no danger from the opinions of the British Cabinet'.[4]

Westmorland's opinion was re-enforced by petitions and resolutions from grand juries throughout Ireland and from the Dublin corporation.[5] Many of these bodies were under the influence of the borough-owning interests associated with the Castle, and the speaker, Foster, was particularly active in encouraging such addresses. In some cases at least the 'protestant' sentiments expressed represented strong feeling, but the demonstration was not impressive and could not conceal for long the fact that the upper and middle class Irish protestants were reconciled to granting the franchise to catholics. The efforts of the 'protestant party' merely delayed matters for a year, and in 1793 Pitt forced the Irish administration to pass the catholic relief bill which granted the franchise but denied catholics the right to sit in parliament or hold senior posts in the army. As the bill was virtually ordered from Westminster, the 'Castle clique' was compelled to carry out a policy which it violently opposed.[6] Held together as they were by patronage, they could hardly resign and lead an opposition, nor, had that been possible, were

---

[4] Westmorland to Pitt, 18 Jan. 1792 (P.R.O.I., Westmorland papers, Fane MSS 45).

[5] P.R.O.I., Rebellion papers 620/19/48; P.R.O.I., Westmorland papers, Fane MSS 46, 68; Plowden, *Hist. Ire. to 1800*, app. pp. 15-19.

[6] Westmorland to Dundas, 21 Jan. 1792 (P.R.O.I., Westmorland papers, Fane MSS 46).

they possessed of the kind of popularity which would have made them effective.

The parliamentary opposition, led by Grattan and supported by the great borough-holding interests of the Ponsonbys, took advantage of the dilemma of the government party by demanding full equality for catholics.[7] This had the effect of forcing government spokesmen to speak against further extension of catholic rights, thus losing any possible gratitude they might have received for introducing the bill. At this juncture Grattan and the Irish whigs made an issue of the Catholic question. They were tireless in exposing the blunders of the administration and the corruption of the borough system, and were at times prepared to call attention to the suffering of the lower classes. Yet apart from exposing abuses, the Irish whigs offered neither effective leadership nor really sound argument. They insisted that constitutional changes, such as borough reform and catholic relief, would remedy social unrest like that caused by the Whiteboys and Defenders.

The fundamental moderation of the Irish whigs and their conviction that the affairs of Ireland could be managed best by the gentry were often obscured by a verbal radicalism and opportunistic manoeuvres to which they were driven by their vanity and their exasperation with Castle policy. As they had no prospect of persuading the British government to accept their programme and no intention of leading a popular revolution themselves, they wasted their eloquence in a futile battle with the purchased majority of the Castle. A few of the younger whigs, like Lord Edward Fitzgerald, joined the United Irish, but most, when confronted with the threat of revolution, like Grattan himself, withdrew temporarily from politics and some ended by joining the Orange lodges.

The radical movement which emerged after the volunteer convention of 1784 drew its main support from the dissenters of Ulster who had sympathized with the American rebellion and for a long time accepted whig leadership. This movement, however, included some catholics and many nominal members of the established church. It represented a general middle class as well as dissenter radicalism. Among its leaders were both convinced revolutionaries and adventurers, but the Irish

[7] *P.R.*, 27 Feb. 1793, xiii. 327.

middle class and the dissenters[8] in particular, despite their taste for radical literature and oratory, felt they had much to lose and were thus as little inclined toward revolution as the gentry. When the cause of radicalism became identified with illegal conspiracy and a rising of the catholic peasantry, the Irish middle class drew back and many of its erstwhile radicals took refuge in the Orange lodges.

Most of the radical leaders had joined the whig clubs founded under the tutelege of Charlemont in Dublin in 1787 and in Belfast in 1790. However, the middle class radical leaders hoped to play a part in national politics and, under the influence of the French revolution, came to believe they could. An able spokesman was found in Theobald Wolfe Tone who turned to radical politics after his efforts to make a career along more conventional lines proved unsuccessful.[9] He published a pamphlet attacking the whigs as false friends of liberty and invoking the 'rights of man' to justify full equality for catholics.[10] In October 1791 Tone and his friends founded the society of United Irishmen in Belfast. It stood for complete religious equality and parliamentary reform, and was to be national in scope, open to all religious denominations, and would maintain contact with the Jacobin Club in Paris, the Revolution Society in England and the Committee for Reform in Scotland.[11]

The programme of the society was moderate,[12] but it was controlled by revolutionaries who hoped to guide the cautious and timid.[13] Tone wrote, 'I have alluded to the Catholics but so remotely as not to alarm the most cautious Protestants... to fear the Catholics is a vulgar and ignorant prejudice. Look at France and America; the Pope burnt in effigy at Paris, and the

---

[8] Belfast constitutional compact, 1 Oct. 1790 (P.R.O.I. Westmorland papers, Fane MSS 8, 8a).

[9] Wolfe Tone, *Life*, p. 18.

[10] Ibid., p. 25; For whig reaction to Tone, see *Charlemont MSS*, ii. 142, 160.

[11] P.R.O.I., Rebellion papers 620/19/24; Wolfe Tone *Autobiography*, ed. S. O'Faolain, pp. 36–8.

[12] Statement of United Irishman Robert McCormick, n.d., McCance collection, in P.R.O.N.I., 272/6.

[13] Drennan-Bruce letters in P.R.O.N.I., DOD 553/43; Westmorland to Pitt, 1 Jan. 1792 (P.R.O.I., Westmorland papers, Fane MSS 35); Tone to ——, n.d., cited in Patrick Duigenan, *An answer to Henry Grattan*, p. 77.

English Catholic at this hour seceding from his church; a thousand arguments crowd at me, but it is unnecessary to dwell on them'.[14]

Tone secretly favoured a republic on the American model with toleration for all and no established church.[15] His radicalism, like Grattan's liberalism, ignored the intensity of the peasant land-hunger and under-estimated the power of the longstanding border feuds. He was, no doubt, misled by the American example and by the apparent ease with which middle class catholics and protestants worked together in Dublin and Belfast. In America, however, the population was largely of protestant and British stock, and religious antagonism had yet to mature fully. Moreover, neither in America nor in the Irish cities was there a land question.

After establishing branches of the United Irish society in Belfast and Dublin,[16] Tone, lacking an independent income, was forced to seek employment.[17] This was supplied by Joseph Keogh, the head of the Catholic Committee which had been founded in 1759 under the direction of the upper clergy and remnants of the old catholic nobility. After the outbreak of the French revolution, the middle class catholics, led by Keogh, took control of the movement from its aristocratic founders,[18] and re-organized it on a more democratic basis. The services of Richard Burke, the son of Edmund Burke, were secured to plead the catholic cause in Britain. When it became evident that Burke could achieve little,[19] he was thanked and dismissed,[20] and Wolfe Tone hired to assist in the calling of a catholic convention to be composed of delegates from all over

[14] Tone to Chambers, June, 1790 (P.R.O.I., Rebellion papers 620/19/24).
[15] Tone, *Autobiography*. ed. S. O'Faolain, pp. 36-8.
[16] Declaration of the society of United Irishmen of Dublin, 9 Nov. 1791 (P.R.O.I., Rebellion papers 620/19/33).
[17] Tone, *Life*, pp. 67, 100.
[18] Report and resolutions of the general committee of the Catholic Association, 18 Feb. 1791 (P.R.O.I., Westmorland papers, Fane MSS 72); Westmorland to Dundas, 21 Nov. 1791 (ibid., 24); Westmorland to Pitt, 1 Jan. 1792 (ibid., 35); Westmorland to Hobart, 7 May [?] (ibid., 210).
[19] Westmorland to Dundas, 14 Jan. 1792 (P.R.O.I., Westmorland papers, Fane MSS 42); Westmorland to Dundas, 21 Jan. 1792 (ibid., 46); Dundas to Westmorland, 29 Jan. 1792 (ibid., 49) R. Hobart to Earl of Hillsborough, 12 Sept. 1792 (P.R.O.N.I., Downshire MSS).
[20] Tone, *Life*, p. 72.

Ireland. This convention sent delegates to London to bring pressure on Pitt on behalf of catholic interests.

The existence of the convention raised transitory hopes among the Dublin radicals that it might be pushed into the role of the states general in France, but neither the appeals of the United Irish societies nor Tone's personal association with the Catholic Committee made any substantial impression on the majority of catholics. Some catholics were perhaps influenced by the hostility of the church hierarchy to a radicalism which it associated with Jacobin France. More important, however, was the fact that the catholic association with the United Irishmen would give offence to the crown and offer little compensation in return. With the outbreak of war in 1793, the United Irish counted less on winning over the catholics than on the prospect of military help from France, but the arrest of the French agent, Jackson, compromised most of the United Irish leaders, and led to the suppression of the movement and Tone's exile.[21] The subsequent illegality of the society frightened away many of its middle class sympathizers, and it was some time before it could be reconstituted as an underground movement with a new leadership.

Meanwhile, Grattan enjoyed a brief revival of influence when the liberal Lord Fitzwilliam was made lord lieutenant of Ireland. After consulting with Grattan and the Ponsonbys, the new viceroy concluded that the war could only be made popular in Ireland by granting full equality to catholics, making some concession in the way of parliamentary reform, and breaking the power of the 'Castle clique', including Fitzgibbon and the Beresford interest.[22] Fitzwilliam had been instructed not to make an issue of the catholic question, but he struck at the power of Fitzgibbon by dismissing Beresford, and he wrote to Portland for power to act on the catholic question.[23]

The Beresford interest at once set to work to undermine Fitzwilliam's position in England.[24] However, the viceroy had already exceeded his instructions and the king now declared

[21] Wolfe Tone, *Autobiography*, ed. by his son, i. 77–84.
[22] Lecky, *Ire.*, iii. 244–6.
[23] Grattan, *Memoirs*, iv. 194–5; John Beresford, *Correspondence*, ii. 88.
[24] Lord Auckland to Lord Henry Spencer, 6 Mar. 1795 (Lord William Auckland, *Journal and correspondence*, iii. 292).

The Growth of Orangeism amongst the Peasantry, 1795-6

himself absolutely opposed to catholic emancipation.[25] Short of resigning, Pitt had no choice but to dismiss Fitzwilliam. This was done 23 February 1795.[26] Thus, in the year the Orange lodges were founded a new and inevitably unpopular Irish viceroy,[27] Lord Camden came to office to wrestle with the problems of the United Irishmen, the war, and Defenderism. The United Irish were already in contact with France, and if they could effect a liaison with the Defenders, they would be allied to the only powerful revolutionary force in eighteenth century Ireland—the catholic peasantry. No such liaison had been effected by 1795, and the troubles in Armagh which led to the formation of the Orange lodges at first seemed to create further obstacles to the United Irish idea. The border counties, however, were one of the few areas in Ireland where middle class radicals could offer effective assistance to the catholic peasant without immediately becoming involved in illegal activity. Such assistance soon became necessary because of the defeat of the catholics at the Diamond and the protestant reprisals that followed.

2. The Armagh Outrages

After the 'battle of the Diamond' the protestant peasantry began a series of night raids, soon known as the 'Armagh outrages', which had as their purpose the driving of catholic tenants from the county.[28] The extent to which the newly organized Orange lodges were associated with the outrages is not easy to establish. The lodges had been founded under the pressure of the Defender menace, when moderation seemed to the peasants a reasonable price to pay for the support of the gentry. With victory secure, however, the need for landlord patronage ceased to be urgent and the temptation to take advantage of victory proved irresistible.[29]

[25] King to Pitt, 6 Feb. 1795 (Earl Stanhope, *Life of Pitt*, see appendix).
[26] Ibid., ii. 307.
[27] Jonah Barrington, *The rise and fall of the Irish nation*, p. 208; Grattan, *Memoirs*, iii. 226.
[28] *P.R.*, 22 Feb. 1796, xvi. 107, 118; Cooke to Pelham, 16 July 1798 (B.M., Add. MS 33102); A.M., Blacker MSS i. 241-3; R.I.A., Stowe MS pp. 39-42.
[29] Dalrymple to Pelham, 9 Oct. 1795 (B.M., Add. MS 33101); A.M., Blacker MSS i. 241.

The Growth of Orangeism amongst the Peasantry, 1795-6

The resulting action against catholic tenants in Armagh hurt landlord interests by attracting unfavourable attention to the county and causing rents to fall. This alienated the gentry and put Orange sympathizers such as the Verners and Atkinsons in a difficult position. Violence was also deplored by many small merchants who had joined the Orangemen for protection and business reasons.[30] However, the most active element in the lodges at this time were the men involved in the fight at the Diamond, many of whom must have been involved in the 'outrages'. Even moderate Orangemen may at first have sympathized with what seemed to them 'legitimate vengeance', but matters were soon out of hand. Cottages occupied by catholic tenants were papered with notices inviting them 'to hell or Connaught'.[31] Neglect of such warnings meant raids in which furniture and weaving looms were destroyed. Fire was seldom applied as the raiders were often prospective tenants of the premises.[32] Killing and bodily injury were rare. The number of catholic families driven from Armagh to Connaught became a matter of controversy. William Blacker insisted that about 180 families were affected,[33] some of whom destroyed their own cottages to get compensation money under the Whiteboy act. Figures as high as 1400 have been suggested.[34] Lord Altamount, a great land-owner in Connaught, reported that nearly 4,000 fugitives had sought refuge in county Mayo[35] which suggests a figure of about 700 families.[36]

It cannot be established that Orangemen, acting as such, organized the raids. It seems more likely that miscellaneous protestant bands including sworn Orangemen were responsible.[37] Many such expeditions had probably been planned at the

[30] A.M., Blacker MSS i. 240.
[31] Evidence of Lord Gosford, *Rep. on Orange lodges I*, H.C. 1835 [377], xv. 231; P.R., 22 Feb. 1796, xvi. 108; A.M., Blacker MSS i. 242; *Morning Chronicle*, 11 Feb. 1825.
[32] A.M., Blacker MSS i. 243. [33] Ibid., i. 244.
[34] Curran's estimate, in Cleary, *History of the Orange Society*, p. 67.
[35] Altamount to Cooke, 27 Nov. 1796 (P.R.O.I., Rebellion papers 620/26/82); Wesley Doyle, *Considerations vitally connected with the present state of Ireland in reference to the Roman catholic question and the Orange system*, p. 53.
[36] *View of the present state of Ireland 1797*, p. 23 (P.R.O.I., Rebellion papers 620/34/53); *N.S.*, 17 Oct. 1796.
[37] *F.J.*, 5 Dec. 1795, 5 Jan. 1796; *N.S.*, 31 Dec. 1795; R. Madden, *United Irishmen, their lives and times*, i. 106-8.

inns of Jim Sloan and Dan Winter, with or without their approval. Yet even if the Orange leaders had restrained sworn members from participating in the raids, the superior organization which the lodges gave to the more numerous and better armed protestants made it impossible for the Defenders to organize effective resistance.

Contemporary with the 'Armagh outrages', an effort was made by the gentry and Dublin placemen to form a society in aid of civil power to suppress Defenderism.[38] Nearly all its members later became Orangemen, and a few at least were aware of the society founded by James Sloan. Lord Carhampton, the commander-in-chief, supported the movement, but it was premature and checked by the Castle. Lord Camden wrote, 'I have had a great deal of trouble with an association which was proceeded in by Lord Carhampton—and several other friends of government. They were giving every encouragement to a new version of the Volunteers.'[39]

A number of such loyal associations were organized, but only one appears to have been connected with the early Orangemen. It was an association of the noblemen and gentlemen of the barony of Dungannon,[40] headed by Lord Northland whom Blacker named as an early patron of Orangeism.[41] Northland probably contemplated uniting his gentlemen's club with the Orange peasantry, but had to abandon the plan because of government hostility to loyal associations and the 'Armagh outrages'. A contemporary report of General Dalrymple, the commander in Belfast, suggested that a section of the gentry had aroused his suspicions. He reported, '... protestant acts of revenge against Catholics for past injuries,' and expressed fear that the 'ingenuity of some of the country gentlemen and other inhabitants' might make the feud permanent. He declared his determination to treat 'Greek and Trojan' alike.[42] Troops were scattered over the disturbed area in detachments of from thirty to 300.[43] The presence of the military appears to have quieted

---

[38] Hamilton to Pelham, 5 Oct. 1795 (B.M., Add. MS 33101).
[39] Camden to Pelham, 3 Oct. 1795 (ibid.); Dalrymple to Pelham, 23 Oct. 1795 (ibid.).
[40] *F.J.*, 16 Oct. 1795.   [41] A.M., Blacker MSS i. 240.
[42] Dalrymple to Pelham, 3 Oct. 1795 (B.M., Add. MS 33101).
[43] Ibid.

the disturbances at first,[44] but it was wartime and the troops, recently recruited, inadequately disciplined, and dispersed in small detachments which could not cover all possible areas of disturbance, soon ceased to be a deterrent.

Newspaper accounts of meetings of magistrates to denounce Peep O'Day Boy activities and offers of rewards for information concerning offenders appeared frequently in late October and November.[45] One such meeting in Armagh on October 26 urged all landlords 'to bring their tenants together and require them to engage in the most solemn manner to keep the peace' and declared that those 'who absent themselves from their houses at night' should be considered as ill-disposed persons.[46] An account in the United Irish *Northern Star* a month later maintained that a total of seventy-six peaceful inhabitants of Armagh 'were dragged from their beds by a party of Orangemen headed by two of Colonel Ogle's crimp sergeants, falsely charged with desertion and released at the eleventh hour by an unnamed magistrate'.[47] The failure of the troops and the county meetings of landowners to quiet the disorders was emphasized by the burning of a Portadown linen manufacturer's house by protestants late in December.[48] A man named McCann, probably a Defender, was shot while sitting by his fire, and newspapers reported 'two or three Orangemen, or Peep O'Day Boys, as they are called, were killed'.[49]

These incidents and others apparently induced the governor of the county, Lord Gosford, to call a meeting of landowners, including James Verner, the member of parliament. Six resolutions were passed denouncing the actions of 'parties unknown'[50] and a committee was appointed to take information against offenders of every description. Lord Gosford was evidently interested in using this meeting to attract the attention of a wide public, as he had printed a strongly-worded address which was distributed to influential people in Dublin.

[44] Dalrymple to Pelham, 9 Oct. 1795 (ibid.); S. Hamilton to ——, 29 Sept. 1795 (ibid.); *F.J.*, 24 Oct. 1795; Lindsay to govt., 12 Oct. 1795 (P.R.O.I., Rebellion papers 620/22/45).
[45] *N.S.*, 5 Nov. 1795; *D.E.P.*, 10 Nov. 1795. [46] *D.E.P.*, 10 Nov. 1795.
[47] *N.S.*, 23 Nov. 1795. [48] *F.J.*, 28 Dec. 1795; *D.E.P.*, 29 Dec. 1795.
[49] *F.J.*, 28 Dec. 1795.
[50] *B.N.L.*, 28 Dec. 1795; *Rep. on Orange lodges I*, H.C. 1835 [377], xv. 229–30.

The handbill read, 'A persecution, accompanied with all the circumstances of ferocious cruelty which have in all ages distinguished that dreadful calamity, is now raging in this county. Neither age, nor even acknowledged innocence as to the late disturbances, is sufficient to excite mercy, much less afford protection'. Gosford went on, 'The only crime which the wretched objects of this merciless persecution are charged with, is a crime of easy proof; it is simply a profession of the Roman Catholic faith. A lawless banditti have constituted themselves judges of this species of delinquency, and the sentence they pronounce is equally concise and terrible; it is nothing less than a confiscation of all property and immediate banishment'. Gosford declared, 'These horrors are now acting...with impunity. The spirit of impartial justice...has for a time disappeared in the county.'[51]

James Verner later asserted he had no recollection of such an address being made to the meeting itself.[52] Nowhere is the word 'Orangemen' mentioned nor is it suggested that the outrages were inspired by an organization. Forty years later, Gosford's son, who was hostile to Orangeism, when asked before a parliamentary committee whether he thought the banditti referred to in the resolutions were Orangemen, replied, 'I should think [it] alluded to parties of Protestants banded together, but whether under the form of Orangemen, I cannot say'.[53] Gosford, like other landowners, may have felt called upon to protect his catholic tenants. Castle influence had made him governor of county Armagh in 1791, displacing Lord Charlemont.[54] As Charlemont had consistently opposed outside influence in the county and insisted that order could best be secured by some system of volunteering, it was possible that Gosford shared the government's suspicion of volunteering, and was not reluctant to speak out about the deficiencies of local magistrates in maintaining impartial justice.

Gosford's efforts attracted attention to but did not end the

[51] *Rep. on Orange lodges I*, H.C. 1835 [377], xv. 229.
[52] James Verner to Joseph Pollock, 9 Mar. 1807, in Gowan, *Orangeism*, pp. 147–50.
[53] Evidence of Lord Gosford, *Rep. on Orange lodges I*, H.C. 1835 [377], xv. 231, 258.
[54] *Charlemont MSS*, ii. 134.

outrages. Grattan brought the matter up in parliament in February 1796[55] when the government was asking for new repressive legislation in the form of an indemnity bill and an insurrection bill. The first measure was designed to protect from future prosecution officers of the crown who had acted outside the law against Defenders in Connaught. The second bill gave magistrates the right to enter houses in search of arms, to arrest strangers unable to give an account of themselves, and compelled the inhabitants of localities which were proclaimed in a state of disturbance to remain indoors between sunset and sunrise. The government claimed that the activities of the Defenders and the United Irishmen had made this legislation essential, while Grattan accused the Castle of using its power only against catholic and republican disturbers of the peace. He compared 'those insurgents, who call themselves Orangemen, or Protestant Boys' to the followers of Lord George Gordon. The crimes of the Defenders, he maintained, were punished by a multitude of hangings, but 'with the crimes of the Orange Boys, he could make no such boast.'[56]

Grattan went on to read Lord Gosford's address and he declared the government's zeal to maintain order did not seem to apply to county Armagh. Pelham, the Irish secretary, answered that Colonel Craddock had been sent to Armagh to do what he could, and he pointed out that the Orange 'outrages' were an additional reason for passing the repressive legislation. Colonel Craddock then rose to explain that he had not found the local magistrates cooperative in Armagh, and when they had cooperated, little could be done because juries and witnesses had been intimidated. He became convinced that his troops could do nothing, and had recommended to the Castle that he be recalled. The current outrages could be put down, he said, but pointed out that in September the Defenders had been the aggressors.[57]

The caution with which government spokesmen discussed the Armagh outrages and the fact that reprisals against the Defenders in the south had been severe lent plausibility to the rumour that the government was secretly sympathetic to the Orangemen.[58] Yet three weeks before Grattan's speech, Camden had

[55] *P.R.*, 22 Feb. 1796, xvi. 107–11.   [56] Ibid.   [57] Ibid.
[58] *P.R.*, 13 Oct. 1796, xvii. 4.

written to the duke of Portland, 'The Armagh protestants, finding themselves more numerous, have been induced to commit acts of the greatest outrage and barbarity against their catholic neighbours. This circumstance has been owing to the magistrates of the county having imbibed the prejudices which belong to it, and having been swayed by their predilections in the discharge of their duty'.[59]

Camden wrongly assumed that the magistrates were capable of controlling the peasantry, but he understood that some of them hoped to profit from rising protestant sentiments. The Verners, Atkinsons, and others more difficult to identify had in mind a society similar to Lord Carhampton's Dublin Association. This would include in its ranks not only the more respectable elements who had fought at the Diamond, but would also combine protestant landlords and tenants for mutual security against Defenderism, revive the Orange tradition, and further the political ambitions of its landlord patrons. The first step towards the creation of such a society had been taken in September 1795 but further action was delayed for nearly a year because of the Armagh outrages and the hostility of the government.

The outrages continued throughout the winter and were only brought to a halt by the vigorous action at the Armagh spring assizes of Attorney-General Wolfe, a member of the Beresford faction. Over 200 offences had been reported by the time of the assizes, and Orangemen, rather than Peep O'Day Boys, were named as the offenders in the press.[60] Wolfe announced that the prosecution would be undertaken to 'convince His Majesty's subjects, whatever their religious profession might be ... that they might rely on receiving protection from every species of oppression'.[61] Two Defenders and two Orangemen were sentenced to death.[62] If Sibbett, the Orange historian, is to be relied on, the convicted Orangemen were followers of Wilson from Dian, who had not yet merged his forces with Sloan's lodges.[63]

[59] Camden to Portland, 22 Jan. 1796 (Lecky, *Ire.*, iii. 434).
[60] *D.E.P.*, 2 Apr. 1796; *N.S.*, 11 Apr. 1796; *F.J.*, 4, 12 Apr. 1796.
[61] *B.N.L.*, 4 Apr. 1796.
[62] Corry to govt., 1 Apr. 1796 (P.R.O.I., Rebellion papers 620/23/61); Wolfe to govt., 1 Apr. 1796 (ibid., 620/23/62).
[63] Sibbett, *Orangeism*, i. 217–8.

The Growth of Orangeism amongst the Peasantry, 1795-6

At the assizes Colonel Ogle was compelled to pay damages for offences of his recruiting sergeants the previous December, while the Whiteboy act, which forced local inhabitants to pay damage for property destroyed in cases where no offender was brought to trial, was invoked for the benefit of catholics. The United Irish newspaper, the *Northern Star*, commented, 'The Attorney-General on the part of the Crown has evinced the utmost impartiality. Catholic witnesses had been in general deterred from coming forward for fear of the Orangemen, but a military guard was granted to protect them.'[64] A man named Levery was convicted for trying to induce a soldier to be 'true to the Duke of York and his committees',[65] which suggests that some Orangemen were claiming connection with the aristocratic Orange and Blew Society as a means of winning over the military.

The spring assizes appear to have been fairly effective in curtailing the outrages in Armagh, but a good part of the protestant fury was, by that time, probably spent, and more violent elements found an outlet for their energies in county Down.[66] There as early as March 1796 Lord Downshire's estate manager, Thomas Lane, reported the necessity to take measures against Orangemen from county Armagh who were influencing protestant tenants to attack the catholics.[67] The show of government hostility towards 'wreckers'[68] no doubt served to remind the protestant bands of a need for association with the gentry and may have been exactly what the leaders of the Orange lodges required to bring the movement under their control. The 'partial' magistrates[69] and landlords favourable to Orangemen may well have feared the consequences of the wrecking and have been relieved to see the government undertake the unpopular repressive action. Moreover, after

[64] *N.S.*, 4 Apr. 1796.
[65] *D.E.P.*, 2 Apr. 1796.
[66] Lane to Downshire, 24 Mar. 1796 (P.R.O.N.I., Downshire MSS); Cooke to Pelham, 14 July 1796 (B.M., Add. MS 33102); Laurence to Pelham, 11 Mar. 1796 (P.R.O.I., Rebellion papers 620/23/48).
[67] Lane to Downshire, 24 Mar. 1796 (P.R.O.N.I., Downshire MSS).
[68] *F.D.J.*, 21 Jan. 1796.
[69] Lane to Downshire, 27 Jan. 1796 (P.R.O.N.I., Downshire MSS); Kelly to Pelham, 28 Jan. 1796 (P.R.O.I., Rebellion papers 620/23/16); *N.S.*, 8 Feb. 1796; *F.J.*, 14 Apr. 1796.

several months of fury, a reaction in favour of moderation was to be expected.

By June 1796 a number of the gentlemen class who were either members or patrons of the movement felt the occasion favourable to renew the scheme attempted in October to establish the respectability of the Orange movement and to found a new 'loyal association' which could, at the earliest convenient moment, admit Orangemen to its ranks.[70] The prime movers in this project were magistrates Thomas Knox of Dungannon and Holt Waring of Waringstown, neither of whom were classed as 'supine magistrates' by the government, Lord Gosford or General Dalrymple. The plan was favoured by the decline of the 'outrages' in Armagh which permitted some of the expelled catholics to return. Orangemen were now concerned with saving the protestants capitally convicted at the spring assizes. They indulged in an occasional show of strength such as the illumination of the countryside with bonfires when a stay of execution was granted William Trimble,[71] described as a captain of the Orangemen. A month later Lord Gosford appealed for Trimble's life on the ground that it was 'the general opinion of the county, particularly among the protestants, that if Trimble's life be saved, all animosities and religious disputes would be at an end.'[72] This quiet in Armagh, however, had to be viewed in the light of outrages in the other counties.

Holt Waring, whatever his Orange sympathies, forwarded a letter from his son, also a magistrate, to the government. The young Waring wrote, 'The mistaken lenity of government in not hanging the men convicted at Armagh has occasioned all the mischief that has happened since and the gentlemen of that county who represent to government that all was subsided are to blame as it was by no means true.'[73] In Waring's neighbourhood, a mill owner named Magill had his mill burned after he

[70] Knox to govt. 25 June 1796 (P.R.O.I., Rebellion papers 620/28/202); F.D.J., 5 Apr. 1796.

[71] Corry to govt., 20 Apr. 1796 (P.R.O.I., Rebellion papers 620/23/80); Madden, *United Irishmen*, i. 119; Evidence of P. McConnell, *Rep. on Orange lodges III*, H.C. 1835 [476], xvi. 72.

[72] Gosford to S. Hamilton, 19 May 1796 (P.R.O.I., Rebellion papers 620/23/115).

[73] H. Waring to his father, 2 June 1796 (ibid., 620/23/141).

had been warned to dismiss his catholic employees.[74] Lord Downshire's estate manager reported incendiary letters being dropped and a 'rooted implacability between Protestants and Papists'.[75] Another Down magistrate, Waddell, reported wrecking[76] while Charlemont's Belfast correspondent wrote that fifty-seven houses had been wrecked since the assizes in county Down by the 'Orange-boys' and ten in Armagh.[77] Charlemont agreed that there was trouble in Down, but insisted that Armagh was quiet.[78] Gosford also wrote of the quiet in Armagh, but added that the people 'wait for a favourable opportunity to revive the spirit of religious quarrel'.[79]

It is evident that the Orange leaders and their patrons had no control over the Down wreckers who were certainly acting contrary to the policy and interests of the movement. However, the activities of Armagh protestants in Down could hardly have been sustained without the support of a federated society. The mere existence of such a society provided opportunities for groups within it to organize raids without the sanction of the leaders. Nor could the leadership take action against them without attracting unfavourable attention.

The wrecking in Down jeopardized the Orangemen's plans to establish their respectability by a peaceful demonstration on July 12. General Dalrymple stated early in June that the magistrates and others considered the project dangerous, but they were unwilling or unable to take preventative measures. He wrote, 'Great preparations are making everywhere for the celebration of the 12th of July and ... I need make no observation on the consequences that may possibly attend such a parade. They are obvious and the business ought to be prevented if possible. Mr Brownlow and Mr Obins who live near Lurgan are sufficiently acquainted with this business and I apprehend the chief rendezvous will be thereabouts.'[80]

A week later General Dalrymple wrote that he considered the

[74] Ibid.; *N.S.*, 6 June 1796.
[75] Lane to Downshire, 3 June 1796 (P.R.O.N.I., Downshire MSS).
[76] Waddell to Ross, 1 July 1796 (P.R.O.I., Rebellion papers 620/23/141).
[77] Haliday to Charlemont, 26 June 1796 (*Charlemont MSS*, ii. 275).
[78] Charlemont to Haliday, 2 July 1796 (ibid., p. 276).
[79] Lord Gosford to ——, July 1796 (Lecky, *Ire.*, iii. 437).
[80] Dalrymple to Cooke, 10 June 1796 (P.R.O.I., Rebellion papers 620/23/164).

The Growth of Orangeism amongst the Peasantry, 1795-6

Orange parade within the scope of the Whiteboy act and urged government to prevent it as his 'hopes of activity in the magistrates were very limited'.[81] Against Dalrymple's opinion, the government could set a report from Holt Waring, who appears to have been the first to report favourably on the Orangemen. 'I have not the least apprehension of any ill consequence [of the coming parade]', he wrote, 'as from the best information that I have been able to make, they mean not to have arms of any kind, and they have declared against using any kind of spirits on that day. It is said they will be 20,000 strong. With every inquiry I have been able to make I cannot learn who are the principal people concerned in conducting this business.'[82] Waring could hardly have been ignorant of the people concerned in Orangeism and was probably consulted by them about the proposed parade. On July 8 the *Northern Star* printed an attack on Orangeism, threatening to expose its leaders, and published an apparently authentic version of the secret Orange oath. Several magistrates assured Dalrymple that there would be no violence on July 12, but William Brownlow, named by Blacker as an early patron of the lodges,[83] requested troops be present at Lurgan in case of trouble.[84] When the day of the parade arrived, Dalrymple wrote, 'the behaviour of the people at the Orange festival on the 12th was faultless. I have received a great many assurances that in the future no countenance will be given any outrages, and I am inclined to believe them. In the County of Armagh they are chiefly over, but in Down and Antrim they still prevail.'[85]

The *Northern Star* reported, 'The gentlemen called Orange Boys who had desolated the County of Armagh during the last year, paraded publicly in large numbers through the towns of Lurgan, Waringstown, and Portadown. This banditti... parade in open day, under banners bearing the King's effigy and sanctioned by the magistrates. Irishmen! Is this not plain

[81] Same to same, 19 June 1796 (ibid., 620/23/183).
[82] Holt Waring to Cooke, 4 July 1796 (P.R.O.I., Rebellion papers 620/24/11).
[83] A.M., Blacker MSS i. 240.
[84] Brownlow to Dalrymple, 9 July 1796 (P.R.O.I., Rebellion papers 620/24/27).
[85] Dalrymple to Pelham, 13 July 1796 (B.M., Add. MS 33101, this letter is dated in the Add. MS as 1795, but from its context it is clearly 1796).

enough?'[86] In the same issue, an anonymous letter to the editor asked, 'Is it a truth that higher powers have hired men called Orange-men at five guineas per man and one shilling per day to disturb, destroy, and harass harmless inhabitants, because they are Irishmen?'

Taking a similar tone, the hostile *Dublin Evening Post* reported, 'The procession consisted of 14 companies and formed a motley group of turncoats, Methodists, Seceders and High Churchmen'.[87] The failure to mention presbyterians was deliberate, as both the *Post* and *Northern Star* published long articles denying that presbyterians were responsible for the 'Armagh outrages'. It would be surprising if no presbyterians had joined the parade. There were no dissenting clergymen or prominent dissenters among the early patrons of Orangeism.[88] However, the Peep O'Day raiders, who were widely reported as presbyterian farm labourers, clearly acted without the approval of their church or middle classes.[89] The dissenting members of the peasantry were as much alarmed by the rise of Defenderism[90] as the episcopalians and many of them fought at the Diamond. It seems likely that they were prepared to support the Orange movement in spite of its connection with the established church because of the need they felt for the patronage of the gentry.

An independent witness, unsympathetic to Orangeism, reported, 'Three or four thousand protestants [i.e. Anglicans] and dissenters paraded and dispersed peacefully'.[91] The numbers given vary. The *Belfast News-Letter* mentions 2,000.[92] Another source gives 2,500.[93] Blacker, the Trinity College student present at the Diamond battle and the Lurgan parade, claims the total number of lodges[94] at this time as ninety. Participating in the demonstration with Blacker were several

[86] *N.S.*, 15 July 1796. [87] *D.E.P.*, 21 July 1796.
[88] Evidence of W. Verner, *Rep. on Orange lodges I*, H.C. 1835 [377], xv. 10.
[89] *F.J.*, 5 Jan. 1796; *N.S.*, 31 Dec. 1795; see also Memorial of the presbyterian congregation of Drumbanagher, county Armagh, in *N.S.*, 18 Feb. 1796; Lord Altamount to govt., 16 July 1796 (P.R.O.I., Rebellion papers 620/23/34).
[90] S. Hamilton to ——, 29 Sept. 1795 (B.M., Add. MS 33101).
[91] Jones to govt., 27 July 1796 (P.R.O.I., Rebellion papers 620/24/60).
[92] *B.N.L.*, 15 July 1796.
[93] O'Neil to govt., 19 July 1796 (P.R.O.I., Rebellion papers 620/24/20).
[94] A.M., Blacker MSS ii. 25.

The Growth of Orangeism amongst the Peasantry, 1795-6

Trinity College students who joined during the summer holidays and provided a nucleus for an Orange lodge in Dublin.⁹⁵ The day was marred by a single incident when soldiers of the Queens' County militia attacked some marchers, tearing off Orange insignia. McMurdie, a protestant, struck one of the soldiers and was killed by a bayonet thrust.⁹⁶

The July 12 demonstration in 1796 was an Orange triumph that impressed the gentry and military favourably and alarmed the enemies of Orangeism. At Dublin Castle, however, the Orangemen were still regarded as another dark cloud on an exceptionally gloomy horizon. Cooke wrote to Pelham:

> The procession of the Orangemen to the Diamond on the 12th went off quietly. About 5,000 paraded without arms. Their banners, King George on one side, King William on the other. The Orangemen are beginning persecutions in the County of Down and the magistrates are not sufficiently active. This persecution works on the Catholics in other places and naturally breathes revenge... I fear the Militia will be tainted with this religious quarrel and the United Irishmen, in order to seduce the Militia and Catholics, promise to join them both against the Orange Boys.⁹⁷

3. The Dungannon Plan

The developments described above were in process in early July when Thomas Knox forwarded to government the resolutions passed by his 'loyal association', which were known at the time as the 'Dungannon resolutions' or 'Dungannon plan'. His evident intention was to create a legally armed society that Orangemen could join. The resolutions ran, 'If His Majesty in his wisdom shall require our further exertions, that we will embody ourselves... under such officers as he shall commission and will train and discipline ourselves so as to be able to render him more effective service and frustrate the hopes of traitors and banditti... who rely upon finding the country naked and defenceless, should regular troops be drawn off to oppose an invading enemy'.⁹⁸ Knox described the supporters

⁹⁵ Ibid.
⁹⁶ Cooke to Pelham, 14 July 1796 (B.M., Add. MS 33102).
⁹⁷ Ibid.
⁹⁸ Knox to govt., encl. 25 June 1796 (P.R.O.I., Rebellion papers 620/23/202).

of the resolutions as intelligent men known personally to him who 'will not proceed until after the Assizes and not then if government disapprove ... failure to disapprove in no way commits government'.⁹⁹ Answering for the viceroy, Cooke wrote Knox, 'His only objection to measures of this kind arises from an apprehension that others may be grafted on them of a questionable tendency. The resolutions, however, which you have adopted appear to be cautiously guarded'.¹

Knox's project was considered as a possible model for a series of loyal associations to be formed in disturbed areas. In places where the gentry were of Orange persuasion, they would inevitably provide the lodges with a legal basis for existing as armed bands. If the gentry were inclined otherwise, they could, in theory, be used to put down 'wrecking'. Knox's scheme proved more attractive in Antrim and Down, where the United Irish were stronger, than in Armagh. An Armagh magistrate critical of Orangeism wrote, 'Lord Gosford wrote me a note respecting the plan of associating adopted in Tyrone by Knox. I don't know that the gentlemen of this County would wish to engage in such an association ... such as I have conversed with are against it. The quiet state of this County at present ... will probably fortify them in that disinclination.'² Another magistrate who had difficulties with Orangemen wrote, '... if they [the government] adopt the plan and embody Protestants they will have a handsome force of well-affected men'.³

Meanwhile, the success of the July 12 parade had strengthened the Orangemen and made them bolder. At the summer assizes in Armagh, Orangemen presented to the magistrates 'An humble petition of the Protestant association forming the Loyal Union of Orange', in which they declared they modelled their institutions on the Boyne Club, an earlier Orange society, and they announced their willingness to support the civil authority, maintaining that:

... every act of violence and outrage ... is imputed to us. We deny the charge with contempt; our principles binding us in a most

⁹⁹ Knox to govt., 4 July 1796 (P.R.O.I., Rebellion papers 620/24/1).
¹ Cooke to Knox, 9 July 1796 (ibid., 620/24/24).
² Corry to Cooke, 23 July 1796 (P.R.O.I., Rebellion papers 620/24/48).
³ Waddell to ——, 22 Aug. 1796 (ibid., 620/24/22a).

secret and solemn manner to the contrary. We abhor and detest every act of outrage committed by Defenders, Peep O'Day Boys, or others, and declare ourselves separate from such violators, ... as our own principles are as sacred and so distinct, as that venerable body of brotherhood called Free Masons.[4]

In forwarding the petition to government, Dalrymple commented, 'I cannot but be pleased with and consider it as some proof of intentions',[5] but a week later, he thought, 'The Orange Societies have agreed on monthly meetings. What such frequent assemblies have to do with the memory of King William, I know not'.[6]

A day previous, Holt Waring had written from Waringstown:

The Orangemen ... did assemble accordingly and paraded through this town with many flags and emblems of loyalty, in number from 2,500 to 3,000 ... They were perfectly regular, sober, no arms, not even a stick among them ... I must beg to observe to you that a distinction must be made, between these Orangemen and those of the County Armagh under that denomination who have wrecked and made such horrid waste and depredation for some time past.[7]

In spite of the orderly parades, loyal addresses and reports of general quiet in the county, an Armagh magistrate, Thomas Kemmis, reported two Orangemen convicted capitally for posting notices, rioting, and appearing in arms. 'There were several tried the same day', he wrote, 'but not any convicted though the proof was beyond question ... The gentlemen of the County have not attended. It was with the greatest difficulty Grand Juries were made up.'[8] A few days later, he commented on the absence of Knox and Richardson from the assizes.[9]

The magistrates and landlords, who had hitherto remained in the background as patrons, such as the Verners, Blackers, Knox and the Warings, were now prepared to come forward

---

[4] Dalrymple to Pelham, encl. 20 July 1796 (B.M., Add. MS 33101).
[5] Ibid.
[6] Dalrymple to Cooke, 24 July 1796 (P.R.O.I., Rebellion papers 620/24/53).
[7] Holt Waring to Cooke, 23 July 1796 (ibid., 620/24/46).
[8] Thomas Kemmis to ——, 24 July 1796 (P.R.O.I., Rebellion papers 620/24/55).
[9] Same to ——, 27 July 1796 (ibid., 620/24/88).

The Growth of Orangeism amongst the Peasantry, 1795-6

more openly in defence of Orangeism. One result of this was their sons' parading with the Orangemen on July 12 without family disapproval. In districts where such relationships between Orangemen and gentry had been established, 'outrages' were rare. The outrages committed in Antrim and Down during the summer of 1796 were mostly in districts where there was little connection between the Orangemen and gentry. In such areas, it was difficult to distinguish between miscellaneous protestant bands and 'sworn' Orangemen, as local Orangemen were in a position to act independently of the leaders of the movement.

The persistence of 'outrages' in areas outside their influence made it impossible for magistrates like Knox and Waring to undertake an unqualified defence of Orangeism and still remain in the confidence of the Castle. They were, therefore, prepared to acknowledge the faults of Orangeism, but, at the same time, undertook to collect and report all information favourable to the lodges. This cautious advocacy of Orangeism was undermined by magistrates supporting their own loyal associations, who reported adversely on the Orangemen. One of these, Captain Waddell, wrote to Cooke, 'I have taken all the pains I could to come at the real intentions of the people in this county associating under the name of Orangemen, who have kept this neighbourhood in alarm for some time past. They deny any connection with those people who have been racking houses'. Waddell had a copy of their rules which, he said:

> ... were not contrary to law ... most of them activated by fear of the Papists and ignorance. The masters of the different bodies have declared before Magistrates Waring, Magennis and James that they shall be immediately disbanded and released from their obligation which I think will be done and you will have advice of it. I shall keep a very steady outlook and if I see the least prevarication or double dealing, I shall have their captains taken up and committed for administering unlawful oaths.[10]

A week later Knox wrote to Cooke, 'As to the Orangemen, we have a rather difficult card to play; they must not be entirely discountenanced—on the contrary, we must in a

---

[10] Waddell to Cooke, 5 Aug. 1796 (P.R.O.I., Rebellion papers 620/24/82).

certain degree uphold them, for with all their licentiousness, on them we must rely for the preservation of our lives and properties, should critical times occur. We do not suffer them to parade, but at the same time applaud them for loyal professions'.[11] Knox undoubtedly hoped to incorporate the Orangemen in his loyal association, but had to move cautiously lest he discredit the whole Dungannon project. His argument, however, made little impression on the government which remained hostile to Orangeism and was very conscious of the dangers involved in permitting the organization of 'loyal associations'. Camden wrote, 'Knox's association is construed into a Protestant combination, supported by the government, against the Roman Catholics'.[12] That the government continued to be hostile to Orangeism is shown clearly by Cooke who wrote at the end of July, 'The irritating conduct of the Orangemen in keeping up persecution against the Catholics does infinite mischief. It has been made the handle of seducing many of the Militia'.[13] In the same letter, he wrote, 'All my information coincides in the increasing activity of the disaffected... and insurrection after the harvest, aided by invasion'.

A point had been reached where it appeared necessary to accept the risk involved in permitting the gentry-armed associations of loyal elements to meet the danger of threatened invasion and uprising after the harvest. The model selected for such an organization was the yeomanry, a type of part-time volunteer cavalry already maintained in England. The measure had been suggested as early as 1795 by Fitzwilliam and Grattan, who assumed that such an armed corps under the leadership of a liberal gentry would prove an auxiliary to a whig government. Lord Charlemont could see only good in the measure, although it was now being pressed on the government largely by members of the Beresford interest and others hostile to Charlemont's principles. With the volunteers still in mind, the government found the decision painful, but neither Cooke nor Camden appear to have foreseen the manner in which the yeomanry would strengthen the Orange lodges. In mid-July, Cooke wrote, 'I fear there will be a necessity for Yeoman

[11] Knox to ——, 13 Aug. 1796 (P.R.O.I., Rebellion papers 620/24/106).
[12] Camden to Pelham, 13 Aug. 1796 (B.M., Add. MS 33102).
[13] Cooke to Pelham, 27 July 1796 (ibid.).

Cavalry. The Attorney-General, the Speaker, the Chancellor, and Sir John Parnell, are for the measure.'[14]

On July 30, the viceroy wrote to Pelham, 'We are aware on our part that the Orangemen in the North and the Defenders in the West are only kept down by force, which is stationed there ... it is impossible to have much confidence in some of the Militia Regiments and we have often agreed there is not much dependence to be placed upon our generals'. He went on to state, 'I have been called upon by almost all those whom we usually consult to establish some corps on the model of our Yeomanry Cavalry and Infantry in England'.[15]

The decision of the government not to discountenance loyal associations at the time Knox presented his proposals was, in effect, a reversal of the policy adopted towards Carhampton's societies in 1795, and gave the gentry sufficient latitude to take the first steps towards organizing yeomanry corps before official sanction was given.[16]

Two extracts from a letter written by Haliday to Charlemont on August 7 indicate the relationship of the Orangemen to the organization of the new corps. Haliday wrote:

On Friday, there is to be a general assembly of the Down nobility and gentry at Newtownards, at the requisition of the most noble marquis of Downshire, for the purpose of effectuating this new measure of a yeomanry cavalry... The 'Orange Boys' parade in great numbers in the vicinage of Lisburn; a clergyman of the Marquis of Hertford harangues them, after the service is over, from the pulpit, exhorting them to firmness and perseverance (their object is the banishment or extermination of the Catholics) tendering them the oath of allegiance, and promising them, it is said, arms from the Government.[17]

The clergyman was Reverend Philip Johnson who, years later, told how he had submitted a plan along the lines of the 'Dungannon scheme' to Lord O'Neill who forwarded it to the government. Johnson wrote, 'I soon after formed five or six parishes, being a principal part of Lord Hertford's estate, into small bands, including every loyal Protestant, who were in some degree organized and prepared to check the progress

[14] Cooke to Pelham, 14 July 1796 (B.M., Add. MS 33102).
[15] Camden to Pelham, 30 July 1796 (ibid.).
[16] Camden to Pelham, 28 Aug. 1796 (B.M., Add. MS 33102).
[17] Haliday to Charlemont, 7 Aug. 1796 (*Charlemont MSS*, ii. 278-9).

of sedition and withstand the open attempts of the disaffected'.[18] These bands were recruited from Orangemen, and Johnson himself soon joined. 'When I saw that the Institution was founded on principles in which all loyal Protestants could join and that it could not be suppressed without injuring the cause of loyalty, and that it might be highly useful if properly directed, and how, like everything that is good, it might be subject to abuse... I could not afterward refuse when called upon to take a lead in it'.[19]

In a report which dwelt on the reluctance of the gentry to form associations of men of property, General Nugent, the military commander in Johnson's district, wrote, 'Lord Hertford's agent [Johnson] has attempted this, but he is much too insignificant to succeed in any degree'.[20] The *Northern Star* commented, 'A Reverend Gentleman, not 100 miles from Lisburn, it is said, has taken up the trade of the Armagh Magistrates, and is industriously fomenting disturbances in that neighbourhood'.[21]

4. THE UNITED IRISH MOVEMENT SPREADS TO THE SOUTH

Cooke was receiving abundant evidence that the 'Armagh wrecking' had driven the Defenders into collaboration with the United Irish society. A widely believed, but wholly unfounded, rumour that each Orangeman took an oath 'to be true to the king and government and that I will exterminate as far as lies in my power the Catholics of Ireland' was spread.[22] There is no evidence that even the Peep O'Day Boys took such an oath, but it was credited by whigs and radicals, and by Plowden, the English catholic historian.[23] As early as May 1796 the name

---

[18] Philip Johnson to Lord Hardwicke, July 1804 (Michael McDonagh, *The Viceroy's post-bag*, p. 27).

[19] Ibid.

[20] Nugent to Cooke, 20 Aug. 1796 (P.R.O.I., Rebellion papers 620/24/132).

[21] *N.S.*, 22 Aug. 1796.

[22] Lane to ——, 16 July 1796 (P.R.O.N.I., Downshire MSS); Dalrymple to Cooke, 10 June 1796 (P.R.O.I., Rebellion papers 620/23/164); *B.N.L.*, 23 Oct. 1797.

[23] Plowden, *Hist. Ire. to 1800*, (Philadelphia, 1805), iv. 186; Madden, *United Irishmen*, iv. p. xv.

of 'Orangeman' was sufficient to cause panic among the excitable catholic peasantry. Edward Hudson wrote Charlemont from Portglenone, county Antrim:

A few days previous to a fair which was lately held in the town of Antrim, a report was circulated that a number of 'Orangemen' (from the moon, I suppose) were to be there in order to fall on the Catholics. However absurd and improbable such reports are, in the present state of things here they have spread a panic amongst that description of people which we who love union have not been able to dispel, though I assure you no pains have been spared for that purpose.[24]

Fear of the Orangemen spread to Connaught by means of the Armagh refugees, and, with the enthusiastic assistance of the United Irish, throughout Ireland. The manner in which the United Irishmen were able to exploit this fear of Orangeism was best described in the testimony of three of their leaders, which is fully supported by all contemporary sources. They claimed:

To the Armagh persecutions is the union of the United Irishmen most exceedingly indebted. The persons and properties of the wretched Catholics of that country were exposed to the merciless attacks of the Orange faction, which was certainly in many instances uncontrolled by the justices of the peace, and claimed to be in all supported by Government... We will remark that, once for all, what we solemnly aver, that wherever the Orange system was introduced, particularly in Catholic Counties, it was uniformly observed that the numbers of United Irishmen increased most astonishingly. The alarm which an Orange Lodge excited among the Catholics made them look for refuge by joining together in the United system, and as their number was always greater than that of bigoted Protestants, our harvest was ten-fold.[25]

In a comprehensive report sent on August 6 to the duke of Portland, Camden summarized the information he had on the growth of the disturbances. He noted, 'The United Irish of Belfast, who had been engaged in forming democratic societies ... took advantage of this ill conduct of the Dissenters in

[24] Hudson to Charlemont, 29 May 1796 (*Charlemont MSS*, ii. 273).
[25] Memoir or detailed statement of the origin and progress of the Irish union delivered to the Irish government by Messrs. Emmett, O'Connor and McNevin (Castlereagh, *Memoirs and correspondence*, i. 356–7).

The Growth of Orangeism amongst the Peasantry, 1795-6

Armagh to form a junction with the societies of Defenders in the Western and Midland Counties'. He went on to report, 'They are indefatigable in their attempts to seduce the Army and Militia and they privately boast of success among the latter, in which, I fear, they are but too well grounded, especially among those Militia men who are Roman Catholic and whose feelings may have been irritated by the ill behaviour of the Dissenters or Orangemen in Armagh'.[26]

Camden considered the repressive action early in the year had quieted the Defenders, but that they had revived since their union with the republicans. The relative quiet of the country could be attributed to the plans the United Irish were working out for an insurrection after the harvest in conjunction with a French invasion. Of the Orangemen, Camden wrote, 'The party of Dissenters called Orangemen keep up a system of terror at least, if not outrage, in Armagh, and have begun to carry their vexations to the Catholics into the County of Down. Some of them were recently apprehended by a spirited magistrate, but in prosecution at the late Assizes, the Catholics, on whose examinations they had been taken up, through terror or other causes, prevaricated on trial, and the offenders escaped'. Camden assured Portland he would 'use every possible exertion to prevent these outrages of the Dissenters against the Roman Catholics, which however, though not aimed immediately at the Government, are perhaps more dangerous than even direct conspiracies, as they justly irritate the Catholics and give a pretext for the disaffected to act upon'.[27]

In spite of these sentiments, Camden felt compelled to accept the measure which placed the government in a *de facto* alliance with the Orange lodges. On August 28, he wrote to Pelham, 'I do not like to resort to Yeomanry Cavalry or Infantry... if I can help it... but I see no other recourse in the present times. The army must be withdrawn from many of its quarters and must be drawn together to act in larger bodies than it has lately done. I have sent for the Chancellor and the rest of the King's servants to concert with them the best... means of

---

[26] Camden to Portland, 6 Aug. 1796 (P.R.O.I., Rebellion papers 620/18/18).

[27] Camden to Portland, 6 Aug. 1796 (P.R.O.I., Rebellion papers 620/18/11).

resorting to this species of force.'[28] By permitting the gentry to raise a force of part-time soldiers similar, in many respects, to the volunteers, the government unintentionally provided the means of creating a national Orange movement. The yeomanry could not be recruited without the cooperation of the lower class protestants, and the Orange lodges were to be both an agency for employing the energies of the protestant peasants and a means of keeping them under some degree of gentry control.

[28] Camden to Pelham, 28 Aug. 1796 (B.M., Add. MS 33102).

III

GENTRY SUPPORT OF ORANGEISM, 1796-7

~~~~~~~~~~~~~~~~~~~~~~~~~

1. UNITED IRISH MILITARY STRENGTH

AT THE TIME of the July 12 parades in 1796, the Orange Order numbered perhaps several thousand organized into about ninety lodges,[1] enjoying the cautiously-exercised patronage of a minority of Ulster landowners and magistrates who were strongly opposed to catholic emancipation. Of these, the Verner family was, perhaps, the most important. By July 12 of the next year, the Orange lodges had gained a recognized position in Ulster with the open support of a powerful section of the gentry and were accepted, if reluctantly, as allies by the government. This astonishing progress was the result of the reaction of the government and a section of the gentry to the menace of a powerful military underground force organized by republicans and Defenders,[2] and the rise of this force is, therefore, part of the history of Orangeism.

The illegal military force of the United Irish had two elements—the educated doctrinaire republicans and the agrarian rebels. The theories of the former were of no interest to catholic peasants. Nor were the middle class republicans interested in the

---

[1] A.M., Blacker MSS ii. 35.
[2] Fleming to govt. 27 Jan. 1795 (P.R.O.I., Rebellion papers 620/22/19); Wolfe to Westmorland, 9 May 1796 (P.R.O.I., Westmorland papers, Fane MSS 108).

land question as such. They were, however, opposed to church establishment and hence to tithes, and were prepared, for the sake of their allies, to revise the system of rents. The 'Armagh outrages' and perhaps the hope of help from France had convinced the Defenders that the government would do nothing for them and that their best chance was to join the United Irish in an attempt at revolution.

The republican leaders had, at first, counted little on the catholic peasants as allies. However, the disbanding of the old volunteers left them without a military organization. They were further disorganized by the exile of their leaders, Hamilton Rowan,[3] Tandy[4] and Wolfe Tone[5] in 1794-5. This loss was compensated for when they were joined by men from higher stations of life, among whom were the lawyer, Arthur O'Connor, a prominent member of parliament and a relative of Lord Longueville, William James MacNeven, a former leader of the Catholic Committee, Thomas Addis Emmet, and Lord Edward Fitzgerald, a brother of the duke of Leinster. They joined the movement in the spring of 1796 after having persuaded themselves that further efforts to achieve equality for catholics and parliamentary reform by constitutional means were useless.

The new republican leaders shared their predecessors' doubts about the catholic peasantry and rested their main hopes on French invasion. Of the Defenders, they wrote, 'They were composed almost entirely of Roman Catholics, and those of the lowest order, who, through a false confidence, were risking themselves and the attainment of redress by premature and unsystematic insurrection.'[6] They were themselves somewhat surprised at their success in winning over the Defenders, and in organizing an extensive underground armed force.

The numbers gathered in this force are difficult to estimate. Those who took the United Irish oath may have been well over 200,000 by 1798.[7] In Ulster in the autumn and winter of

[3] Pollock to Westmorland, 15 Apr. 1795 (P.R.O.I., Westmorland papers, Fane MSS 111).

[4] Ibid.

[5] Tone sailed for America on 22 June 1795, see *D.E.P.*, 23 June 1795.

[6] Memoir ... of the Irish union by Emmett, O'Connor and McNevin (Castlereagh, *Correspondence*, i. 357-8).

[7] For various statements of the estimated strength of the United Irish in 1797-8 see Report of the secret committee presented by Pelham, 10 May

1796–7, there were perhaps 40,000 sworn United Irishmen armed in some manner and acting under the leadership of elected officers who recognized the authority of a central directory. Although it was better organized and led, this movement had most of the limitations of the Whiteboys and Defenders. It could best make its influence felt by paralysing the normal functioning of government, intimidating witnesses and juries,[8] murdering and otherwise terrorizing loyalists and neutrals.[9] Any large-scale rising it conducted would have the character of a Jacquerie and, as such, could hardly hope to achieve more than a temporary or local success unless aided by the French[10] or a defection of a major portion of the crown forces. The last danger gave the Orangemen a special value as their presence in inadequately-disciplined military units, such as the yeomanry and militia, whatever other difficulties it created, served as an insurance against United Irish influence. Had the armed forces been in a high or even normal state of efficiency such insurance would not have been considered, but Castle authorities were hardly able to make a free choice.

2. CROWN FORCES

At the disposal of the Crown were three categories of troops—regulars, including Scottish fencibles, Irish militia, and yeomanry. The fencibles were raised as a substitute for militia in Scotland to serve for the duration of hostilities, but were not available for foreign service. Recruited with some care by the aristocracy among highland clans untouched by the levelling spirit of the French revolution, they were the troops least likely to fraternize with, or commit outrages against, the civil popu-

[8] Evidence of John Macara, 27 Aug. 1797 (B.M., Add. MS 33105).
[9] Pelham to ——, 1 Nov. 1797 (ibid.).
[10] Wolfe Tone, *Life*, ed. by his son, ii. 30–5.

1797 (P.R.O.I., Frazer MSS); Higgins to Cooke, 27 Sept. 1797 (P.R.O.I., Rebellion papers 620/18/14); Report of Wicklow United Irish, 22 Jan. 1798 (ibid., 620/35/55); John Maxwell's notebook on United Irish, 1 May 1797 (ibid., 620/34/54); R. Ross to Downshire, 25 Apr. 1798 (P.R.O.N.I., Downshire MSS); Cooke to ——, 21 Feb. 1797 (B.M., Add. MS 33103); see also document delivered to Cooke by Reynolds, in W. H. Maxwell, *History of the Irish rebellion in 1798*, p. 333.

lation.[11] Yet desertion from their ranks was not unknown, nor were clashes between them and the civil population uncommon. The regulars were in a particularly unfortunate state as the best men had been taken to serve with the British field forces, and had been replaced by recruits. The years between 1794 and 1798 were years of military defeats in the Low Countries and on the French coast, and of costly victory in the West Indies.[12] England could not spare her best troops for duty in Ireland. Not only were many of the troops hastily recruited and inadequately trained, but a number of the junior officers were men whose principal qualification for command had been the ready cash with which to purchase a commission.[13] Another difficulty sprang from the fact that too many regulars, although recruited in England, were Irish. To the Irish labourers who crossed St George's Channel in search of work, the bounty money offered for enlistment was an attraction. Those who joined in England were drawn from the classes most affected by the revolutionaries, and many had actually been forced to accept military service as a punishment for their political activities.[14]

Far more alarming was the state of the Irish militia. When this force was raised, it was hoped that the peasantry who, as a rule, made excellent soldiers, would make no serious objection to being drafted into a force of militia. This expectation was unfulfilled. A rumour was circulated that the militia was being raised for the purpose of sending on foreign service those men who had signed petitions of the Catholic Committee. Resistance to conscription was general throughout Ireland,[15] and small uprisings took place in some localities. Ultimately a compromise was reached whereby men were induced to enlist on a voluntary basis by offers of large bounties from the landed gentry, who also undertook to see that the families of drafted men would not suffer while the men were away on service. Yet the result was very unsatisfactory.[16] The officers were, for the most part, dependents of the gentry, irresponsible in their conduct of duty

[11] J. R. Western, 'Formation of Scottish militia, 1797', in *Scottish Historical Review*, xxxiv, no. 117, p. 8 (Apr. 1955).
[12] J. W. Fortescue, *British army 1783–1802*, pp. 41–3, 106.
[13] Ibid., pp. 52–4, 77.
[14] *P.R.*, 3 Feb. 1796, xvi. 47.
[15] Pelham to Portland, 26 Oct. 1796 (B.M., Add. MS 33113).
[16] Ibid.

and given to treating their men with contempt.[17] Sir John Moore, who had units of the Irish militia under his command in 1798, was appalled by the conduct of the officers. He wrote:

When the Militia was first formed, had pains been taken to select proper officers and to introduce discipline they might in time have been respectable troops; but, like everything else in this country, the giving of regiments was made an instrument of influence with the Colonels, and they made their appointments to serve electioneering purposes. Every sort of abuse has been tolerated, and, it is, I fear, now too late to amend them. The officers are in general profligate and idle, serving for the emolument, but neither from a sense of duty nor of military distinction.[18]

Moore went on to say, 'The officers in the Militia are in general Protestants, the men Roman Catholics; the hatred between these two persuasions is inveterate to a degree, and the officers have so little sense or prudence as not to conceal their prejudice'.[19]

In militia regiments, the sergeants and the band were, as a rule, protestant, and the other ranks catholic. The catholic militiamen garrisoning areas where Orangemen were active, like the Limericks stationed in Armagh, were naturally sympathetic to the victims of 'outrages'. As shown previously,[20] this could lead to attacks on Orange parades. It also provided a pretext for clashes between catholic and protestant regiments which, in one case, made it necessary to confine the Downshires to barracks while the Limericks were marching through.[21]

The catholic militiamen had, apart from the natural inclination towards rowdyism common to under-disciplined troops, a sense of legitimate grievance which made secret societies attractive. Moreover, republicans could offer hospitality to soldiers serving away from their own counties. Of republican work in the militia, the United Irish leader, MacNeven, wrote:

[17] Lord Clare to Auckland, 2 Jan. 1797, in *Some Fitzgibbon letters*, ed. R. B. McDowell, p. 305; Pelham to Camden, 3 Oct. 1797 (B.M., Add. MS 33105).
[18] Sir John Moore, *Diary*, pp. 273–5, entries dated 16 Feb., 4 Mar. 1798.
[19] Ibid.
[20] See above p. 41.
[21] Matthews to Downshire, 27 Oct. 1796 (P.R.O.N.I., Downshire MSS).

The impression ... made ... on the defenders gave the United Irishmen a ready access to the militia regiments, as they arrived in the north. These were mostly composed of catholics, having come from the other provinces; in many instances they were already defenders, that association having spread into the counties where they were raised. The progressive steps were now made easy, the catholic soldier had no reluctance to become a defender; the defender was quickly induced to follow the example of those where he was quartered and become a United Irishman. The union thus spread among them very extensively, and the militia regiments were often vehicles by which both systems were carried to different and remote districts.[22]

The number of sworn Defenders and United Irishmen in the militia cannot be established. Musgrave, the contemporary Orange historian, considered that by November of 1797 there were 700 United Irishmen among the 4,000 militiamen in Antrim, 200 out of 4,200 in Armagh, 1,000 out of 2,700 in Tyrone, 1,000 out of 1,100 in Down, and 700 out of 2,000 in Donegal.[23] Government had received ample reports of United Irishmen in the Kerry,[24] Tipperary,[25] Dublin,[26] Louth,[27] and Meath[28] regiments, while some of the regular units such as the 9th Dragoons, Fencibles,[29] and Royal Irish Artillery[30] were affected as well. The large number of desertions, the clashes between militia and loyal units, and informer reports to the government suggest that these figures were not much exaggerated. However, the sacrifices which sworn United Irishmen in the militia would make for the 'cause' were limited. By making an example of a few ringleaders, officers could usually put an end to republican influence.

It is not surprising, then, that protestant militiamen sta-

[22] J. W. MacNeven, *Pieces of Irish history*, pp. 120–1.
[23] Musgrave, *Memoirs*, p. 210.
[24] Higgins to Cooke, 23 Sept. 1797 (P.R.O.I., Rebellion papers 620/18/14); Sir George Hill to Pelham, 5 July 1797 (ibid., 620/31/205).
[25] Lake to Knox, 27 Aug. 1797 (N.L.I., Lake MSS 56).
[26] Nugent to Pelham, 25 June 1797 (B.M., Add. MSS 33104); Knox to Pelham, 14 Apr. 1797 (B.M., Add. MS 33103).
[27] *B.N.L.*, 2 June 1797.
[28] Dalrymple to Pelham, 17 Apr. 1797 (P.R.O.I., State of the country papers 408/591/8).
[29] Lake to Knox, 29 Apr. 1797 (N.L.I., Lake MSS 56).
[30] Lake to Pelham, 13 Mar. 1797 (B.M., Add. MS 33103).

tioned in areas where Orangeism flourished would be attracted to the movement. On 3 December 1796, Major Matthews, a militia officer, wrote to Lord Downshire that he found 'the system of Orange Clubs have really taken place in the Regiment [the Downshire] ... that Sergeants Bulmer and Ker are at the head of it, and that it is insinuated through the Regiment that your Lordship approves of the Orange Men ... I will take every means to put a stop to this business'.[31] A few days later he wrote, 'There is nothing surer than that Orange Men, if it goes on, will be the means of making United Irishmen, and our neighbours, the Queen's, are, I believe, very willing to undertake the business'.[32]

Although as Matthews suggested, United Irish cells in the militia could result from a reaction against Orangeism, the opposite was more likely to be true as the Defenders existed before the Orangemen were organized. It cannot be established how and when the first Orange lodges were founded in protestant regiments in the 'disturbed areas'. Matthews' letter is the first indication of Orangeism in the militia, and it would be logical to assume that the first military warrants were issued to the Downshires some time late in 1796 at a time when some units of newly-raised yeomanry were openly displaying their Orange badges. While the militia was subject to both republican and Orange influence, only the latter was at first important in the yeomanry. Because the United Irish considered they had little prospect of capturing the new corps, they denounced the yeomanry as Orange, and directed their efforts towards discouraging enlistment.[33] This not only left the field free to Orangemen, but added to their prestige by seeming to confirm their assertion that they had government support. Later, when the yeomanry became established, the United Irish made belated efforts to gain influence within it with limited success.[34]

[31] Matthews to Downshire, 3 Dec. 1796 (P.R.O.N.I., Downshire MSS).
[32] Same to same, 5 Dec. 1796 (ibid.).
[33] Letter to editor signed R.C., in *N.S.*, 19 Dec. 1796.
[34] Knox to Pelham, 17 May 1797 (B.M., Add. MS 33104); Knox to Pelham, 22 May 1797 (ibid.); Pelham to Knox, 20 May, 1797 (ibid.); Lord Cavan to Knox, 20 Aug. 1797 (N.L.I., Lake MSS 56); Sir George Hill to Cooke, 10 July 1797 (P.R.O.I., Rebellion papers 620/31/216).

3. The Raising of the Yeomanry, 1796–7

As shown previously,[35] the enlistment of the Irish yeomanry was preceded by the organization of a series of 'loyal associations', some of which were controlled by gentlemen close to the Orange lodges. The county meetings in August 1796, however, were intended to provide for a wider participation of the gentry in raising the new corps. The political attitude of the corps would presumably depend on the local landlords, few of whom were yet sympathetic to Orangeism. The Orangemen, however, were the only 'enthusiastic loyalists', and as the United Irish and Catholic Committee discouraged enlistment, those engaged in recruiting were in no position to discountenance Orangemen.

The manner in which yeomanry were enlisted where landlords were of Orange sympathies was described by Colonel William Blacker:

> I was enabled to transmit to the Castle a list of nearly a thousand good men... The arrangement was not finally completed until October and on the 30th of that month, I found myself elevated to the rank and title of Captain William Blacker of the Seagrove Infantry... which consisted of four sergeants, one of these permanent, a drummer and 100 privates. I had now a very difficult task to perform, that of selecting from so many candidates... However, by taking into council a number of the Orange leaders, deciding to select a certain proportion from each lodge the thing was... well managed. The candidates were drawn out on the green after church one fine Sunday in November and the selection was made.[36]

In the Churchill district, James Verner raised an infantry corps whose officers were listed in *Faulkner's Journal* on October 29.[37] Two days later the Churchill Orange lodge was formed with two of the younger Verners in office, David as master and John as secretary.[38] The close association between Orangemen and yeomanry was probably also maintained on Lord Hertford's estate where Reverend Philip Johnson was active,[39] and

---

[35] See above p. 31.   [36] A.M., Blacker MSS ii. 67–8.

[37] *F.D.J.*, 29 Oct. 1796; see also W. Richardson, *History of the origin of the Irish yeomanry*, p. 34.

[38] A.M., Churchill Orange lodge minute book 1802–17, p. 1.

[39] Letter to editor signed United Irishman, in *N.S.*, 10 Oct. 1796; Castlereagh to Pelham, 4 Nov. 1796 (P.R.O.I., Rebellion papers 620/18/11).

with more cautious management in Dungannon and Waringstown where Thomas Knox and Holt Waring were influential.

In some areas, the gentry felt compelled to respect government policy, if somewhat reluctantly, by enrolling a few catholics. J. N. Everard wrote to Lord Downshire, 'We would not have enrolled any Papists but that Mr Pelham's speech in Parliament disavowed the idea of making any objection to them'.[40] On October 10 a letter-writer to the editor of the *Northern Star* maintained that the only section of the people consulted by the administration in raising the yeomanry were Orangemen of Armagh.[41]

The *Northern Star* also delighted in reporting recruiting difficulties and continually asserted that, except for Armagh, Ireland was peaceful.[42] In districts where the United Irish were strong and there were no Orangemen, recruiting went slowly. One letter in government files written in Armagh at this time declared that gentlemen putting down their servants' names had turned 'the country against loyal associations' and further stated that 'Charlemont who supported the yeomanry scheme had been deserted by those he thought he could depend on'. The author revealed his sympathies by stating that, 'Orangemen have committed many excesses, yet I believe on inquiry, they will be found less compared to what has been alleged'.[43] The gentlemen's servants were probably catholics while the word 'country' probably referred to Orangemen.

The gentry who deliberately evaded government policy by not enlisting catholics were few, but Orangemen could frequently get their way by refusing to serve with catholics. Lord Downshire, while raising yeomanry in the Newry area, wrote, 'I am happy to say that there are some very respectable and loyal Papists among them, but the yeomanry infantry are not so liberal as the cavalry; their condition of service is, that no Papist should be enrolled with them ... They are chiefly Orangemen, and all agree in not admitting a Papist, however recommended'.[44]

---

[40] Everard to Downshire, 17 Oct. 1796 (P.R.O.N.I., Downshire MSS).
[41] *N.S.*, 10 Oct. 1796.   [42] *N.S.*, 17 Oct. 1796.
[43] N. Alexander to Henry Alexander, 8 Nov. 1796 (P.R.O.I., Rebellion papers 620/26/31).
[44] Lord Downshire to ——, 25 Nov. 1796 (Lecky, *Ire.*, iii. 473).

The yeomanry movement increased the influence of Orangeism only in districts where it was already established. Many Ulster units raised in the fall of 1796 were little affected by Orange influence and those outside Ulster not at all. Grattan at first joined the yeomanry but later resigned, while Keogh, the catholic leader, offered to raise a catholic corps, but on being told that denominational corps would not be acceptable, he denounced the movement as partisan. Radical and liberal opinion opposed recruiting and in Belfast no corps could be raised. However, the support given by Lord Downshire and, above all, by Lord Charlemont, who went to Armagh in September of 1796 to raise a corps, proved decisive. A military body which numbered among its sponsors the old commander of the volunteers and the founder of the Whig Club could hardly be represented as a horde of armed Orangemen. Charlemont remained an enemy of Lord Clare and the Beresfords, but he conceived it his duty to support the authority of the crown, even though disliking its ministers. He wrote, 'No man detests more heartily than I do the present administration and its measures, yet should that detestation prevent me from endeavouring to save my country from destruction even while swayed by Mr. Pitt?'[45] Charlemont could hardly have approved of the Orange lodges, but he may well have been prepared to tolerate Orangemen among his yeomen as he had formerly tolerated radicals among the volunteers.

It is difficult to make an accurate estimate of the number of yeomanry raised in the autumn of 1796. In a letter to Portland in December, Camden mentioned that 20,000 had come forward, of whom 9,000 were armed,[46] while Pelham wrote, 'The Yeomanry Corps are now become so numerous that the Lord Lieutenant has determined to suspend all new offers excepting in the disturbed parts of the country'.[47] The number of yeomen was to be greatly increased during the next year, and once the corps was established, United Irish policy was modified. In some districts United Irishmen continued a campaign against the corps, boycotting yeomen and threatening their lives;[48] in

---

[45] Charlemont to Haliday, 12 Sept. 1796 (*Charlemont MSS*, ii. 283).
[46] Camden to Portland, 26 Dec. 1796 (Lecky, *Ire.*, iii. 474).
[47] Pelham to Downshire, 3 Dec. 1796 (P.R.O.N.I., Downshire MSS).
[48] Arbuckle to Downshire, 15 Mar. 1797 (ibid.).

others, they adopted a conciliatory attitude and endeavoured, with considerable success, to win them over.

While the yeomanry was being recruited, the question of Orangeism was raised again in parliament. In the speech from the throne, the government expressed its regret at the Armagh atrocities, and dwelt at length on the growing menace of internal disorder.[49] On October 24 it asked and received the right to suspend the habeas corpus act, thus arming its officials with additional powers.[50] Grattan made an eloquent attack on this measure, calling attention to the Armagh outrages and pointing out the failure of officials to make adequate use of the existing powers against the Orangemen.[51] James Verner, using this occasion to defend the Orangemen from Grattan's attack, maintained that the Armagh outrages were exaggerated, that the Defenders had started the quarrel at the Diamond, and that Orangemen were loyal members of the established church. His speech probably excited more curiosity than sympathy, and is remarkable only as the first defence of Orangeism in parliament.

Although violence subsided in the autumn of 1796, no serious effort was made to disarm the population. Much of the quiet was the result of the increased steadiness of the United Irish underground while it awaited the expected French invasion.[52] United Irish morale was maintained by frequent assemblies on various pretexts such as digging potatoes for imprisoned republicans,[53] which served both as a drill and a show of force. The quiet which accompanied the new strength of the republicans removed immediate pressure from the government, which could find some consolation in the failure of disturbances to spread beyond Ulster. It might have been hoped the repressive legislation and new yeomanry would keep the province under control if the crown forces did not succumb to an invasion.

The French arrived late in December taking both the Castle and the United Irish by surprise, but were kept from landing by

[49] *P.R.*, 13 Oct. 1796, xvii. 3-71.
[50] Ibid., 24 Oct. 1796, xvii. 51-66.
[51] Ibid., 31 Oct. 1796, xvii. 4.
[52] Castlereagh to Lady Castlereagh, Sept. 1796 (Ione Leigh, *Castlereagh*, pp. 78-80).
[53] Carhampton to Hamilton, 8 Nov. 1796 (B.M., Add. MS 33102); *N.S.*, 21 Oct., 8 Nov. 1796; Lord Moira to Pelham, 8 Nov. 1796 (P.R.O.I., Rebellion papers 620/27/31).

adverse winds and poor seamanship.[54] News of the French fleet off the coast rallied most of the country to the crown.[55] Troops marching southward toward the threatened point at Bantry Bay were cheered on by southern peasants who cleared snow from roads and supplied them with food.[56] The militia marched in good spirits as catholic peasants joined the Bantry yeomanry, and protestant yeomen were mobilized to relieve regulars in the north. Only in Belfast and certain areas in Ulster did the rebellious spirit remain unshaken.

The disheartening effect which this had on the revolutionaries and the hope that the British cabinet might replace Lord Camden by the prince of Wales[57] led Grattan to an eleventh hour attempt at compromise. Some United Irishmen would have gladly returned to loyal opposition had the government offered concessions but it is to be doubted that the defection of a few upper and middle class leaders could have halted the forces which the republicans had put in motion.

Grattan's reform measure won only thirty votes,[58] indicating gentry acceptance of Castle leadership. Yet the gentry itself was fast losing influence over the peasantry, and apart from the placemen and Orangemen there were few who regarded the government as better than a necessary evil. The degree of government unpopularity at this time is shown by the way in which the circulation of subsidized newspapers such as the *Belfast News-Letter* fell when it defended Castle policy.[59] Some Castle journalists like John Giffard, editor of *Faulkner's Dublin Journal*, and Francis Higgins of the *Freeman's Journal*, also acted as Castle secret agents,[60] and were vitriolic enemies of catholic emancipation.[61] As their sentiments and policy were Orange, it

[54] Tone, *Life*, ii. 234.
[55] Higgins to Cooke, 31 Dec. 1796 (P.R.O.I., Rebellion papers 620/18/14); Camden to Portland, 10 Jan. 1797 (Grattan, *Memoirs*, iv. 265); Dalrymple to Pelham, 25 Dec. 1796 (B.M. Add MS 33102).
[56] Pelham to duke of York, 26 Dec. 1796 (B.M., Add. MS 33113); see also *Times*, 11 Mar. 1823.
[57] Charlemont to prince of Wales, June 1797 (*Charlemont MSS*, ii. 302).
[58] *P.R.*, 15 May 1797, xvii. 570.
[59] A. Aspinall, *Politics and the press*, pp. 109-112.
[60] W. J. Fitzpatrick, *Secret Service under Pitt*, pp. 118-9; P.R.O.I., Rebellion papers 620/18/14; see also Brian Inglis, *Freedom of the press in Ireland 1784-1841*, p. 56.
[61] Earl Stanhope, *Life of Pitt*, iii. 164.

is remarkable that there is no evidence they played a part in the Orange movement before 1797[62] when a gentleman's lodge was organized in Dublin.

Apart from Higgins and Giffard, the Castle had many sources of information on republican activities. Pitt's secret service watched Irish exiles in France,[63] while the town major of Dublin, Charles Henry Sirr, kept an assortment of detectives and informers who spied on the public. Sirr became an Orangeman in 1797, but seems to have had no previous connection with the lodges. Orangemen do not appear to have been a useful source of information to the Castle, as intelligence they supplied would naturally be looked on with suspicion. Also Orangemen were usually known to United Irishmen and there were far better sources available within the republican movement itself.

Sources of intelligence were not, however, the main problem of the Castle at the beginning of 1797. In spite of the disappointment at Bantry, republican forces grew in numbers and steadiness and spread beyond Ulster. Reports were received of the disintegration of civil power—the murder of loyalists, suspected informers and yeomen, attacks on gentry active against rebels, the systematic disarming of non-republicans, and forced recruiting into the underground army.[64] Lord Camden wrote a full description of the situation to Portland on March 9. 'The endeavour to arrest the progress of this system', he said, 'if it is possible, is the more necessary as infinite pains are taken to spread its influence over other parts of the kingdom. In the counties of Fermanagh, Louth, Kildare, and in King's County, it has appeared and also in the County of Mayo, and if effectual means are not taken to stop it, I think that the North of Ireland will not be the only part of this kingdom in a state little short of rebellion.'[65]

To restore its authority, the government had to discover and arrest the leaders of the United Irish and to disarm their rank and file. A network of informers, many of them within the republican system, facilitated the first part of the task, but the disorganized

---

[62] Inglis, *Freedom of the press*, p. 69.
[63] Fitzpatrick, *Secret service under Pitt*, pp. 19, 93.
[64] See B.M., Add. MS 33103, Jan. to Apr. 1797.
[65] Camden to Portland, 9 Mar. 1797 (Lecky, *Ire.*, iv. 18).

state of the armed forces made it impossible to act with humanity or efficiency. The measures undertaken were accurately described by republicans and whigs as 'the dragooning of Ulster'. This dragooning had to be carried out in the face of unrestrained criticism in the British and Irish parliaments, a vocal and critical gentry as well as a press which, until May, included the United Irish *Northern Star*. Few military commanders have undertaken a task of this kind under similar difficulties. The commanders responsible were Lieutenant General Lake, who commanded the north, usually from Belfast, Brigadier General Nugent at Hillsborough, and Brigadier General Knox at Dungannon.

4. THE DISARMING OF ULSTER, 1797

When the decision was made to disarm Ulster, it was fully expected that no direct assistance from the Orangemen would be required. The ineffectiveness of the attempts at disarming in the autumn of 1796 was partly due to the readiness with which magistrates permitted those taking the oath of loyalty to retain their arms. It was now intended to disarm all those who were not clearly 'loyal and respectable', and refusal to assist the civil power was to be considered sufficient grounds to confiscate arms. By special order of the viceroy, no action was to be taken to disarm the disaffected in Belfast.[66]

The new policy commenced officially by a proclamation of General Lake on 13 March 1797,[67] when all those not serving the crown in some capacity were ordered to bring in their arms. From the beginning the policy proved a failure. The republicans, warned of the proclamation, simply hid their arms in bogs and hedges, and it was often the neutral and loyal who were disarmed.[68] Lake wrote to Pelham, 'My declaration has yet been of very little use in making people give up their arms... From the want of more troops we have failed in our search.'[69] Insufficient force was, of course, less a problem than

---

[66] Pelham to Lake, 3 Mar. 1797 (P.R.O.N.I., Downshire MSS).
[67] *B.N.L.*, 13 Mar. 1797.
[68] Anderson to Downshire, 14 Mar. 1797 (P.R.O.N.I., Downshire MSS); Lake to Knox, Mar. 1797 (N.L.I., Lake MSS 56).
[69] Lake to Pelham, 15 Mar. 1797 (B.M., Add. MS 33103).

the quality of the troops. The yeomanry in particular were a disappointment. To General Knox, Lake wrote, 'I am sorry to say that those of the Yeomanry (between ourselves) are not much to be depended upon'.[70] To Downshire he wrote, 'Should the Yeomanry of [the Newry area] be inclined not to come forward, I think their arms ought to be taken from them'.[71] On the other hand, in districts where the yeomanry were active, they embarrassed the military by their excesses. Lake wrote again to Knox on 21 March 1797, 'I fear the Yeomanry are not to be trusted in their search for arms; their prejudices ... will lead them to improper acts',[72] while to Pelham he wrote, 'I really do not know of any excesses committed by the military since this unpleasant mode of warfare has commenced. I rather believe the Yeomanry may have shown some dislike to their neighbours ... but I do not believe they have been guilty of any great act of violence'.[73]

From every area Lake received discouraging information—complaints about military excesses and demands for more troops. The gentry asked for soldiers in each district, often insisting that they be highlanders.[74] The ineffective measures appeared merely to have driven reformers and neutrals into the republican camp, and actually strengthened the United Irish organization. Lake wrote to Pelham that 'the system of terror as practised by the United Irish has completely destroyed all idea of exertion in most of the magistrates and gentry throughout the country'.[75] Matters were not improved by news that the merchants corps of the Dublin yeomanry had, in the spirit of the 'old volunteers', insisted on their right to deliberate.[76] The *Northern Star* reported that the Cavan militiamen were taking whiskey and money instead of arms.[77] Lake's exasperation with the performance of his troops appears to have reached a point where military excesses seemed less dangerous than ineffective action. He was stopped by Camden on March 25 from promoting a sergeant who had killed a prisoner to prevent his being

[70] Lake to Knox, Mar. 1797 (N.L.I., Lake MSS 56).
[71] Lake to Downshire, 19 Mar. 1797 (P.R.O.N.I., Downshire MSS).
[72] Lake to Knox, 21 Mar. 1797 (N.L.I., Lake MSS 56).
[73] Lake to Pelham, 17 Mar. 1797 (B.M., Add. MS 33103).
[74] Lake to Pelham, 19 Mar. 1797 (ibid.).
[75] Same to same, 21 Mar. 1797 (ibid.).
[76] *B.N.L.*, 3 Apr. 1797. [77] *N.S.*, 3 Apr. 1797.

rescued,[78] and Lake soon became convinced that nothing short of burning the houses of men suspected of concealing arms would effectively disarm the province.[79] The belief was further strengthened when the assizes closed in Down without a single conviction.

The assizes were followed by a meeting of Armagh nobles and freeholders who passed a resolution that 'the British Constitution is enjoyed in name only', and demanded parliamentary reform, catholic emancipation, and the dismissal of the present ministers.[80] The *Northern Star* commented, 'Armagh ... once again proudly rears her head'.[81] Shortly thereafter, Lake wrote to Knox, 'Our situation grows worse every day as there can be no dependence upon our troops. I even fear some of the Fencibles are not free from infection'.[82] So startling was the evidence of United Irish influence in the ranks that Lake feared the consequence of a thorough investigation. He wrote to Pelham, '... between ourselves I am a little at a loss how to act at the moment, perhaps ... lay upon my oars ... as I fear by investigating other regiments too closely I may find so many guilty that I shall not know what to do with them'.[83]

Meanwhile, Lake's brigadier at Dungannon, General Knox, began to put forward a series of proposals in a manner which suggested that they were merely the consequence of his reflections on immediate circumstances. However, it is impossible not to notice the family connection of Knox with Lord Northland, whom Blacker named as an early patron of Orangemen. Nor can the similarity between his programme and that advanced by Thomas Knox of Dungannon, probably a kinsman of the general, be ignored. General Knox argued that the only section of the population upon which the government could rely was the Orangemen,[84] that they had become more respectable since the 'Armagh outrages' and could be kept under control, and that in any case it was necessary to undertake the risks

[78] Lake to Pelham, 25 Mar. 1797 (B.M., Add. MS 33103); Pelham to Lake, 29 Mar. 1797 (ibid.).
[79] Lake to Pelham, 16 Apr. 1797 (ibid.).
[80] *N.S.*, 21 Apr. 1797.
[81] *N.S.*, 24 Apr. 1797.
[82] Lake to Knox, 29 Apr. 1797 (N.L.I., Lake MSS 56).
[83] Lake to Pelham, 1 May 1797 (B.M., Add. MS 33104).
[84] Knox to Pelham, 19 Apr. 1797 (ibid., 33103).

involved in accepting their support. He wrote Lake on March 18:

> I have arranged a plan to scour a district full of unregistered arms, and this I do, not so much with a hope to succeed to any extent, and to increase the animosity between Orangemen and the United Irish. Upon that animosity depends the safety of the centre counties of the North. Were the Orangemen disarmed or put down, or were they coalesced with the other party, the whole of Ulster would be as bad as Antrim and Down.[85]

He added he would make no attempt at a 'genuine search and seizure of arms in Armagh, except in the wild country around Fews'.[86]

The practice of allowing Orangemen to keep their arms, however, proved insufficient to secure their safety. Three weeks later, Knox wrote, 'Loyalists are under the impression of terror. The Yeomanry are not what they were. Even the Orangemen on whose loyalty and firmness I had the most perfect reliance are shaken, but on that point I shall refer you to Mr Verner whom I shall see to-morrow'.[87] His conversation with Verner resulted in a suggestion which he forwarded to Pelham. 'Mr Verner informed me he could enrol a considerable number of man as supplementary Yeomen to be attached to his corps without pay, if Government would give them arms. They would consist of staunch Orangemen, the only description of men in the north of Ireland that can be depended upon. He reckons upon two or three hundred. May I encourage him to proceed?'[88]

About the same time as this was written, a man named Bisset proposed to Pelham that a special fencible regiment (regular troops) of Orangemen be raised.[89] Knox approved, but Pelham could see no legal way of raising a corps on the basis of a religious distinction. He put the project aside, giving as his reason the impending peace negotiations with France.[90] The consideration of the fencible corps, however, had the effect of delaying

[85] Knox to Lake, 18 Mar. 1797 (N.L.I., Lake MSS 56).   [86] Ibid.
[87] Knox to Pelham, 11 Apr. 1797 (B.M., Add. MS 33103).
[88] Same to same, 19 Apr. 1797 (ibid.).
[89] Pelham to Knox, 20 May 1797 (ibid., 33104).
[90] Pelham to Bisset, 23 June 1797 (ibid., 33103); Pelham to Knox, n.d. (N.L.I., Lake MSS 56, no. 77).

Knox's original plan to increase Verner's yeomanry corps,[91] and Knox was distracted from his plans to employ the Orangemen by a quarrel with Lord Carhampton over the militia.[92]

The internal history of the Orange movement up to this time is obscure. It can be assumed that the original leaders, such as James Sloan, were making plans in conjunction with Verner, and perhaps Knox, to bring the movement out in the open. A meeting of Orange leaders was planned for May 21 in Armagh city[93] where, a month before, nobility, clergy and free-holders had passed anti-government resolutions.[94] Knox was in contact with the Orangemen and was prepared to forward their resolutions to Pelham. The immediate purpose of this move was evidently to counteract the impression made by the anti-government resolutions of the April 19 meeting. A few days before the Orange meeting, Knox wrote to Pelham, 'Macan, the Sovereign of Armagh, ... was, in general, believed to be a United Irishman,' and that 'a great proportion of several Corps of Yeomanry in the neighbourhood of Armagh have become United Irish'.[95] He requested authorization to put the corps in question to a test by insisting that each yeoman swear he had never taken the United Irish oath.[96] Pelham, not caring to publicize disloyalty in the yeomanry, decided against applying the test, and insisted it would be sufficient to disarm yeomen under suspicion.[97] The meeting on May 21 at Armagh was attended by masters of various Ulster Orange lodges, with James Sloan, who had been secretary since 1795, acting as chairman.[98] A declaration of principles was published 29 May 1797 in the *Belfast News-Letter*. It read in part:

1. We associate to defend ourselves and our property.
2. We deny that we are sworn to extirpate and destroy [the

[91] Bisset to Pelham, 6 June 1797 (B.M., Add. MS 33104); Pelham to Knox, 20 May 1797 (N.L.I., Lake MSS 56).
[92] Lake to Knox 13 May 1797 (N.L.I., Lake MSS 56); Lake to Pelham, 14 May 1797 (B.M., Add. MS 33104); Pelham to Knox, 12 May 1797 (ibid.).
[93] Knox to Pelham, 21 May 1797 (B.M., Add. MS 33104).
[94] See above p. 66.
[95] Knox to Pelham, 17 May 1797 (B.M., Add. MS 33104).
[96] Ibid.
[97] Pelham to Knox, 20 May 1797 (B.M., Add. MS 33104).
[98] *B.N.L.*, 29 May 1797.

Roman Catholics] ... loyal, well-behaved men shall fear no injury from us.

3. We request that members of the Government do not enter into calumnies against us.

4. We further warmly invite gentlemen of property to reside in the country, in order that we may enrol ourselves as district corps under them; and as two guineas is not a sufficient sum [the government allowance for yeomanry equipment] for clothing a soldier, we entreat gentlemen to subscribe whatever they may think proper for that purpose—many an honest fellow having no personal property to contend for, nor any other objects than the laudable patriotic ties of our association.[99]

The Orangemen also pledged themselves to the king, the constitution, the protestant ascendancy, and the maintenance of the established church. The last point was, no doubt, the result of support the movement had received from clergymen such as Philip Johnson. If this was regretted by the numerous dissenters in the movement, they perhaps accepted it as a price worth paying to acquire government favour. The Orangemen outside county Armagh and adjacent districts at this time had formed no effective liaison with the gentry, and did not succeed in doing so until the Armagh precedent had been established. On the day of the meeting, Knox wrote to Pelham that the Orangemen had passed very satisfactory loyal resolutions and that with their help he could put down the United Irish in Armagh, Cavan, and parts of Tyrone.[1] Pelham assured Knox that any means of suppressing the United Irish was desirable, but 'at the same time, party and religious distinctions have produced such consequences in the county of Armagh that it will [take] the utmost prudence and dexterity in the management of such an undertaking. I leave the matter to your discretion, but wish to be informed of any particular plan.'[2]

In replying to this, Knox did not hesitate to comment freely on general policy. 'If the only object of the British government', he wrote, 'was to settle Ireland, it might be done in two months ... I proposed some time ago ... through Mr Elliot that the Orange Men might be armed and added to some of the loyal

---

[99] Ibid., see also Knox to Pelham, 21 May 1797 (B.M., Add. MS 33104).
[1] Knox to Pelham, 21 May 1797 (B.M., Add. MS 33104).
[2] Pelham to Knox, 20 May 1797 (N.L.I., Lake MSS 56).

corps as supplementary Yeomen. This scheme did not at the time seem to meet with approval. If government is resolved to resist Catholic Emancipation, the measure of adding strength to the Orange party will be of the greatest use. But they are bigots, and will resist Catholic Emancipation'. Knox continued, 'A. W. Atkinson has spoken to me on the subject of arming a body of these men (100) of the Church of England. He is a very loyal man and a stout magistrate, but I understand illiterate and of rude manner. He had written to you, but had not received an answer. A Corps might be entrusted to him with good effect'.[3] In the same letter, Knox stated, 'The loyal corps in this neighbourhood have purged themselves already, but a good many Yeomen are casuist enough to reconcile the oath of allegiance and the United Irish oath'.

On receiving the Orange resolutions from Knox, Pelham wrote, 'Nothing can be better than the resolutions of the Orange Men', but added, 'I confess that I still feel considerable difficulty in requiring any test excepting that provided by act of Parliament, although I perfectly agree with you in thinking that it may, in many instances, be very desirable'.[4] In reply, Knox expressed the opinion that a union of the Irish and British parliaments was desirable, and that parliamentary reform and catholic relief should accompany union.[5] These comments set him apart from his associates, the Orange gentry, who strongly opposed concessions to the catholics, but were not really inconsistent with his conviction that the only means of putting down the rebellion, apart from sending more British troops, was accepting support from the Orangemen. He pointed out that catholic emancipation would only benefit the catholics of property, of which there were none in Ulster where the United Irish were strongest.[6] Its immediate effect would be to lose the Orangemen without gaining the catholics.

On May 17, while Knox was arranging the liaison with the Orangemen, the viceroy-in-council issued a new proclamation of martial law.[7] Military officers could now act without

[3] Knox to Pelham, 22 May, 1797 (B.M., Add. MS 33104).
[4] Pelham to Knox, 26 May 1797 (N.L.I., Lake MSS 56).
[5] Knox to Pelham, 28 May 1797 (B.M., Add. MS 33104).
[6] Ibid.
[7] Lake to Knox, 21 May 1797 (N.L.I., Lake MSS 56).

authority from the civil magistrates, and the burning of houses in districts known to be seditious became a policy. The effective system of informers[8] enabled the government to arrest several United Irish leaders, and measures were taken to restore discipline in the militia'.[9]

5. MILITARY INCIDENTS

Unpleasant incidents could hardly be avoided. One of the first of these involved the Monaghan militia which had been stationed in Belfast since June of 1796, and as a result, a considerable number of militiamen had become United Irishmen.[10] By May 1797 the regimental officers decided to take action and called a special parade to deal with the danger. At this parade seventy men came forward, admitting themselves sworn United Irishmen.[11] Of these, four were court-martialled and shot; the rest were pardoned.[12] The former republicans sought to atone for past offences by assuming an attitude of extreme hostility towards the population of Belfast.[13] On May 19 a party of the Monaghan regiment raided the offices of the *Northern Star*, which had long defended the United Irish point of view, and smashed the printing apparatus.[14] The troops acted without orders, but their officers, including Lake himself,[15] approved their actions and made no serious effort to punish them.[16] It is likely the Monaghan militia founded an Orange lodge in its

[8] Pelham to General Cotte, 27 May 1797 (B.M., Add. MS 33104).
[9] Pelham to Loftus, 27 May 1797 (B.M., Add. MS 33104); Loftus to Pelham, 29 May 1797 (ibid.); Wynne to Pelham, 29 May 1797 (P.R.O.I., State of the country papers 408/591/43); *B.N.L.*, 2 June 1797.
[10] Col. Chas. Leslie to Lake, 25 Apr. 1797 (B.M., Add. MS 33103); Lake to Pelham, 26 Apr. 1797 (ibid.); *B.N.L.*, 8 May 1797.
[11] Lake to Pelham, 1 May 1797 (B.M., Add. MS 33104).
[12] Duke of York to Pelham, 9 June 1797 (ibid.).
[13] Pelham to ——, 1 Nov. 1797 (ibid., 33105); Pelham to Lake, 6 June 1797 (ibid., 33104); Lake to ——, 4 June 1797 (ibid.); Lake to ——, 17 May 1797 (N.L.I., Lake MSS 56); Lane to Downshire, 25 May 1797 (P.R.O.N.I., Downshire MSS); *B.N.L.*, 26 May 1797.
[14] Lane to Downshire, 21 May 1797 (P.R.O.N.I., Downshire MSS); Mrs. M. McTier to W. Drennan, 19 May 1797 (W. Drennan, *The Drennan letters*, p. 256); Sir Henry MacAnally, *The Irish militia*, p. 115.
[15] Lake to Knox, 21 May 1797 (N.L.I., Lake MSS 56).
[16] Lake to Pelham, 1 May 1797 (B.M., Add. MS 33104).

ranks at this time.[17] They were to hold warrant no. 47, which made them senior to the lodges in the Cavan, Armagh and Fermanagh regiments, all of which were in existence by 1798.[18]

The people of Belfast sensed the growing hostility of the Monaghans, for on June 1 Lake reported that they were endeavouring to get the regiment sent away.[19] On June 5 Reverend Edward Hudson wrote Charlement that 'the military in Belfast is making ample use of the power vested in them. Not a day passes without hearing of some act of outrage. This summary mode of punishing I do not like much, even when it falls on fit objects. There is a danger, too, that these gentlemen in red may not exactly know where to stop; and, being both judge and executioner, their mistakes may not easily be remedied'.[20]

The second serious military incident involved the Welsh fencible regiment, the Ancient Britons, and the yeomanry near Newry.[21] Having arrived from Scotland about 10 April 1797,[22] the Ancient Britons were mentioned by Lake for work at Forkhill on May 14.[23] It is possible they made some contact with Armagh Orangemen in that area, and carried the Orange spirit with them to Newry. The Newry area was United Irish, and had, until June, successfully evaded government efforts to seize arms. The Britons may have been encouraged to act with severity or simply followed the example of the yeomen, but their action was soon out of hand and their 'terrible' deeds became legendary. The witnesses against them are impressive. John Giffard, the Castle agent and journalist, generally considered to have been a loud and violent Orangeman,[24] wrote to Cooke on 5 June 1797 that 'the Welsh burned a great number of houses, and the object of emulation between them and the Orange Yeomen seems to be, who shall do the most mischief to the wretches who certainly may have seditious minds, but who are, at present, quiet and incapable of resistance'. In describing a search for arms, he wrote:

[17] *B.N.L.*, 14 July 1797. [18] Gowan, *Orangeism*, p. 196.
[19] Lake to Pelham, 1 June 1797 (B.M., Add. MS 33104).
[20] Hudson to Charlemont, 5 June 1797 (*Charlemont MSS*, ii. 300).
[21] Pelham to Lake, 6 June 1797 (B.M., Add. MS 33104).
[22] *B.N.L.*, 10 Apr. 1797.
[23] Lake to Knox, 14 May 1797 (N.L.I., Lake MSS 56); Lake to Pelham, 14 May 1797 (B.M., Add. MS 33104).
[24] Madden, *United Irishmen*, ii. 291-6.

I was directed by the smoke and flames of burning houses, and by the dead bodies of boys and old men slain by the Britons, though no opposition whatever had been given by them, and, as I shall answer to Almighty God I believe a single gun was not fired, but by the Britons and Yeomanry. I declare there was nothing to fire at, old men women, and children excepted ... From ten to twenty were killed outright; many wounded, and eight houses burned.[25]

Giffard is a very damning witness against the Britons. The only personal reason which might have induced him to attack the behaviour of this regiment so severely is that they killed a member of his own unit, the Dublin Militia. But the action of these Welsh fencibles is condemned by so many sources that there is no reason to believe they have been slandered by biased witnesses.[26] Yet such was the state of the country that even the viceroy hesitated to condemn them. Pelham wrote to Portland that, from their activity and loyalty, [the Ancient Britons] had become the terror of the disaffected, 'and in some instances have proceeded too far, but I have written to General Lake to make inquiries'.[27]

There is no doubt that the reputation which the Ancient Britons established by indiscriminate killing had a sobering effect on the population, and this reputation served as a deterrent to republican sympathizers. If the Ancient Britons could be unleashed by the government, the population of any district would hesitate to give aid and comfort to the United Irish. It was by such terrorist methods that the Ulster republicans were overawed.

Apart from the Belfast riot and the 'outrages' of the Ancient Britons, which were undoubtedly the most serious incidents, the Castle received various reports about the conduct of its forces and the Orangemen. The most disturbing of these was a report on June 18 that a catholic chapel at Tartaraghan had been destroyed by Orangemen of Verner's corps, who asserted they acted on Verner's orders.[28] Verner denied it at once, and

[25] John Giffard to Cooke, 5 June 1797 (P.R.O.I., Rebellion papers 620/31/36).
[26] Grattan, *Memoirs*, iv. 378; Plowden, *Hist. Ire. to 1800*, iv. 267; MacNeven, *Pieces of Irish history*, p. 202.
[27] Pelham to ——, 1 Nov. 1797 (B.M., Add. MS 33105).
[28] Owen Creilly to T. Burgh, 20 June 1797 (P.R.O.I., Rebellion papers 620/31/131).

offered the testimony of a sergeant and private of the Fay fencibles, who were employed to drill his yeomanry, that members of the corps did not participate, but merely stood by and watched the chapel being pulled down, although 'one or two yeomen were throwing stones'.[29] Robert Lowry wrote from Dungannon complaining that the yeomanry went out without their officers day and night to 'scour the county, destroying houses, furniture, stab and cut in the most cruel manner... We are beginning the County Armagh business, papering and noticing Roman Catholics to fly on or before such a day or night'.[30] Pelham wrote to Lowry at once that no yeomanry corps henceforth be allowed to act without officers.[31] The overall effect of military and Orange action was to renew the flight to Connaught.[32] Victims fleeing this time, however, were often United Irish terrorists and not altogether innocent victims.[33]

The inability of the Orange leaders to restrain their followers had its counterpart in the inadequate control which the United Irish exercised over their local contingents. The United Irish leaders insisted, no doubt truthfully, that they never countenanced the assassinations and murders committed in the name of the republican cause. It was, in fact, impossible at this time to organize a popular movement among the Irish peasants for the purpose of employing physical force without opening the door to excess. Fanatics and criminals were bound to seek shelter in the movement and the consequence of enforcing too rigid a discipline would be to dampen the enthusiasm on which the success of the movement depended.

Orangemen were more given to excess outside the areas where they were associated with the gentry. Captain O'Beirne of the Longford regiment, writing from Keady near the Monaghan border, reported, 'Orange boys headed by officers in full yeomanry uniforms [committing] robberies, murders

[29] Verner to govt., 1 July 1797 (ibid., 620/31/190); Verner to Pelham, 3 July 1797 (ibid., 620/30/196); *B.N.L.*, 14 July 1797.
[30] Lowry to Pelham, 29 June 1797 (P.R.O.I., Rebellion papers 620/31/171).
[31] Pelham to Lowry, 2 July 1797 (ibid., 620/31/171).
[32] R. Livingston to Charlemont, 8 Nov. 1797 (*Charlemont MSS*, ii. 310-11).
[33] H. Browne to Pelham, 31 May 1797 (P.R.O.I., Rebellion papers 620/30/271).

and shameful outrages and claiming government sanction'.[34] There was also adverse mention of the Orangemen by Lord Blayney of Castle Blayney, who was very active against the United Irish in Monaghan. He protested that the Orangemen were committing crimes and claiming government sanction. As he was known for his opposition to government policy, he hesitated to act against the Orangemen lest he be thought sympathetic to the United Irish. He asked, 'Why sanction a mob of any kind, sir? You have force enough without such assistance ... government should contradict reports that it protects Orangemen'.[35] Lord Blayney found no comfort in the government reply that it did not favour one party more than another. He wrote again to say that the 'Orange Men ought certainly to be shewn some countenance, but under that cloak robbers and assassins will shelter themselves'.[36]

In areas where Orangemen had no connection with the gentry, local authorities continued to regard them as another species of rebel. The men at the Castle were inclined towards the same view, but by permitting General Knox to encourage the Orangemen, the government had unwillingly given them a special status. The inconsistency between arming them in Armagh and suppressing them in Monaghan could hardly be ignored. The government was unable to devise a solution to this dilemma, but it was, in some measure, solved after the Dublin lodge was founded 4 June 1797.[37] The large numbers of gentry and placemen of all classes joining the Dublin lodge were soon using their influence in the country to organize or recognize local Orange lodges and grant them the status they enjoyed in Armagh. But there was no Castle policy, and local magistrates, landlords and military commanders were permitted to work out their own policy towards Orangeism.

[34] Capt. O'Beirne to Marshall, 3 June 1797 (P.R.O.I., Rebellion papers 620/31/27).
[35] Blayney to govt., 2 June 1797 (ibid., 620/31/12).
[36] Same to same, 10 June 1797 (ibid., 620/31/71).
[37] Evidence of W. Verner, *Rep. on Orange lodges III*, H.C. 1835 [476], xvi. 252.

6. Dublin Lodge supported by protestant party

The founding of a gentlemen's Orange lodge in Dublin was the first step toward the creation of a national movement. Although Thomas Verner—with his Armagh connections—became its first master, this lodge drew its strength from Patrick Duigenan, members of the Beresford faction, and others who had constituted an informal 'protestant party' since the catholic relief act of 1793. Members of this party had been responsible for efforts to establish anti-Defender associations in the fall of 1795,[38] which had been abandoned in the face of government hostility. The Orange lodges were ideally suited to their needs, but their dependence upon government prevented them from supporting any movement until the spring of 1797. By that time, the influence of Grattan's supporters in the Dublin yeomanry had aroused fears that the corps might be politicalized in the manner of the volunteers. To prevent such a development, the 'protestant party' united to suppress discussion in the Dublin corps. In rendering this service to the Castle, they had acted as a faction, and as their continued existence as a faction appeared to be a necessary check to opposition influence in the yeomanry, the government could hardly prevent them from creating a formal organization.

Yet at the time of its founding in June 1797, the Dublin lodge added little, if any, prestige to the more plebeian branch of Orangeism in Ulster. Thomas Verner, its master, was certainly not of very great influence. Yet by March of the following year it numbered among its members several noblemen, a Beresford, Major Sirr, Jonah Barrington of literary fame, and a host of other Castle supporters[39] and Church of Ireland clergy, thus becoming the most powerful club in Dublin and the nucleus of a national Orange movement. In Ulster there was a three-fold increase in membership by the late spring of 1797, partly as a result of the support offered the lodges by General Knox and partly because of the success of General Lake's measures against the United Irish.

---

[38] See above p. 33.
[39] Evidence of W. Verner, *Rep. on Orange lodges II*, H.C. 1835 [475], xvi. 252; Gowan, *Orangeism*, pp. 189–90.

Gentry Support of Orangeism, 1796–7

Under the terms of Lake's proclamation of May 17, all those not guilty of crime, but who had become involved in republicanism, could clear themselves by taking a loyalty oath. After the Belfast military riot and the episode of the Ancient Britons at Newry, many came forward to take the required oath.[40] It is likely that large numbers of repentant United Irish sought shelter in the Orange movement. Among them, perhaps, were many who had joined the republicans under the pressure of terror and were happy to rally to the government. A notice of an Orange meeting in Belfast on June 23, with James Montgomery as master,[41] establishes that by now Orangeism had reached the former citadel of radicalism, while the general rallying to the government was further indicated by a series of loyal resolutions passed by representatives of thirty-four free masonic lodges of Armagh who acknowledged that some of their members had become United Irishmen and they 'wished to wipe away that stigma'.[42]

At this time, Orangemen felt strong enough to establish a central leadership by forming a grand lodge of Ulster. A general demonstration of strength and of government support was planned for 12 July 1797 when plans for the grand lodge were to be announced.[43] Having granted permission for a series of parades, General Lake rode out from Belfast, escorted by the Belfast yeomanry, to review 3,000 Orangemen at Lisburn and possibly 12,000 at Lurgan.[44] It is unlikely that the total number parading in 1797 exceeded 5,000. Of the Lisburn parade, Haliday wrote:

We had a display here yesterday morning of the whole force the 'Orange Boys', 'Orange' wenches, and 'Orange' children could muster, for many miles around; it was supposed there might have been three thousand of the motley crew, including the various corps of yeomen. I do not understand the nature of the 'Orange Boy' establishment. I should have rejoiced in the profusion of 'Orange' badges could I have considered them as anything better than those of tame submission on one hand, and rancorous religious bigotry on the other; but I was exceedingly offended with the figure of the best

---

[40] Andrew Newton to ——, 18 June 1797 (P.R.O.I., Rebellion papers 620/31/114).
[41] *B.N.L.*, 23 June 1797.   [42] *B.N.L.*, 26 June 1797.
[43] Gowan, *Orangeism*, p. 187.   [44] *B.N.L.*, 14 July 1797.

of kings, miserably depicted on divers banners... rather like a great fool. The pageant was over by noon, and with abundance of sheepskin noises, to which we are so well accustomed in this garrison. There was no rioting, though those who remembered the 5th of June... had their apprehensions.⁴⁵

The day was marked by one incident involving a party of Kerry militia who raided Stewartstown while the younger inhabitants had gone to Lurgan for the Orange parade.⁴⁶ The 24th Dragoons rode back to Stewartstown, and a fight ensued during which seven militiamen were killed and six wounded.⁴⁷

Sometime before the formation of the Ulster Grand Lodge in 1797, the Orangemen had established an inner circle or higher order. Such devices are common to secret societies and for the Orangemen, it provided a means by which gentlemen and reliable plebeians might exercise control over the unruly rank and file. It is impossible to tell the degree of exclusiveness maintained by this inner circle, which took the name of Purplemen. In the later period of the lodges, the Order of the Purple was conferred on any Orangeman who had a record of good behaviour in his lodge. Colonel William Verner testified in 1835 that the Purple Order was withheld only from the recently-recruited Orangeman who, the lodges had decided, was undesirable.⁴⁸ At first, the higher order was called the Orange Marksmen. Its members were given a separate set of secret signs and passwords, and were bound by a special oath requiring higher standards of behaviour than those demanded of ordinary Orangemen. A special requirement of the Orange Marksman was that he 'induct no man into the Order on the road or hillsides',⁴⁹ by which clause, it was hoped that various officers of the Orange lodges, who would naturally belong to the higher order, could be prevented from recruiting disorderly

⁴⁵ Haliday to Charlemont, 13 July 1797 (*Charlemont MSS*, ii. 303).
⁴⁶ Hamilton to Pelham, 14 July 1797 (P.R.O.I., Rebellion papers 620/31/230); —— to Cooke, 14 July 1797 (ibid., 620/31/231); Lord Northland to Pelham, 15 July 1797 (ibid., 620/31/234); A.M., Blacker MSS iii. 19; *B.N.L.*, 17 July 1797.
⁴⁷ Pelham to Portland, 1 Nov. 1797 (B.M., Add. MS 33105); *B.N.L.*, 17 July 1797.
⁴⁸ Evidence of W. Verner, *Rep. on Orange lodges I*, H.C. 1835 [377], xv. 29; Evidence of Stewart Blacker (ibid., p. 112).
⁴⁹ See appendix A, iii.

Gentry Support of Orangeism, 1796-7

elements by irregular methods. During an attack on the lodges in 1823 in the British parliament, it was claimed that the Purple Order was connected with the 'introduction into the army of the Orange lodges'.[50] Some evidence for this exists in a letter written to Captain J. W. Maxwell in 1798 by an Orangeman who complained that the selection of men to be enrolled in the yeomanry corps under Captain Maxwell had been 'taken to the higher degree'.[51] Sometime early in 1797, the Orange Marksman became the Purpleman, and hence the lodges had two orders—the Orange and the Purple.[52] Later so-called Black lodges came into existence as a further inner circle of Orangeism, but these were, in the early years, against the rules of the Orange Order and membership in them was forbidden.[53]

The Orange movement continued to grow in strength and influence throughout the remainder of 1797. Its chief centre of strength remained county Armagh and its adjacent districts, where the gentry and military accepted Orange support. Lord Blayney continued to oppose Orangeism in Monaghan,[54] and as its influence spread northward from Dungannon, it was opposed by Sir George Hill of Derry. Hill announced he would not permit the formation of an Orange lodge unless ordered to by government, and he gave as grounds for his opposition that any society formed by dissenters in his district would soon become seditious.[55]

At the September assizes in Armagh and Down, juries resumed their normal functions, convicting large numbers of persons of a variety of crimes.[56] Convictions in Down included two 'calling themselves Orangemen', who were charged with house robbery.[57] Attacks on catholics in Orange districts were less frequent, but not unknown.[58] Captain Lindsay in Dungan-

[50] Abercromby's speech in H.C., in *Times*, 6 Mar. 1823.
[51] John Murphy to Captain Maxwell, 28 May 1798 (P.R.O.N.I., T 1023(150).
[52] Evidence of Swan, *Rep. on Orange lodges I*, H.C. 1835 [377], xv. 84.
[53] Evidence of S. Blacker (ibid., pp. 112–3).
[54] Blayney to govt., 20 Nov. 1797 (P.R.O.I., Rebellion papers 620/31/71).
[55] Hill to Cooke, 23 Sept. 1797 (ibid., 620/32/139).
[56] Wolfe to Pelham, 12 Sept. 1797 (P.R.O.I., Rebellion papers 620/32/116); Wolfe to Cooke, 13 Sept. 1797 (ibid., 620/32/122); *B.N.L.*, 22 Sept. 1797.
[57] *B.N.L.*, 28 Sept. 1797.   [58] *B.N.L.*, 2 Oct. 1797.

non reported that the houses of loyal catholics were attacked the moment he withdrew his picquets and patrols.[59] The flight of Ulster catholics to Connaught had been noticeable in early summer, but was little mentioned in the autumn of 1797. However, the large numbers of catholics already in Connaught had exhausted their resources and were subsisting on public funds.[60] They and others driven from Ulster had made certain that tales of Orange terrorism and the extermination oath were widely diffused in the other provinces. The effect this had was to win for the United Irish new strength in the south to compensate for the defeat inflicted upon them by the Orange and military forces in Ulster.

[59] Lindsay to Pelham, 14 Sept. 1797 (P.R.O.I., Rebellion papers 620/32/126).
[60] Lord Altamount to ——, 18 Oct. 1797 (ibid., 620/32/172).

IV

THE REBELLION OF 1798

1. The Orange Bogey

GENERAL LAKE'S DISARMING of Ulster, with the aid of the Orangemen, achieved a surface tranquillity in the north. Yet, even as this was being effected, the forces of rebellion were spreading through the hitherto loyal provinces in the south.[1] The liaison which the republicans had established with the Defenders in the early part of 1796 had taken nearly a year to mature, but, by the end of 1797, the major part of the catholic population in Ireland had been brought under the United Irish system.[2] The relative ease with which this was accomplished was made possible by the terror that the word 'Orangeman' was able to evoke among the catholic peasantry,[3] and the continual assertion on the part of Orangemen that they enjoyed government support.[4] Had there been no Orangemen, however, the military outrages of government forces in Ulster might have been sufficient to generate the same degree of fear among

---

[1] Ross to Downshire, 27 Mar. 1798 (P.R.O.N.I., Downshire MSS); Pollock to Downshire, 16 Mar. 1798 (ibid.); Connor to Pelham, 25 Feb. 1798 (P.R.O.I., Rebellion papers 620/35/155).

[2] D. Browne's notebook on United Irish activities (P.R.O.I., Rebellion papers 620/54/7); John Maxwell's notebook, May 1797 (ibid., 620/34/54).

[3] F. Archer, Justice of the Peace for Carlow, to govt., 3 Jan. 1798 (ibid., 620/35/11).

[4] Haliday to Charlemont, 7 Aug. 1797 (*Charlemont MSS*, ii. 278–9); see also MacNeven, *Pieces of Irish history*, pp. 178, 186.

The Rebellion of 1798

the excitable peasantry.[5] But the republicans chose to concentrate their propaganda against Orangemen, so that during the summer and autumn of 1797, the 'Orange bogey' became a factor in Irish politics which far exceeded in importance the movement itself.[6] The rumours that were spread through the southern Irish provinces have been likened to those which roused the catholic peasantry in 1641. So seriously were these tales taken that in county Carlow, a rumour that Orangemen were coming was sufficient to induce part of the population to flee from their homes,[7] for it was believed that Orangemen were sworn to exterminate catholics, and that the majority of the protestant population were Orangemen.[8]

Cooke, the under-secretary at Dublin Castle, accepted as authentic an informer's report which suggests that such rumours were deliberately and cynically spread by United Irish leaders. He wrote to Pelham 26 December 1797:

I learn from my friend that Lord Edward Fitzgerald received an order from Paris to urge an insurrection in order to draw troops from England. In consequence, there was a meeting of the Head Committee where he and O'Connor proposed arming 500 men with short swords . . . that this body should repair to all the Mass Houses at Midnight Mass on Christmas morning . . . and raise a cry that the Orangemen were murdering the Catholics.

The report continued 'having raised the uproar, they should begin their attacks on the Castle . . . Emmet and Chambers opposed and the Bishops, who were opposed to outrage, put off Mass until the morning'.[9]

The fear of Orangeism in the south had little relation to Orange strength as the movement there was small and without substantial influence. The agencies by which Orangeism advanced southward were the northern military units and the gentry who had joined the Dublin lodge. The United Irishmen

[5] View of present state of Ireland 1797 (P.R.O.I., Rebellion papers 620/34/53).
[6] Evidence of Emmet before select committee of the Irish house of lords, 10 Aug. 1798, in MacNeven, *Pieces of Irish history*, p. 215; Musgrave, *Memoirs*, p. 377; Plowden, *Hist. of Ire. to 1800*, iv. 299.
[7] *F.D.J.*, 13 Jan. 1798; P.R.O.I., Rebellion papers 620/35/11.
[8] Cooke to Pelham, 23 Dec. 1797 (B.M., Add. MS 33105).
[9] Same to same, 26 Dec. 1797 (ibid.).

The Rebellion of 1798

gained adherents in the south by way of their converts among the Defenders. Many of these were parish priests who, in defiance of the catholic hierarchy, were active in the revolutionary movement.[10] Thus the republicans in the south had a very different character than their middle-class-led counterparts in Ulster. The idea of winning protestants, or even Orangemen, to the United Irish cause was not considered in the south. There the republican movement followed the lines of the Whiteboys and Defenders. It accepted the name, signs, organizational system and passwords of the United Irish, but had little understanding of their political objectives.

As the United Irish won over catholics in the south, enthusiasm for the movement waned in the north. Fear of the consequences of a catholic-dominated revolution, combined with General Lake's repressive measures in Ulster had, by the eve of the rebellion of 1798, driven many erstwhile republicans into the Orange Order.[11] Of this shift in alliance, Hudson wrote to Charlemont, 'Your old Ballymascanlan Volunteers, who six months ago were almost all United Irishmen are now complete Orangemen, which is more congenial with their feelings. A gentleman who had just come from Cork told me that this system is beginning to spread in the south. I understand they reckon on the countenance of government, and, I fancy, not without reason'. Hudson went on:

They are, I am told, loyal; but I foresee many evils from the establishment of parties in a country. I could wish that this party (if there must be parties) had taken the name of 'loyalist' or any other than that of Orangeman. For this latter tends to frighten and alienate the Catholics who are, here at least, well affected... In speaking of this astonishing increase of Orangeism, I forgot to mention the most part wonderful of it, that immense numbers of them are in Belfast.[12]

Yet in spite of the desertion of republicanism by a substantial number of United Irishmen, the movement kept alive in the north.[13] The government was thus in no position to reduce its

---

[10] Major Cawerass to Pelham, 18 Apr. 1797 (P.R.O.I., Rebellion papers 620/29/277).
[11] Evidence of W. Blacker, *Rep. on Orange lodges III*, H.C. 1835 [476], xvi. 248.
[12] Hudson to Charlemont, 19 May 1797 (*Charlemont MSS*, ii. 323).
[13] Lake to Pelham, 27 Jan. 1798 (B.M., Add. MS 33105).

Ulster garrison to meet the new threat developing in the south. Rumours of a second French invasion increased the anxiety of the men at the Castle,[14] while attacks in parliament added to their embarrassment. The latter were made in the British and Irish houses of lords by Lord Moira, who denounced the army and Orangemen for the outrages committed during the disarming of Ulster. These denunciations, applauded only by the Foxite whigs, would have passed as a minor irritation had not the Castle been confronted with an internal crisis partly of its own making.

2. The Appointment of Abercromby

The Irish commander-in-chief, Lord Carhampton, had long been a source of annoyance to the Castle because of his quarrelsome temperament and Irish political connections. In November 1797 Lord Camden succeeded in having him replaced by General Abercromby,[15] a professional soldier without Irish connections, who, the viceroy assumed, would ensure the efficient and impartial conduct of military affairs. This view made no allowance for Abercromby's reaction to the state of the army, his necessary ignorance of Irish politics, and the difficulties involved in managing the diverse forces under his command. On arrival, the new commander-in-chief went on a tour of inspection in the south, and he sent a series of letters to London in one of which he stated, 'The dispersed state of the troops is really ruinous to the service. The best troops in Europe would not long stand such usage ... I have found the cavalry in general unfit for service and more than one-half the infantry dispersed over the face of the country, in general, under officers very little able to command them.'[16] Abercromby recommended that regulars and militia be concentrated to deal with possible foreign invasion, and the yeomanry assigned the task of policing the interior. This was sound enough, but as the yeomanry was not sufficient to protect all estates from the United Irish, the gentry was alarmed and offended. Further

---

[14] Hostile preparations in French ports in February and March, 1798, in Castlereagh, *Correspondence*, i. 165–8.
[15] Brownrigg to Pelham, 7 Nov. 1797 (B.M., Add. MS 33105).
[16] Abercromby to Pelham, 23 Jan. 1798 (B.M., Add. MS 33105).

weakening Abercromby's position was the fact that he was personally disliked by two of the most important generals in the Irish command—Lake and Dalrymple.[17]

In times of peace, the office of commander-in-chief had been of small importance, and even in wartime, it was clearly subordinate to that of the viceroy. However, Abercromby, before coming to Ireland, had insisted on and had been granted full control of the military. Such control was resented by the 'Castle clique' as an usurpation of its authority. A more tactful general might have maintained his position by keeping the confidence of the viceroy, but the manner in which Abercromby proceeded soon convinced Camden that the appointment had been a mistake. He wrote Pelham on 25 December 1797 'Elliott has gone to Abercromby in consequence of a letter he has written him [complaining of the dual direction of the army] which shews he is a person not to carry on business with as I had imagined. He appears desirous of having unlimited power and does not brook even any pauses in executing his orders'.[18]

Abercromby was essentially the simple military man placed in circumstances calling for a soldier who was something of a diplomat and intriguer. He accepted office under protest, and acted without making allowance for vested interests and personal feelings.[19] It was inevitable that he would provoke the wrath of such competent intriguers as Lord Clare[20] and the Beresfords, and that they, in turn, would precipitate his resignation. The crisis developed over the question of martial law. As a step towards halting military outrages, the commander-in-chief issued a strongly worded general order on 26 February 1798 declaring the 'army to be in a general state of licentiousness which must render it formidable to everyone but the enemy'.[21] He instructed all officers to give strict attention to 'the standing orders of the kingdom, which at the same time that they directed military assistance to be given at

[17] Knox to Pelham, 29 Nov. 1797 (ibid.); Lake to Pelham, 27 Jan. 1798 (ibid.).
[18] Camden to Pelham, 25 Dec. 1797 (ibid.).
[19] Ross to Downshire, 27 Mar. 1798 (P.R.O.N.I., Downshire MSS).
[20] Clare to Auckland, 23 Mar. 1798 (Lord Auckland, *Journal and correspondence*, iii. 393–5).
[21] General orders of Sir Ralph Abercromby, 26 Feb. 1798, in Grattan, *Memoirs*, iv. 352).

The Rebellion of 1798

the requisition of the civil magistrates, positively forbid the troops to act (but in case of attack) without his presence and authority and the most clear and precise orders are to be given to the officer commanding the party for this purpose'.[22] This order, which became known to the public, confirmed from an official source the charges which, quite independently of Abercromby, had been made in the house of lords by Lord Moira. Neither Abercromby nor Moira had overstated the case, but the effect of such a declaration under such circumstances could hardly contribute to public tranquillity.[23] Not only did the commander-in-chief's order disturb public opinion, it was in conflict with the proclamation of 18 March 1797[24] which instructed the military to act without the intervention of civil authority. Lake, the military commander in Belfast, upon hearing the order, wrote, 'I understand Sir Ralph talks much of conciliation and says that the troops should not act without magistrates ... I pity him and imagine he is quite in his dotage. I agree with you in thinking but for coercion, as it is called, the North of Ireland would have been lost'.[25]

After issuing his general orders, Abercromby left Dublin for an inspection of Ulster, thus giving the 'Castle clique' an opportunity to conspire against him. What followed was very much as it had been in the Fitzwilliam affair. Fitzgibbon, Beresford, and Cooke immediately wrote to England attacking Abercromby's actions. Camden and Pelham offered a lukewarm defence of the commander-in-chief, but they, too, were offended by his overly candid criticism and direct methods of meeting problems. Abercromby's view, however, was supported wholeheartedly by regular officers such as Sir John Moore. Moore, whose sentiments were probably similar to those of many of the British officers sent to Ireland at the end of 1797, wrote:

The argument used by the Chancellor of Ireland in the late debate upon Lord Moira's motion seems to me very weak. He says that conciliation (meaning with respect to the Roman Catholics) had already been tried, but instead of contenting them, it had only

---

[22] Ibid.
[23] Beresford to Lord Westmorland, 29 Mar. 1798 (Beresford, *Correspondence*, ii. 154).
[24] *P.R.*, 18 Mar. 1797, xvii. 129.
[25] Lake to Knox, 25 Feb. 1798 (N.L.I., Lake MSS 56).

created discontent; that in each new concession, the people professed themselves contented and grateful, and yet, within a month or two afterwards, their discontent and turbulence returned with increased vigour.

Moore asked, 'Can it then be sound policy in a Government to favour one part of its inhabitants against nineteen who are oppressed... That so much has been granted to the Roman Catholics is a bad argument for withholding from them the little that remains'.[26]

To professional soldiers like Moore and Abercromby, politics in the army seemed inexcusable. They were unwilling to make concessions to the feelings of the Irish gentry, and attempted to impose on them and their satellites—the militia officers—a degree of discipline to which they were wholly unaccustomed. Abercromby's general orders, which the officers rightly took to be directed against themselves, were bitterly resented.[27] Moore wrote, 'The principal officers, who had hitherto been used to being complimented, could not bear the language of truth. They had the folly to call out and make public what was meant for their private guidance and correction, and they had done so with all the effrontery of innocence and rectitude'.[28]

From Moore's and Abercromby's dislike of politics among officers, it can be inferred that they would hardly tolerate Orange lodges among the men. Moore was explicit on this point. He wrote on March 17:

I made a speech yesterday to the troops. I reprobated some meetings of Orange Boys (Protestants), which, as I heard, had taken place. I said that if by such meetings they intended to form a union to defend their country, they were unnecessary as every good man was already determined in his heart to do so, and they, as soldiers, had already sworn to do it; but, if it was to create a distinction and separate interest from the Catholics, it was wicked, and must be punished.

Moore told the troops that Ireland was composed of catholics and protestants and that government had entrusted both equally with her defence. He ended his address by saying, 'A

[26] Sir John Moore, *Diary*, i. 275, entry 4 Mar. 1798.
[27] Ross to Downshire, 5 Mar. 1798 (P.R.O.N.I., Downshire MSS).
[28] Moore, *Diary*, i. 283, entry 29 Mar. 1798.

union of both was necessary for this purpose. Distinctions of this kind were illiberal and for a man to boast of his religion was absurd.'[29]

Moore's reasoning would have been sound enough had there been sufficient officers of his calibre in Ireland to give proper attention to the morale of the troops. Secret societies of any kind could, in such circumstances, be dealt with effectively by alert regimental officers. However, as the character of the average officer of the Irish militia was, by Moore's own testimony, very poor, and the republicans were making efforts to plant cells among the troops,[30] Orangemen were useful. If they served no other purpose, they were a possible point of contact between officers and the men. It would be next to impossible for a republican organization to make headway in a regiment where an active minority of Orangemen would report any suspicious behaviour. Moreover, a United Irish agent would hesitate to agitate among troops known to have Orangemen in their ranks. The lodges, therefore, although their general effect on discipline may have been bad, did offer a makeshift means of counteracting republican infiltration in militia units where the ranks were disaffected[31] and the officers of doubtful quality. If this sort of officer was to be retained, and political influence tolerated in the army, Orange lodges were, perhaps, the best insurance of loyalty. Lake and Knox, who were not prepared to attack the great political interests with which they were personally associated, found the Orangemen useful. Abercromby and Moore, who were determined to break political interests and find competent officers, distrusted self-appointed loyalists.

In justice to the judgment of officers like Lake and Knox, it must be pointed out that the senior officers, arriving in Ireland from service overseas, under-estimated the danger of rebellion. While parading about the countryside with their troops, they found the peasantry quiet, and concluded that reports of disaffection were exaggerated,[32] forgetting, perhaps, that their

[29] Moore, *Diary*, i. 279, entry 17 Mar. 1798.
[30] Lane to Downshire, 1 Feb. 1798 (P.R.O.N.I., Downshire MSS).
[31] Lake to Knox, 17 Feb. 1798 (N.L.I., Lake MSS 56).
[32] Lake to Knox, 22 Jan. 1798 (N.L.I., Lake MSS 56); Abercromby to Pelham, 10 Jan. 1798 (B.M., Add. MS 33105).

The Rebellion of 1798

presence would frighten the peasantry into a temporary submission. It is probable that Abercromby, if given a free hand, might have handled the incipient rebellion better than did the 'Castle clique'. But to permit Abercromby to carry on in face of the opposition of the lord chancellor would have involved a reversal of the policy of supporting the Irish government, which Pitt had made clear by his recall of Fitzwilliam in 1795. This was too drastic a step, and Abercromby was sacrificed. The circumstances of the commander-in-chief's resignation were described by Moore who wrote:

> It was during his tour to the north that the cabal was formed against him, and it was not until his return to Dublin that he found his orders had been subject to discussion, and his character and conduct traduced and misrepresented, both in this country and in England. He had done all he could with Lord Camden to show him the danger of the measures pursued. His Lordship agreed with him, but could not resist the other party.[33]

Abercromby resigned, but was induced by the viceroy to remain in office for the time being. Meanwhile, the use which Lord Moira and Fox were able to make of Abercromby's general orders gave the English cabinet no cause to regret his resignation. Moreover, the letters written by Clare and Beresford to Lord Auckland, Lord Buckingham, and other friends in England, had supplied Westminster with the Castle's version of the Irish situation.[34] As a rule, the English cabinet was inclined to restrain the Irish government, but in the spring of 1798, it appears to have considered Clare and his friends as the best means of controlling Ireland, and supported them against the advice of the senior officers. The viceroy had been carried along, frequently against his better judgment, by Clare and the 'Castle clique'. Camden had hoped to restrain their power, and had the new commander-in-chief proved more tactful and the viceroy more forceful; this effort might have succeeded. Camden, however, was a tired man who had repeatedly asked to be recalled, and Abercromby was wholly wanting in political judgment.

[33] Moore, *Diary*, i. 287, entry 16 Apr. 1798.
[34] Beresford to Westmorland, 20 Mar. 1798 (Beresford, *Correspondence*, i. 153); Clare to Auckland, n.d. (Auckland, *Correspondence*, iii. 395–7).

3. GRAND LODGE EFFORTS TO CONTROL THE ORANGEMEN

While this internal crisis in the government was developing, the Orange lodges gained steadily in strength. The founding of the Ulster Grand Lodge, and the adherence of the Beresfords and a powerful section of the gentry to the Dublin lodge, had given the movement enormous prestige.[35] Sloan, the innkeeper who had headed the lodges in 1795 and was still active at the founding of the grand lodge in the spring of 1797, was by this time no longer of sufficient prominence to head the movement. High offices were henceforth to be filled by the gentleman class. The Orange movement had established its worth in Ulster by ensuring the loyalty of the militia, filling the ranks of the yeomanry, and actively assisting in the policy of dragooning. Valuable as this assistance was, its militant protestant character was embarrassing to a government supported by bodies of catholic loyalists[36] and worried about conciliating the majority of its subjects. It was, therefore, the responsibility of the gentlemen leaders of Orangeism to insist on some gesture of goodwill towards catholic loyalists. At least one public gesture was made by Orangemen in December 1797 after several catholic parishes in the north had, under the influence of their clergy, passed resolutions denouncing the United Irishmen who 'have led many of our body into deep designs' and assuring 'all our Protestant brethren ... our sincere affection for them, and our absolute determination to co-operate and join with them by every means in our power for the suppression of rebellion'.[37]

In response to these loyal addresses, a group of Orange leaders, headed by William Blacker and Wolsey Atkinson, passed a resolution which read:

We have, in the public papers, with much satisfaction, read the declarations of the Roman Catholic inhabitants of several parishes of this province ... We have no doubt of the sincerity of such declarations, and that the Catholics of Ireland, sensible of the bene-

---

[35] Knox to Pelham, 29 Nov. 1797 (B.M., Add. MS 33105).

[36] Cooke to Pelham, 3 June 1798 (ibid.); Rev. S. Cupples to Rev. Forster Archer, 28 Dec. 1797 (P.R.O.I., Rebellion papers 620/33/180); *B.N.L.*, 15, 22 Dec. 1797, 5 Jan., 5 Mar. 1798.

[37] Proclamation of catholics of Culfaghtrim and Grange of Innispollin, county Armagh, in *B.N.L.*, 15 Dec. 1797.

The Rebellion of 1798

fits they enjoy, will not suffer themselves to be made dupes of by wicked and designing men ... We earnestly declare we are not enemies of any body of people on account of their religion, their Faith, or their mode of worship; we consider every peaceful and loyal subject as our brother, and they shall have our aid and protection.[38]

As the republicans were successfully playing on public suspicions, Orangemen thought it expedient to bring their activities more into the open. This, combined with the need to control their fast growing membership, induced Orange leaders to organize the movement on a national basis by moving the grand lodge from Ulster to Dublin. A meeting of deputies was held in that city 8 March 1798 at which the more important lodges and districts were represented. Present were William Blacker, grand master of Armagh, Thomas Verner, who held the grand masterships of counties Tyrone, Londonderry and Fermanagh, Captain Beresford of the Dublin cavalry, Lieutenant-Colonel Rochford, grand master of county Carlow, and eleven sergeants from militia regiments of counties Cavan, Armagh and Fermanagh. The Armagh militia was represented by five sergeants of lodges numbers 222 and 235.[39] As at least one lodge existed in the Monaghan regiment, this meeting could not have included representatives from all military lodges. Nor was the Westmeath regiment, in which Moore discovered Orange Boys, represented.

At the meeting the framework of a national organization was established. Grand lodges already formed in several counties were declared subordinate to the grand lodge of Ireland to be established in Dublin. Each county was divided into districts under a district master chosen by the lodges in each district, and each county was to have a grand lodge. The meeting further decided that the grand lodge of Ireland should be formed of members balloted for by each county grand lodge, and that the grand masters of Dublin lodges should be members because of their residence in Dublin. All masters of county lodges were to have the power to choose one member by ballot.

[38] *B.N.L.*, 5 Mar. 1798; see also *B.N.L.*, 20 Nov., 29 Dec. 1797, 15 Jan., 26 Jan., 2 Mar. 1798; James Verner to viceroy, 7 Feb. 1798 (P.R.O.I., Rebellion papers 620/35/120).
[39] Gowan, *Orangeism*, p. 196.

Grand lodge elections were to be yearly during the first days of June. The first meeting of the grand lodge was to be held 9 April 1798 at the home of Thomas Verner. A copy of eleven resolutions, embodying the above points, was sent to every lodge in Ireland.[40]

Thomas Verner, the first Irish grand master, whose name is associated with the Orange movement almost from its beginning, appears to have been the driving force behind the lodges during the 'respectable' period. Besides being the son of the member of parliament and prominent Armagh land-owner, James Verner, he was the brother-in-law of the wealthy Lord Donegal. The first official meeting of the Irish grand lodge was attended by such diverse elements as the marquis of Drogheda, Sir Richard Musgrave, a later historian of the rebellion, Captain Blacker, and Sergeant Holmes of the Armagh militia. The general secretary was Wolsey Atkinson of Portadown who had taken that office at a meeting of the Orange lodges of county Armagh on 12 February 1798.[41] Fermanagh, Cavan, Kildare and Waterford were represented by their grand masters, and the three militia regiments of Fermanagh, Armagh and Cavan were again represented by committees of sergeants. The main business of the meeting was to give official sanction to the recommendations made at the March 8 meeting, and to assign Harding Giffard the task of preparing rules for the use of all Orange societies. When this was done the meeting adjourned until November as the threat of rebellion claimed the attention of those present.[42]

While these meetings were taking place, the more influential Orangemen were doing what they could to present the lodges in a favourable light to the English cabinet. The manner in which they gained the ear of the duke of Portland is obscure. But by March 20, he was persuaded of the Orangemen's usefulness and respectability. He wrote, 'I heard yesterday that the Orange Association in Ulster has been joined by all the principal gentry and well-affected persons of property in that province, for the purpose of protecting themselves by an oath to defend the King and Constitution'. Portland went on:

[40] Ibid., p. 197.
[41] *B.N.L.*, 23 Feb. 1798; see also Gowan, *Orangeism*, pp. 196–8.
[42] Gowan, *Orangeism*, p. 200.

Associations of any sort unless authorized by the Government are not generally to be countenanced, but, considering the circumstances of these times, and the necessity of counteracting the attempt of our domestic enemies, exertions of this kind may do more than all the military force you could apply towards the establishment of order. The example may produce the best effects in other parts of the Kingdom, and may give you a disposable force to be carried to the South. The sense of danger and the proper spirit which has prompted this combination may dispose those who have entered into it to allow your Excellency to methodize, and bring them into the state of subordination which may enable you to employ their zeal to the best advantage.[43]

Lord Camden, to whom the above was addressed, was still wary of Orangemen. He replied, 'I think them likely to increase and although it is possible they may be useful, if disorders in the country take a still more serious turn; at present any encouragement of them much increases the jealousy of the Catholics, and I should therefore think it unwise to give an open encouragement to this party, although it is not expedient to suppress them'.[44]

Without the support of the British government, the viceroy was not strong enough to oppose the wishes of the Beresford faction. As this faction had managed to go over his head and secure British support in the person of the duke of Portland, Camden's hesitation in the matter of government collaboration with the Orangemen made little difference. Evidence that Camden's efforts to influence the duke against the lodges had little effect is found in a letter Portland wrote April 2 in which he stated:

One association is formed by Orangemen of Ulster, which consists already of 170,000 persons, and has been joined by all the principal gentry and well-affected persons of property in that province, for the purpose of protecting themselves against the combinations which have been formed by the United Irish ... It seems to me, that such proof of energy on the part of the country, would be likely to do more than all the military force you can apply.[45]

---

[43] Portland to Camden, 20 Mar. 1798 (P.R.O.I., Rebellion papers 620/40/1); Froude, *Ire.*, iii. 331.

[44] Camden to Portland, 23 Mar. 1798 (P.R.O.I., Rebellion papers 620/40/6).

[45] Portland to Camden, 2 Apr. 1798 (P.R.O.I., Rebellion papers 620/40/8); Lecky, *Ire.*, iv. 247.

The Rebellion of 1798

It is difficult to believe that Portland accepted the obviously false figure of 170,000 as the real strength of the Orangemen. It must have been clear to him that if such prominent landlords as Charlemont and Gosford were not with the Orangemen, the lodges had not been joined by 'all well-affected persons of property'. Yet no matter what Portland thought privately about the strength of Orangeism, his letters show that, for the moment at least, he was prepared to countenance a 'protestant policy' as outlined by Lord Clare and Duigenan as early as 1793. It meant rallying the protestant interest in support of the Crown, and the abandonment of all political concessions to catholics. Duigenan had established to his own and Lord Clare's satisfaction that the dogma of the catholic church made it impossible for its adherents to be loyal subjects of a protestant king, and that, therefore, concessions to them could not buy their loyalty. Basing his reasoning on Duigenan's thesis, Clare insisted that the only formula for tranquillity in Ireland was for the protestant colony to renounce its liberalism, and for the British government to make no further concessions to catholics.[46]

In the spring of 1798 there was much to lend strength to Duigenan's argument. The situation was summarized by Cooke, the Irish under-secretary who certainly could not be described as an anti-papist fanatic. 'The popish spirit', he wrote, 'has been set up against the Protestants by reporting every Protestant to be an Orangeman, and by inculcating that every Orangeman has sworn to exterminate the Papists; to these fictions are added the real pressure of high rents from the undertakers of land, and high tithes'.[47] The only course which appeared open to the government was to accept the fact that the bulk of the catholic population had been won over to the rebels,[48] and to collaborate with the loyal protestant faction while at the same time endeavouring to control the latter's excesses. The Irish gentry had this in mind when they took charge of the Orange movement. Such an open course could not, however, be adopted by the government. Instead, it merely extended its informal alliance with Orangemen, in existence since the formation of the

[46] Clare to Castlereagh, 16 Oct. 1798 (Castlereagh, *Correspondence*, i. 393).
[47] Cooke to Auckland, 19 Mar. 1798 (Auckland, *Correspondence*, iii. 392).
[48] Cooke to Pelham, 8 Jan. 1798 (B.M., Add. MS 33105).

yeomanry, by arming irregular bodies of Orangemen,[49] and making no attempt to suppress Orange societies in the armed forces. To explain how this worked it is necessary to consider the course of events during the rebellion.

4. THE SUPPRESSION OF THE REBELLION

Between the brief gathering of Orangemen in April and the following November there occurred that series of outbreaks and punitive actions which are summed up as the 'rebellion of 1798'. As informers had kept the government aware of the main activities and plans of the rebel leaders, it was possible for the Castle to choose its own moment to strike. Rebel plans had matured to the point where the directory of the United Irish had decided to risk rebellion without French aid.[50] This decision was forced partly by the alarm caused by the disarming of Ulster and partly by the hopes aroused by the progress of the United Irish system in the south. The rebels concluded that by waiting passively for French help they would run the danger of having their organization smashed by 'dragooning' on the Ulster model. They resolved, therefore, to strike with their own resources.

Before they had matured fully, their plans were made known to the government by an informer named Reynolds. On Reynolds's information that a meeting of the republican executive was to be held March 12 in Dublin, the government struck and arrested eighteen members.[51] The next move was against the various units of the underground army. Local leaders were arrested and their followers disarmed when possible. But the Abercromby crisis created a difficulty. It would hardly do to have the commander-in-chief resign on the eve of a major punitive action. It was equally illogical to leave operations in

---

[49] Pelham to Knox, 23, 26 May 1797 (ibid., 33104); Elliott to Knox, 16 Apr. 1798 (N.L.I., Lake MSS 56); Lake to Knox, 30 May 1798 (ibid.); Castlereagh to Knox, 30 May 1798 (ibid.); *B.N.L.*, 23 Apr. 1798; Castlereagh to Maxwell, 23 May 1798 (P.R.O.N.I., Verner papers T 1023/149).

[50] Hill to Pelham, 4 June 1798 (B.M., Add. MS 33106); *B.N.L.*, 18 Sept. 1798.

[51] Stanhope, *Life of Pitt*, iii. 108–9; Maxwell, *Hist. of the Irish rebellion of 1798*, p. 42.

charge of an officer who disapproved of the policy he was expected to enforce.

In spite of these difficulties, martial law was proclaimed on March 30.[52] Abercromby was given explicit instructions to use the military without waiting for the authorization of the civil magistrates in the disturbed counties of Kildare, Tipperary, Limerick, Cork, King's, Queen's, and Kilkenny. Troops were quartered on the civilian population, and the people were ordered to give up their arms on pain of having their houses burned.[53] Until April 25 this policy was carried out by Abercromby who did what he could to strike a balance between humanity and effectiveness.

His successor, General Lake, applied the policy of dragooning with the ruthlessness which had proved effective in Ulster. Meanwhile, the rebels were able to replace by new men most of their leaders who had been arrested on March 12, and they benefited to some degree by the services of Lord Edward Fitzgerald, who remained concealed in Dublin until May 19.[54] As their organization was being destroyed, the rebels were under the necessity of acting at once. May 23 was the day set for the insurrection. On that day, the mails were to be stopped as the signal for a general rising, and the troops at Loughlinstown and the artillery at Chapelizod were to be surprised. Like most republican projects, this, too, was betrayed by an informer. Two of the key United Irishmen in the plot, the Sheares brothers,[55] tried to win over Captain John Armstrong of the King's County militia who, on the instruction of his regimental commander, pretended to join the conspiracy.[56] Armstrong learned that a network of republican cells existed in the militia regiments, but that no officers were involved. The republicans assigned him the task of winning over his own regiment, and promised him a colonelcy in the United Irish army as a reward. Armstrong did not learn the names of the executive committee nor the exact date of the rising, but his information confirmed

[52] Moore, *Diary*, i. 285.
[53] Moore, *Diary*, i. 286, 289, entries 5 Apr., 27 May 1798.
[54] *B.N.L.*, 25 May 1798; Cooke to Auckland, 20 May 1798 (Auckland, *Correspondence*, iii. 417–8).
[55] *B.N.L.*, 25 May 1798.
[56] Fitzpatrick, *The secret service under Pitt*, pp. 308–10; Madden, *United Irishmen*, iv. 251–2.

The Rebellion of 1798

reports received from other quarters. Thus warned, the government was able to frustrate the rebel plans for seizing Dublin and raising a mutiny among the militia.[57] On May 23, however, several of the mail coaches going to Dublin were stopped,[58] and a series of local uprisings took place.[59] The insurrection found government forces alerted, and in most localities, the uprisings were suppressed at once.[60] Nowhere could the undisciplined peasants, armed with pikes, stand against organized troops. Lane reported to Downshire, 'At Belfast General Nugent is flogging away at a fine rate. We hear of its good effect and that great discoveries are making'.[61] The expected republican mutiny in the militia did not occur, and the militia proved as zealous as the Orange yeomanry in dealing with the rebels.[62] General Lake wrote to Knox, 'The Militia had behaved uncommonly well. None better than the Dublin Militia which, I dare say, will astonish you'.[63] Many former Belfast republicans wanted to join the yeomanry to prove 'their loyalty'.[64] In Ulster, long the heart of the United Irish movement, no outbreak took place until June 7.[65] Only in the county of Wexford did the underground army of the republicans meet with a temporary success.[66]

At the outbreak of the rebellion, Orange lodges in Wexford were located near the Wicklow border towns. Ogle Gowan, who organized Canadian Orangeism, wrote that his father, Captain John Hunter Gowan, a magistrate of Mount Nebo, was holding a lodge in the burned remains of his country home when he received news that the rebels had attacked troops heading for

---

[57] *B.N.L.*, 25, 26 May 1798.
[58] Griffith to Pelham, 12 June 1798 (B.M., Add. MS 33106); Ross to Downshire, 24 May 1798 (P.R.O.N.I., Downshire MSS).
[59] Ibid., see also James Verner to Maxwell, 23 May 1798 (P.R.O.N.I., Verner papers T 1023/148); Beresford to Auckland, 24 May 1798 (Auckland, *Correspondence*, iii. 427–8); *B.N.L.*, 25 May 1798.
[60] *B.N.L.*, 26 May 1798.
[61] Lane to Downshire, 29 May 1798 (P.R.O.N.I., Downshire MSS).
[62] Lake to Knox, 3 June 1798 (N.L.I., Lake MSS 56); Castlereagh to Knox, 5 June 1798 (ibid.).
[63] Lake to Knox, 30 May 1798 (ibid.).
[64] Mackey to Downshire, 1 June 1798 (P.R.O.N.I., Downshire MSS).
[65] Maxwell, *Hist. of the Irish rebellion of 1798*, p. 203.
[66] Cooke to Pelham, 9 Aug. 1798 (B.M., Add. MS 33106); Beresford to Auckland, 28 May 1798 (Auckland, *Correspondence*, iii. 430–1).

The Rebellion of 1798

Carnew.[67] The lodge was closed and its members marched to support the troops. They were joined by yeomanry from Carnew, Tinahely, and its neighbourhood which were, like Gowan's corps, 'members of the Orange lodges of those places'.[68] In the same account, Gowan claimed that the rebel attack on Hacketstown was repulsed by fifty men of the Antrim militia, assisted by the armed Orangemen of Hacketstown, Coolattin, Shillelagh, and Upper Talbotstown. The Orangemen were commanded by a minister, James McGhee of Coolkenna lodge.[69] Edward Cooke, the under-secretary at the Castle, claimed that the Orange associations 'which were formed and promoted by Colonel North [fast?] and some other gentlemen in the centres of Wexford and Carlow . . . have operated very mischievously', though he could give 'no particular facts to support my opinion'. He added that 'it is undoubtedly the object of the chiefs of rebellion to flame religious dissension'.[70] Edward Hay, in the history of the rebellion, asserts that 'the Orange system made no appearance in the county of Wexford until the beginning of April on the arrival of the North Cork militia . . . in [which] there were a great number of Orangemen'.[71]

Other accounts of the Wexford rebellion give the Orangemen no prominence, and it may be assumed that their influence in the course of local events was slight. Nevertheless, the organization of even a few lodges would be sufficient to disturb the catholic peasantry which would interpret such activity as a prelude to the Armagh type 'outrages', especially as rumours of impending Orange massacres[72] were deliberately spread. The rebel force in Wexford under the leadership of a protestant, Bagenal Harvey, and a catholic priest, Father John Murphy, established a camp near Enniscorthy on Vinegar Hill after seizing the towns of Enniscorthy and Wexford. From the beginning of the rising, the leaders had little control of their half-wild forces.[73] The revolt took the character of a war of religion, and

---

[67] Gowan, *Orangeism*, pp. 237-8.
[68] Ibid., p. 238.
[69] Ibid., p. 229.
[70] Cooke to Pelham, 3 June 1798 (B.M., Add. MS 33105).
[71] Edward Hay, *History of the Irish insurrection of 1798*, p. 57.
[72] Plowden, *Hist. Ire., 1801-10*, i. introduction p. 100; Hay, *Hist. of the Irish insurrection of 1798*, pp. 56-9, 69-70.
[73] Cooke to Pelham, 9 Aug. 1798 (B.M., Add. MS 33106).

The Rebellion of 1798

protestants were massacred on suspicion of being Orangemen.[74] On May 27 the catholic archbishop of Dublin, Dr Troy, ordered an address to be read from all altars each Sunday exhorting the rebels to 'give up your arms and unite with your peaceful fellow citizens to put down the insurrection'.[75]

Castlereagh, who replaced Pelham as chief secretary, described the Wexford situation as:

... a religious phrensy. The Priests lead the rebels to battle; on their march, they kneel down and pray, and show the most desperate resolution in their attack... They put such Protestants as are reported to be Orangemen to death, saving others on condition of their embracing the Catholic faith. It is a Jacobinal conspiracy throughout the Kingdom, pursuing its object chiefly with Popish instruments; the heated bigotry of this sect being better suited to the purpose of the republican leaders than the cold, reasoning disaffection of the northern Presbyterians.[76]

The atrocities committed by the United army were frightening enough, but in the reports circulated in Ulster they were greatly exaggerated.[77] By far the worst of these was the massacre of loyalist and protestant prisoners at Scullabogue.[78] News of this and other outrages could not but dampen the enthusiasm of the more ardent United Irishmen in the north. Republicanism was all but extinguished amongst the presbyterians[79] and thousands of erstwhile United Irishmen swelled the ranks of the Orange lodges.[80] James McKey of Belfast described this change of attitude, writing to Lord Downshire, 'The number of disaffected fellows now in this town under arms for the protection of their property would astonish you. To see Presbyterian ministers, with rich republican shopkeepers, sitting in the

---

[74] Alexander to Pelham, 26 July 1798 (ibid.); Beresford to Auckland, 31 May 1798 (Auckland, *Correspondence*, iii. 439); Clare to Auckland, n.d. (ibid., iv. 7–8).

[75] *B.N.L.*, 5 June 1798.

[76] Castlereagh to Wickham, 12 June 1798 (Castlereagh, *Correspondence*, i. 219).

[77] *B.N.L.*, 26 June, 10, 13, 24 July 1798.

[78] Lecky, *Ire.*, iv. 394; *B.N.L.*, 10, 24 July 1798.

[79] Public declarations by dissenters on their loyal sentiments, in *B.N.L.*, 6, 10, 27 July, 3, 7, 17 Aug. 1798.

[80] Castlereagh to Portland, 3 June 1799 (Castlereagh, *Correspondence*, ii. 325–6).

The Rebellion of 1798

guard room at daylight in the morning with their guns, had, in my eyes, a wonderful appearance'.[81]

The full impact of the events in the south was not felt among the bulk of the Irish protestants until some weeks after the rebellion was broken. The attempt of the rebel army to invade county Kilkenny was repulsed at New Ross with a loss of 3,000,[82] while another attempt to carry the rebellion beyond Wexford was crushed at Arklow on June 9.[83] The rebels were thus forced back on the defensive to become the scourge of county Wexford until the government could bring up sufficient reinforcements to overwhelm them. Eight thousand troops were brought from Britain, including 2,000 guards. A total of about 15,000 men advanced in four divisions on the main rebel encampment on Vinegar Hill, arriving on June 21. The rebel forces were scattered and Vinegar Hill taken, but retreating rebels massacred protestant prisoners held at Wexford.

The belated revolt in the north which broke out on June 7 in Antrim under Henry Joy McCracken,[84] was speedily dealt with by troops sent from Belfast by General Nugent. An attempted outbreak in Derry was prevented by General Knox, while near Ballynahinch in county Down, a rebel encampment held out for three days against government forces.[85] Within a week the Ulster rebellion had fizzled out. Nowhere in the north did the rebellion take on the character of a religious war even though known Orangemen were often killed as a matter of course. The underground army had been disorganized by the dragooning policy of Lake, the raids of the Orangemen, and the arrest of its leaders so that it was incapable of serious action. The general population of Ulster, which had been, on the whole, sympathetic to the republican cause, was intimidated by the military and Orange terrorism, and frightened by news of the predominantly catholic character of the United Irish movement in the south. The part played by the Orange lodges in the rebellion of 1798

---

[81] McKey to Downshire, 14 June 1798 (P.R.O.N.I., Downshire MSS).

[82] Major Vesey to Pelham, June 1798 (B.M., Add. MS 33105).

[83] Castlereagh to Pelham, 13 June 1798 (ibid.).

[84] Castlereagh to Elliott, 13 June 1798 (ibid.); Maxwell, *Hist. of the Irish rebellion of 1798*, p. 204.

[85] George Stephenson to Downshire, 12 June 1798 (P.R.O.N.I., Downshire MSS); James McKey to Downshire, 13 June 1798 (ibid.).

may be considered from three aspects. By their arrogance they helped to provoke the outbreaks. Their predominant influence in the yeomanry turned this corps into enthusiastic counter-revolutionaries while their presence in the militia and in some of the fencible and regular units helped to secure the loyalty of these troops, even if at the expense of undermining discipline. Finally, the Orangemen acted as irregular auxiliaries to the government forces, providing small bodies of men to fight beside the yeomanry and other authorized troops. The extent to which Orange provocation drove the catholics into active rebellion can easily be over-estimated. As indicated previously,[86] the 'Orange bogey', created by United Irish propaganda, was most effective where there were no Orangemen. In Wexford, where the rebellion was most furious, there had been no Orange outrages, although the Orangemen in the militia and yeomanry behaved in a most provocative manner.[87]

The part which the Orangemen played in the yeomanry has been discussed already.[88] Their greatest service was, perhaps, in filling the ranks of the Ulster corps organized in the autumn of 1796. After that, their principal service was keeping up the morale of the various units to which they belonged. In yeomanry corps in the south, where no or few Orangemen existed, desertions to the enemy were not uncommon.[89] Yet the fact that so many of the non-Orange corps in the south proved effective against the rebels detracts from the Orangemen's claims to have been the only loyal element in the yeomanry. However, the Ulster Orangemen did provide a hard core which kept the others loyal and discouraged mutiny and desertion. Without them, the yeomanry could not have functioned.

As the question of the loyalty of the militia is controversial, the value of having Orange lodges in it is not easy to estimate. Clare had declared as early as 1793 that an Irish militia composed of catholics would be untrustworthy, and his opinion seems to have been shared by a large section of the gentry. Yet the militia proved loyal, both at the time of the attempted

[86] See above p. 81.
[87] Camden to Pelham, 3 June 1798 (B.M., Add. MS 33105); Cooke to Pelham, 3 June 1798 (ibid.).
[88] See above chapter III.
[89] Cooke to Pelham, 8 June 1798 (B.M., Add. MS 33105).

The Rebellion of 1798

French landing at Bantry and during the rebellion.[90] Sir John Moore considered the ranks of the militia sound, and blamed only the officers. However, there remains the conspiracy in the King's County militia, exposed by Captain Armstrong, and lesser conspiracies in other regiments.[91] On the eve of the rebellion when it was thought expedient to execute four men of the Monaghan regiment, the knowledge that certain regiments of the militia were Orange was undoubtedly a comfort to the Castle. William Verner told the house of commons in 1835 that regiments, known to have Orangemen in their ranks, were hurried to Dublin during the rebellion. He claimed that 'at the period of the rebellion in Ireland, the Cavan militia, [was] ordered by forced marches into Dublin, in consequence of the disturbed state of that metropolis from disaffection, and he remembered the Armagh and Fermanagh regiments being detained to do the duty of that garrison because the men were chiefly Protestants, most of whom were Orangemen'.[92]

The question might be raised whether these protestant regiments would not have been reasonably reliable even had there been no Orange lodges within their ranks. Yet as the United Irishmen appealed to Irish of both denominations, the politically-minded privates and non-commissioned officers who joined the lodges might very well have become republicans if they had not become Orangemen. Moreover, the Orangemen undoubtedly raised the morale of protestant regiments by presenting action against the rebels as a sort of continuation of the campaign of 1690. The value of the Orange lodges in catholic militia regiments was of a different order. Orangemen may have at times served as spies against the United Irishmen in the ranks, but such service was unnecessary because of the abundance of informers among the republicans. They could, however, make the activities of the United Irish propagandists difficult, and, by the mere fact of being organized, protect protestant soldiers against intimidation by the Defenders and United Irish.

In addition to their services in the yeomanry and militia,

---

[90] Castlereagh to Pelham, 8 June 1798 (B.M., Add. MS 33105); Lake to Knox, 3 June 1798 (N.L.I., Lake MSS 56).

[91] Marshall to Elliott, 2 June 1798 (B.M., Add. MS 33105); Griffith to Pelham, 4 June 1798 (ibid.).

[92] *Hansard 3*, xxx. 281; Lake to Knox, 5 June 1798 (N.L.I., Lake MSS 56).

The Rebellion of 1798

bodies of Orangemen, as such, were armed by the government and permitted to act as auxiliaries to the forces of the crown. Membership in the lodges was thus treated, for the time being, as equivalent to an oath of allegiance. In a sense, a precedent for such action had been set when General Lake reviewed unarmed detachments of Orangemen 12 July 1797.[93] It might be argued also that the volunteers of 1778 were allowed to serve with approximately the same status. The reasons the Castle did not simply swear these men in as yeomen and thus avoid an open association with a political faction seem to have been want of time, the fact that many Orangemen were not fit physically for military service, and that the existing system of the yeomanry was not prepared to integrate these political clubs into its organization.

The manner in which Orange bands were taken into government service was described by Colonel Blacker, who, as a captain in the Trinity College yeomanry, had been called upon by Lord Castlereagh to raise an Orange contingent. Blacker said, 'I was taken into the presence of the secretary at the Castle, and I was asked by him if I had not a certain degree of influence in my neighbourhood as well as being a captain in the yeomanry corps; I said that I had reason to think that I had, among the Orangemen in particular; he asked me what number of persons I thought I could bring forward in aid of the Government; I said, I thought I could bring them 1,000 men in a few hours'. Blacker went on, 'What makes me remember the circumstances so well is, that he gave me one of his own peculiar laughs upon the occasion as if he did not believe me; however, he sent me down to the north by the mail coach that night with an order for 100 stand of arms, to be taken out of the depôt of Charlemont'.[94] Blacker stated he gave the guns to 100 picked Orangemen, and that after the emergency was past, the guns were returned to the yeomanry. About the same time, Lord Auckland, who was in communication with Beresford, noted, 'No stir in the north except on the right side. The people called Orange-men keep the country in check, and will overpower the rebels should they stir. If we can keep the North quiet, I do not

---

[93] Evidence of W. Verner, *Rep. on Orange lodges I*, H.C. 1835 [377], xv. 20.
[94] Evidence of W. Blacker, *Rep. on Orange lodges III*, H.C. 1835 [476], xvi. 217.

fear soon subduing the rebels, and I hope to see this country more quiet and settled than it has been for a long time'.[95]

The confidence the Castle placed in Orangemen can be further established by the testimony of Lieutenant Colonel William Verner, an Orangeman, who, speaking in the house of commons in 1835, read an extract from the orderly book of the Royal Artillery dated Belfast, 19 June 1798, stating 'Detail for guard tomorrow as usual. Field officer for the day to-morrow, Lieut. Colonel Durham. Fife Fencibles. The Belfast Yeomen are to do duty with the Fifeshire, which make them upon an equal footing with the Monaghan Militia, both Corps having 500 fit men for duty. There are 228 Orangemen and Castlereagh Yeomen; one half of them are to be attached to the Monaghan and the other half to the Fifeshire.'[96]

In many accounts of the rebellion the words 'Orangeman' and 'loyalist' are used as though they were inter-changeable. This was often true, but there were a number of loyalist bands which did not seem to have been associated in any way with the Orange lodges.[97] Known loyalists were permitted to keep their arms and small groups, sometimes including catholics, gave active aid to the military during local outbreaks.[98] In places under immediate threat of attack, any man capable of bearing arms—who professed loyalist sentiments—was not likely to be refused the right to fight.[99] In general, however, Orange lodges seemed the principal liaison between the loyalist population and government.

Against the services rendered by Orangemen to the government during the rebellion must be balanced the ill-will and animosity excited by their behaviour. The extent to which they were responsible for provoking the rebellion has been discussed already, but what of their conduct during its suppression? In the north where former United Irishmen were joining the Orange lodges, there was no record of Orange atrocities during the outbreak. Most of the northern rebels who took arms were protestants. The largely catholic Monaghan militia was, in fact, one of the mainstays of the government's forces in the north.

---

[95] Notes on the civil war by Lord Auckland (*Fortescue MSS*, iv. 226); Beresford to Auckland, 1 June 1798 (Auckland, *Correspondence*, iii. 442).
[96] *Hansard 3*, xxx. 282.   [97] *Times*, 6 Mar. 1823.   [98] Ibid.
[99] Lake to Knox, 30 May 1798 (N.L.I., Lake MSS 56).

In the south, however, there is a great deal of evidence that irregular Orange bands, Orange yeomen, and Orange militia were guilty of burnings, murder, and other outrages against suspected enemies of the government.[1] To the government's policy, harsh enough as it was, the Orangeman added much bitterness and partisan fury. In the months that preceded the rebellion, many who had become active rebels came forward to take loyalty oaths.[2] After the outbreak, however, a profession of loyal sentiments was not considered sufficient; districts were occupied by troops and only those who came forward to give up arms were considered loyal. Sir John Moore noted that in areas where he was engaged in disarming the population, no arms were given up until a house or two had been burnt.[3]

Innocent people undoubtedly suffered as the result of the methods used by military officers and the gentry to separate the real from the suspected rebels. Men informed against or taken in arms were arrested and beaten, sometimes tortured in the hope that they could be forced to give information against others.[4] In cases where they refused, they were frequently hanged.[5] More often, they were transported.[6] Such measures were an inevitable reaction to the United Irishmen having made normal legal procedure impossible. Where the punitive measures were carried out by relatively humane officers, employing disiplined subordinates, gross brutality and injustice were usually avoided. But in times of civil war, naturally brutish elements often gain sufficient authority to turn themselves into petty tyrants and commit crimes which have no relation to political necessity.

Many such crimes were attributed to Orangemen and with justice, but they were by no means confined to them. Catholic

---

[1] Cornwallis to Ross, 24 July 1798 (Cornwallis, *Correspondence*, ii. 368–9); Maxwell, *Hist. of the Irish rebellion of 1798*, pp. 288, 291, 293.

[2] Knox to Pelham, 16 July 1797 (B.M., Add. MS 33104).

[3] Moore, *Diary*, i. 289, entry 27 May 1798.

[4] *B.N.L.*, 8 June, 13 July 1798; Lane to Downshire, 29 May 1798 (P.R.O.N.I., Downshire MSS).

[5] Lake to Pelham, 30 Nov. 1798 (B.M., Add. MS 33105); Stephenson to Downshire, 21 June 1798 (P.R.O.N.I., Downshire MSS); *B.N.L.*, 13 July 1798.

[6] Stephenson to Downshire, 21 June 1798 (P.R.O.N.I., Downshire MSS); *B.N.L.*, 13 July 1798.

troops proved no less savage then Orange yeomen, and among the worst behaved of all units was the Hompesch regiment of German mercenaries.[7] On the other hand, units of English militia and Scottish fencibles had records of good behaviour. It cannot be said that the savagery of repressive measures was the sole responsibility of Orangemen,[8] but the purely military outrages were of relatively short duration and ceased once the troops were brought under control. Moreover, atrocities committed by non-Orange soldiery were the result of simple brutality, and when they added insult to injury, they did not employ insults associated with long-standing animosities. Orangemen, however, losing no opportunity to relate current humiliations to past defeats of catholic Ireland, had a way of making their persecution cut deeper than that of the others.

Such activity was certainly not carried out on orders. Orange leaders repudiated religious hatred. In response to a declaration of loyalty by a body of catholics shortly after the outbreak of the rebellion,[9] the lodges of Ulster published the following statement:

We have, with the greatest pleasure, seen declarations of loyalty from many congregations of our Roman Catholic brethren, in the sincerity of which we declare our firm confidence, and assure them, in the face of the whole world, and of the Being whom we both worship, though under different forms, that, however the common enemies of all loyal men may misrepresent the Orangemen, we consider every loyal subject as our brother and friend, let his religion be what it may. We associate to suppress rebellion and treason, not any mode of worship. We have no enemies, but the enemies of our country.[10]

This statement was yet another attempt to discredit the rumour, circulated by republicans, that Orangemen were sworn to exterminate catholics. If it was also intended by Orange leaders as a warning to their unruly rank and file, it certainly had

---

[7] Lecky, *Ire.*, iv. 471; Maxwell, *Hist. of the Irish rebellion of 1798*, p. 243.

[8] Connelly to Castlereagh, 7 Aug. 1798 (P.R.O.I., State of the country papers 408/601/23); see also State of things in Wicklow, 20 Aug. 1798 (ibid., 408/601/64).

[9] *F.D.J.*, 24 May 1798; *B.N.L.*, 5 June 1798.

[10] *Report on the state of Ireland, report from the select committee, with minutes of evidence*, H.L. 1825 [181], ix. 351; *B.N.L.*, 20 July 1798.

The Rebellion of 1798

little effect.[11] John Claudius Beresford, a captain of the yeomanry and the most active Orangeman in the Beresford family, is reported to have had a whipping post set up in his stables where suspects were questioned and beaten amid the taunts of Orange yeomen.[12] Perhaps the most unfortunate aspect of the Orange outrages was that they were not only a reminder of past insults, but as Orangemen were Irish, a promise of future trouble. For the Orange movement was an organization capable of renewing persecution when the German mercenaries and Welsh fencibles had gone elsewhere and the militia had been disbanded.

Wolfe Tone and the United Irishmen had done their best to direct Irish hatred against Britain, and later republican historians have spoken vaguely about atrocities by British troops. This suited the political purposes of Irish nationalism, but in reality, the rebellion of 1798 had as much the character of a civil war as a war of independence. It had its beginning in an attempt by Belfast radicals to challenge the authority of the Castle, but as the traditional alignment in Irish disputes had been the English government with the protestant gentry and Ulster protestants on one side, and the catholic peasantry and any foreign allies it could find forming the other, whenever politics took a violent turn, this pattern re-asserted itself. Ulster radicalism, like the liberalism of the gentry, had matured while the catholic peasantry was politically dormant. When the peasantry awakened in 1798, this radical sentiment died and Orangeism took its place. Henceforth, Irish nationalism was to be based almost exclusively on the catholic population. News of the United Irish outrages in the south, in combination with the defeat of the feeble revolt in the north, accelerated the flow of repentant radicals into the lodges. This was partly a reaction against the 'papist' turn the southern outbreaks had taken, and partly a rallying to the winning side.[13] However, while former rebels were swelling the ranks of Orangeism, another change took

[11] *Rep. on Orange lodges I*, H.C. 1835 [377], xv. 14–5; Report of attacks on catholic houses near Dungannon, 27 Feb. 1798 (P.R.O.I., Rebellion papers 620/35/160).

[12] John Beresford to Auckland, 30 May 1798 (Auckland, *Correspondence*, iii. 433); MacNeven, *Pieces of Irish history*, p. 147; Plowden, *Hist. Ire. to 1800*, iv. 330.

[13] Beresford to Auckland, 13 June 1798 (Auckland, *Correspondence*, iv. 18).

place in the Irish government which was soon to result in a cooling of relations between Orangemen and the Castle.

5. THE CORNWALLIS ADMINISTRATION

Lord Camden, who had never given whole-hearted approval to Lord Clare's policy, felt increasingly isolated after the recall of Abercromby. This feeling was sharpened when Pelham, the chief secretary, proved too ill to carry on and was replaced by young Lord Castlereagh. The viceroy had repeatedly urged that his office could best be filled by a military man,[14] and the outbreak of the rebellion finally induced the British government to act on his advice.[15] On June 20 Lord Cornwallis, who is best remembered for his defeat at Yorktown, arrived to take office as lord lieutenant. He was primarily a military man, but, unlike the former commander-in-chief, he was a man of considerable tact and some political understanding. The original purpose in sending a general of Cornwallis's standing—the crushing of the rebellion—had been accomplished by the previous administration. His task, therefore, was to restrain the excesses of loyal forces and to quiet the fury of the Castle party. Cooke, General Lake and others associated with the Irish administration were determined to make the outbreak of the rebellion the occasion for destroying, root and branch, the conspiracy which had disturbed the countryside since the resignation of Lord Fitzwilliam. Moved by strong partisan zeal, they were unlikely to allow considerations of humanity or even long-term policy stay their hand in carrying out the ruthless measures they considered essential in smothering the flames of rebellion. As Lord Camden could not restrain them, the arrival of Cornwallis proved timely.

Like Abercromby and Moore, the new viceroy took a somewhat detached view of Irish politics, and saw no purpose in encouraging reprisals.[16] The government had arrested more men than it was able to convict by fair trial even though most of them were guilty of being implicated in the plot. Cornwallis

[14] Camden to Pelham, 6 June 1798 (B.M., Add. MS 33105).
[15] Pitt to Windham, 12 June 1798 (William Windham, *Windham letters*, ii. 72).
[16] Griffith to Pelham, 11 July 1798 (B.M. Add. MS 33106).

The Rebellion of 1798

solved this problem by a compromise which enabled many leaders, who might have been tried for a capital offence, to be exiled instead.[17] Amnesty was offered to the more humble rebels not guilty of criminal offences, who surrendered voluntarily.[18] This clemency aroused furious indignation among Orangemen,[19] but the viceroy's position was made easier by the support of Lord Clare.[20]

Clare had long been the strong man of the 'Castle clique', and openly held views identical with those of Duigenan. This won him the hatred of his whig, catholic, and United Irish contemporaries and signalled him out for attack by liberal and nationalist historians. Yet few men knew Ireland better. Lord Clare combined his political conservatism with a genuine sympathy for the peasantry, and was not without charity towards his enemies.[21] He had, for example, permitted Tone to go into exile when he was implicated in the Jackson affair in 1794.[22] There is, therefore, no inconsistency in his agreeing with Cornwallis on the question of clemency. As Clare destroyed his private papers, his attitude towards the Orange lodges is difficult to establish. He was not an Orangeman like his friend, Dr Duigenan. But Duigenan, the Beresfords, and the placemen closely associated with the Castle, who had joined the Orange movement by way of the Dublin Lodge, were government supporters first and Orangemen second. As their power was dependent on remaining in the government, they could be compelled to carry out the viceroy's policy even though it was contrary to their opinions. Yet many Orangemen were not directly dependent upon the Castle for favour, and were thus free to offer opposition to the new lord lieutenant.[23]

Their conduct at this time was described by a former viceroy, the marquis of Buckingham, who had returned to Ireland with his regiment of English militia. Buckingham wrote to Lord Grenville:

---

[17] Ibid.   [18] Elliott to Pelham, 20 July 1798 (ibid.).   [19] Ibid.
[20] Cooke to Pelham, 9 Aug. 1798 (ibid.); Clare to Auckland, 1 Aug. 1798 (Auckland, *Correspondence*, iv. 39).
[21] Cooke to Pelham, 3 June 1798 (B.M., Add. MS 33106).
[22] Lecky, *Ire.*, iii. 373-4.
[23] Griffith to Pelham, 11 July 1798 (B.M., Add. MS 33106); Alexander to Pelham, 26 July, 4 Aug. 1798 (ibid.).

The Rebellion of 1798

This proclamation and the general tenor of Lord Cornwallis's very meritorious conduct has raised much ferment amongst the very violent Orangemen, who have formed a very dangerous society, professing very loyal principles, but certainly united as a body almost in every town in Ireland in contra-distinction to the Catholics; and wherever they have not been suffered to be formed, namely, in the Counties of Kerry, Clare, Galway, Sligo and Mayo, all of which are Catholic Counties, not a man has stirred, nor has a United Irishman taken arms. It is, however, understood that the Catholics are only quiet because the Protestants are so. Now this sort of loyal association upon Jacobin principles must be grappled with, or the Government must be given up to them; and yet I protest I don't know what in theory to advise.[24]

Buckingham who had ended his period as viceroy at a time when religious antagonism was fast ebbing away, was shocked at the extent to which it had revived. He went on to suggest to Grenville to 'instantly recall or strike off one half of your generals who are worse than useless, and particularly your brigadiers of Irish Cavalry and Irish connections, for whom there cannot be the slightest occasion, and from whom there is much to be feared, and nothing to be hoped'. His second suggestion was 'to send some of your best skeleton or weak corps in exchange for the Irish corps, and to spare no trouble to complete a regular efficient army in the room of that which Lord Camden's (must I say) weakness, Lord Carhampton's mad violences, and above all, Sir R. Abercromby's total insufficiency and fatal order for free quarters have completely ruined'.[25]

While Cornwallis was endeavouring to put Irish affairs in order with a minimum of bloodshed and ill feeling, an epilogue to the rebellion did much to reveal the inherent weakness of the Irish government's position. Late in August, when the rebels still in arms had been reduced to a handful, the French arrived with a token force at Killala Bay in the west.[26] On landing they were at once joined by some local peasantry[27] who were given arms and uniforms. Lake concentrated about 2,000

---

[24] Buckingham to Grenville, 23 July 1798 (*Fortescue MSS*, iv. 265).
[25] Ibid., p. 266.
[26] Griffith to Pelham, 29 Aug. 1798 (B.M., Add. MS 33106); *B.N.L.*, 28 Aug. 1798.
[27] *B.N.L.*, 4, 11 Sept. 1798; *A narrative of what passed at Killalla*, pp. 17, 23.

The Rebellion of 1798

troops, mostly cavalry, at Castlebar to confront about 900 French regulars[28] and a few peasants. As a result of some confusion, Lake's cavalry was ordered to withdraw just as the French were about to retreat and the sight of their own cavalry moving to the rear so alarmed the Irish militia that they began a disorderly retreat that was turned into a rout by a French bayonet charge.[29] The infantry units involved were the Kilkenny and Longford militia—both catholic regiments, while the cavalry was Roden's fencibles, a protestant unit consisting largely of Orangemen. Lake lost his guns, and some of the scattered militiamen joined the enemy, but Lord Roden's men made an orderly retreat.[30]

As Connaught was undisturbed by the trouble in 1798, no large force joined the French.[31] The peasants who rallied to them were said to have done so for the sake of the uniforms,[32] and no militia deserted until after the defeat.[33] Had the French landed a few weeks earlier at Wexford, their handful of trained men might have prolonged the revolt. Landing too late and in the wrong place, the French force's principal damage was to General Lake's reputation. The small French column, commanded by Humbert, was soon surrounded by 20,000 men under Lake and Cornwallis and compelled to surrender.[34] On this occasion, the Orange Armagh militia won distinction by a brilliant bayonet charge.[35]

Another French expedition, carrying Wolfe Tone, was intercepted and the founder of the United Irish was taken, tried, and condemned to death, but managed to cheat the executioner by suicide.[36] Contemporary with the events surrounding Tone's death, Napper Tandy, whose military experience was limited to that gained as a captain in the Dublin volunteer artillery, had

---

[28] Griffith to Pelham, 3 Sept. 1798 (B.M., Add. MS 33106).
[29] *B.N.L.*, 11 Sept. 1798; Clare to Auckland, 3 Sept. 1798 (Auckland, *Correspondence*, iv. 53, see footnote).
[30] Maxwell, *Hist. of the Irish rebellion of 1798*, p. 235; Lecky, *Ire.*, v. 52.
[31] Griffith to Pelham, 29 Aug. 1798 (B.M., Add. MS 33106).
[32] Diary of the bishop of Killalla, entry 27 Aug. 1798, in Maxwell, *Hist. of the Irish rebellion of 1798*, p. 257; see also *A narrative of what passed at Killalla*, pp. 24-7.
[33] Alexander to Pelham, 5 Sept. 1798 (B.M., Add. MS 33106).
[34] *B.N.L.*, 4 Sept. 1798. [35] *B.N.L.*, 11 Sept. 1798.
[36] *B.N.L.*, 23 Nov. 1798.

persuaded the French to make him a general and to place at his disposal the brig *Anarcreon*. Tandy landed on the Isle of Arran September 16, issued a number of proclamations, and became so drunk that he had to be carried back on board.[37] As the local populace showed no enthusiasm, the expedition returned to France after eight hours on Irish soil.

During the French landings in August and September, the membership of the Orange lodges was being swelled by the influx of protestant loyalists throughout Ireland, but principally by the presbyterians in Ulster.[38] Repentant Jacobins and opportunists who had previously avoided political affiliation rallied to the winning side. In 1795, to be an Orangeman was dangerous. By the autumn of 1798, it involved little risk and had become fashionable. Edward Hudson described this development in a letter to Charlemont 6 October 1798, when he wrote:

The Orange 'mania' has broke loose amongst us, and spreads with a rapidity almost incredible. It made its appearance here (but lately) through the means of a corps of yeomanry that has been quartered here some time. They bit a few of my corps, at first; but within this week they have had a dispute with their officers on the subject. They are both excellent men, but by endeavouring to check the progress of the association, incurred the reputation of leaning to the Catholics. This had produced its usual effect, and, the business is assuming somewhat of a religious appearance, all denominations of Protestants are taking it up. The officers of the other corps have got matters settled very properly for the present; yet within these forty-eight hours, the number of 'Orangemen' is trebled in this town.[39]

In the course of the rebellion, the Orangemen and the forces of the crown had intermingled to such an extent that it became difficult to distinguish one from the other. As magistrates, yeomanry and militia officers were active Orangemen, it was all but impossible for the public to discover to what extent the government countenanced the activities of Orangemen.[40] Hudson wrote Charlemont in October about a paper signed by

---

[37] Moore, *Diary*, i. 325, entry 23 Sept. 1798; Lecky, *Ire.*, v. 68–72.
[38] Castlereagh to Portland, 3 June 1799 (Castlereagh, *Correspondence*, ii. 325–6).
[39] Hudson to Charlemont, 6 Oct. 1798 (*Charlemont MSS*, ii. 336).
[40] Lord Blayney to ——, 2 June 1797 (P.R.O.I., Rebellion papers 620/31/12); A. T. Stuart to ——, 14 Mar. 1797 (ibid., 620/29/69).

The Rebellion of 1798

William Atkinson 'captain commandant of the armed Orangemen', granting permission to retain arms.[41] Atkinson was high constable of Belfast and grand master of county Antrim. The paper was, no doubt, the result of authorization which Castlereagh had given Blacker and others to raise Orange bands, and was originally intended as a means of confining the distribution of arms to trustworthy Orangemen. However, documents of this kind, signed by Orange grand masters who were also high constables, could be used by minor Orange leaders to claim official status. Searches for arms, even raids on catholic homes, could be represented as official business by Orangemen waving their captain commandant's authorization. Hudson took up the matter with the military and later reported that Atkinson had asked that all such papers signed by him be taken up by the local military commanders.[42]

The suppression of the rebellion gave the protestant peasantry the same kind of ascendancy they had enjoyed after the battle of the Diamond, and they naturally pressed their advantage. In October, which seemed to open the outrage season, Hudson wrote, 'Rancour and animosity prevail to an astonishing degree. Papers have been put up with the old inscription: to hell or Connaught'.[43] As in the time of Lord Gosford's protest in 1795, the persons responsible for these outrages were not identified clearly as Orangemen. Yet it is almost certain that Orangemen were involved.[44] Some lodges attempted to curb these abuses by threatening to expose and prosecute any member charged with committing outrage. One resolution ran:

We, the undersigned members of the different Orange Lodges in Clogher, Augher, Ballygawly and Aughnacloy, having been informed that many irregularities have been committed in some Orange Lodges in this district, and that a few members of the same have been guilty of disorder... We will meet every month to receive information against any Orangeman charged with improper conduct, and should the charge be well-founded, will deliver up the offender to the J. of P., and at our expense, the prosecution will be carried against him.[45]

[41] Hudson to Charlemont, 27 Oct. 1798 (*Charlemont MSS*, ii. 337).
[42] Same to same, 15 Nov. 1798 (ibid., ii. 340).
[43] Same to same, 27 Oct. 1798 (ibid., ii. 337).
[44] Hudson to Charlemont, 7, 15, 30 Nov. 1798 (*Charlemont MSS*, ii. 340–1).
[45] *B.N.L.*, 9 Nov. 1798.

The Lurgan Orangemen also repudiated the charge that 'a leading feature of their Institution is a spirit of inveteracy and persecution towards their Catholic fellow subjects', and they warned, 'particularly anxious and zealous shall we be in bringing to punishment any Orangeman who, under whatever pretence, shall be so forgetful of his obligation . . . as to commit an act of wanton outrage'.[46] It was impossible for a society, including as many important people as the Orangemen boasted, to countenance lawless activity. The grand lodge in Dublin, which was more sensitive to public opinion than the Ulster lodges, at once took action to disclaim Orange responsibility for the attacks on catholics.

The second meeting of the Irish grand lodge was set for 20 November 1798 when it was intended to regularize the organization and print rules and by-laws. The November meeting was thus the obvious occasion for the Orange Order to make a public statement, explaining and defending its actions. But the growing hostility of Cornwallis's administration,[47] combined with the well-founded suspicion that Orangemen were responsible for the renewed attacks on catholics in the north, caused the Orangemen to act sooner. On September 10, at a gathering called to make plans for the grand lodge meeting, the chairman, Reverend J. F. Knife, made a statement declaring that the Orange lodges were not an anti-catholic body. The lodges, he maintained, were merely opposed to sedition, and had no quarrel with catholics on the grounds of their religion. The lodges disclaimed responsibility for attacks on catholics, and Knife pointed out that in the early part of the year, they had inserted a clause in their rules stating '. . . no person do persecute or upbraid anyone on account of his religion'.[48]

When the grand lodge met on November 20, further efforts were made to defend the movement against charges of religious intolerance. It was asserted that disorderly elements were impersonating Orangemen[49] and that unknown parties had circulated forged Orange rules and by-laws purporting to show

[46] *B.N.L.*, 30 Nov. 1798.
[47] *Times*, 3 Oct. 1798; Cooke to Auckland, 25 Jan. 1799 (Auckland, *Correspondence*, iv. 83).
[48] *Rep. on Orange lodges I*, H.C. 1835 [377], xv. app. 3, p. 2.
[49] Evidence of W. Verner, ibid., xv. 15.

The Rebellion of 1798

that Orangemen were sworn to exterminate catholics.[50] It was also felt necessary to contradict reports that Orangemen had been opposed to non-conformists as well as catholics. The efforts of the grand lodge appear to have had the two-fold purpose of disassociating the lodges from outrage and warning the plebeian Orangemen that membership in the lodges would not ensure them immunity from justice. Orangemen participating in raids probably acted independently of even their local lodge masters. Nor should it be doubted that criminals impersonated Orangemen and republicans forged Orange rules. However, Duigenan, who was, in a sense, an intellectual supporter of Orangeism, gave fear of catholics an air of learned respectability. The attacks on catholics were too widespread not to have included among the raiders a substantial number of sworn Orangemen, and the memory of past protection which protestants, guilty of outrage, had received from gentlemen who were now Orangemen, probably weighed more heavily with unruly rank and file Orangemen than did the warnings from the grand lodge. Yet the efforts of the grand lodge cannot be dismissed as a mere face-saving device. It was in the interest of the Orange leaders to discipline their membership, but they could not press such control too far without undermining the anti-catholic spirit which gave Orangeism its driving force. There was also a danger that too heavy a hand might shatter the movement into a series of independent bands all calling themselves Orangemen.

Not only was the word 'Orange' applied loosely to all protestant bands, but it was used by organizations not recognized by the grand lodge. The history of these 'Black Lodges' is obscure. The name 'Black Lodge' appears to have been applied to unauthorized Orange lodges which sometimes included individuals belonging to the regular movement who regarded the Black lodges as a higher form of Orangeism.[51] Only by publicly defining what constituted membership in the Orange Order, and what the lodges stood for could the grand lodge hope to control its followers and avoid responsibility for the acts of unauthorized persons styling themselves Orangemen. Harding Giffard, who had been assigned the task of drawing up rules

[50] *Hansard 2*, viii. 475; Sibbett, *Orangeism*, ii. 83.
[51] Evidence of S. Blacker, *Rep. on Orange lodges I*, H.C. 1835 [377], xv. 112, 122.

The Rebellion of 1798

and by-laws for the grand lodge, presented his report, in which it was stated that 'many persons have introduced various orders into the Orange Society, which will very much tend to injure the regularity of the Institution; the Grand Lodge disavows any other orders but the Orange and Purple, and there can be none other regular, unless issuing from and approved of by them'.[52]

It was decided that the grand lodge should meet the first Thursday of each month at 'Harrington's at seven o'clock and the third Thursday at three o'clock in the same place'. Delegation of authority in local lodges was to be from above, with the master of each lodge appointed by the grand lodge and he in turn was to appoint a deputy master, treasurer and secretary. To make voting legal, a lodge was required to have ten or more members present. Meetings were to open with a prayer followed by a reading of the general rules. Members were then to be proposed, reports of committees heard, names of proposed members called for, members balloted for and made, and the meeting to close with a prayer.[53] This procedure involved no serious departure from previous Orange practices, and was, in many respects, similar to that followed by contemporary masonry.

After thanking Giffard for drawing up the rules, the grand lodge passed a resolution authorizing a collection to be made for the families of loyalists who had suffered as a result of the rebellion. No other business of importance seems to have been conducted. With the meeting of November 20, the Orange lodges were firmly established on a national basis with a central leadership meeting regularly to guide their activities. Thus, after the third anniversary of the battle of the Diamond the Orange lodges evolved from an obscure rural protestant society in Ulster into the strongest political movement in Ireland.

With the crushing of the rebellion and the destruction of the United Irish conspiracy, the government no longer required the services of Orangemen. The catholics were, for the moment, humbled, but as the fear inspired by counter-revolutionary terrorism wore off, catholics were bound to resume political activity. Of more immediate importance was the decision of the

---

[52] Rules of the Orange society adopted 20 Nov. 1798 (ibid., app. 3, pp. 2–6).
[53] Ibid.

The Rebellion of 1798

British government to force the Irish parliament to end its independent existence. By the beginning of 1799, the issues arising out of this project split the Orange movement. Thus the Orange lodges, which within three years had become the most powerful party in Ireland, were to lose this favoured position within a few months.

V

UNION WITH GREAT BRITAIN
1799–1801

THE IDEA OF A LEGISLATIVE UNION between the Irish and British parliaments had, in the early part of the eighteenth century, found such persuasive advocates as Swift and Molyneux who spoke in what they conceived to be the interest of Ireland. Opposition at that time came, not from the Irish, but from the English merchant interests who feared Irish competition. By the middle of the century, however, Irish opinion solidly opposed union, while influential Englishmen interested in Ireland regarded the measure with favour. Most of the later viceroys, as well as Adam Smith, Pitt, Wilberforce and the king looked on union as the best solution to Ireland's difficulties.[1]

Grattan's 'revolution of 1782', by making the task of governing Ireland more difficult, made union more attractive at Westminster. Yet it was obvious that any project of union—coming from an English source—would only serve to unite Ireland against the measure. As the British cabinet was not prepared to force union on the Irish in the face of united opposition, the project had to await a crisis which made united opposition impossible.

Prior to the catholic relief bill of 1793 no prominent Irish political leader favoured union. Placemen, whigs and radicals were, for different reasons, agreed in their opposition to any

[1] Lecky, *Ire.*, v. 120–219.

scheme for abolishing the Irish parliament. Yet placemen could be bribed or coerced by Westminster, and party loyalties were far stronger in Ireland than national sentiments. With the exception of the Irish republicans, who had tied themselves to an alliance with France, there was no group in Ireland which would not favour union if they could be persuaded it was essential to their class or party interest. However, it was not until the passage of the catholic relief bill of 1793 that an influential Irishman saw the salvation of his party and class in union.

During the debates on the catholic relief act, Fitzgibbon had stated clearly that he considered the alternative before the Irish parliament was the rejection of the bill or union with Britain. Fitzgibbon maintained that once the catholics were given political rights, it would be only a matter of time before protestants would find themselves a minority in the Irish parliament.[2] With the passage of the bill, Fitzgibbon henceforth favoured union. Other opponents of the catholic relief bill such as the speaker, John Foster, Sir John Parnell, and Duigenan did not conclude with Fitzgibbon that union was the only salvation for protestant Ireland. Neither the placemen nor the Orange section of the gentry had any enthusiasm for union. In favouring it, Fitzgibbon was virtually alone among the Irish protestant ascendancy group. He could, therefore, do little more than inform his friends in England of his sentiments.

In the minds of English statesmen, however, the question of union was bound up with that of catholic relief. They saw in it a means whereby Irish catholics could be given equality without endangering the security of the protestant minority. Such a move would, they hoped, satisfy the majority of Irishmen, do justice to all, and strengthen the empire. Clare, on the other hand, wanted union as a means of securing protestant control of Ireland. He was absolutely opposed to having the measure combined with a catholic relief bill.[3]

In the summer of 1798 Pitt commenced discussions with a number of influential men in both countries on the subject of

---

[2] Clare's speech in the Irish house of lords, 17 Mar. 1793, in Froude, *Ire.*, iii. 98–104; Clare to Auckland, n.d. (Auckland, *Correspondence*, iv. 8).

[3] Clare to Castlereagh, 16 Oct. 1798 (Castlereagh, *Correspondence*, i. 393); Cornwallis to Pitt, 25 Sept. 1798 (Cornwallis, *Correspondence*, ii. 413–4).

union. After some exchange of opinion and a violent protest from Clare, the idea of combining the union project with catholic relief was abandoned, a decision which was regretted by Lord Cornwallis and his newly-appointed secretary, Lord Castlereagh,[4] to whom Pitt had entrusted the delicate task of securing the passage of an act of union in the parliament of Ireland. Castlereagh had been appointed acting chief secretary in Pelham's place during the summer of 1798, and by autumn he was given the post in his own right.[5] Cornwallis was not, as antiunionists later insisted,[6] sent over with instructions to work for union, but he and Castlereagh at once agreed to its expediency. In this they were supported by Cooke, the under-secretary, who was in charge of subsidies to the press, and who, under Camden's administration, had reluctantly collaborated with Orangemen. By the autumn of 1798, the viceroy, his chief secretary, the under-secretary, and the chancellor were working to put Pitt's project of the union into effect.

Although these men filled the four most important posts in Ireland and had the full backing of the British government, they had to proceed cautiously as union was the one question which might unite Orangeman, whig, catholic and republican in a common opposition to British influence.[7] The placemen, especially, had to be treated with care, as the measure would destroy the parliament which was their main source of income. Yet, it was hoped, that in the disturbed state of the country, a considerable section of the Irish might be persuaded to welcome union as the best possible solution to their country's difficulties. In this calculation the government proved partly right. The catholics, who were being hounded by the military and Orangemen, had little enthusiasm for preserving the protestant Irish parliament. Most of them regarded union with indifference, but many—perhaps to annoy protestants—and in the hope that any change would be for the better, gave the measure their

[4] Cornwallis to Ross, 30 Sept. 1798 (Cornwallis, *Correspondence*, ii. 415); Cornwallis to Pitt, 25 Sept. 1798 (ibid., p. 414); Clare to Auckland, 21 Oct. 1801 (*Some Fitzgibbon letters*, ed. R. B. McDowell, p. 306).

[5] Camden to Castlereagh, 31 Aug. 1798 (Castlereagh, *Correspondence*, i. 324–5).

[6] Jonah Barrington, *The rise and fall of the Irish nation*, p. 226.

[7] Drennan to Mrs. McTier, 19 Jan. 1800 (Drennan, *Letters*, p. 296); Francis Hardy to Charlemont, 6 Nov. 1798 (*Charlemont MSS*, ii. 338).

support.[8] The catholics who actively opposed the measure were few. Among the ex-republicans and presbyterians there was some lukewarm support, but no enthusiasm.[9] Of the leading politicians of the country, some of the great borough owners, such as Lord Ely and Lord Shannon, were favourable at first,[10] but most expressed misgivings on the ground that public opinion was strongly opposed.

There was, in fact, a hard core of resistance to the idea of union, based on three powerful vested interests: the legal profession,[11] whose members played such a prominent part in the politics of the independent parliament; the landed gentry,[12] who owned most of the boroughs and enjoyed the pageantry that went with being the nobility of a semi-independent kingdom; and, finally, there were the leading citizens of Dublin,[13] who had no wish to see the capital reduced to the status of a provincial city. These three elements were in a much better position than the government to influence Irish opinion.

The question of union was kept carefully from the press until late in November 1798.[14] The Castle newspaper, *Faulkner's Journal*, even took the trouble to denounce as Jacobin propaganda that such a measure was contemplated.[15] Having sounded public opinion throughout the country, the men at the Castle were painfully aware of the hostility the project was likely to arouse. Cooke was assigned the task of writing an anonymous

---

[8] Castlereagh to J. Beresford, 24 Nov. 1798 (Castlereagh, *Correspondence*, ii. 16); Marquess of Waterford to Castlereagh, 9 Sept. 1799 (ibid., ii. 394); Buckingham to Grenville, 25 Dec. 1798 (*Fortescue MSS*, iv. 423).

[9] Castlereagh to Wickham, 23 Nov. 1798 (Cornwallis, *Correspondence*, ii. 443-4); Mrs. McTier to Drennan, 13 Dec. 1798 (Drennan, *Letters*, p. 284); Mrs. McTier to Drennan, 28 Jan. 1799 (ibid., p. 287).

[10] Castlereagh to Portland, Nov. 1798 (Casltereagh, *Correspondence*, ii. 24-5).

[11] Castlereagh to Wickham, 19 Nov. 1798 (Castlereagh, *Correspondence*, ii. 8); Castlereagh to Foster, 24 Nov. 1798 (ibid., 17-8); Cornwallis to Portland, 25 Jan. 1799 (Cornwallis, *Correspondence*, iii. 48); *B.N.L.*, 14 Dec. 1798.

[12] Cornwallis to Portland, 23 Jan. 1799 (Cornwallis, *Correspondence*, iii. 42-3).

[13] Cornwallis to Viscount Brome, 27 Dec. 1798 (ibid., iii. 24); *B.N.L.*, 21 Dec. 1798.

[14] *B.N.L.*, 2 Nov. 1798.

[15] *F.D.J.*, 16 Oct. 17, 27 Nov. 1798.

pamphlet stating the government's case for union.[16] A draft of his pamphlet was circulated among prominent union sympathizers and it underwent considerable revision before publication. Meanwhile, the government-subsidized press was instructed to give its full support to union. Cooke's pamphlet was recognized at once as a statement of official opinion and the reaction to it was immediate.[17] Numerous pamphlets attacking the idea of union were rushed into print, and vested interests opposed to the project prepared to act.[18] A meeting of the lawyers was called for December 6 by Saurin, a distinguished member of the profession and an Orangeman. Union was declared 'an innovation which it would be highly dangerous and improper to propose at the present juncture'.[19] This was followed by a meeting of Dublin bankers and merchants[20] on December 18. They expressed their loyalty to the crown, but condemned union. On this occasion catholic merchants, whose economic interests were tied to Dublin, joined protestants in protest. Among the independent gentry who opposed union were Foster,[21] the speaker of the Irish house of commons, Sir John Parnell and George Ogle, all supporters of the government and members of the Dublin Orange lodge. Not even the Beresford faction, which was closely associated with Clare, rallied to the government's side.[22]

The question of legislative union was considered at the opening of the Irish parliament in January. This allowed only a few weeks for discussion,[23] but before the end of December protestant opinion in Ireland had been thoroughly aroused against the measure. Nor is this extraordinary. Cooke argued that protestant Ireland was dependent on England for defence

[16] *An address to the people of Ireland for and against an union by a friend to Ireland.*

[17] Barrington, *The rise and fall of the Irish nation*, p. 226.

[18] Granville Leveson-Gower to his mother, 14 Jan. 1799 (Granville, *Correspondence*, i. 236).

[19] *B.N.L.*, 14 Dec. 1798.

[20] *B.N.L.*, 21 Dec. 1798; Cooke to Castlereagh, 18 Dec. 1798 (Castlereagh, *Correspondence*, ii. 47–8).

[21] Clare to Auckland, 23 Dec. 1798 (Auckland, *Correspondence*, iv. 74).

[22] Beresford to Castlereagh, 19 Dec. 1798 (Castlereagh, *Correspondence*, ii. 50–1).

[23] Clare to Auckland, 5 Feb. 1799 (*Some Fitzgibbon letters*, ed. R. B. McDowell, p. 306).

Union with Great Britain, 1799–1801

and cited as evidence of this the recent rebellion.[24] Orange yeomen and the gentry who had led them in the rebellion immediately took offence. It was, they insisted, their all but unaided efforts that had overwhelmed the United Irish. As large-scale reinforcements in the form of English militia were not hurried to Ireland until the back of the rebellion had been broken,[25] there was some justice in their claim. They regarded themselves as the saviours of Ireland for the British crown,[26] and, being already irritated by Cornwallis's conciliatory policy towards rebels, they took Cooke's arguments as the final provocation.[27] They were furious but there was a helplessness about such fury. Nearly every organization to which they belonged was officered, in part, by men financially dependent on the Castle. There were few of them who did not enjoy some authority in local government or in the militia which could be withdrawn by the Castle. Moreover, they remained an unpopular, if dominant, minority and their opposition to union had the effect of persuading catholics and some republicans such as Neilson and Hamilton Rowan that union was worth supporting. Yet by attempting to push the measure quickly through parliament, the government had under-estimated the opposition of the protestant Irish and their ability to resist.

The question of union began to trouble the Orange lodges at the time of the meetings in December 1798.[28] They could not, as Orangemen, openly oppose a government measure without renouncing their claim to a semi-official status and risk losing the support of the numerous placemen in their ranks. Yet most Orangemen were among the violent anti-unionists.[29]

[24] *An address to the people of Ireland for and against an union by a friend to Ireland.*
[25] Camden to Pelham, 6 June 1798 (B.M., Add. MS 33105); see also Resolution of the Dublin corporation, Nov. 1806, in Sibbett, *Orangeism*, ii. 109.
[26] *Times*, 6 Mar. 1823.
[27] Buckingham to Grenville, 2 Jan. 1799 (*Fortescue MSS*, iv. 435); Same to same, 19 Jan. 1799 (ibid., p. 445).
[28] Resolutions of Orangemen, 13 Dec. 1798, 5 Jan. 1799, in *Rep. on Orange lodges III*, H.C. 1835 [476], xvi. 253; see also Evidence of W. Verner, ibid., [377], xv. 28.
[29] Buckingham to Grenville, 2 Jan. 1799 (*Fortescue MSS*, iv. 435); Same to same, 22 Jan. 1799 (ibid., p. 447); Earl of Carysfort to Grenville, 28 Jan. 1799 (ibid., p. 458); Leveson-Gower to his mother, 14 Jan. 1799 (Granville, *Correspondence*, i. 236).

Union with Great Britain, 1799–1801

To avoid splitting their organization and provoking an open clash with government, Orange leaders adopted a policy of discouraging the discussion of union at meetings.[30] In Dublin, the enforcement of this rule had obvious difficulties. J. C. Beresford, a half-hearted enemy of union, wrote Castlereagh on December 12:

> The opinions of the other body of men, I mean, the Orangemen of Dublin, I cannot so accurately tell, as it has been my principal aim at all times to prevent them from debating political questions, which would be very dangerous in a community where their numbers are so great, that we should be actually reduced to that miserable situation of being governed by clubs, which, in my mind, has been the cause of half the miseries of France.

Beresford went on to tell Castlereagh, 'But, talking to them individually at the monthly meeting, which met the first Wednesday of this month, I found them mostly adverse to the measure, and one gentleman attempted to introduce a debate on the subject, which I immediately put a stop to. I would by all means advise you not to attempt to procure a declaration from them; it is ten to one they will not be on the side you wish, and, if they should even, you will lay a dangerous precedent'.[31]

Beresford's advice was probably unnecessary as Castlereagh had adequate information on the attitude of the Orangemen. A few days later Cooke wrote asking, 'Would the *Star* and *Courier* fight for a Union (by abusing the Orangemen and praising Lord Cornwallis)?'[32] Prominent Orangemen such as Sir Jonah Barrington, Richard Jebb and Charles Bushe published anonymous pamphlets attacking union, but never as Orangemen.[33] Castlereagh was, no doubt, relieved when his assistant private secretary, Knox, informed him:

> There was a meeting of the Masters of the Orange Lodges in this city [Dublin] and they came to the resolution that, having associated merely to resist insurrection, it did not concern them to interfere with respect to any other political concern; and that, though they

---

[30] Resolutions of Orangemen, 13 Dec. 1798, 5 Jan. 1799, in *Rep. on Orange lodges III*, H.C. 1835 [476], xvi. 253; Evidence of W. Verner, ibid., and [377] xv. 28.

[31] Beresford to Castlereagh, 12 Dec. 1798 (Castlereagh, *Correspondence*, ii. 42).

[32] Cooke to Castlereagh, 15 Dec. 1798 (ibid., p. 44). [33] Ibid.

did not individually pledge themselves to any side on the Union, and should hold themselves at liberty to come forward on the subject in their towns and counties as citizens and freeholders, yet that, as Orangemen, they should be perfectly neuter, and take no side whatsoever. This a strong Orangeman who visited me this morning (John Hill, the brother of Sir George Hill) thinks will be universally adopted.[34]

As Hill predicted, the Orange lodges throughout Ireland followed the lead of the Dublin meeting.[35] But even with that, the neutrality of the lodges had yet to be made official and all but a few Orangemen remained anti-union. Duigenan, after some hesitation, became converted to the idea of union. In his opinion, many supporters of union within the Orange movement were 'afraid openly to proclaim their opinions, convinced that they would, by so doing, lose their popularity, which they may in proper season use for purposes beneficial to Church and State'. Duigenan claimed 'we have succeeded in preventing the Aldermen of Skinner's Alley, a very numerous society of citizens in Dublin, and eminently loyal, from canvassing the business [union] and the different Orange Lodges throughout the kingdom, composed of the bravest, most active and loyal Protestants, have been prevailed on to adopt the same line of conduct'.[36] Duigenan, who was especially bitter about Lord Cornwallis's policy of conciliation, attributed protestant opposition to union to the viceroy. He commented, 'I must plainly tell you that the unaccountable conduct of the present Lord-Lieutenant, which has rendered him not only an object of disgust, but of abhorrence, to every loyal man I have conversed with since my return from England, has induced many persons to oppose a Union'.[37]

Castlereagh wrote to the duke of Portland January 22:

The inflammation in Dublin is extreme, but is, as yet, confined to the middling and higher classes. The lower orders are naturally

---

[34] Knox to Castlereagh, 16 Dec. 1798 (Castlereagh, *Correspondence*, ii. 44–5).
[35] Cornwallis to Portland, 2 Jan. 1799 (Cornwallis, *Correspondence*, iii. 29).
[36] Duigenan to Castlereagh, 20 Dec. 1798 (Castlereagh, *Correspondence*, ii. 52–3).
[37] Duigenan to Castlereagh, 20 Dec. 1798 (Castlereagh, *Correspondence*, ii. 52–3).

indifferent to the question, but will be easily set in motion should their co-operation become of importance to the leading opposers of the measure... Mr Saurin has been but too successful among the officers of the attorneys and merchants corps in persuading them to lay down their arms. Dr Duigenan, whose opinions on the question are strongly favourable, is, I understand, shaken by the Protestant cabal in the city, with which he is much connected.[38]

What Saurin proposed amounted to a strike of the yeomanry who, in protest against union, would resign en masse.[39] The obvious agency through which such a design might be put into effect on a national scale was the Orange movement. In most matters the Ulster Orangemen took their lead from the capital and the resignation by the Dublin yeomen would have been intended as an example for others to follow.

The north of Ireland, however, did not have the same stake in the fight against union as Dublin. Presbyterians were largely indifferent to the survival of the parliament as it stood,[40] and perhaps were a little weary of being in opposition. William Drennan, a former associate of Wolfe Tone, wrote from Dublin on December 7, 'None here seem agitated about Union, except the yeomanry lawyers who enlisted in the English army a while ago, and now are for independence, or, rather, the old corrupt, incoherent connection which is called by Grattan and Giffard 'The Irish Constitution'.[41] His Belfast correspondent, Mrs McTier, replied, 'Union or no Union seems equally disregarded in Belfast'.[42]

If Dublin Orangemen had decided to launch a campaign against union along the lines suggested by Saurin, and the north had followed, it is not clear that a mass resignation of the yeomanry would have forced the British government to reverse its policy. There were enough British troops in Ireland to sustain the authority of the crown in the more important centres, and the yeomanry was useful mainly for police work in rural areas. If the protestant yeomen had followed Saurin's plan of turning in

[38] Castlereagh to Portland, 2 Jan. 1799 (ibid., pp. 80-3).
[39] Cornwallis, *Correspondence*, iii. 29.
[40] Castlereagh to Wickham, 23 Nov. 1798 (ibid., ii. 443), Mrs. McTier to Drennan, 13 Dec. 1798 (Drennan, *Letters*, p. 284).
[41] Drennan to Mrs. McTier, 7 Dec. 1798 (ibid., p. 284).
[42] Mrs. McTier to Drennan, 13 Dec. 1798 (ibid.).

their weapons and disbanding, they would have simply deprived themselves of the power and prestige they had been building up for the last three years. It is not surprising, then, that Saurin, after a few weeks of blustering, did not attempt to carry out his threat. On 5 January 1799 the grand lodge of Ireland passed a resolution which confirmed the policy already in effect of forbidding members, as Orangemen, to take sides on the question of union.[43] Shortly after this, Saurin had a long talk with Lord Castlereagh, and he left the chief secretary with the impression that he would not persevere in his project.[44]

Castlereagh decided to raise the question of union at the January session of parliament despite the failure to win public opinion. Waiting for a more opportune moment would, he considered, encourage opposition, and he wished to make it clear to the Irish upper classes that the British government was determined on union.[45] Castlereagh was not confident that the measure would succeed, and in spite of the grand lodge resolution he was worried about Orangemen. On the eve of the opening of parliament he wrote, 'The violent part the Orangemen have taken up seems to have made a considerable impression on some of our most Protestant (if this is the correct word) supporters. Lord Shannon's opinion is materially changed, and I think the Chancellor is a little shaken'.[46]

In the speech from the throne on 22 January 1799, the mention of the advantages Ireland might enjoy as a result of union provoked an instant attack from the opposition. After debates lasting until January 24, the government was finally defeated by a narrow majority when parliament voted to reject the section of the speech dealing with union.[47] This victory for the opposition was dampened, however, when an amendment proposed by W. B. Ponsonby which would have prevented the

---

[43] Resolution of the grand lodge, 5 Jan. 1799, in *Report on the state of Ireland, report from the select committee with minutes of evidence*, H.L. 1825 [181], ix. 354.

[44] Castlereagh to Portland, 7 Jan. 1799 (Cornwallis, *Correspondence*, iii. 38–9); Cornwallis to Portland, 16 Jan. 1799 (ibid.).

[45] Buckingham to Grenville, 2 Jan. 1799 (*Fortescue MSS*, iv. 435).

[46] Castlereagh to Portland, 21 Jan. 1799 (Castlereagh, *Correspondence*, ii. 128).

[47] *Report on the debate of union*, Jan. 1799, p. 154.

government from introducing the question again was defeated by 105 to 106.[48]

The debate on the throne speech marked the first open break in the ranks of those who had stood together against the catholic relief bill of 1793. Ogle, who later became grand master of the Orange lodges, and the speaker, John Foster, left the government, while John Claudius Beresford, who opposed union to please his constituents, gave up office to avoid dismissal. The head of the Beresford family, John Beresford, remained to support union and thus the huge patronage controlled by the family was not lost. From the government's point of view, the defeat was serious, but not overwhelming. It meant the government would be forced to exert pressure on those enjoying patronage, and undertake the expensive and distasteful business of buying the support of a sufficient number of borough owners to ensure the ultimate passage of the bill. It was clear that neither appeals to what the Castle declared to be the long term interest of the Irish protestants, nor the reaction against the horrors of the rebellion were sufficient to persuade the vested interests in control of the Irish parliament to vote for union.[49]

The contest between the Castle and the anti-unionists during 1799 took the form of a series of negotiations whereby many of the great borough owners, who controlled the votes in parliament, were prevailed upon to give their support to the government in return for honours, office, or financial settlements. Cornwallis wrote, 'My occupation is now of the most unpleasant nature, negotiating and jobbing with the most corrupt people under heaven'.[50] Once gained for the Castle, the borough proprietor, unless he had sold the seat to the incumbent, could compel the men he had sent to parliament to vote for union, and induce his tenants and others subject to his influence to petition for the project. There were, of course, a few great borough owners who supported union in this manner without hope of reward from the Castle. Most of these, however, were absentee landowners with English as well as Irish property.[51]

---

[48] Ibid., p. 91; Cooke to Auckland, 23 Jan. 1799 (Auckland, *Correspondence*, iv. 79).

[49] Cornwallis to Viscount Brome, 27 Dec. 1798 (Cornwallis, *Correspondence*, iii. 24).

[50] Cornwallis to Ross, 8 June 1799 (ibid., p. 102).   [51] Ibid., iii. 319.

Cornwallis spent much of 1799 touring the country, visiting members of the gentry, securing their support by any means at his disposal, and encouraging the various sections of the population to send in loyal addresses in favour of union. As there was little opposition and some lukewarm support among catholics and former United Irishmen, his efforts produced results. He looked on the project of union as a means of taking power from the victorious loyalist faction in the late rebellion. He came to believe that, had the Irish parliament been sensitive to the true feeling of the country, the government's campaign of bribery would have been unnecessary. What he hoped was to gain the necessary parliamentary majority by the means described above, thus making union legal, and, at the same time, offer the loyal addresses in favour of union as evidence that the measure enjoyed some popularity. By the end of the year he had the necessary majority, procured from borough owners, and enough addresses to give the measure the appearance of widespread popular support.[52]

The enemies of union were vigorous in their criticism, but not united in action. As the year progressed, one antiunionist after another defected from the cause, demoralizing the ranks of the opposition. Those who were not bought out by the government hesitated to appeal to the lower classes, or to undertake such action as the strike of the yeomanry proposed by Saurin. They realized that the majority of the lower classes were either indifferent to the fate of parliament over which they had no control, or were not disposed to sacrifice themselves for the sake of the upper and middle classes.[53] Cornwallis wrote, 'The mass of the people do not care one farthing about Union, and they equally hate both government and opposition'.[54]

Cornwallis had taken pains to win the confidence of the catholic priests who, after some hesitation, gave formal support to the measure. In the north, the presbyterian clergy took, for the most part, an attitude of benevolent neutrality towards union.[55]

[52] Cornwallis to Portland, 13 Aug. 1799 (Castlereagh, *Correspondence*, ii. 372–4).
[53] Cornwallis to Ross, 2 July 1799 (Cornwallis, *Correspondence*, iii. 111).
[54] Ibid.
[55] Luke Fox to Castlereagh, 7 Oct. 1799 (Castlereagh, *Correspondence*, ii. 414).

Union with Great Britain, 1799–1801

This left the anti-unionists outside the city of Dublin relatively isolated, yet not without resources.

Opposed to union were the forces which had founded the volunteer movement of 1782. The questions of catholic relief and parliamentary reform had split their ranks, but union brought them together. Wealth and influence were in the hands of the anti-unionists as well as the government, and could be used in the same manner if a determined leadership could be found. The obvious agency through which the protestant gentry could organize their followers among the lower classes was the Orange movement. Through it they might reach the ranks of the yeomanry and even the militia and, perhaps, by a show of force in the manner of 1782, frighten the British government and Castle into abandoning the project.

However, the Orangemen, unlike the volunteers, had a strong central leadership. The creation of this centralized control had been one of the prices the lodges had paid for receiving government support during the rebellion, and gaining the adherence of the gentry. This was unfortunate for the anti-unionists as the Castle could exercise a control over the movement by pressure on its leaders. The grand lodge was led by Thomas Verner, a unionist, and its secretary was J. C. Beresford, a lukewarm anti-unionist who could be influenced by Duigenan and other friends of the Castle. They were able to force the Orange leaders to adopt a policy of neutrality at the beginning of 1799 but this policy was not completely enforceable even then, and as the year wore on, Orangemen became increasingly restless.[56] But there was little they could do unless given leadership by more prominent members of their organization. J. C. Beresford, who might have led the anti-union campaign, was much too cautious, ,[57] while Harding Giffard, who had drawn up the rules and by-laws of the grand lodge, acted as a restraint on Orange firebrands who wanted to bring the lodges into the anti-union movement.[58]

In the north, where many United Irishmen joined the lodges, it appeared to one officer that Orangemen were working with republicans against union. Thomas Conolly, the lieutenant-

[56] Evidence of W. Verner, *Rep. on Orange lodges I*, H.C. 1835 [377], xv. 28.
[57] Barrington, *The rise and fall of the Irish nation*, p. 480.
[58] Evidence of W. Verner, *Rep. on Orange lodges I*, H.C. 1835 [377], xv. 28.

colonel commandant of the Londonderry militia, wrote Castlereagh in February 1799 that 'this monstrous coalition between the United and Orangemen in Parliament will keep us in hot water for a long time, as they will not let their differences sleep... the first from disappointment, the latter from their love of power and plunder, from both of which they are afraid of being kept out by Lord Cornwallis's conduct'.[59] As there were no United men in parliament, Conolly apparently used the term loosely. What he probably meant was the alliance of whigs such as Ponsonby, and Orangemen such as Foster. Yet the journalist, Higgins, reported to Cooke 'the United Irishmen... in league with the Orangemen on the measure of an Union being agitated'.[60]

In county Armagh, the birthplace of Orangeism, the activity of the Verners seems to have kept the Orangemen in check, despite the fact that so prominent a man as Sir Richard Cope was opposed to union. The head of the family, James Verner, wrote Castlereagh at the end of 1799:

I have observed declarations published from every county of this province on the subject of Union, from whence such may be expected, save the County Armagh. Previous to the election held in this county, it was thought prudent by the friends of Union (most of whom support Colonel Cope) to be silent on that topic. Since that, Lord Gosford has taken much pain to write letters, and consult those gentlemen who agreed in sentiments with him; and I have not the least doubt but those persons who are in earnest are exerting themselves with much zeal. But I fear a very strong majority of this county are, and will use every indirect means to frustrate our endeavours.[61]

Verner warned, 'For the reasons I have assigned, your Lordship cannot expect a splendid number of signatures, but I am in hopes a respectable publication will appear'. Verner admitted he did not think Cope was opposed to union for solid reasons, and hoped, therefore, to change his point of view.[62]

As there is little mention of the Orangemen in the correspondence between the Castle and the British government

---

[59] Conolly to Castlereagh, 8 Feb. 1799 (Castlereagh, *Correspondence*, ii. 169).
[60] Higgins to Cooke, 21 Dec. 1799 (P.R.O.I., Rebellion papers 620/18/14).
[61] Verner to Castlereagh, 16 Dec. 1799 (Castlereagh, *Correspondence*, iii. 18).
[62] Ibid.

during 1799,[63] it is evident that high circles did not regard the Orangemen as too serious a problem during that year. However, after the opening of parliament in January 1800 some of the lodges broke the discipline imposed on them by the grand lodge.[64] The occasion for this was the campaign undertaken by the opposition in what amounted to a last minute effort to defeat union. When the opposition was defeated in the division that followed the moving of the throne speech, it became clear that the government could introduce a specific measure for union and carry it at will.[65] The last hope of the opposition was to bring the pressure of Irish public opinion to bear on the government. The viceroy and Lord Castlereagh had asserted that the country favoured union, and offered as evidence of this the favourable reception Lord Cornwallis had received on his tour and the numerous loyal addresses calling for union.[66] To disprove this, the opposition sent a letter throughout the country calling for petitions against union.[67] The chief sponsors were W. B. Ponsonby, Lord Downshire and the new Lord Charlemont. They resolved to fight the government with its own weapons—to bring pressure on their dependents to sign petitions and even to collect money with which to win placemen away from the government.

This campaign was an invitation to disaffected elements and adventurers to fish in troubled waters.[68] It received more support than its leaders cared to countenance, such as anonymous handbills calling Orangemen and catholics to unite in a common front against union. One of these asked if 60,000 armed Irishmen should stand by and see their parliament taken from them.[69] Dublin yeomen paraded to honour Grattan who returned from

[63] Ibid., ii. 120–210; see also Cornwallis, *Correspondence*, iii. 29–160.
[64] Sibbett, *Orangeism*, ii. 84–95; Gowan, *Orangeism*, 252–70; Grattan, *Memoirs*, v. 55–6.
[65] Cornwallis to Portland, 16 Jan. 1800 (Cornwallis, *Correspondence*, iii. 163–4).
[66] P.R.O.I., State of the country papers 516/92/1; *B.N.L.*, 3, 7, 14, 17 Jan. 1800.
[67] Petition from Downshire, Charlemont and Ponsonby, 20 Jan. 1800 (Cornwallis, *Correspondence*, iii. 171).
[68] Drennan to Mrs. McTier, 25 Jan. 1800 (Drennan, *Letters*, p. 297).
[69] Cornwallis to Ross, 21 Jan. 1800 (Cornwallis, *Correspondence*, iii. 167–8).

Union with Great Britain, 1799–1801

retirement to fight union.[70] Once the opposition called for an active campaign against union, the influence of the handful of Orange unionists proved insufficient to keep the entire movement in check. Three Dublin lodges broke the discipline imposed on them by the grand lodge, declaring, 'We cannot think it a duty of an Orangeman to submit implicitly to the directions of a lodge which is principally composed of persons who are under a certain influence ... and while a lodge under such influence shall give the law to all Orangemen, we fear that our dearest interests will be betrayed'.[71] The rebel lodges protested:

against its injunctions of silence, and declare as Orangemen that we consider the extinction of our separate Legislature as the extinction of the Irish Nation. We invite our brother Orangemen to elect, without delay, a Grand Lodge which will be composed of men of tried integrity who shall be unplaced, unpensioned, unbought, and shall avow this best qualification for such a station, that they will support the independence of Ireland and the constitution of 1782.[72]

Although the grand lodge again appealed to the Orangemen 'to avoid a discussion of Union',[73] the revolt of the Dublin Orangemen found imitators. First to respond was Armagh lodge2 53, which met on February 21 at Charlemont. The lodge recommended that the grand master be elected annually, and suggested that George Ogle, an opponent of union, be made grand master, with J. C. Beresford re-elected as secretary 'on account of their uniform support of the interest and independence of Ireland'.[74] The members also recommended that county grand lodges meet on March 12 so that their resolutions could be communicated to the secretary before March 17. A meeting of thirty-six lodges of Armagh and Monaghan followed on March 12 at the home of James McKean, Armagh, where resolutions protesting against union were adopted.[75] Similar steps were

---

[70] Castlereagh to Portland, 18 Jan. 1800 (Cornwallis, *Correspondence*, iii. 166); Alexander to Pelham, 15 Jan. 1800 (ibid., p. 161).
[71] Declaration of Dublin lodge no. 500, Jan. 1800, in Sibbett, *Orangeism*, ii. 91.
[72] Ibid.   [73] *B.N.L.*, 24 Jan. 1800.
[74] Declaration of Armagh lodge no. 253, 21 Feb. 1800, in *B.N.L.*, 25 Feb. 1800.
[75] *B.N.L.*, 18 Mar. 1800.

taken at a meeting of thirty-one lodges of Antrim and Down, held at Maze on March 1, when it was resolved that 'We consider a legislative Union with Great Britain as the inevitable ruin to peace, prosperity, and happiness in this Kingdom'.[76]

While these Orangemen were denouncing union, other lodges such as the eighteen which met in February at Killilea,[77] county Armagh, the district of O'Neiland East lodges which met at Lurgan on April 3[78] and Belfast lodge 145[79] resolved to abide by the orders of the grand lodge. The extent to which the movement was rent by the question of union was indicated in a declaration of March 8, made by the grand lodge of county Antrim meeting at Belfast. 'With the most sincere regret', the declaration read, 'we observe an appearance of division and discord arise among Orangemen, instead of that unanimity which has hitherto prevailed and which alone can give strength and respectability to our association. It is with reason, therefore, that we hold in high estimation the wholesome advice and saluatory orders of the Grand Lodge issued on January 21, 1800'. The Antrim grand lodge went on to say, 'We know that the laws give us no right as Orangemen to discuss political subjects, and any attempt on our part to over-awe the legislature by our numbers would only bring down upon us the merited scourge of those laws. We urge our brethren not to become the tools of any Party or degenerate into factious members of so many debating clubs'.[80] This declaration was largely the handwork of Reverend Philip Johnson who was then district master of Lisburn. Johnson, when writing to the viceroy in July 1804 to seek a preferment at Ahoghil, described how he had prepared and brought forward the above declaration which was subsequently published by the Antrim grand lodge. Johnson claimed from that time forward 'they were never known, as Orangemen, to give an opinion on that or any other political question'.[81]

Too much importance should not be attached to this partial revolt of the Orangemen. It annoyed the Castle, but the Pon-

[76] Ibid., 4 Mar. 1800. [77] Ibid., 25 Feb. 1800.
[78] Ibid., 8 Apr. 1800. [79] Ibid., 18 Feb. 1800.
[80] *B.N.L.*, 21 Mar. 1800.
[81] Johnson to govt., July 1804, in McDonagh, *The viceroy's post-bag*, pp. 24–8.

sonbys, Foster, and Lord Downshire were regarded as the more serious enemies of union, and the Orangemen were only one of the agencies through which these men worked. A meeting called in county Down by Lord Downshire was attended by representatives of all religious denominations,[82] the Orangemen only incidentally. This was followed by similar meetings in other counties. In some cases, they were convened by sheriffs of counties, in others, by private members of the gentry. The purpose was to collect petitions of freeholders against union. It may be doubted that the gentry who convened these meetings were particularly anxious to give them an Orange character. As they wanted to appeal against Union on the widest possible basis, signatures of enfranchised catholics were as good as those of Orangemen. In all, over 110,000 signatures were collected on petitions against union. As the loyal addresses, so painstakingly secured by Lord Cornwallis, were signed by about 7,000, the opposition showing, though futile, was impressive.[83]

The importance of the Orangemen in this campaign stemmed from their special position in the yeomanry. When a substantial section of Orangemen disobeyed the injunction of the grand lodge, doubts arose about the loyalty of the yeomanry and more English troops were requested by the viceroy.[84] On January 24 Cornwallis wrote, 'There can, I think, now be no doubt of our Parliamentary success, although I believe that a great number of our friends are not sincere wellwishers [of] Union ... In Dublin and its vicinity the people are all outrageous against Union; in the other part of the kingdom the general sense is undoubtedly in its favour'.[85]

A few days later he wrote:

The clamour against the Union is increasing rapidly and every degree of violence is to be expected. As none of the English Regiments have yet arrived, I have been under the necessity of ordering the Lancashire Volunteers from Youghal to Dublin ... the apprehensions of our friends rendered this measure absolutely necessary.

---

[82] Cornwallis to Ross, 21 Jan. 1800 (Cornwallis, *Correspondence*, iii. 167).
[83] Cornwallis to Portland, 5 Mar. 1800 (ibid., 202).
[84] Same to same, 27 Jan. 1800 (ibid., 173).
[85] Same to Bishop of Lichfield and Coventry, 24 Jan. 1800 (ibid., 169).

The Roman Catholics, for whom I have not been able to obtain the smallest token of favour, are joining the standard of opposition.[86]

The lord lieutenant could have been strongly influenced by the atmosphere of the capital. It must have seemed to him that his patient work throughout 1799 was being nullified by the last minute efforts of the opposition. The fury of Dublin could not but affect the temper of the placemen, on whom Cornwallis was dependent for his majority. 'In the present temper of affairs', wrote the viceroy, 'I am not prepared to say that dangerous tumults will not arise... and it is with real concern that I express my fears that some defections may take place among those from whom we had a right to expect support'.[87]

The danger was that the yeomanry might, after the manner of the dissenting Orange lodges in Ulster, declare that union constituted a betrayal of the constitution which they were sworn to uphold. If they followed such a declaration with an armed demonstration in the capital amid the applause of the Dublin populace, it would be an heroic placeman indeed who would vote for union. As the ease with which part-time soldiers could turn to politics in Ireland had been demonstrated in 1782, Cornwallis had reason to be worried.

At this time another incident occurred which gave further cause for alarm. Lord Downshire, in his endeavours to collect anti-union signatures, sent petitions to the Downshire regiment[88] of which he was colonel-in-chief. The men were not ordered to sign, but a special parade was held at which they were given the opportunity to sign, of which most of them availed themselves.[89] This was, undoubtedly, an abuse of privilege as great as that committed by the unionists. When this action was reported to the Castle, Lord Downshire was removed as colonel-in-chief of his regiment, dismissed as governor of county Down, and his name erased from the rolls of the privy council.[90]

Such drastic action no doubt made the desired impression

---

[86] Same to Ross, 31 Jan. 1800 (ibid., pp. 174–5).
[87] Cornwallis to Portland, 4 Feb. 1800 (ibid., pp. 178–9).
[88] *B.N.L.*, 28 Feb. 1800.
[89] Ross to Littlehales, 7 Feb. 1800 (Castlereagh, *Correspondence*, iii. 233–4).
[90] Portland to Cornwallis, 17 Feb. 1800 (Castlereagh, *Correspondence*, iii. 241).

on other anti-union Irish aristocrats. Many of them had been willing to court popularity by opposing the government as long as they believed their influence sufficient to ensure them against reprisals. Lord Downshire, who perhaps put principles above privileges, was not typical of the Irish nobility. Yet men like Downshire, Ponsonby, Grattan, and Foster were, under no circumstances, likely to countenance extra-legal activity of any kind. It was not from them that the most violent invective against the Castle came, but from the lawyers and merchants of Dublin such as Saurin. Yet even these men were more given to violent abuse than to violent action. The presence of British troops in and around Dublin was a guarantee that there would be no Orange insurrection. The half-disciplined yeomanry was in no position to cross swords with regulars. Union was debated on 5 February 1800 with 278 of the 300 members of parliament present. When the division took place at one o'clock the following day, the government had 158 votes while the opposition had 115. Cornwallis and Castlereagh had triumphed.[91] Once union had become an established fact, opposition to it died. The issue had strained but not broken the unity of the Orange movement. Henceforth, Orangemen were to be the first among unionists.

[91] Cornwallis to Portland, 6 Feb. 1800 (Cornwallis, *Correspondence*, iii. 181); *B.N.L.*, 2 Jan. 1801.

VI

THE CONSOLIDATION OF THE ORANGE MOVEMENT, 1800–3

WITH THE PASSAGE OF THE ACT OF UNION, Irish history entered a new century and a new phase. The bitterness aroused by the struggle between unionists and anti-unionists did not prove lasting. As Clare had said, 'The Irish were easily aroused and easily appeased'.[1] Few of the Orange and whig anti-unionists cared to struggle against the accomplished fact, and even Grattan was disposed to make the best of things by working within the framework of the new system. The dying embers of the 1798 rebellion left the state of the countryside so disturbed[2] that Castlereagh thought it necessary to ask for a coercion bill in 1801. Although the United Irish were named responsible for the disturbances, their influence was all but extinct. The protestants, except for a few die-hards and exiles, had abandoned republicanism, and the catholic peasantry was not sufficiently interested in continuing a republican movement of their own. Wolfe Tone's efforts to unite Irishmen of both denominations in a nationalist movement had killed radical nationalism in Ulster without planting it firmly in the south.

Union, however, did not solve the all important land ques-

[1] Hay, *Hist. of the Irish Insurrection of 1798*, p. 48.
[2] Capt. Aldney to ——, 16 Apr. 1801 (P.R.O.I., State of the country papers 791/54); Maj.-Gen. Myers to govt., 7 May 1801 (ibid., 408/791/12); Higgins to ——, 23 May 1801 (P.R.O.I., Rebellion papers 620/18/14); Higgins to Marsden, 24 June 1801 (ibid.); *B.N.L.*, 20 Mar. 1801.

tion, and if the catholic peasant had lost interest in republicanism, he had not lost interest in revolt. From the time of the Whiteboys at the close of the Seven Years War until well into the nineteenth century, the discontent of the catholic peasantry was a force which any disaffected minority or foreign power might hope to utilize for purposes of its own. When no such external influences were present, the catholic peasants created, after the fashion of the Whiteboys, simple agrarian secret societies which sometimes included in their oaths a declaration of loyalty to the king. Thus, when the United Irish organization was destroyed, new and more primitive groups arose to take its place.[3]

A contemporary report stated:

The peasants still retain the most rancorous antipathy against the Orangemen and every fresh act of outrage adds fuel to their passive and keen desire for revenge. Being made to believe that those outrages are committed on them under the authority and sanction of government, their antipathy against it and against the Orange party is exactly the same, for they conceive on this account, the government to be the real source of all this . . . suffering.

The report continued:

They now have a general mistrust in every gentleman and they have been for a considerable time past organizing in many counties, although I cannot say to what ends. They admit no gentlemen into their secret, but choose leaders of their own body who had, upon former occasions, given satisfactory proof of their courage and resolution. Their object, as far as I can learn, is self defence against the Orangemen . . . It's safer to be a rebel than to stay home as reprisals are indiscriminate.[4]

These miscellaneous groups worked for limited objectives by terrorist methods, and presented an obstacle to any faction attempting to organize the peasants for serious political action. Such issues as an Irish republic, catholic emancipation, and later, repeal of union, could only interest the peasants insofar as

[3] Myers to govt. 7 May 1801 (P.R.O.I., State of the country papers 408/791/12); Higgins to ——, 23 May 1801 (P.R.O.I., Rebellion papers 620/18/14).

[4] Littlehales to ——, 23 Dec. 1800 (P.R.O.I., State of the country papers 408/733/6).

these objectives could be associated in their minds with the land question.

Immediately after the passage of the act of union, there was no politically-minded minority willing and able to organize the peasantry. The catholic hierarchy and most of the middle-class catholics hoped that their helpful attitude towards union would induce Pitt and the Castle to grant them full equality. Pitt, Cornwallis and Castlereagh were fully prepared to do so,[5] and in the view of such competent judges of Irish opinion as Secretary Cooke and Grattan, the majority of the protestant gentry were willing to give their support. Opposed were Clare, the Orangemen, and a group of lords in England. The viceroy considered that such opposition could be overcome. Cornwallis and Castlereagh did not expect that catholic emancipation by itself would quiet the unruly Irish peasantry. They considered that it should be combined with regular payments to catholic clergy and increased payments to presbyterian clergy, and that some arrangements for commutation of tithes should give relief to the over-burdened catholic peasantry.[6] Whether this programme would have brought tranquillity to Ireland is a matter of speculation, but it certainly would have forestalled the growth of O'Connell's associations.

The failure to follow union by a catholic relief act made it all but inevitable that the chronically discontented catholic peasantry would be organized by some one or some group to support a movement for such an end. Once organized, it would attract few supporters in Ulster, tend to keep the Irish divided along religious lines, and give the Orange movement an opportunity to retain its influence. The history of Orangeism from 1800 until 1829, therefore, revolves largely, but not entirely, around Orange opposition to catholic emancipation.

The failure of Pitt to insist on a measure of catholic relief in 1801 sprang from causes independent of Orangeism. It was the king's refusal to consider the measure under any circumstances which proved decisive,[7] and the men who appeared to influence the king on this question were not Orangemen. Duigenan and

[5] Curtis, *Ire.*, p. 347.
[6] Castlereagh to Portland, 28 Jan. 1799 (Castlereagh, *Correspondence*, ii. 139); see also McDonagh, *Viceroy's post-bag*, p. 1.
[7] Curtis, *Ire.*, pp. 347–50.

perhaps Musgrave may claim an indirect influence because of their close association with Clare. The lord chancellor himself and Lords Auckland, Malmesbury, Hobart, and Westmorland, who were in the best position to bring pressure on the king, were not Orangemen.

Cooke, who always had been closely associated with Clare, decided in favour of the catholics after union, and he attempted to persuade the lord chancellor to the same view. He argued that a few catholic members of parliament and peers could not endanger the protestants after union. In the manner of the bishop of Derry and Wolfe Tone, he asserted that the catholics were a decayed and dying sect, kept alive by the discriminations imposed upon them. Cooke maintained also that the majority of the protestant gentry were reconciled to the measure, but that, '... if the banner of protestantism was displayed, the Orange spirit would show itself in a universal fury'.[8] Clare, of course, was not convinced and did what he could to unfurl the protestant banner by speeches in the British house of lords. The lord chancellor had only another year to live, and died a disappointed man, not realizing, perhaps, that the will of the king would delay catholic relief for another quarter century.

The Orange fury, which Cooke feared, was not aroused. Pitt, unwilling to oppose openly the royal will, resigned, and helped Addington form a 'protestant' ministry. Cornwallis and Castlereagh resigned their offices a few days after the new ministry was formed, and Lord Hardwicke took the viceregal office, assisted by Charles Abbot as chief secretary.[9] Meanwhile, the Orangemen were making efforts to put their house in order. Although the division over the question of union had left their organization intact, it was obvious that they were discredited at the Castle. Cornwallis, whom they had called 'Croppy Corny',[10] and Castlereagh had no sympathy for the Orange lodges, and the Orangemen had reason to fear that the Castle or imperial government would take measures to counter their dominant position in the yeomanry, and their influence in the militia, and in county affairs.

The movement was still annoyed by the presence of Black

[8] Cooke to the Lord Lieutenant, 10 Feb. 1801 (Castlereagh, *Correspondence*, iv. 45–6).
[9] *B.N.L.*, 2 June 1801.   [10] Plowden, *Hist. Ire. to 1800*, v. 78.

lodges, which did not take orders from the grand lodge of Ireland. As the Orangemen were anxious to disclaim responsibility for the acts of violence carried on by individuals and groups said to be Orangemen, they took measures to deal with Orangemen who would not accept discipline. For example, on 12 April 1800 the following notice appeared in the *Belfast News-Letter*:

Caution to all Orangemen. We, the Masters of Nos 75, 113, 125, and 287 Lodges of Orangemen, having fairly tried and considered the conduct of D... M... of Diomone are unanimously agreed that the said D... M... ought to be excluded from all Societies of Orangemen in this Kingdom, and he is thereby excluded from our Societies, of which all Orangemen are hereby required to take notice. Given under our hand at Diomone this 12th day of April, 1800. Signed John Waring, District Master, Chris. Quin, District Master, John Smith, Master, William McDade, Master, John Irvine, Master.

Two months later, a notice appeared in the same newspaper disclaiming responsibility for local outrages. It read:

Advertisement to Orangemen:— We, the undersigned Masters and Brothers of Lodge No 676, do hold in abhorrence and detestation all such atrocious acts of robbery as have been committed in our neighborhood; and we hereby pledge ourselves to each other to suppress any such acts upon information, or we will give timely notice to bring the perpetrators of any such acts to condign punishment. Given under our hands in our Lodge room at Cullybackey, June 2nd, 1800. Signed by order James Watson, Master, W. Keinahand, Treasurer, Thomas Level, Secretary.[11]

The Orangemen claimed that the disorders were the result of the activities of surviving republicans and Defenders, and it is reasonable to suppose that these robberies and murders were the work of uncontrollable elements who, no matter what their affiliation, acted on their own. Many, no doubt, were Orangemen who counted on the influence of their lodge to grant them immunity from punishment. However, the Orange leaders were now of a very different sort from those who had founded the movement in 1795. James Sloan, at whose inn the first lodge was organized, had, after the establishment of the grand lodge of Ireland, ceased to be in the inner circle of Orangeism. Another

[11] *B.N.L.*, 12 June 1800.

link with the founders of the lodges was broken early in 1801 when Thomas Verner, who had first persuaded the gentry to support the movement, resigned as grand master. He was replaced by the Right Honourable George Ogle, the man whom the anti-unionists had suggested as his successor in 1800,[12] and who had been elected representative for Dublin to the imperial parliament. It is possible that Verner's resignation is explained by his loss of popularity in 1800,[13] yet more important was the fact that, although he was a country gentleman and the son of a member of the Irish parliament, he was less prominent than the man who replaced him. As the lodges grew older, they outgrew their founders, and began to attract men higher in the social scale. The movement depended a good deal for its prestige on the connections it could claim in high places. It was, therefore, important that the titular head of the movement should come from as exalted a station as possible. Verner was thanked for his services and he continued to play a part in the movement.

Besides having more prestige than Verner, Ogle was an able speaker, capable, if need be, of making an effective defence of Orangeism in debate. Serving with him as grand secretary was Patrick Duigenan, who replaced J. C. Beresford. At the same time the rebellion historian, Sir Richard Musgrave, was grand treasurer. The presence of these three at the head of the movement may be taken as an indication of the new phase Orangeism was entering. With the rebellion at an end, the lodges were to be less fighting societies, and more political and fraternal clubs. They needed some sort of 'ideas' to hold them together, and Duigenan and Musgrave were men of ideas. It was Duigenan who had supplied Clare with the arguments he had used to such effect in denouncing the catholic relief bill in 1793, and perhaps later in convincing the king that further concessions to catholics would involve a violation of his coronation oath. Musgrave's *Memoirs of the Different Rebellions in Ireland*, published in 1802, was a defence of the protestant ascendancy. Duigenan and Musgrave were, by no standards, great political theorists, but they were the best the Orange movement could produce and good enough to satisfy the needs of the Orangemen.

[12] See above p. 133.
[13] Evidence of W. Verner, *Rep. on Orange lodges I*, H.C. 1835 [377], xv. 28; Gowan, *Orangeism*, p. 270.

Duigenan and Musgrave explained the evils of the times in terms of 'papist plots' and justified their arguments by references to alleged actions of the catholics in past centuries. Their works abound in analogies between 1641 and 1798 and lurid stories of the inquisition. Taken as entertainment, they were much better than the works of Thomas Paine and Wolfe Tone. Amateur politicians who formerly discussed the 'rights of man' in Ulster taverns could satisfy the same appetites by talking learnedly of '1641 and papist plots'.

The Orange movement thus offered an outlet for the political energies previously supplied by the volunteer clubs and the United Irish. The level of discussion in taverns and drinking clubs may not have been high, but the ideas of Musgrave and Duigenan were easier to understand and more congenial to Ulstermen than the radical doctrines which had been formerly popular. Discussion, however, was never to become the main activity of the Orange movement. Armed demonstrations and street fights were better suited to the temperament of Orangemen and indeed to most of their Irish contemporaries. And when they felt the government unlikely to repress them, they indulged those inclinations to the full.

They had particular reason to expect trouble from Cornwallis's successor, Lord Hardwicke, who had been in Ireland during the rebellion as commander of the Cambridgeshire militia. On discovering Orange lodges in his regiment, Hardwicke had issued a regimental order, dated 17 April 1798, which read, 'Several lodges and societies exist in this town, and other parts of Ireland, formed for party and other mischievous purposes, under various denominations... Officers [are requested] not to suffer themselves to become members, and all non-commissioned officers and soldiers are strictly forbidden to become members of any such lodge or societies, or to frequent them under any pretence'.[14] As this order was issued when the Orangemen were engaged in anti-union activity, it is possible that the future viceroy had at first tolerated the lodges, but banned them only when he considered the issue of union was likely to make them dangerous.

Hardwicke, however, came to Ireland in 1801 convinced that the country needed a period of despotic government to repress

[14] Plowden, *Hist. Ire. 1801–10*, i. 117.

The Consolidation of the Orange Movement, 1800–3

the disorderly elements and bring about a return to normal conditions.[15] No action was taken against Orangemen; their influence in the militia, yeomanry, and in local government remained. In Dublin Sirr's detective force was left intact, and subsidies to Castle newspapers continued. Unlike recent viceroys, Hardwicke made no efforts to keep on good terms with the catholic hierarchy.[16] From the Orange viewpoint, he was the perfect viceroy.[17] His administration was, on the whole, popular, and as tranquillity gradually returned to the countryside, even Grattan commented on his competence. Hardwicke's success, however, owed as much to circumstances as to his policy. Protestant radicalism was dormant, not only because of the fears aroused by the rebellion, but because the grievances which had inspired it were removed. Commercial equality had been granted, and the disabilities against dissenters removed, while sums paid to individual presbyterian ministers were increased.[18] The question of parliamentary reform for Ireland was merged into the larger question of reform of the imperial parliament. The catholics, although disturbed at the failure to remove their disabilities, were persuaded by Cornwallis and Castlereagh that the resignation of Pitt would soon compel the British government to act.

With quiet returning to the country, Orangemen lost no opportunity to demonstrate their power and importance. The July 12 demonstrations in 1798 had been marred by the rebellion,[19] and in 1799 and 1800[20] by the divisions in the Orange ranks over union. In 1801 the Orangemen paraded in full regalia.[21] Five lodges of the 8th Armagh regiment of militia marched behind the regimental band which played Orange tunes.[22] With them were members of the Orange lodge of the Royal Artillery's regular unit and members of five civilian

---

[15] Hardwicke to ——, May 1801 (McDonagh, *Viceroy's post-bag*, p. 8).

[16] Higgins to Marsden, 24 June 1801 (P.R.O.I., Rebellion papers 620/18/14).

[17] Sibbett, *Orangeism*, ii. 97.

[18] Bankhead to Castlereagh, 8 Oct. 1800 (Castlereagh, *Correspondence*, iii. 388).

[19] Address to the Orangemen of Ulster by James Verner, 30 June 1798, in *B.N.L.*, 3 July 1798.

[20] *B.N.L.*, 15 July 1800.   [21] *B.N.L.*, 12 June, 21, 31 July 1801.

[22] *B.N.L.*, 21 July 1801.

lodges from the Coleraine area.²³ They paraded to the parish church of Ballyaugrin and in the evening returned to Coleraine where members of the military and civil lodges dined together. A vote of thanks was given the commander of the Armagh regiment for allowing the band to accompany the parade. The regiment was commanded, significantly enough, by a Major Cope.²⁴ At Downpatrick, the Orangemen of Upper Iveagh and Lecale district were received cordially by their county grand master, the earl of Annesley, and later paraded to church at Old Abbey.²⁵ The Orangemen of Belfast and Lisburn, headed by Thomas Verner, paraded to the 'Diamond' to the tune of 'Boyne Water' and 'Protestant Boys'.²⁶

Hardwicke, meanwhile, was showing special favour to the Dublin yeomanry who less than a year before had been on the verge of mutiny. He met the yeomanry captains of the Dublin district at a dinner on July 3 and on the 10th he received delegations from ten companies of yeomanry who requested his presence at a dinner. The dinner was held 29 July at the Rotunda where Captain J. C. Beresford, president of the yeomanry association, greeted the viceroy.²⁷ This would have been impossible under the Cornwallis administration, but Hardwicke was uncertain of the temper of the country and counted more on the armed strength of the yeomanry than on a policy of conciliation towards catholics. The absence of disorders, however, caused the viceroy to release the yeomanry from some of their duties in the autumn. In the spring of 1802 when the treaty of Amiens was signed with France and the danger of revolt and invasion seemed past, the imperial parliament gave a vote of thanks to the Irish yeomanry for their services. The Orangemen were not mentioned by name, but it was taken as a compliment to themselves.²⁸

The end of the war in Europe had a quieting effect in Ireland, but the brief peace did not pass without its ugly incidents. The funeral of Lord Clare in 1802 was marked by hostile demonstrations, the work of about fourteen people under a leader, rather

²³ Ibid.
²⁴ *B.N.L.*, 21 July 1801.
²⁵ *B.N.L.*, 31 July 1801.   ²⁶ *B.N.L.*, 21 July 1801.
²⁷ Sibbett, *Orangeism*, ii. 101; Plowden, *Hist. Ire. 1801–10*, i. 109.
²⁸ *Hansard's parliamentary history*, xxxvi. 1698.

The Consolidation of the Orange Movement, 1800–3

than a spontaneous act of the Dublin population.[29] Had Clare been an Orangeman, the lodges would have avenged the insult. In Kilrea, county Derry, the leader of a masonic lodge led an attack on eleven armed Orangemen who took refuge in a house and fired on their assailants, wounding two.[30] A week later in Downpatrick two Orangemen were acquitted on a charge of murder, but found guilty of riot.[31] In Londonderry, a riot between Freemasons and Orangemen resulted in five fatalities.[32] Clashes between yeomanry and United Irish were reported in Belfast in 1803, and there were rumours that at Saintfield money was offered for the head of an Orangeman.[33]

Orangemen in many districts resumed the practice of the Armagh volunteers in 1788[34]—that of marching armed, wearing Orange insignia through hostile neighbourhoods for the purpose of provoking attack. When menaced they would protest their peaceful intentions until some act of violence against them provided an excuse to fire in 'self-defence'.[35] To discourage such riots, the governor of Derry, Lord Donegal, a relative of Thomas Verner, called a meeting of the county magistrates, many of whom were Orangemen, and issued a declaration condemning the disturbances. Similar action was taken in Down. In the absence of regular constabulary, nothing more could be done by county authorities short of asking for troops. However in this instance, the moral authority of the magistrates proved sufficient to check further disorders. These northern disturbances showed that Orangeism was still vigorous. Yet with the relaxing of the revolutionary threat, and the gradual liquidation of the war establishment of the militia and yeomanry, the movement lost much of its importance. The Orange movement flourished on discord and violence.[36] When these

---

[29] Lecky, *Ire.*, v. 462; Plowden, *Hist. Ire. to 1801*, i. 121.
[30] Sibbett, *Orangeism*, ii. 102; Plowden, *Hist. Ire. 1801–10*, i. 173.
[31] Mrs. McTier to Mrs. Drennan, 12 July 1802 (Drennan, *Letters*, p. 319); James McCleland to Marsden, 24 Aug. 1802 (P.R.O.I., State of the country papers, 408/793/5).
[32] Plowden, *Hist. Ire. 1801–10*, i. 173.
[33] Pollack to ——, 3 Jan. 1803 (P.R.O.I., State of country papers 408/902/1).
[34] See above p. 10. [35] *Hansard 3*, xiii. 1223.
[36] Evidence of W. Verner, *Rep. on the state of Ireland, Report from the select committee with minutes of evidence*, H.L., 1825 [181], ix. 327.

were wanting, its decline was inevitable. However, the European war was resumed in May 1803, and as Napoleon massed troops at the Channel ports, the danger of invasion again became serious. Militia units and yeomanry corps were brought up to full strength, thus reviving the influence of Orangemen in the military.[3]

The grand lodges of various counties in the north issued statements announcing their loyalty to the empire and their confidence in victory. Of these, the statement of the Antrim lodges is typical. It mentioned that '... the number of internal enemies is greatly diminished, but Orangemen are called to be on their guard against them, to be ever ready, like watchful sentinels at their posts'.[37] In keeping with the previously declared policy of the lodges, it was reiterated, 'We entertain no enmity against any man, whatever may be his religion, who is not an enemy of the state'. The extent to which anti-unionist feeling had disappeared among Orangemen is indicated by part of the resolution adopted in county Tyrone. It read:

We feel a particular gratification in declaring that we are not now the divided, rebellious people which recently disgraced this island, as we perceive and acknowledge the indispensable necessity of a compacted Union in order to promote our mutual prosperity and we hail with rapture the propitious moment which has rendered concord complete among the ranks and denominations of men in every corner of the British dominions.[38]

A month later an incident occurred which, though it gave republicanism a martyr, proved to contemporaries that the United Irish movement was dead.[39] In July 1803 Robert Emmet in Dublin and Thomas Russell in Belfast made a gallant but irresponsible effort to revive the dying embers of Irish republicanism. 'Emmet's Rebellion', as it came to be known, took place within a year of a similar effort by Colonel Despard in London. Russell, who was to organize the rising in the

[37] Declaration of the Antrim Orange lodge, in Sibbett, *Orangeism*, ii. 104.
[38] Declaration of county Tyrone Orange lodge, in Sibbett, *Orangeism*, ii. 105.
[39] Brig. Gen. Hart to Littlehales, 29 Aug. 1803 (P.R.O.I., State of the country papers 408/902/34); Rev. Dr Cupples to Rev. Archer, 26 Sept. 1803 (ibid., 408/902/3).

north,[40] was unable to gather more than a dozen followers of the 'lowest rank and most desperate character',[41] chiefly from counties Antrim and Down. These were all that could be found in what had been the cradle of the United Irish society. Emmet, working in Dublin, was able at least to organize an uprising. He gathered arms secretly and was able to have thousands of pikes manufactured without being detected by Major Sirr's hitherto effective secret police.[42] A manifesto was prepared instructing his imaginary legions throughout the country to make all British troops in Ireland prisoners of war, and ordering, 'That all Irish Militia, Yeomen, or Volunteer Corps, or bodies of Irish, or individuals, who, fourteen days from the promulgation and date hereof, ... found in arms, shall be considered as rebels, committed for trial and their properties confiscated'.[43]

To the Orangemen he addressed a special threat and an invitation to join his forces. His proclamation read, 'Orangemen, add not to the catalogue of your follies and crimes; already you have been duped, to the ruin of your country, in legislative union ... Attempt not an opposition which will carry with it your inevitable destruction; return from the paths of delusion—return to the arms of your countrymen who will receive and hail your repentance'.[44] Emmet thus recognized the Orangemen as a distinctly Irish body, not mere hirelings of the Castle, but Irishmen who had to be won over or intimidated. It was, indeed, a source of surprise and bitterness to the surviving radicals that a substantial section of the population, whose credentials as Irishmen could not be disputed, had become zealous defenders of the British connection. The self-confident rationalists, convinced that time was on their side, found themselves defeated and isolated by men and ideas they regarded as anachronistic and doomed. Emmet's appeal to the Orangemen, like his appeal to the Irish nation, was unheeded. On July 23 he distributed pikes and a few firearms to a whiskey-

[40] George Stephenson to Littlehales, 28 July 1803 (ibid., 408/902/2); Mrs. McTier to Drennan, 13 June 1803 (Drennan, *Letters*, p. 324); —— to Pollack, 3 Jan. 1803 (P.R.O.I., State of the country papers 408/402/1).
[41] Maxwell, *Hist. of the Irish rebellion in 1798*, p. 405.
[42] Plowden, *Hist. Ire. 1801–10*, i. 166–7.
[43] Emmet's manifesto, in Madden, *United Irishmen*, iii. 552.
[44] Ibid., p. 555.

laden band of several hundred.⁴⁵ As they moved towards Dublin Castle, passers-by were compelled to join their ranks. On the way Emmet's followers met and brutally murdered Lord Kilwarden, who, as Attorney-General Wolfe, had taken action against the Orangemen during the early Armagh outrages.

The attack on Kilwarden was noticed by three soldiers on their way to an Orange meeting at Peter Daly's hotel. This establishment served not only as a meeting place for Orangemen, but a depôt for yeomanry arms. Two lodges were meeting when the soldiers reported the riot. The seventy or so Orangemen in attendance thereupon armed themselves from Daly's stores and Major Swan, who had been visiting one of the lodges, took command and led them against Emmet's followers.⁴⁶ A general alarm brought small detachments of yeomanry, regulars and armed civilians—probably Orangemen—on the scene, but before most of them arrived Emmet's few hundred men had been scattered.

This last flicker of republicanism ends the first phase of the history of the Orange lodges. With the state no longer in immediate danger, Orangemen could henceforth devote their main energies to the defence of the protestant ascendancy. Their organization had become the recognized carrier of the Orange tradition, acknowledged by the Ulster peasants, the protestant clergy and gentry, and the Dublin placemen who together made up the 'protestant interest'. The principal battle of this interest during the next generation was to be fought against catholic emancipation in the parliament of the United Kingdom. In this conflict Irish Orangemen were to find allies among the ultra tories in Great Britain. It is, therefore, necessary to consider the manner in which Orangeism took root in Britain and the efforts of its British leaders to make it an agency of the tory party.

⁴⁵ Ibid., pp. 348–50.   ⁴⁶ Gowan, *Orangeism*, pp. 279–81.

VII

BRITISH ORANGE LODGES
1798–1822

THE EXCHANGE of Irish and English militia units in 1798 and the founding of Orange lodges in British regiments serving in Ireland[1] provided the means by which Orangeism took root in Britain. The first recorded instance of an authorized Orange lodge travelling to England was in 1798 when Colonel Stanley's regiment of Lancashire militia carried Orange warrant number 220 to Manchester. The regiment was disbanded shortly afterwards, but some of the ex-militiamen who had been lodge members kept the warrant and remained organized as Orangemen. Thus a civilian lodge was established.[2] In 1799 the second battalion of the Manchester and Salford volunteers returned to Manchester carrying Orange warrant number 1128. After this, numerous regiments including Lord Wilton's Lancashire volunteers and Sir Watkin Williams Wynne's Ancient Britons brought Orange warrants to England. Lodges were founded at Oldham, Bury, Stockport, Ashton-under-Lyne, Rochdale and Wigan, but Manchester, where the first English lodge was established, remained the stronghold of the movement.[3]

At first these English lodges were little more than clubs of ex-soldiers, but gradually they began to include ordinary civ-

---

[1] Buckingham to Grenville, 19 Jan. 1799 (*Fortescue MSS*, iv. 445); Colonel, West York Militia to Gordon, 6 Sept. 1809 (P.R.O., H.O. 51/171).

[2] Sibbett, *Orangeism*, ii. 114–5.

[3] *Rep. on Orange lodges IV*, H.C. 1835 [605], xvii. 32, 43 and app. 15, 118.

ilians in their membership. They seem to have functioned mainly as protestant friendly societies and took little active part in politics. As there were many more lodges than available warrants, the claim of these organizations to be Orange societies authorized by the grand lodge of Ireland is open to doubt. English lodges with warrants in theory paid dues and corresponded with the Irish grand lodge, while the groups meeting without warrants did not. In both cases the Irish insignia and ritual were used or at least imitated.

It is probable that most of the men joining these lodges were Irish protestants who had enlisted in English militia regiments or who had come to England to work. A large number of catholic Irish were settled in Manchester and smaller numbers were scattered throughout the various industrial communities of England. This meant that the protestant Irish who came to England—comparatively few in number—constituted a minority within a minority. Such a group might well desire to set itself apart from the catholic Irish immigrant by forming separate protestant societies in which the English and Scots were welcome. In this manner they might hope to protect themselves against the hostility of catholic Irish immigrants and, at the same time, win the approval of the English who normally regarded Irish immigrants with contempt.

As long as the Orange lodges in Britain refrained from public displays they were ignored by the majority of Irish immigrants. Yet once the movement was firmly established, it was inevitable that British Orangemen would attempt a July 12 parade through a catholic district, thus provoking a riot. The first of these Orange riots occurred in Manchester on 12 July 1807, when Orangemen, carrying banners and marching to Orange tunes, joined a number of English friendly societies in a parade to the collegiate church of Reverend Ralph Nixon. On their return they were attacked by Irish catholics.[4] The military was called out and a number of persons arrested.

The riot could not have greatly disturbed the city of Manchester as one of its newspapers, the *British Volunteer*, did not find space to print a letter from Nixon in its July 18 issue.[5] In his letter, printed on July 25, Nixon described the riot as an attack

---

[4] *British Volunteer*, Manchester, 25 July 1807.
[5] *British Volunteer*, Manchester, 18 July 1807.

by Irish catholics on a peaceful Orange parade. 'Orange principles', Nixon declared, 'are imperfectly known in England, and those who attacked them were misled by an erroneous opinion that our views are hostile and directed against papists. Orangemen are zealously attached to the King and admire our matchless constitution'.[6] The Manchester Orangemen interpreted the riot as a British 'battle of the Diamond' and made it the occasion for reorganizing and expanding their movement. A county lodge was established in Lancashire,[7] and lodges were founded in Liverpool, Leeds, Birmingham, York and Bradford. Two had already been founded in London and three in Scotland by 1807. The Argyle fencibles had introduced the order into Scotland some time before this date, the first lodge being established at Maybole, the second in Glasgow, and the third in Argyleshire.[8]

The expansion of the movement after the riot encouraged Nixon to believe that British protestants could be organized in a national Orange movement capable of winning the patronage of the upper classes. With the object of creating such a national movement, he visited the London Orangemen and wrote to Ireland for authority to found a British grand lodge. The visit to London made it clear that British Orangeism would have to make its headquarters in the Midlands. Nixon wrote, 'On our arrival in London, we were disappointed to find the society neither so numerous nor quite so respectable as we anticipated, or as the nature of such an establishment requires'.[9] Nixon's estimate of the London lodges is confirmed by a printed notice of one of their meetings held a year later. The Middlesex and Surrey lodges met in a public house known as the 'Moon and Seven Stars' on Stanhope street, Clare Market. At this meeting they elected Henry Stanton, a former Irish yeomanry officer, as their grand master and permanent master of the two lodges. Two sets of resolutions were passed, the first to the effect that the members were loyal and protestant, and determined not to

---

[6] Ibid., 25 July 1807.
[7] R. Nixon to John Verner, 3 Sept. 1808 (*Rep. on Orange lodges IV*, H.C. 1835 [605], xvii. app. 21. pp. 174–5).
[8] Sibbett, *Orangeism*, ii. 116; Gowan, *Orangeism*, p. 285.
[9] R. Nixon to John Verner, 3 Sept. 1808 (*Rep. on Orange lodges IV*, H.C. 1835 [605], xvii. app. 21 pp. 174–5).

encourage political or religious discussion. The second set of resolutions called all loyal brothers to attend the next meeting and declared that the lodges would meet on the second and fourth Wednesday of each month at 'Brother Harcourt's public House'.[10] A vote of thanks was tendered to Stanton for being present. It is difficult to resist the conclusion that Stanton was a vain young man who had courted the honours conferred on him by buying the drinks.[11]

In any case the title of county grand master was ridiculous for two lodges which met jointly twice a month. Nor did the London organization progress much during the next decade. C. E. Chetwood, an Irish Orangeman who went to London about 1818, stated that the only lodge then functioning held fortnightly meetings attended by about twenty persons, mostly of the lower orders, at a public house in Clerkenwell called the 'Coach and Horses'.[12] When Nixon visited London there may have been two other lodges, but it is safe to conclude that the strength of the London movement was insignificant during the early years of Orangeism in England.

On his return from London, Nixon decided to organize the British grand lodge in Manchester. He took up the matter with John Verner who was then Irish grand secretary. Verner admitted that the Irish lodge could not exercise adequate control of Orangemen in England, but he expressed concern about the difficulties involved in maintaining a uniform system if the movement was to have two heads.[13] Verner seemed in no hurry to have Nixon establish a separate leadership in Britain, but could offer no strong argument for delay as he had admitted that the Irish grand lodge had all but ceased to exist.[14]

Nixon's first task was to find a gentleman to accept the office of grand master. The choice was very limited as the Manchester movement was composed almost entirely of workingmen. The two most obvious candidates were Colonel Taylor of Moston, near Manchester, and Colonel Fletcher of Bolton

[10] Gordon to Jenkinson, 19 Sept. 1809 (P.R.O., H.O. 50/413).
[11] Henry Stanton to Dundas, Sept. 1809 (P.R.O., H.O. 51/171).
[12] Evidence of C. E. Chetwoode, *Rep. on Orange lodges IV*, H.C. 1835 [605], xvii. 3.
[13] R. Nixon to John Verner, 3 Sept. 1808 (ibid., app. 21. p. 174).
[14] Same to same, 21 Nov. 1808 (ibid., p. 175).

who appears to have been a personal friend of the influential 'ultra tory' peer, Lord Kenyon,[15] a recent recruit to Orangeism. Nixon first approached Taylor requesting him to become grand master. Colonel Taylor had raised and equipped at his own expense the Manchester and Salford rifles, and, like Thomas Verner of Armagh, was a man of consequence in local politics. According to the Orange historian, Sibbett, he made careful enquiries about the aims and objectives of the movement before placing himself at its head,[16] and was only convinced of its worth when Nixon presented him with a copy of the rules and by-laws published by the grand lodge of Ireland.[17] He must have had some hesitation about risking his reputation by becoming the chief of a movement whose members were drawn from the lower orders and obviously included rowdy elements. It was not until May 1808, almost a year after Nixon first approached him, that Taylor consented to accept office and the British grand lodge was established.[18]

The formal organization of the British grand lodge took place at the Star hotel, Manchester, which had hitherto been the meeting place of the county lodges of Lancashire. Officers appointed were Colonel Taylor, grand master, Colonel Fletcher, deputy grand master, W. A. Woodburne, a solicitor of Manchester, grand treasurer, and Nixon grand secretary.[19] The Irish grand lodge was informed of the action and assured that all the rules of the Irish order would be upheld by the English lodge.[20]

Irish warrants held in England were cancelled and all lodges were compelled to acquire new ones from the British grand lodges.[21] The first of these was issued on 26 October 1808 to Griffith Ellis Henderson of Manchester and was signed by Taylor, Fletcher and Woodburne. Warrants were issued to lodges at Oldham, Manchester, Stockport, Wigan, Rochdale, Ashton under-Lyne, Gorton, Halifax, Glossop, Shaw, Bardsley, Gee

[15] Evidence of Lord Kenyon (ibid., p. 122).
[16] Sibbett, *Orangeism*, ii. 116; Gowan, *Orangeism*, p. 286.
[17] R. Nixon to Taylor, 20 May 1808 (*Rep. on Orange lodges IV*, H.C. 1835 [605], xvii. app. 21. p. 174).
[18] R. Nixon to Verner, 21 Nov. 1808 (ibid., p. 175).
[19] Evidence of Lord Kenyon (ibid., p. 122).
[20] R. Nixon to Verner, 21 Nov. 1808 (ibid., p. 175).
[21] Ibid., rep. p. iv.

Cross, Mottram and Dobb Cross.[22] In that manner the British grand lodge was founded ten years after the first military lodge crossed the Irish Sea.

Orangeism, however, could not flourish in Britain except in cities like Manchester which had large Irish populations. Here where the recently arrived Irish were held together by being in an alien community and organized to some degree by their church and revolutionary societies, there was a rough parallel with conditions in Armagh. The Irish catholic immigration, which posed an apparent threat to British living standards, excited fears and resentment among British labourers. This feeling, which had its root in a dislike of the Irish, could find expression in the Orange lodges.

In other areas, as the state of the London lodge suggests, Orangeism was an exotic movement introduced by Irish protestants and maintained by adventurers and rowdies with a taste for pageantry and an eye for patronage. The only conceivable circumstance likely to recommend the British movement to the government or ruling class was a republican uprising in Britain on the United Irish model. Like the Irish peasantry, the neglected and restless industrial population was a revolutionary force which could be used by upper and middle class radicals able to associate themselves or their party with the idea of improving the condition of the people. It may be doubted, however, that such discontent could have been harnessed by the divided and not always popular British radicals, or that effective leaders could have risen from the lower classes. Certainly, there was nothing on the scale of the United Irishmen, and spontaneous movements—such as the Luddites—were less formidable than the Defenders.

Yet if this all but leaderless discontent was not to result in revolution, it was more than sufficient to alarm the comfortable classes. The widespread fear of revolution was a political fact which could be exploited by British Orange leaders like Nixon, Fletcher and Taylor. And if they could participate in any capacity, however insignificant, in measures taken against a real or imaginary revolutionary conspiracy, Orangemen could henceforth claim to be preservers of the state. It is indeed sur-

[22] Sibbett, *Orangeism*, ii. 117–8; *Rep. on Orange lodges IV*, H.C. 1835 [605], xvii. app. 15, p. 118.

prising that the Orange lodges, centred as they were in Manchester where disaffection was rife, did not make more of their opportunity.

During the Luddite troubles of 1812, Colonel Taylor and Colonel Fletcher along with a man named Lloyd of Stockport, all Orangemen, were, in their capacity as magistrates, active against those creating disorder. Orange magistrates swore in a number of Orangemen as special constables[23] and, as most of these were working men, they probably used some of them as police spies. Chetwoode denied that they acted as spies, but Nixon wrote the earl of Yarmouth that 'signs and passwords cannot be dispensed with [as] they were found absolutely necessary during the late disturbance in this and adjoining counties to enable our brethren to recognize each other in their laudable endeavours to discover the secret machinations of the disaffected'.[24]

Acting as informers was not a normal Orange practice, however, as Orangemen preferred open violence to under-cover work. The government, moreover, had an abundance of informers and was clearly not dependent on Orangemen for that type of assistance. Against Luddism the Orangemen did little more than serve as special constables under a few Orange magistrates, although the Irish grand lodge gave them credit for saving England. In a declaration dated 12 July 1813 the Irish grand lodge claimed, '... The seditious agitators are stung to madness by the knowledge of the Union between the British and Irish Orangemen, which every day acquires new power and more wide extension. Following your loyal example, the British Orangemen have saved their country by suppressing the treasonable bands calling themselves Luddites'.[25]

Some Orangemen were present during the clash in 1819 between the troops and the crowd, which had assembled to hear Hunt, that became known as the 'Peterloo massacre', but as special constables they played a minor role. Colonel Fletcher, who supplied the government with a constant stream

---

[23] Nixon to Stockdale, 11 June 1814 (*Rep. on Orange lodges IV*, H.C. 1835 [605], xvii. app. 21. pp. 179–80).

[24] Nixon to earl of Yarmouth, 13 Nov. 1813 (ibid., p. 179).

[25] *Rep. on the state of Ireland, report from the select committee with minutes of evidence*, H.L. 1825 [181], ix. 352.

of letters of an alarmist nature, was active[26] as a magistrate in suppressing the riot. For this activity, he was subjected to an attack in parliament on 22 December 1819[27] when a member named Bennett presented a petition from John Lever, of dubious character, calling for an enquiry into the conduct of Colonel Fletcher during the riot. Lever claimed that Colonel Fletcher had had him committed to gaol on a charge of murder because he had refused to act as a spy in York and Derby in 1812. Bootle Wilbraham, another member of parliament, pointed out that the petitioner had waited seven years before making his complaint against a man 'who, for 22 years had performed the duties of a magistrate to the satisfaction of every loyal man'.[28] But, Wilbraham added, Colonel Fletcher was one of those who had acted at Manchester 16 August 1819 and hence he was exposed to the 'hostility of a certain class who were now endeavouring by petitions, to cast reflections on all the magistrates concerned upon that occasion'.[29]

Unlike their Irish counterpart, the English Orangemen had no influence in the yeomanry[30] which had been called out by the magistrates to suppress the riot. This is explained by the fact that the English yeomanry was composed entirely of mounted troopers recruited from the more prosperous farmers while the Orangemen in England were largely urban labourers. There were, of course, lodges in the regular units and militia, but among the well-disciplined troops in Britain this does not seem to have made much difference.

General Maitland, the military commander in the Midlands, did not share Colonel Fletcher's anxieties about the revolutionary spirit of the lower classes. His principal worry was the extravagant demands for military protection made by property owners. Although he does not mention the Orangemen in his communication to the home office,[31] it is likely that Maitland would have encouraged them or any other society which undertook to organize special constables instead of demanding military protection.

[26] P.R.O., H.O. 40/1, 8, 24 Apr., 1 May 1812.
[27] *Hansard*, xli. 1445–9.   [28] Ibid.   [29] *Hansard*, xli. 1448.
[30] Evidence of Chetwoode, *Rep. on Orange lodges IV*, H.C. 1835 [605], xvii. 33.
[31] Maitland to Sidmouth, 22 June 1812 (P.R.O., H.O. 40/1).

Although the British movement was not powerful, its limitations could be concealed, and the indisputable importance of the Irish Orangemen might be offered as evidence of the potentialities of the British lodges. Nixon and members of the grand lodge insisted that if only a substantial number of ultra tories would found a London counterpart of the original Dublin lodge, the country would respond and the British movement would grow to Irish proportions. This idea of a popular movement strongly opposed to catholic emancipation was undoubtedly attractive to ultra tory peers and even to the dukes of York and Cumberland. Association with the Orangemen, however, presented difficulties. Whigs and radicals had always asserted that the movement was encouraged by government and they made the most of any scraps of evidence connecting men in high places with Orangemen. The character of the lodges as oath-bound secret societies raised doubts as to their legality and the existence of lodges in the army was clearly contrary to law. The history of British Orangeism during its early years revolves around efforts to keep the lodges within the letter of the law and to win tory support, and the attempts of their enemies to expose Orange 'conspiracies' and make the lodges illegal. The cabinet, while feeling no particular sympathy towards Orangemen, had no intention of suppressing them at the demand of whigs and radicals.[32]

According to Nixon, the founding of the grand lodge resulted in a steady growth of the British movement.[33] Over two years passed before all Irish warrants were replaced by new ones issued from Manchester, putting Orangemen in Britain under the authority of the British grand lodge. Meetings at this time were usually held in public houses, often with the encouragement of the proprietors.[34] About a fifth of the entire membership consisted of military lodges[35] and there was some overlapping between the military and civil lodges. It was not uncommon for soldiers in uniform[36] to attend lodge meetings and,

[32] *Hansard*, xxxi. 1089–98; ibid., xli. 896, 1392.
[33] Nixon to Giffard, 11 Feb. 1811 (*Rep. on Orange lodges IV*, H.C. 1835 [605], xvii. app. 21. p. 177.
[34] Evidence of James Whittles, ibid., p. 159.
[35] Nixon to Sergeant Green, 6 Feb. 1813 (ibid., app. 21. p. 178).
[36] Ibid., p. 160.

if no civil lodge was nearby, the military lodges could, subject to permission from the grand lodge, acquire civil members.

The first serious difficulties arising from the existence of military lodges occurred in the summer of 1809. A magistrate of Worcester named St. John arrested a razor-grinder who, on being searched, was found to possess an Orange certificate made out to Private William Hall of the First West York militia. It was printed on good paper and had the royal coat of arms with a yellow ribbon attached to it by a wax seal and stamped with the image of William III crossing the Boyne.[37] St. John sent the certificate to the Horse Guards[38] whereupon the military secretary, Colonel Gordon, wrote the officer commanding the First West York militia who replied that Private Hall was a man of excellent character who had probably lost his Orange certificate while on a recruiting tour. 'The Lodge', wrote the commanding officer, 'has existed for ten years in this Regiment; [it] is a society of loyal and philanthropic tendency like Free Masonry. There are, I understand similar lodges held in many Regiments and most towns of the Kingdom'.[39]

Had the duke of York been at the Horse Guards instead of Sir Henry Dundas, this letter might have been sufficient to end the investigation of Orangeism. Dundas, however, was not satisfied with the colonel's reply and instructed Gordon to put the matter before Lord Liverpool,[40] then home secretary. In reply, Liverpool's secretary wrote, 'I am directed by His Lordship to tell you that His Majesty's Government considers such associations to be of the most dangerous tendency and that as it is understood that oaths are administered ... it is material that the Lt.-Colonel of the 1st West York Militia should be apprized that all such oaths are illegal'.[41] Liverpool also requested further information on the lodges in the army and gave instructions that in all places where lodges were thought to exist the commanding officers were to inform their men the government considered such societies illegal.

---

[37] Colonel Gordon to Jenkinson, 9 Sept. 1809 (P.R.O., H.O. 50/413).
[38] St. John to Colonel Gordon, 27 Aug. 1809 (ibid.).
[39] Colonel, First West York militia to Colonel Gordon, 6 Sept. 1809 (P.R.O., H.O. 51/171).
[40] Colonel Gordon to I. Beckett, 9 Sept. 1809 (ibid.).
[41] Jenkinson to Colonel Gordon, 18 Sept. 1809 (P.R.O., H.O. 51/171).

British Orange Lodges, 1798–1822

Before this correspondence was completed, Henry Stanton, who has been mentioned previously as head of the London Orange lodges,[42] wrote to Dundas applying for a commission in the regular army. To the letter he attached printed pages of testimonials, twelve in all, given him by 'gentlemen, field officers, clergymen, and M.P.'s', including John Claudius Beresford. Most of the names had some connection with Ireland. Attached to the printed testimonials was an affidavit which read:

Henry Stanton, Gentleman, son of Surgeon Stanton, who died of wounds received in His Majesty's service, grandson of Rev. Joseph Bennett, D.D., Justice of the Peace, and nephew of P. Downe, Esq., Captain of the 5th Regt., killed at Bunker Hill, came before me and made oaths that he has vouchers of the propriety of his former conduct from the following noblemen, field officers, and gentlemen.[43]

A list of names followed and it was signed by a London alderman. Enclosed with the testimonials was a printed notice of the meeting at which Stanton had been made Orange grand master of the counties of Middlesex and Surrey. Gordon sent the letter, along with the enclosures, to the home office. In reply he was instructed that:

Henry Stanton is to be informed that it appears from Paper No. 1 (the notice of the Orange lodge meeting) that he is a member of a certain society called an Orange Society, and that, it being considered that oaths are administered to the members of such societies, it is thought right that he should be informed that all such oaths are illegal. Under 37 Geo. 3. c. 123, 39 Geo. 3. c. 79, members are liable to imprisonment and transportation.[44]

Undaunted, Stanton wrote a long letter to Colonel Gordon in which he offered his sincere thanks for the trouble Gordon had taken in favouring him with certain opinions and statutes relating, as was supposed, to the Orange society. He explained that the acts quoted could not possibly apply to a patriotic society, and commented, 'There are generals and colonels who allow and encourage lodges of Orangemen in their Regiments and at least 100 Members of Parliament have been initiated and

---

[42] See above p. 153.
[43] Henry Stanton to Dundas, Sept. 1809 (P.R.O., H.O. 51/171).
[44] Beckett to Colonel Gordon, 22 Sept. 1809 (P.R.O., H.O. 51/171).

enrolled in various parts of the United Kingdom'.[45] He claimed there were 1,700 lodges and 150,000 members. At the end of his letter he wrote out the Orange oath. The figure of 100 members of parliament was the number allotted to Ireland in the united parliament and Stanton assumed they were all Orangemen. The 150,000 members were acquired probably by taking the highest numbered lodge he had heard of and multiplying by some convenient number. His statistics were nonsense as he should have known from the weakness of his own lodge.

As a result of the above correspondence some action was taken to suppress Orangeism in the army, but it was far from effective. Nixon knew of Liverpool's judgment by way of Stanton and the West Yorkshire lodge. He realized that the acts, as interpreted by the home secretary, would apply to civil as well as military lodges. To prevent legal action being taken, Nixon went to great pains to keep the military lodges under control and to give all lodges the character of friendly societies. To Giffard he wrote:

To shelter the societies from any persecution from the malevolent, and to place them on a legal and permanent footing, the grand lodge has directed that the rules and regulations by which the societies have been hitherto governed, shall be revised so as to fall within the scope and meaning of the proviso 33 Geo. 3 for regulating benefit societies; and this I doubt not, can be done without materially infringing on the spirit of any rule, which is considered the standard of the original principles or discipline of the Orange system.[46]

Nixon hoped that by a few alterations in the rules he could keep the effect of government measures against the lodges at a minimum. He tried to keep unruly elements out of the military lodges and to discourage anything which might give the appearance of defiance of authority. To Hope of the 13th Dragoons he wrote, 'I have particularly noticed your remarks on the irregular conduct of the lodge acting under a duplicate from No. 661—should an application be made for a warrant, you may rely upon it they will meet with an entire refusal'.[47] To Bombardier

[45] Stanton to same, 3 Oct. 1809 (ibid.).
[46] Nixon to Giffard, 11 Feb. 1811 (*Rep. on Orange lodges IV*, H.C. 1835 [605], xvii. app. 21. p. 177).
[47] Same to Hope, 16 May 1809 (ibid., pp. 174-5).

Alexander Sallans, he promised the support of the grand lodge for 'every prudent measure you may adopt for the advancement of the Orange system, and that warrants will be granted to anyone applying with sufficient testimonials of their fitness'.[48] To Sergeant William Hallam, Nixon wrote, 'With respect to the grant of a warrant to the Wiltshire Militia, their number will not be so much regarded as their fitness and steadiness'.[49]

However, the clearly stated attitude of Lord Liverpool on the subject could not but result in regimental officers from time to time taking action against Orangemen in their corps. Nixon attempted to use the influence of Orange officers to discourage such measures, but without much success. On 17 July 1811 he wrote Major Clutterbuck, a brother Orangeman, complaining that lodge number 45 (Northumberland militia) was being prevented from going to church on July 12 by captains of the companies and he expressed surprise that a loyal and benevolent society could be so used. He mentioned, though, that in a military lodge 'it would hardly be prudent to continue the system, contrary to the directions of the commanding officer', and expressed his fears that lodge number 45 might have to be dissolved.[50]

His apprehensions proved justified. On October 9 he sent notice to lodge number 45 and two others (number 42 of the 3rd West York militia and number 59 of the 2nd Battalion 95th Rifle regiment), requesting them to dissolve as the officers commanding their respective regiments had expressed their determination to suppress the lodges. Nixon insisted that the grand lodge could not advise them to act contrary to the commands of their officers.[51] Yet such dissolutions did little to diminish the activities of the Orangemen in the army. On 4 January 1812 Nixon sent reports of the proceedings of the Christmas meetings of the grand lodge to eleven military units scattered about Britain from the Channel Islands to Scotland.[52] When a Major Doyle banned the Orange society

---

[48] Nixon to Sallans, 3 Aug. 1810 (ibid., p. 176).
[49] Same to Sergeant Hallam, 28 July 1809 (ibid.).
[50] Same to Clutterbuck, 19 July 1811 (ibid., pp. 177–8).
[51] Notices to lodges nos 45, 42, 59, 9 Oct. 1811 (ibid., p. 178).
[52] Nixon to ——, 4 Jan. 1812 (ibid., p. 178).

in his unit a year later, Nixon denied that any previous action had been taken against military lodges. He wrote to Sergeant Green, 'This is the first instance of a commanding officer interfering to prevent his men from the enjoyment of a measure tending to link them together in strong ties of brotherly affection'.[53] Perhaps Nixon was counting on influence in high places by this time, for, although he counselled prudence and reminded the sergeant of his duty to obey, he offered to appeal to Sir Charles Imhoff, inspecting officer of the Midlands, who was a friend of the duke of York.[54]

The exact relationship of the duke of York to the Orange societies at this time cannot be ascertained, but he was very close to them and possibly a member. Plowden, the catholic historian, writing in 1811, asserted in a footnote unsupported by further evidence that in 1797 the duke of York encouraged the formation of Orange lodges in regiments stationed in Ireland.[55] This is unlikely.[56] The duke, however, was a member of the Orange and Blew Society, and the similarity of names could have caused confusion. He was not particularly concerned with politics, but was as firm as his father, the king, in opposition to catholic emancipation. This view was shared by his more politically minded brother, the duke of Cumberland, who had become prominent among the anti-catholics or ultra tories.

The ultra tories could hardly avoid some association with avowed Orangemen as they were colleagues of Duigenan, Musgrave, Ogle and Foster, who spoke and voted against concessions to catholics in the united parliament. There appears, however, to have been little or no connection between the Manchester lodges and the Irish Orangemen in parliament. Ultra tory indifference to British Orangemen is evident at the time of the whig cabinet's resignation in 1807 when the king refused to approve a bill granting catholics the right to serve as senior army officers. To counter petitions favouring catholics, the new government, headed by the duke of Portland, sought protestant petitions opposing these claims. The duke of Cumberland used his office as chancellor of Dublin University to secure the desired petitions and the duke of Portland did the same at

---

[53] Same to Green, 6 Feb. 1813 (ibid.).
[54] Ibid.   [55] Plowden, *Hist. Ire.*, *1801–10*, i. 28.
[56] Colonel Brownrigg to Pelham, 7 Nov. 1797 (B.M., Add. MS 33105).

Oxford.[57] Petitions against catholic claims also came from the Dublin corporation.[58] The new cabinet was, in fact, soliciting protestant support in the United Kingdom in much the same way as Fitzgibbon had in Ireland when confronted with the catholic relief bill of 1792.

The protestants who signed the anti-catholic petition at Oxford were not Orangemen, nor does any effort seem to have been made to use the services of the British grand lodge. Irish Orangemen who signed the petition sent by Cumberland to Dublin university and corporation did not sign as Orangemen. Yet Cumberland had sought the petitions, and the men who provided them, in Dublin at least, were known Orangemen. This appears to have aroused Nixon's hopes of a similar collaboration in Britain, and perhaps awakened a suspicion that he did not enjoy the full confidence of the inner circles of Irish Orangemen. Nixon wrote Giffard to enquire 'if his Royal Highness [the duke of Cumberland] was ever initiated an Orangeman? If so, is it likely that his Royal Highness (on an address or deputation being sent him) would deign to honour the societies with his countenance and support?'[59]

The British lodges, as the above indicates, had no contact with the duke of Cumberland in 1811. But some time after this, Nixon, by way of Lord Kenyon or the Irish grand lodge, opened a correspondence with the marquis of Hertford's son, Lord Yarmouth, who was the member of parliament for the family seat in Antrim and a confidant of court circles because of his mother's influence with the prince regent. In corresponding with Nixon, Lord Yarmouth was continuing family tradition. Philip Johnson, the first clergyman to encourage Orangeism in 1796, was attached to his father's estate in Antrim.[60]

Yarmouth appears to have been a party to what amounted to a plot to bring the duke of York into the Orange order. The moment was certainly opportune as the prince regent, under the

---

[57] Plowden, *Hist. Ire., 1801–10*, ii. 508.

[58] Duke of Bedford to Lord Grenville, 20 Mar. 1807 (*Fortescue MSS*, ix. 121–2.

[59] Nixon to Giffard, 11 Feb. 1811 (*Rep. on Orange lodges IV*, H.C. 1835 605], xvii. app. 21. p. 177.

[60] See above pp. 46–7.

influence of the duke of Cumberland, had been converted to his father's view of the catholic question and, much to the disappointment of his former whig friends, announced his opposition to a catholic relief bill introduced by Grattan. In disgust, Earl Grey wrote to Grenville in May 1813:

> The Prince said publicly at his table a day or two before, that nobody would vote for the question who did not wish to endanger his title to the Crown. And they say somebody has really succeeded in putting this notion into his head, which is only saying that he is as mad as his father. What do you think of their having actually established an 'Orange Club' *eo nomine*, which is to meet today for the first time at Lord Yarmouth's, the Duke of York being announced President.[61]

Whether this meeting took place cannot be established definitely, but there is a notice in *The Times* of 27 May 1813 of a Philanthropic Society meeting at St. Paul's Coffee House, at which the duke of York was to preside.[62] This could have been the Orange Club in disguise. Other somewhat confusing evidence that the duke of York became an Orangeman in 1813 is offered in two letters written in 1832 and 1833 by Edmund Swift, an indigent Orangeman and former Castle journalist. In both letters, which are addressed to the grand lodge, Swift stated, 'At that time [1813] I had the distinguished honour to assist at the formation of the Grand Orange Lodge of England, at the residence of Lord Kenyon, when that nobleman and the Marquis of Huntly and other personages were made Orangemen. I also had the honour of swearing into the office of grand master his Royal Highness, the late duke of York'.[63]

As Swift wrote about twenty years after the events mentioned, he could have made mistakes as to details. Lord Kenyon, for example, had joined the lodges in 1808, and it appears unlikely that the duke of York could have been made grand master of the English lodges as Colonel Taylor held that post. Yet as Lord Yarmouth used his influence to secure for Swift the post of keeper of the crown jewels,[64] it is evident that Swift had con-

---

[61] Earl Grey to Grenville, 27 May 1813 (*Fortescue MSS*, x. 341–2).
[62] *Times*, 27 May 1813.
[63] Edmund Swift to grand lodge, 3 June 1834 (*Rep. on Orange lodges IV*, H.C. 1835 [605], xvii. app. 21. p. 155).
[64] Same to same, 8 Feb. 1834 (ibid., pp. 154–5).

nections in upper circles, and he would hardly write a letter to the grand lodge mentioning events which its members would, from their own memory, know to be untrue. What probably occurred in May 1813 was that a single lodge, composed of gentlemen, was formed in London, possibly at Lord Kenyon's, more likely at Lord Yarmouth's home. The duke of York was made master of the lodge and several noblemen were initiated as Orangemen. Kenyon was probably present but not initiated, as Swift claimed, because he was already an Orangeman.

An indication of the ordinary Orangeman's reaction to rumours of Orange influence in court circles is offered in an anonymous pamphlet signed 'An Orangeman', published by J. J. Stockdale who also printed the Orange rules. The author denounced the duke of Sussex for a speech he made at a dinner given by the Friends of Civil and Constitutional Liberty, an organization favouring catholic emancipation. At the dinner the duke had referred to the danger of an Orange party forming in England. The author pointed out that the dinner was held on the birthday of the Pretender, and he expressed fear of the intimacy of Jacobinism and Jacobitism while praising the Orangemen for 'wrestling with King Ludd'. The duke of Sussex was accused of 'conspicuously placing himself at the head of a tavern meeting whose object was to subvert the Constitution', and the duke of Kent, who was also present, was reminded that he was superior warden of the Orange and Blew Society in the 4th Foot. The author informed the duke of Sussex, '... that he shall be happy if, with the manly honour of a British Prince, you will make royal reparation to the Institution, which last week you libelled, in the besotted orgies of a club, where the Prince Regent was insulted'.[65] The author of the pamphlet, who was probably a publican, was, no doubt, secretly flattered that so important a person as the duke of Sussex should refer to Orangeism.

Had all gone well, the new Orange Club formed in London would have replaced the Manchester lodge as the grand lodge of England, and Colonel Taylor would have resigned in favour of the duke of York. But the presence of royalty in the movement provoked a major attack from the opposition in the house of commons. Early in 1813 Nixon had the rules and regulations of

[65] *An address to the duke of Sussex.*

the English lodges printed for the purpose of forestalling legal action against the lodges. In the revised publication the conditional oath, by which Orangemen agreed to 'defend the present King, George III, and his heirs and successors, so long as he or they shall support the Protestant ascendancy',[66] was dropped. The new version of the rules was distributed to members of the house of commons some time in June. This might have been done with the knowledge that Williams Wynn, the member of parliament for Montgomery, was going to call for an enquiry into the activities of the lodges.

When Wynn introduced the subject of Orangeism in parliament, he said he based his objections to the lodges on an earlier pamphlet containing an account of the rules of the society which differed considerably from those contained in the copy of rules just distributed to the members of parliament. The earlier edition of the rules which he had seen was probably that published by the Irish grand lodge in 1810. Wynn warned, 'The existence of such societies in this country was directly in opposition to a specific Act of Parliament, 39 George 3 c. 79—which was passed in the year 1799, for the very purpose of putting down such societies meeting for political purposes, and bound to each other by oaths and tests'.[67]

He admitted the Orangemen might have been of some use to the government during the rebellion of 1798, but asserted that every successive government in Ireland had found them obstructing rather than supporting its authority. Wynn declared that the societies were now to be established in England and warned:

it was impossible to conceive an institution more ill-timed or more mischievous in its operation... In delivering what he had to say upon the subject, he wished to divest himself of every feeling that could have the remotest reference to that great question—Catholic Emancipation—which was necessarily so intimately blended with the societies under consideration... If... he was hostile to the claims of the Catholics, he should equally feel it his duty, as one anxious for public peace, to seek every means of checking them.[68]

[66] Obligation of an Orangeman and the secret articles of the lodges, 20 Nov. 1798, in *Rep. on Orange lodges I*, H.C. 1835 [377], xv. app. 3. p. 3.

[67] *Hansard*, xxvi. 974.   [68] Ibid., pp. 975–6.

Much of the force of Wynn's attack was lost by Nixon's timely issue of the new rules,[69] because Wynn's case was made out largely against the conditional oath. He referred to no instance when Orangemen had been responsible for creating disorders in Britain, but he named places where they had functioning lodges and pointed out that they had branches in the army. The existing laws were thought sufficient to put down the lodges, Wynn said, but if they were not, they should be strengthened. He concluded by moving that a committee of enquiry be appointed to investigate the lodges.[70]

The reaction to Wynn's motion was not altogether favourable. It was asserted that the new rules put the society within the law, and that in any case the rules Wynn quoted referred only to the Irish lodges. Orangemen in the army were declared to be the exclusive concern of the military. The defunct Catholic Committee was attacked by Stewart Worthey, who was probably an Orangeman. Another member denounced the lodges for 'midnight orgies' of songs and toasts while still another member defended them on the grounds that they were in the same category as free masons and friendly societies. The most serious charge came from Whitbread, a member hostile to Orangeism. He asked, 'Ought not the House to enquire into this dark conspiracy?' He went on:

It had been impudently said, that the Prince of Wales and the Duke of York were at the head of these clubs... The law of 1799, when it was passed, was executed with severity, and why was it now to be relaxed? Were the robes of a peer proof against the sword of justice? Was there a magic charm about the great which bewildered the understanding, and made that appear in them a virtue which in others was an unpardonable crime? The blood royal was even polluted by this charge.[71]

Whitbread's attack brought a response from Canning who expressed his personal disapproval of the Orange lodges but did not think them of such importance as to justify a committee of enquiry. He recommended instead that '... a declaration from one of his Majesty's ministers, that the law would be recurred to, if the association was persisted in, would put an end to this despicable society, which if suffered to exist, might shake on its

[69] Ibid., pp. 976–7.   [70] Ibid., p. 979.   [71] *Hansard*, xxvi. 983.

foundation this noble country'.⁷² Castlereagh agreed with Canning, declaring, 'Such associations were ever dangerous, but especially so when extended to military bodies... He trusted that the feelings of the country would re-echo the sentiments of parliament and repress these bodies without the assistance of coercion; for he was convinced the good sense of the people would prefer the empire of the law to the domination of clubs and associations'.⁷³

Wynn withdrew his motion, but the debate ended any possibility of royal patronage being given openly to the lodges for some time to come. Nixon, however, continued his efforts to establish the organization on a legal basis. He wrote the earl of Yarmouth on August 1 telling of a committee being formed to revise the rules and that, in consultation with Lord Kenyon, they had decided it was impossible for them to preserve the present form of the Orange lodges with perfect security on the grounds of their legality.⁷⁴ In Nixon's opinion, secrecy had to be abolished and '... to elude the grasp of the Act, we must act entirely as benefit societies, and however serviceable such a plan may be to those in the humbler walks of life, it is not likely to be embraced or relished by others of more elevated ranks; besides, its adoption would in a great measure destroy the grand object of the Institution'.⁷⁵

Nixon thanked Yarmouth for an offer 'to draw out a proposal for the future regulations of the Orange system', and assured him that 'the Orange Institution, when once placed on terra firma, will shortly become a powerful auxiliary to the Protestant cause'.⁷⁶ Again on 13 November 1813 Nixon wrote Yarmouth expressing his fear that in their efforts to keep the society within the law they would frame rules which made it impracticable to '... maintain that union, influence and observance of the rules so necessary for the wellbeing and perpetuity of the institution'.⁷⁷

The exact manner in which Nixon solved the difficulties cannot be ascertained, as no other letters on this subject are available. In 1814 a new set of rules was issued which included

---

⁷² *Hansard*, xxvi. 985.   ⁷³ Ibid., p. 986.
⁷⁴ Nixon to Lord Yarmouth, 1 Aug. 1813 (*Rep. on Orange lodges IV*, H.C. 1835 [605], xvii. app. 21. p. 179).
⁷⁵ Ibid.   ⁷⁶ Ibid.   ⁷⁷ Same to same, 13 Nov. 1813 (ibid.).

no oath as such but merely a pledge of allegiance to the king and protestant cause. The society thus ceased to be oath-bound. No further attacks were made on the English lodge for several years. But Nixon was still apprehensive about the status of the lodges. On 11 June 1814 he wrote to J. J. Stockdale that he was surprised to hear that '... papistical advocates were likely to attack them in Parliament, but that he believed the prudent measures which had been adopted to render the Orange system free from complaint, would have silenced them forever'. Nixon went on to say, 'It is now obvious that nothing will satisfy such characters, short of the surrender of our privileges, feelings, and principles as Protestants. It is not the threat from Sir H. Parnell or his party that will deter such men as Colonel Taylor of Manchester, Colonel Fletcher of Bolton, and Mr Lloyd, of Stockport, from the support of the Orange system, founded as it is now, upon a legal and independent basis.'[78]

No further events of importance mark the history of the British lodges until 1819. In that year Manchester Orangemen supported civil authority during the Peterloo riots,[79] but the clash of Liverpool Orangemen with the city's mayor attracted more attention. The mayor stopped an Orange July 12 parade[80] which was reported to have carried a mock pope and cardinal to be burned at the church door.[81] The infuriated Orangemen took the matter to court and lost their case which cost them £200. This could only be paid by securing financial help from Lord Kenyon.

The Liverpool incident provoked another attack against the lodges in parliament and an enquiry was asked for. Castlereagh replied that if Lancashire was a county of tory magistrates and Orange clubs, as charged, he could not imagine a more certain means of committing man against man than by an investigation. Canning felt it necessary to remark that the only connection he had with such of his constituents in Liverpool as were members of the Orange societies was to ask their favour. Before and since, he had always expressed his sentiments as directly opposite to Orangemen.[82]

---

[78] Nixon to Stockdale, 11 June 1813 (ibid., app. 21. pp. 179–80).
[79] *Hansard*, xli. 1445–9.
[80] *Rep. on Orange lodges IV*, H.C. 1835 [605], xvii. report xviii.
[81] *Hansard*, xli. 896, 910–11.   [82] Ibid., p. 948.

Contemporary with these events was the renewal of attempts to win royal patronage. At the opening of 1820, the British grand lodge was still in Manchester with Colonel Taylor as grand master. On the death of George III, the Orangemen drew up a declaration of condolence which they sent to Lord Sidmouth who, in turn, presented it to the king.[83] Shortly after, Colonel Taylor died, leaving the office of grand master vacant. The most obvious successor was Colonel Fletcher or Lord Kenyon, but when C. E. Chetwoode, the secretary of the recently founded lodge in London, proposed that the grand lodge be moved to London and the duke of York invited to become head of the British lodges, the grand lodge unanimously agreed.

Chetwoode had joined a Dublin lodge in 1816 or 1817 and shortly after went to London where he found the Orangemen in Clerkenwell were 'mostly drawn from the lower orders'. He then founded a gentlemen's lodge which met fortnightly at the British Coffee House on Cockspur street. Although the meetings were attended by some twelve to twenty people, the location of the lodge in London and the status of its members made it a point of contact between the Orangemen and the ultra tories. Chetwoode no doubt intended it to serve the same purpose as the first Dublin lodge which became the grand lodge of Ireland. Chetwoode's exact status is difficult to discover. He claimed to have been an acquaintance of Sidmouth,[84] but never to have discussed the British Orange lodges with him until the question arose as to the duke of York becoming grand master. In any case, it was Chetwoode who proposed sending the invitation to the duke and it was he who delivered the message.[85] He stated, 'When I first made the proposition ..., his Royal Highness observed, that, as a member of the Royal Family, and from his station and principles, he could not *join* any institution as to the legality of which there was a doubt; but that if it was cleared up to his satisfaction, he should be happy to render it any assistance by his patronage'.[86]

Chetwoode's testimony contradicts a later statement made by Lord Kenyon that the duke joined the lodges in 1819[87] while

---

[83] Sidmouth to Kenyon, 14 Mar. 1820 (*Rep. on Orange lodges IV*, H.C. 1835 [605], app. 21. p. 165).
[84] Evidence of Chetwoode, ibid., p. 36.   [85] Ibid., p. 3.
[86] Ibid., pp. 3–4.   [87] Evidence of Lord Kenyon, ibid., p. 123.

British Orange Lodges, 1798–1822

Taylor was still grand master. As the movement was a secret society, there was considerable difference between public and private adherence to Orangeism. From the events of 1813 and from the duke's intransigent attitude towards catholic emancipation, it might be inferred that he had no objection to joining the Orange order other than the fear that such a step might be inexpedient.

Chetwoode and Kenyon maintained that when the duke expressed doubts about the legality of the lodges they sought legal advice from several prominent lawyers. Foremost among these was Serjeant Lens, chosen because he was known to be in the confidence of the whigs.[88] That legal advice was sought and given is true, but it appears that the duke became grand master of the lodges in February 1821 while the final opinion of Lens was given early in 1822. The duke seems, then, to have acted without too careful investigation into the position of the lodges. On 8 February 1821 he wrote to Orange grand secretary William Woodburne, 'I have to acknowledge the receipt of your letter of the 6th, and to acquaint you, that Mr Eustace communicated to me the Resolution entered into by members of the Loyal Orange Institution, appointing me their Grand Master, and with which I felt much gratified, and I am sorry that my acquiescence should not have been communicated to you'.[89]

Against the duke of York's gracious acceptance of their invitation, the lodges could balance the curt refusal of another duke. In reply to a letter from J. J. Stockdale asking his patronage for the Orangemen, the duke of Wellington wrote:

I confess I object to belonging to a society professing attachment to the throne and constitution from which a large proportion of His Majesty's subjects are excluded ... The principal objection which I have to belonging to this society, is, that its members are bound to each other by an oath of secrecy. If such an oath is legal, which I doubt, I can't swear it consistently with my oath of allegiance and the oath which I have taken as one of His Majesty's Privy Council.[90]

---

[88] Ibid., p. 122; see also Evidence of Chetwoode, ibid., p. 4.

[89] Duke of York to William Woodburne, 8 Feb. 1821, *Rep. on Orange lodges VI*, H.C. 1835 [605], xvii. report vi.

[90] Wellington to Stockdale, Feb. 1821 not sent (Wellington, *Despatches, correspondence, and memoranda 1819–32*, ed. by his son, i. 156).

British Orange Lodges, 1798–1822

This letter was not mailed, probably because the duke received information that the duke of York had joined the lodges. The failure to win Wellington could not have disturbed the Orangemen greatly at this time. With the duke of York at their head, they styled themselves the Royal Orange Lodge. Meetings of the grand lodge of Great Britain were held henceforth at the residence of the deputy grand master, Lord Kenyon.

The Orangemen, by publicizing the patronage which they enjoyed, soon provoked comment in parliament. On 21 June 1821 Sir John Newport directed a question to the government concerning reports he had heard of the duke of York's connection with an organization called the Loyal Orange Association. 'It appeared', he stated, 'that this association had communications with various corresponding societies over which they had no control, that officers were selected and secret obligations entered into, and that in all other respects they came within the spirit and letter of the Acts 39 and 57 of the late King'.[91] Castlereagh replied that his Royal Highness had stated his acquiescence in being elected grand master of the Royal Orange Lodge, but that acquiescence was given under the idea that the objects of the association were merely those of general loyalty, and that it was not a society of a political nature. 'As soon as it was suggested to him that there was some doubt as to the legality of the Association', Castlereagh said, 'he sent a communication to them in which, without imputing to them any intentional breach of the law, he declined all connection with them'.[92]

In his letter of resignation to Kenyon, the duke of York wrote:

The question put to the Marquis of Londonderry yesterday evening in the House of Commons by Sir John Newport and the answer given by His Lordship, place me under the necessity of making in writing that communication to your Lordship which I wished to have deferred until I had the pleasure of seeing you. Your lordship is perfectly aware of the grounds and principles upon which I accepted the Grand Mastership of the Orange Lodge in England. I have within these few days learnt that the law officers of the Crown and other eminent lawyers are decidedly of the opinion that the Orange

[91] *Times*, 22 June 1821.   [92] Ibid.

Associations, under the Oath administered to their members, are illegal.

The duke went on, 'Under that circumstance, and from the moment I satisfied myself of the existence of this objection, it became my duty to withdraw myself from an office and from an association of which I could no longer be a member without violating those laws which it has ever been my study to uphold and maintain'.[93]

This new calling to question of the legality of the lodges caused Kenyon and Chetwoode to redouble their efforts to put the Orange movement within the law. The new rules made little difference in the substance of the organization. It was the object of Kenyon and Chetwoode to keep a body of men together, meeting regularly and willing to take orders from the grand lodge. It mattered little to them how this was done. To avoid all implications of being oath-bound, they administered no oath but admitted only those who had, at some time, taken an oath of allegiance before a notary or some other qualified official. The name of 'lodge' was changed to 'warrant'[94] to avoid the appearance of being a federation under a central leadership. Thus a number of warrant holders were enabled to hold meetings of men who had taken the oath of allegiance to the crown, an oath of abjuration of popery and the Stuarts, and who declared they had never been papists or United Irishmen. Under the new system nothing was changed. Oaths could be administered by Orangemen in their capacity as magistrates and warrant holders could call and conduct meetings without going through the formality of establishing a lodge.

The weakness of the new system was that warrants were issued to individuals, and it thus became difficult to replace a *de facto* lodge master without securing a new warrant. Yet this system served its purpose of satisfying the letter of the law without dissolving the organization.

By 1822 Orangeism had taken root in most industrial areas in Britain and in a substantial number of military units. It was hardly formidable as it stood but was credited by its leaders and its enemies with great potentialities. The duke of York's

---

[93] Duke of York to Lord Kenyon, 22 June 1821 (*Rep. on Orange lodges IV*, H.C. 1835 [605], xvii. report vi-vii.
[94] Ibid., report vii.

brief association with the lodges was a source of immense prestige, and a periodic denunciation of Orangeism in parliament did not harm the movement in the eyes of its members. The manoeuvres of Nixon, the grand secretary, managed to preserve the organization's legality, but failed to make it attractive to the upper classes. The London lodge created by Chetwoode had established promising contacts in tory circles and the office of grand master was left vacant in the hope that royalty might again see fit to take an interest in Orangeism.

VIII

ORANGEISM IN IRELAND
1803–25

1. THE WAR YEARS

EMMET'S BRIEF REBELLION in Ireland and the renewal of the war with France served to rescue the Irish Orange movement from the decline which set in after the union, and Orangeism remained an active irritant in Irish politics until the peace of 1815. During this period the entrenched position that Orangemen held among the magistrates of the northern counties, in the yeomanry, and in the corporation of Dublin was attacked frequently, but never seriously disturbed. Within Castle circles there was a steady increase of Orange influence. Unrest in Ireland was general throughout the war period, the country having to be held down by a garrison of some 25,000 men, and in all but two years had to be governed with the aid of the insurrection act. In such circumstances it was hazardous for the Castle to challenge a powerful vested interest which professed to be loyal. Yet the recruiting of catholics for overseas service, and the obvious necessity for conciliating the majority of the Irish people made it impossible for the Castle to give whole-hearted approval to Orangeism.

Under the firm but by no means hostile hand of the Hardwicke administration there were few of those unfortunate incidents which had made the support of Orangemen embarrassing to past governments. If the interests of the protestant ascendancy—which Orangemen defined as a protestant monopoly of public office—were challenged, however, the response was immediate and violent. In 1805 when a number of aristocratic and middle class catholics formed the first post-union catholic committee, the Orangemen's reaction was immediate. The committee, after a fruitless interview with Pitt, prepared petitions asking for catholic emancipation which the whig opposition agreed to present to parliament. In response to this, John Giffard, who held a government sinecure in the customs department, used his influence to induce the Orange-controlled corporation of Dublin to prepare anti-catholic petitions. Hardwicke would not tolerate such partisan activity from a man in government pay and Giffard was removed from his £700 a year sinecure.[1]

When the catholic petitions were presented in the house of commons, the Irish Orangemen demonstrated both their zeal and inadequacy as parliamentarians. In view of the safe protestant majority, the display was unnecessary. Duigenan and the parliamentary Orangemen may well have hoped that their Irish experience would qualify them to take a leading part in the affairs of a parliament of such strong protestant sympathies. However, their style of speech and argument proved wholly unsuited to the English house of commons. Duigenan's violence and antiquarian learning made an extremely unfavourable impression, as did all the Orangemen in parliament save Foster. It was left to Grattan to uphold the Irish reputation for eloquence, and by taking full advantage of the Orangemen's shortcomings, he established himself as the leading parliamentary advocate of the catholic cause.[2]

The parliamentary rebuff of the Orangemen was followed by a more serious attack on their position in the Irish government which came with the advent of the 'ministry of all talents'. The whig duke of Bedford was made lord lieutenant partly as a gesture of conciliation towards the catholics. Bedford's position was not unlike that of Fitzwilliam in 1795 in that he found himself at the head of a hierarchy of government servants who

[1] Wellesley to duke of Richmond, 13 Mar. 1808 (Wellington, *Civil correspondence and memoranda, Ireland from 20 Mar. 1807 to 2 Apr. 1809*, ed. by his son, London, 1860, p. 361).

[2] *Hansard*, xi. 549–72.

could be counted on to disregard the spirit of the policy he had been sent to implement. He did not repeat Fitzwilliam's mistakes by attempting the dismissal of hostile subordinates, but a number of Orange magistrates were removed and, as a token of good intentions, Grattan, who had been removed from the privy council in 1798, was restored to his place.[3] Efforts were made to discourage anti-catholic comment in government-subsidized newspapers, and plans undertaken to create a Castle press which would present a whig point of view.[4] Finally, in the hope that a liberal policy would quiet the country, the insurrection act was permitted to lapse. As these conciliatory measures removed none of the economic grievances of the catholic peasant, they were no more effective in quieting the country than the catholic relief act of 1793. By the end of 1807, Bedford, in co-operation with Grattan, was preparing repressive legislation as forceful as any enacted by previous administrations.

Bedford was equally unsuccessful in his efforts to keep Orange office holders from anti-catholic agitation. During the crisis which followed the death of Fox, the whigs had pressed for a measure admitting catholics to senior posts in the army, but had been checked by the king. To drive the whigs from office, the anti-catholic tories sought popular support in the country. Orange placemen in Dublin could hardly be expected to remain aloof from such a campaign. In disgust the viceroy wrote:

Mr Giffard, at the conclusion of a speech in which he indulged himself in the most virulent invective against the Catholic body, and the most strained panegyric on the Orangemen, and Sir R. Musgrave's History, moved a petition to the two Houses of Parliament be presented to the Duke of Cumberland ... which was carried on a division of 39 to 13. On the committee appointed to draw up the petition were the names of Mr Alderman Alexander and Major Sirr, both immediately connected with the government, and Mr Alderman King, His Majesty's Stationer.

The viceroy went on:

This, as you may readily conceive, has caused no inconsiderable sensation among the Catholics, and they contrast the present administration (their professed friends) with that of Lord Hardwicke,

[3] *D.N.B.*, xxii. 423.
[4] Inglis, *Freedom of the press in Ireland 1784-1841*, p. 113-15.

which they observe did not suffer such acts to pass with impunity . . .
This will not be the only instance in which the Orange party will
show their disregard of the wishes or authority of the government.[5]

The Orangemen, however, had little to fear from the viceroy
as the elections of 1807 returned a strong anti-catholic majority.
The duke of Portland formed a cabinet absolutely opposed to
catholic emancipation, with Lord Perceval as its strongest
member. Under this new administration, the duke of Richmond,
who is remembered principally for the ball given by his wife
on the eve of Waterloo, was sent to Ireland as lord lieutenant.
With him as chief secretary was the future victor of Waterloo—
Sir Arthur Wellesley.

Never since the days of Camden had a government been so
favourably disposed to Orangeism. On strong recommendations
from the dukes of Cumberland and York, Wellesley re-appointed
John Giffard to his sinecure at the customs.[6] Duigenan was
appointed to the privy council, as was another Orangeman,
Sir George Hill.[7] Far more impressive was the appointment
to the office of attorney-general of William Saurin, who had
been foremost in the Orange revolt against union. Saurin was,
with the possible exception of Foster, the most able of the
Orange leaders. His views on the protestant ascendancy were
consistent and uncompromising. To Peel he wrote:

> We ought not to deceive ourselves. Ireland must be either a Catholic
> or a Protestant state—let us choose. But he is a Utopian who believes
> he has discovered a nostrum by which it can be both, or neither.
> This is the project of Grattan and Plunket, who have taken it up as a
> mere party question, and have with great talent and ingenuity first
> deceived themselves (at which no two men are more expert), and
> next, I am sorry to say, they have misled many others.[8]

Saurin was to remain attorney-general until 1822,[9] rising to
a position approaching that of Lord Clare in pre-union days.

[5] Duke of Bedford to Grenville, 20 Mar. 1807 (*Fortescue MSS*, ix. 121–2).
[6] Wellesley to duke of Richmond, 13 Mar. 1808 (Wellington, *Civil correspondence*, p. 361).
[7] Wellesley to James Trail, 9 Mar. 1808 (ibid., p. 360).
[8] Saurin to Peel, 16 Mar. 1813 (Robert Peel, *Private papers*, ed. C. S. Parker, i. 81).
[9] Wellesley to Lady Blessington, n.d. (Daniel O'Connell, *Correspondence*, ed. W. J. Fitzpatrick, i. 85).

Unlike Clare, though, he was no orator and did not exhibit his power in such a way as to arouse lasting bitterness among his enemies. As attorney-general, he was tireless but usually cautious in his efforts to suppress popular movements, and slow to take action against Orangemen. It is not surprising, then, that with a viceroy sent by an anti-catholic cabinet, and Saurin as attorney-general, the Orangemen took liberties they would not have taken under less favourable circumstances. Yet in the disordered state of the country, it may be doubted that the best of whig viceroys could have kept the Orangemen under control. In the north the Orangemen found themselves in conflict with a catholic secret society known as Ribbonmen. In every respect this organization seemed to be a continuation of the Defenders. Like the Defenders it had a declaration of loyalty to the king in its secret oath and showed no interest in political questions.[10] Although some Ribbonmen were to be found in the south, they were primarily active in the counties of Ulster and those bordering Ulster where they attempted to carry on the protestant-catholic feud by the usual methods of nightly raids on farm houses and individual assassinations.

In the south where there were various catholic societies which continued the tradition and, in one case, the name of Whiteboys, the movements were directed against the landlords and the payment of the tithe, rather than against the government. Only one society, known as the Shaunavests,[11] was considered to be republican in its outlook, and to look for help from Napoleonic France. Of the others, the Threshers, who were strong in the north, were opposed primarily to the tithe, and the Caravats, like the Ribbonmen, gave a formal adherence to the crown.[12] No serious efforts were made to give these societies central leadership or long term objectives, but this in itself made it difficult to inflict on them anything but a temporary and local defeat.

Orangemen had been accused of keeping alive these societies by acts of provocation against catholics. In the south where

---

[10] Evidence of Daniel O'Connell, *Report on the state of Ireland, report from the select committee with minutes of evidence*, H.L. 1825 [181], ix. 147–8).

[11] Wellesley to Lord Hawkesbury, 11 Feb. 1808, encl. 6 Feb. 1808 (Wellington, *Civil correspondence*, pp. 332–3).

[12] Ibid.

troops, sometimes led by catholic magistrates, were the principal agency of law and order, this was certainly nonsense. In the north it is certain that the Ribbonmen, in some degree, were a reaction against the Orangemen. Yet Ulster was the most orderly province in Ireland, and Ribbonism, whatever its origin, was kept in check by the Orange yeomanry.[13] When the clash of interests between protestant and catholic tenants in such places as Armagh and the long established habits of violence among them are considered, it is likely that Ribbonmen or some similar society would have carried on warfare against the protestants even had there been no Orange lodges.

Dealing with Ribbonmen and other catholic secret societies presented little difficulty to the Orangemen as long as they controlled the yeomanry and could count on local magistrates granting them some degree of immunity from the law. Any real or apparent threat of their privileged position they resisted to the point of open defiance. To the Orangeman, permitting catholics to serve in the yeomanry meant giving arms to his traditional enemy. Wearing Orange badges on yeomanry uniforms was, in the Orangeman's view, necessary as a means of overawing the catholic population. It is not surprising, therefore, that several cases of insubordination developed in the yeomanry over the question of wearing Orange badges and the refusal of Orangemen to appear on parade with catholics. As the yeomanry were only part-time soldiers, not under the mutiny act, the Orangemen in the ranks knew that by such insubordination they were risking nothing more than dismissal from the corps. Cases of near mutiny were numerous, but an examination of a few will suffice to reveal the manner in which they occurred.

One such incident took place in Bandon where a pre-1795 Orange club, the Boyne Society, was constituted as a yeomanry corps by Lord Bandon. In July 1809 this unit insisted on parading with Orange lilies in their hats, and when ordered to remove them, the men became unruly.[14] Their officer, Captain Kingston, who tried to control them, had a shot fired into his

---

[13] Evidence of O'Connell, *Rep. on the state of Ireland, report from the select committee with minutes of evidence*, H.L. 1825 [181], ix. 147–8.

[14] Lt. Col. Auriol to Littlehales, 16 July 1809 (*Rep. on Orange lodges III*, H.C. 1835 [476], xvi. app. B.1., p. 18).

house one evening by an unidentified yeoman.[15] Lord Bandon declared their conduct subversive of discipline, and demanded that the yeomen give up their leaders.[16] The corps apologized through their sergeants, but when they assembled again they wore their Orange lilies.[17]

The inspecting officer, Lieutenant-Colonel Auriol, reported they were a steady body of men under arms, but had no respect for their officers. 'Bandon people annually give way to that party spirit', he wrote, 'which I apprehend it is the wish of the Government to have subside, and which Lord Bandon as well as myself hoped would soon decrease'.[18] He further declared that the officers, with one exception—Captain Connor—were doing their best to end party spirit. Connor had protested against the existence of a catholic yeomanry corps by neglecting to order his men to present arms to Auriol. When it was decided to disband the corps, the men wrote to Dublin Castle accusing Auriol of neglecting his duty and protesting their loyalty and good intentions. A year later Lord Bandon wrote that he felt the former members of the Bandon corps could be counted on henceforth to act with moderation if they were reconstituted as a corps. 'The Orangemen', he declared, 'were behaving with the greatest regularity and there was no assemblage on the 12th'.[19]

The Bandon corps was reassembled shortly thereafter, leaving things much as they had been. In the same summer as the Bandon corps was disbanded a clash took place between a party of the Omagh yeomanry and a draft of the King's County militia going overseas. One yeoman was killed and thirty-five militiamen were left in gaol to prevent yeomanry vengeance.[20] A year later the Bann infantry, Scarva yeomanry of Down, and the Warrington cavalry refused to serve with catholics, while the Down county yeomanry laid down their arms rather than serve with catholics.[21] On 21 September 1810 Major General Michel wrote from Belfast, 'I am excessively concerned to

---

[15] Lord Bandon to Littlehales, 9 July 1809 (ibid., p. 19).
[16] Ibid.   [17] Ibid.
[18] Lt. Col. Auriol to Littlehales, 16 July 1809 (ibid., p. 18).
[19] Lord Bandon to Littlehales, 15 July 1810 (ibid., p. 20).
[20] Maj. Gen. Hart to Adj. General in Dublin, 13 Aug. 1809 (*Rep. on Orange lodges III*, H.C. 1835 [476], xvi. app. B. 2, p. 27).
[21] Brigade Maj. Wallace to Littlehales, 19 Sept. 1810 (ibid., app. B.4, p. 30).

add, that the rooted animosity at present subsisting between those yeomen denominated Orangemen and the Roman Catholics, is so inveterate as to hold out but little hopes of reconciliation... the corps in question I have inspected and they are the very best description of yeomanry'.[22] A few weeks later a junior officer wrote to Sir E. B. Littlehales at Dublin Castle questioning 'how far it may be prudent or practical to subdue party spirit'.[23] In June 1812 the Armagh yeomanry refused to serve under Lieutenant Barnes, a protestant who had signed a petition in favour of catholic emancipation.[24]

The government was in a difficult position. Irish catholics were needed to swell the regular army ranks in the Peninsula. Volunteers from the Irish militia were especially welcome as they were trained or partly trained men. It was certainly a matter of expediency and justice that these volunteers be treated with respect and that their relatives and co-religionists be permitted to exercise their legal right of serving in the yeomanry. If only for appearance's sake, it was to the advantage of the Castle to have a few catholics in as many yeomanry corps as possible.

The July 12 parades, which Orangemen often insisted on holding in catholic areas when catholic militia regiments were nearby, were little better than invitations to disorder. Commenting on one such demonstration in Letterkenny, a general officer commanding in the area wrote, 'The Catholics (awed by military force) were obliged to become quiet spectators of the Orange processions; they were much irritated, and will certainly take the first opportunity to proceed to some acts of violence. A Catholic regiment ought not on any account to be stationed in this county, as there are perpetual quarrels with the Orangemen and the Catholics'.[25] It was recommended that detachments of the Clare militia be moved from Letterkenny and replaced by regulars. This was done and there were no immediate outbreaks.

[22] Maj. Gen. Michel to ——, 21 Sept. 1810 (ibid., p. 32).
[23] Capt. Nicholson to Littlehales, 29 Oct. 1810 (ibid., p. 34).
[24] Memorial of officers of Armagh yeomanry to the duke of Richmond, 6 June 1812 (*Rep. on Orange lodges I*, H.C. 1835 [377], xv. app. 7, p. 81).
[25] Lt. Gen. Sir C. Asgill to the commander of the forces, 13 July 1811 (*Rep. on Orange lodges III*, H.C. 1835 [476], xvi. app. B.5, p. 34).

No better examples can be found of the manner in which Orangemen used the yeomanry in their own interests than the riots which broke out at fairs on market days. The original responsibility for such quarrels was about equal on both sides, but the outcome of several such riots seems to suggest that the catholic faction permitted their aggressive instincts to lead them into what appear to have been traps. The riot at Kilkeel on 9 February 1814 is a case in point.[26] A fight broke out between a catholic and a protestant, others joined, and a general fight ensued. The catholics, being more numerous, soon drove the protestants, who were mostly yeomen, into the house of McKibben, the sergeant of the Mourne infantry yeomanry corps, where the unit's arms were stored. A local magistrate, Captain Mathews, who was commander of the yeomanry, offered to intervene but was persuaded by McKibben and another sergeant that everything was under control.

The catholics attacked McKibben's house, throwing stones and tearing slates from the roof. Thereupon, the yeomen armed themselves, fired on their assailants and sallied forth into the town where, with the aid of other protestants, they attacked forty or fifty catholic houses. About ten catholics and eight protestants were found guilty of rioting. The next day a party of armed protestants fired on a party of catholics returning home from Kilkeel, wounding two.[27] Several of the eight protestants found guilty managed to evade their sentences—two left the country and another escaped.[28] Some yeomen were dismissed from the corps as was Captain Mathews, who had neglected to intervene during the early stages of the riot.[29]

In measures taken against those responsible for such riots, catholics invariably were dealt with more severely than the protestants, but protestants were, as the above indicates, tried and punished. Yet the problem of the Orange control of local justice gave the Orangemen a sense of immunity from the law which produced much evil.[30] Instances of Orangemen evading

---

[26] Ibid., app. B.6, pp. 35–9.
[27] Solicitor-general's report on transactions at Kilkeel, 22 Apr. 1814 (ibid., app. B.6, p. 38); see also Alex Stewart to ——, Feb. 1814 (ibid., p. 36).
[28] Brigade Maj. Wallace to Littlehales, 8 Apr. 1814 (ibid., p. 37).
[29] Littlehales to Brigade Maj. Wallace, 12 Apr. 1814 (ibid.).
[30] *Times*, 6 Mar. 1823.

justice through their influence in law courts and especially on juries are too numerous to recount. In Fermanagh in 1810 a prisoner named Hall, who had confessed to breaking into a catholic chapel and stealing vestments, was acquitted by an Orange jury.[31] Grand jurors were known to sit in court wearing Orange ribbons, and a defendant accused by a catholic might hope to intimidate a jury by announcing himself an Orangeman.[32] In the case of King versus Kitson, the father of a man killed in a riot on 11 July 1811, which was in all essentials similar to the riot at Kilkeel, appealed to every magistrate in Fermanagh to prosecute Kitson, an Orangemen, but no magistrate would take up his case.[33] It was only by appealing to Judge Osborn, through a catholic attorney, that the magistrates were compelled to deal with the case. The accused Kitson had shown a guilty conscience by fleeing to America, but despite his absconding, he was acquitted by an Orange jury.[34] A Lieutenant Hamilton of the yeomanry ordered his men to fire into a crowded house, killing a man, and when proceedings were brought against him, the magistrate released him in his father's custody. He fled, and returned several years later.[35]

In 1809 a petition, signed by fourteen Orange justices of the peace, clergymen and yeomanry officers, was sent to the duke of Richmond, the viceroy, requesting mitigation of the death sentence passed on Alexander Bell for attempted murder. A few minutes after the trial was over, two magistrates, William Lofty and Major William Blacker, went to Baron McClelland, the judge, applying to him for clemency for the prisoner on the grounds that 'they apprehended the prosecutor and those who had assisted in the prosecution, would be murdered by friends of the prisoner, if he were executed'.[36] McClelland insisted, however, that his judgment be carried out.

In 1806 a hatter in Armagh named Constantine O'Neill was visited by unknown parties, probably Orangemen, who burned his house and fired several times at his wife and family. O'Neill charged that the party included younger members of

[31] Evidence of Kernan, *Rep. on Orange lodges III*, H.C. 1835 [476], xvi. 71.
[32] Ibid., p. 71.   [33] Ibid., p. 76.   [34] Ibid.
[35] Ibid., pp. 76–7.
[36] Baron McClellan to Sir Charles Saxton, 1 Aug. 1809 (ibid., app. B.3, pp. 28–9).

the Verner family.[37] When no magistrate in Armagh would take up his case, Wilson, a Tyrone magistrate, made a show of collecting evidence but decided O'Neill had no case. Upon the clearing of his sons of the charge, Verner staged a celebration[38] which was attended by Orangemen from Wilson's county. A party of these, numbering about 500, on returning from the Verner festivities, threatened O'Neill's life.

The abuses described above were not, in the view of the ordinary Orangemen, abuses at all, but a continuation of a privileged position protestants had enjoyed throughout the eighteenth century. Bearing arms was considered a lawful protestant monopoly and in catholic yeomen and militia Orangemen saw, not the defenders of the state, but their traditional enemies. Crimes committed against catholics were a continuation of a feud, a form of warfare which protestant courts had no right to punish. The Irish protestant peasant had no reason to think he could rely either on the goodwill of his catholic neighbours or the forces of the crown for his safety. This feeling was the result of his own and, what he believed to be, his ancestors' experience. Added to this general background of fear and antagonism there was a good deal of bravado, drunkenness and rowdyism. Nor can it be denied that common criminals found shelter in the Orange movement, as they did in other political societies.

There was in Ireland no tradition of impartial justice, and the habit of settling disputes by violence, and even a fondness for violence itself was so engrained in the rural population, that it was impossible to give effect to a liberal policy that would do justice to all. Although the root of this difficulty lay in the land question, no solution could be found for that or any other question until violence was effectively restrained. No measure, however right or just in itself, could be enforced unless backed by a police power untainted by party or religious feuds. Ireland was held down by 25,000 regulars, supported by about 31,000 yeomanry. Some 20,000 yeomen were in the nine counties of Ulster; another 6,000 were in Leinster (including Dublin),

---

[37] Letter to Rev. Henry Conwell, parish priest relative to a pamphlet written by Richard Wilson, n.d., in A.M., Blacker MSS; Plowden, *Hist. Ire., 1801–10*, ii. 349–56.

[38] A.M., Churchill Orange lodge minute book, 8 Aug. 1807.

and only 5,000 were provided by Munster and Connaught.[39] As the yeomanry, in all but a few cases, consisted of Orangemen,[40] the crown could not disentangle itself from Orange support without depriving itself of an essential part of its police power. Ulster, where Orange abuses abounded, suffered less than any other province from agrarian crime.[41] When disturbances broke out in the south, as was the case in 1820, Ulster yeomen could be mobilized to release troops for service in troubled areas. This condition of military dependence on Ulster was a legacy of the 1798 rebellion, and persisted in one form or another until the organization of the constabulary in 1822.

By an inconsistency not uncommon to opposition arguments, it was the critics of the Orange outrages who were most reluctant to grant the crown the additional powers and military force which would have made it possible to dispense with Orange support. Grattan, O'Connell, Plowden, Hume, and other tireless enemies of Orangeism were strongly influenced by the theory that Orangemen were goading the catholic peasantry into revolt. This part truth obscured the fact that a show of weakness on the part of the civil power was a greater incentive to revolt than all the Orange abuses as long as the catholic peasantry sought to redress its many grievances by the methods of Whiteboys and Ribbonmen. Disbanding the Orange yeomen would simply be an invitation to the lawless elements among catholics to attack protestants.

If, however, the catholic peasantry could be won away from its primitive methods of resistance, and organized into an orderly political movement, the Orangemen would lose much of their usefulness to the protestant population and to the Castle. This fact seems to have been understood by O'Connell who, after the departure of the whigs from the cabinet in 1807, laid the foundation for a new political movement. Seeing no prospect of winning emancipation by discreet pressure on the

---

[39] *Hansard 2*, viii. 96, 524.
[40] Ibid., pp. 443–90; see also Evidence of Lord Gosford, *Rep. on Orange lodges I*, H.C. 1835 [377], xv. 297; Evidence of W. S. Crawford, ibid., p. 300.
[41] Evidence of M. Sullivan, ibid., p. 38; see also evidence of O'Connell, *Rep. on the state of Ireland, report from the select committee with minutes of evidence*, H.L. 1825 [181], ix. 147–8.

tory ministry, he decided to return to the policy abandoned in 1793—of exerting influence on the government by popular agitation. O'Connell began a two-fold struggle against physical force tendencies among the catholics and against the enemies of catholic equality. He fought another battle with the parliamentary champions of emancipation who preferred the Gallican-type scheme favoured by Castlereagh and Canning, with state subsidies for the clergy and a royal veto over the appointment of bishops.[42] Although this plan was acceptable to English catholics, the Irish bishops and the Vatican, O'Connell held out against it and ultimately carried his point. He used a variety of arguments to support his case, but was probably moved by the consideration that a Gallican-type church would oppose all popular movements and support the union.

Though royalist,[43] O'Connell was a strong nationalist. He had supported Saurin's opposition to union during the Cornwallis administration, stating that he preferred the old penal code with all 'its pristine horrors to Union'.[44] In 1810 he supported a half-hearted move of the Dublin corporation for repeal and announced he would 'trample on emancipation if it interfered with repeal'.[45] It is hardly surprising that O'Connell's early efforts to create a national catholic movement in the face of a hostile cabinet and Attorney-general Saurin's influence at the Castle met with defeat. The catholic committee he organized had local branches which sent delegates to a convention similar to the one originally organized by Tone and Keogh. It was clearly within the scope of the convention act which had last been used to dissolve Keogh's organization in 1793.

O'Connell further challenged the authority of the government by petitioning for the recall of the duke of Richmond and his secretary, Wellesley Pole, who was then chief secretary. With the aid of Saurin, Wellesley Pole proposed a circular ordering the arrest of all persons connected 'actively or passively with the late elections for members or delegates to the Catholic Committee'.[46] O'Connell was

[42] Evidence of A. R. Blake, ibid., p. 105; McDowell, *Public opinion and government policy in Ireland 1801–46*, pp. 92–8.
[43] *Annual Register*, London, 1828. lxx. 148.
[44] Daniel O'Connell, *Speeches*, ed. by his son, i.9.   [45] Ibid., pp. 23–4.
[46] Daniel O'Connell, *Correspondence*, i. 21.

placed on the defensive and he could do no better than replace the illegal committee with a 'catholic board', whose principal activity was defending members of the defunct committee from actions taken by Saurin.[47]

Although anxious to have the convention act used to suppress O'Connell's organization, the Orangemen feared that the friends of the catholics might induce the government to employ it against the lodges. To forestall such a development, the grand lodge of Ireland held a general meeting 10 July 1810 at which new rules were prepared omitting the secret articles. A year later when the government moved against O'Connell's committee, a further effort to avoid official displeasure was made in the form of a grand lodge address appealing to Orangemen to exercise 'charity towards their enemies' and limited processions to a few places in the north. The Orangemen, however, had little to fear in 1811 with Perceval as prime minister and the duke of Richmond as viceroy. Yet the Richmond administration, like its predecessors, found the Orangemen an embarrassment and never gave them its unqualified approval. While Wellesley was chief secretary he wrote Duigenan asking him to refrain from speaking in parliament on the question of catholic claims 'since he had so frequently delivered his opinions on that subject'.[48] On another occasion he objected to the appointment of a police magistrate on the grounds 'he is a Wexford Orangeman. He suffered in some degree in the Rebellion and his mind is irritated against the people.'[49]

In the opinion of the viceroy, the government's policy was far too severe towards the Orangemen. Richmond wrote Peel in August 1812, 'No stone is left unturned to add strength to the Catholics, violent as they are, and cold water is universally thrown on the Protestants' even giving their opinion... Hitherto, however, I have followed the wish of the Cabinet and have been silent. I must own I am nearly tired of this silence, and that I think it hardly fair to the most loyal people in the country.'[50] By the 'most loyal' people, the duke could only

[47] O'Connell to O'Connor, 13 July 1813 (ibid., p. 21).
[48] Wellesley to Duigenan, 25 May 1808 (Wellington, *Civil correspondence*, p. 440).
[49] Wellesley to James Trail, 10 July 1808 (ibid., p. 471).
[50] Richmond to Peel, 9 Aug. 1812 (Peel, *Private papers*, i. 71).

mean Orangemen. His bitterness against the catholics was, undoubtedly, the result of the personal attacks made on him by O'Connell's followers, and the influence of Saurin.

The assassination of Perceval in 1812 resulted in the replacing of a cabinet absolutely opposed to catholic emancipation by the Liverpool ministry which merely wished to avoid making emancipation an issue. For the Orangemen, this was a misfortune but hardly a disaster. Sir Robert Peel became Irish secretary, and from that day until he left the country it was Peel, rather than the successive viceroys, who was the real governor of Ireland. He co-operated with Saurin in most matters, and undertook to defend Orangemen from attacks in parliament, but treated them with caution and a good deal of suspicion. Shortly after taking office, he attempted to discipline Orange journalists receiving government subsidies. One of these, Edmund Swift,[51] who objected that it was against his principles to abandon his anti-union policy, was told, on being dismissed, that 'it was his pen was needed by the Government and not his principles'.[52] Peel also made an attempt to use John Giffard to obtain information from the inner circle of Orangeism but received only a 'panegyric on his [Giffard's] civil and military exploits'.[53]

Peel's attitude towards leading Orangemen is well illustrated by his letter to Saurin a month after taking office. He wrote:

I entirely agree with you in your opinion upon the service which the Protestant cause would derive from the active exertions of an Irishman in the House of Commons, who would share with Dr. Duigenan in zeal but would temper it with a little more discretion. At the same time, I must own that I could not bring myself to propose to Dr. Duigenan to resign his seat from Parliament, after all his labours, and all the obloquy he has braved and will brave in the cause of the Protestant Ascendancy.[54]

To O'Connell's followers the chief secretary was 'Orange Peel',[55] nor have Orangemen hesitated to claim him as their

[51] See above p. 166.
[52] Swift to grand Orange lodge, 3 June 1834 (*Rep. on Orange lodges IV*, H.C. 1835 [605], xvii. app. 21, p. 155).
[53] Inglis, *Freedom of the press in Ireland 1784–1841*, p. 156.
[54] Peel to Saurin, 2 Oct. 1812 (Peel, *Private papers*, i. 45–6).
[55] O'Connell, *Correspondence*, i. 40.

champion.⁵⁶ Friend to their expressed principles he was, but there was a quality about his friendship which tended to smother the movement. In commenting on Orangeism to Lord Liverpool, Peel wrote:

> We find it, I assure you, a most difficult task when anti-catholicism (if I may so call it) and loyalty are so much united as they are in the Orangemen to appease one without discouraging the other. I believe, however, that the administration of justice (so far at least as the exercise of mercy by the Lord-Lieutenant is concerned) has not been impeached, and that there is no impression whatever on the mind of the Catholic that the case of each party has not been viewed through a medium perfectly impartial.⁵⁷

During the first two years of Peel's secretaryship, attacks upon Orangeism were frequent. The British lodges were attacked briefly in 1813,⁵⁸ and to protect themselves further from anticipated parliamentary action, the Irish lodges again had their rules re-written in 1814. Following the lead of the British lodges, they dropped the conditional oath.⁵⁹ Sir Henry Parnell presented petitions against the Orange lodges in June 1814, which declared the Orange oath to be illegal, and the Orange demonstrations in the north the cause of civil disorder.⁶⁰ A further debate took place in November when Sir John Newport accused Peel of protecting and encouraging the societies. He moved that all copies of addresses from the Orangemen to Peel be submitted to the principal secretary. Peel seconded the motion, denying he had received addresses as such. He had, however, received an address from the grand jury of Fermanagh expressing appreciation of his conduct. He read his reply to this address and offered a copy of the document itself declaring that the house then was in possession of all correspondence between himself and the Orange lodges. He also stated that many of the signatures on the petitions against the Orangemen were in the same handwriting. Newport was challenged to cite an instance of Peel's partiality toward the Orangemen. Peel

---

⁵⁶ See vote of thanks to Peel passed by the grand lodge, in *Rep. on Orange lodges IV*, H.C. 1835 [605], xvii. report p. xix.

⁵⁷ Peel to Lord Liverpool, 15 Oct. 1813 (Peel, *Private papers*, i. 122).

⁵⁸ *Hansard*, xxvi. 974–86.

⁵⁹ *Rep. on Orange lodges I*, H.C. 1835 [377], xv. app. 3. pp. 11–5.

⁶⁰ *Hansard*, xxviii. 34–7

admitted, however, that some abuses had occurred as a result of the Orange societies.[61]

At the time of these debates in parliament, Peel had cooled considerably towards the lodges. He wrote the viceroy:

> Supposing them to be perfectly legal, I must confess that I cannot look upon this, or any other political association in Ireland that is controlled by any other authority than that of the Government, without jealousy... I admire the principles that the Orangemen maintain and avow. But when I find among their rules direct reference to the 'officers, non-commissioned officers, and privates of respective regiments', I cannot conceal from myself the possible danger of such an institution.[62]

On the same day he wrote, 'I suppose I shall be blamed by the one party for going too far in the vindication of the Orangemen, and by the other for not going far enough. The more I think upon the subject, the more I am convinced that even the most loyal associations in Ireland for political purposes are dangerous engines. We may derive a useful lesson from the Volunteers[63] [of 1782].'

Peel was aware of the possible danger of the lodges becoming the 'over-mighty' subject, but he did not consider the danger immediate. He was prepared to defend them against attacks which he considered unfair, and would in any case resist opposition-inspired efforts to bring action against the lodges. Parnell renewed his attack on 4 July 1815 when he called for a parliamentary investigation of the lodges. He mentioned the conditional oath and declared the lodges responsible for the disturbances in Ireland which Orange magistrates neglected to suppress. Fourteen petitions, Parnell claimed, had been presented by Sir John Newport respecting these associations.[64] Peel answered that even if the facts stated by Parnell were true, no good could possibly arise from such an investigation. 'It was wholly inexpedient and highly injudicious', Peel claimed, 'if this commission were instituted, it would only operate to the exasperation of irritations which were already too much to be

---

[61] *Hansard*, xxix, 606–14.
[62] Peel to Lord Whitworth, 23 July 1814 (Peel, *Private papers*, i. 159).
[63] Peel to Gregory, 23 July 1814 (ibid., pp. 159–60).
[64] *Hansard*, xxxi. 1090; N. Gash, *Mr. Secretary Peel*, p. 148.

lamented. In that case they would only have appointed commissioners to receive exaggerated details of both parties, and to review judicial cases which had received the formal decision of the law'.[65]

A friend of O'Connell, Maurice Fitzgerald, the knight of Kerry, supported Parnell, arguing that the administration of the duke of Richmond and his successor, Lord Whitworth, had departed from the policy of the previous viceroys, and 'the laws were not as generally exercised towards all parties in the community as they ought to be, owing to a sort of implied encouragement which was attributed to certain quarters, relative to the Orange system'.[66] Several other members spoke in support of Peel, and Parnell's motion was voted down by eighty to twenty.

2. THE EBB-TIDE OF ORANGEISM

After 1815 Orangeism ceased to be a serious problem. The end of the war removed one source of difficulty by bringing about the disbanding of the militia. O'Connell's Catholic Board had degenerated into a debating society and was finally suppressed.[67] In parliament many who had favoured catholic emancipation as a necessary wartime measure now lost interest, and Grattan, who had been introducing catholic relief bills against a declining majority, found the votes against the measure increased in 1815. Irish protestants had more reason to feel secure, and lost interest in the Orangemen. Agrarian disorders continued in 1816 but a partial famine in 1817 dampened, rather than inspired, the spirit of revolt. In 1818, the year Peel left Ireland, it was not thought necessary to renew the insurrection act.

Left without active opposition, the Orangemen became involved in internal disputes[68] which the annual meetings of the grand lodge were unable to resolve. Orangemen in office were hostages for the good behaviour of the lodges and, through the agency of the grand lodge, used their influence to ensure

[65] Ibid., pp. 1092–93.   [66] Ibid., p. 1094.
[67] Whitworth's proclamation, 3 June 1814, in O'Connell, *Correspondence*, i. 32.
[68] Sibbett, *Orangeism*, ii. 157–8.

the movement's good conduct. This restraint which office-holding Orangemen attempted to impose on the local lodges was at the root of the movement's internal troubles. From 1800 on the grand lodge had insisted there were only two orders in the lodges—the Orange and the Purple. Yet certain lodges, particularly in Armagh, formed higher orders or 'inner circles' which went by such names as 'Scarlet', 'Black' and 'Royal Arch Purple'. They satisfied a desire for the mysterious, but endangered the whole legal status of the lodges. Moreover, some of the unauthorized rituals looked ridiculous and annoyed the gentry and Dublin lawyers in the grand lodge.

Serious trouble began in 1811 when Thomas Seaver, the grand secretary of Armagh, and Henry Sling, deputy district master of Armagh city, were charged with introducing irregular orders. The grand lodge issued a statement reminding Orangemen that only two orders were to be tolerated.[69] Again in 1813 a new order appeared in Donegal which was suppressed.[70] But the problem persisted. The absence in the 1817 edition of the rules and regulations[71] of the paragraph reminding members that there were only two orders suggests that the grand lodge had decided to tolerate, without approving the unauthorized 'inner circles'.

The Orange movement was to remain dormant for several years until the renewal of serious agrarian disturbances, the visit of the king, a new vice-regal administration and the re-emergence of O'Connell's movement brought about an Orange revival in the early years of the new decade. A year after Peel's departure there were outbreaks in the south, principally by a new secret society called Rockites,[72] after a mythical Captain Rock whose name was affixed to the society's proclamations. This movement, which was directed against rents and tithes, was not considered at first to justify a renewal of the insurrection act, but involved the transfer of additional troops to Ireland in 1820. Quiet returned and, with the coming of George IV to the throne, all parties adopted a policy of waiting. The Orangemen

---

[69] Grand lodge resolution, 1811, in Sibbett, *Orangeism*, ii. 157.
[70] William McIntosh to John Giffard, 16 Jan. 1813 (ibid., pp. 157–8).
[71] Grand lodge address 7 July 1817 (ibid., p. 158).
[72] Evidence of M. Barrington, *Report on the state of Ireland, report from the select committee with minutes of evidence*, H.L. 1825 [181], ix. 305.

had much to fear and little to hope from the new king who, in his youth, had been a friend of the catholics, but, as avowed loyalists, they had no choice but to show enthusiasm.

It was made plain to them that displays of Orange badges at the coronation celebrations would be unwelcome, but Orange colours appeared nevertheless. On July 1 the Newry yeomanry defied the orders by appearing on parade with Orange lilies in their hats. When given the alternative of removing the lilies or laying down their arms, they chose the latter course.[73] The lord mayor of Dublin further irritated the Orangemen by posting an official notice requesting the citizens of Dublin to refrain from the traditional practice of dressing King William's statue on July 12 since it might mar the forthcoming visit of the king by arousing party spirit.[74] The order was respected reluctantly.

On 27 August 1821 the king entered Dublin amid the general rejoicing of the population. O'Connell was prominent among those who did him homage. No catholic petitions were pressed upon the king, and the Orangemen almost succeeded in concealing party spirit. But on one occasion, they broke the official truce between the 'Orange and the Green'. After the king's departure from a public banquet in Dublin, Alderman Beresford was asked to give the 'glorious, pious and immortal memory' toast. When he declined, he was then asked to propose the health of the deputy grand master of the Orangemen—Alderman Darley. After this was drunk, Darley rose, thanked the assembly and then proceeded to give the party toast,[75] but made a point of apologizing to the chief secretary the next day. After the king returned to England, the party truce in effect during his visit lasted barely a fortnight. Yet it would be a mistake to under-estimate the importance of the royal presence. It was a compliment to Ireland and flattered the national pride of all parties.

There is no reason to believe O'Connell insincere in his homage to the king, or his proposal that a permanent royal residence be established in Ireland. And in spite of the incident at the banquet, the Orangemen never showed more restraint

[73] Sibbett, *Orangeism*, ii. 187.
[74] O'Connell, *Select Speeches*, ii. 132–7; Sibbett, *Orangeism*, ii. 187.
[75] Ibid.

than during the king's visit.[76] Whether a more prolonged stay or more frequent visits would have reconciled the 'Orange and the Green', it is impossible to say, but certainly nothing else did. When the king departed without promising catholic emancipation, O'Connell and his followers did not conceal their disappointment. Nor could they find much comfort in the actions of parliament. Plunkett's introduction of the catholic emancipation bill caused only dismay as it included the royal veto. O'Connell was at first relieved when the bill was thrown out by the lords,[77] but the nature of the opposition was alarming. Henceforth, the strongest opposition to catholic emancipation was centred in the upper house, with the royal dukes of York and Cumberland its most conspicuous leaders. The king was undecided on the issue, and the prime minister determined to keep his cabinet intact by postponing the measure. The pro-catholic element in the cabinet, however, was strengthened by the adherence of the Grenville whigs—Grenville, Buckingham, and Wellesley.

3. THE WELLESLEY ADMINISTRATION

The presence of the Grenville whigs in the cabinet led to the appointment of Lord Wellesley as Irish viceroy. He faced a task similar in many respects to that of his whig predecessors—Fitzwilliam and Bedford. Like them, he was confronted with agrarian disturbances which made necessary the renewal of the insurrection act at the time he took office. And as in the case of the other whig viceroys, he was expected to use his reputation as a friend of the catholics to conciliate their feelings without granting any substantial concessions. While Fitzwilliam and Bedford accomplished nothing but retained their popularity, Wellesley, a more able man, accomplished a good deal at the expense of his popularity. He had the advantage of being an Irishman by birth, enjoyed a great reputation for past service to the state, and was the elder brother of the duke of Wellington. He perhaps understood that the one solid benefit he could offer catholics was to eliminate Orange influence at the Castle.

---

[76] Evidence of A. R. Blake, *Report on the state of Ireland, report from the select committee with minutes of evidence*, H.L. 1825 [181], ix. 108.

[77] O'Connell to his wife, 14 Apr. 1821 (O'Connell, *Correspondence*, i. 71)

He began his administration by dismissing Attorney-general Saurin and replacing him by Plunkett.[78] Wellesley might have contended that Plunkett's appointment was offset by making Goulburn, 'a staunch protestant', the chief secretary. Efforts were made by the viceroy to renew the party truce, which had been in effect during the king's visit, by inviting Orange grand masters and catholic bishops to mingle at viceregal levees. The ascendancy men, however, considered the balance was against them and treated Saurin's dismissal as a challenge.

Meanwhile, the outbreak of agrarian violence aroused the Orange movement from the torpor which had set in during Sir Robert Peel's secretaryship. The old guard active in 1798 had largely died out. Duigenan died in 1816 at the age of 80, in the act, it is claimed, of eating an orange. Sir Richard Musgrave died in 1818 and John Giffard in 1819. In 1818 George Ogle resigned as grand master and was replaced by General Archdall, the member of parliament for county Fermanagh. The new grand master was a soldier who had lost an arm in Egypt serving under the old foe of Orangeism—General Sir Ralph Abercromby. In 1820 the grand lodge renewed its efforts to eliminate unauthorized 'orders', and to increase the power of the Orange leaders. Taking advantage of rumours that the secret signs and passwords had been betrayed to Ribbonmen, the grand lodge held a special meeting in January 1820 at which the authority of the central leadership was strengthened by having the grand lodge meet twice a year, in February and August, and by leaving the conduct of the movement's business in the interim to a committee. A new set of rules was published[79] which specified that Orangemen 'could not assist at, nor sanction the making of any member in any other order purporting to be part of the Orange System, than the Orange and Purple'.

By restoring this rule, the grand lodge provoked a protest from a group of Orangemen, headed by Thomas Seaver, now district master of Carneough, and Henry Sling, who issued circulars to all lodge masters requesting the maintenance of what they called the 'Diamond' system and rules of 1798.[80]

[78] Wellesley to Lady Blessington, n.d. (O'Connell, *Correspondence*, i. 85).
[79] Grand lodge circular, 19 Jan. 1820, in Sibbett, *Orangeism*, ii. 181–2, 164.
[80] Ibid., p. 164.

As a result of this protest, a number of lodges remained outside the movement because they refused to adopt the new system. This internal quarrel of the Orangemen never received a satisfactory solution. Organizations known as Black Knights and Knights of Malta continued to claim an affiliation with Orangeism unrecognized by the grand lodge. The prominence which this question occupied in the internal politics of Orangeism during its years of decline was the result of general inactivity. It was the kind of dispute involving personalities and local vanity likely to develop in any organization of a political nature when it has nothing else to do.

In 1821 Orangeism was at a low ebb, not only because of the internal dispute, but also because the bulk of the members had been called to serve in the yeomanry, thus disrupting the routine of the local lodges. By the autumn of 1821 the efforts of the grand lodge aided, no doubt, by the growing disorders in the south, and the renewed fear of a change in the government's attitude towards the catholics, began to have results. The report of the grand lodge in February 1822 stated that only a few lodges were holding out against the 'new system', and that twelve new lodges had been founded. 'The serious appearance', the report read, 'which the unhappy disturbance in the South has assumed, and the insurrectionary spirit which has been found to prevail elsewhere, has had the effect of causing members to take shelter beneath the wings of the Association'.[81]

To this anxiety over the unrest among catholics was added an uneasiness about the viceroy's attitude towards the catholic question. The Orangemen as professed loyalists, bitter as they were about Saurin's dismissal, were reluctant to give open defiance to the king's representative. Moreover, the viceroy's statements, made shortly after his arrival, that he had come to enforce the laws not to change them,[82] disappointed O'Connell and the catholics, and offered some consolation to Orangemen. Had the viceroy not attempted to prevent the July 12 demonstrations, he might have suffered nothing more from the Orangemen than an attitude of hostile neutrality. However, when the lord mayor of Dublin endeavoured to make the banning of

[81] Grand lodge report, 22 Feb. 1822, in Sibbett, *Orangeism*, ii. 193.
[82] O'Connell to Wellesley, 11 July 1822 (O'Connell, *Correspondence*, i. 84).

the traditional dressing of King William's statue, which was imposed for the king's visit, a precedent for banning the ceremony permanently, Wellesley supported his action. At the same time, O'Connell wrote the viceroy declaring such ceremonies illegal, and reminded him he had armed forces at his disposal and offered the help of catholic special constables.[83]

With the gauntlet thus thrown down, the Dublin Orangemen defied the lord mayor and viceroy by dressing King William's statue. This led to a clash with O'Connell's men on the evening of July 12.[84] The Orangemen, who, for the first time since the Cornwallis administration assumed an attitude of open hostility to the viceregal administration, were virtually without a friend at court. Wellesley, however, does not appear to have been greatly disturbed by their enmity and he proceeded with measures to quiet the country. These struck at the roots of Orange influence. A new constabulary force was organized which was designed to make the police duties of the yeomanry superfluous. The new force was to be divided equally between protestants and catholics, and was to be well armed and kept under military discipline. Orangemen could not be prevented from joining such a force, as indeed they did,[85] but it could not be dominated by them. It would not, like the yeomanry, make unofficial raids on catholics, and the wearing of Orange badges would be punished by dismissal from the service.

Orange influence was further weakened by the introduction of stipendiary magistrates who were independent of local politics.[86] These measures were combined with a move to improve the position of catholic peasants by granting them the right to arrange commutation of the tithes. Although these changes undermined the position of the 'ascendancy', their effect was not immediate. The insurrection act was still in force and the Castle could not govern Ireland without the use of troops and yeomanry.

In November 1822 action was taken against the Ribbonmen

---

[83] Ibid.   [84] F.J., 13 July 1822, in O'Connell, *Select speeches*, ii. 174.
[85] Evidence of Inspector-General Stovin, *Rep. on Orange lodges I*, H.C. 1835 [377], xv. 321.
[86] Major Willcocks to the lord lieutenant, 30 Dec. 1824 (*Report on the state of Ireland, report from the select committee with minutes of evidence*, H.L. 1825 [181], ix. 17.

who were beginning to consolidate lesser secret societies under their banner and to carry out attacks against individual protestants in Ulster.[87] Some appear to have been repeating among themselves a prophecy that heretics would be driven from Ireland in 1825. As they were led largely by tavern keepers of dubious honesty, and were without support from any section of the educated classes or a foreign power, Ribbonmen had little hope of carrying their activities beyond the point of guerrilla warfare. They undoubtedly offered a means of protecting the interest of the peasant, but their attacks on landlords were indiscriminate, striking at the undefended rather than the bad. O'Connell fully approved government measures against Ribbonmen, taking pride in the extent to which catholic magistrates aided in these repressive measures.[88] Numerous Ribbonmen were brought to trial in November by Plunkett who gave Orangemen no cause to complain of his energy.

The banning of the July 12 celebration had not been forgotten, however, nor had the viceroy repented. On October 29 an order was issued against decorating King William's statue on the coming Orange holiday of November 4. The order was defied, but Orangemen dressing the statue were stopped by police and soldiers.[89] At a civic banquet that night, Orange toasts were omitted from the programme. The deficiency, however, was supplied by the newly appointed sheriff, Thorpe, who offered a spontaneous toast so that the day would not pass without some tribute to the cause.

The determination of the viceroy to prevent outdoor demonstrations convinced Orangemen they must indicate their feelings as dramatically as possible.[90] They chose December 14, the night on which Wellesley was to make a public appearance at a performance of *She Stoops to Conquer*. It was a gala occasion with most of Dublin society present. When Wellesley arrived he was hissed by Orangemen in the theatre and during the first act, shouts were raised for the singing of 'God Save the King'. The cast complied by singing the national anthem, but while the singing was in progress shouts of 'no popery', and 'a

---

[87] Evidence of O'Connell, *Report on the state of Ireland, report from the select committee with minutes of evidence*, H.L. 1825 [181], ix. 147–8.
[88] Ibid. [89] *Hansard 2*, viii. 1161. [90] *Hansard 2*, viii. 995.

groan for the lord mayor' came from the gallery. An attempt was made to resume the play but it was interrupted a second time by cries of 'a groan for the lord lieutenant', the 'glorious, pious and immortal memory', and 'no popish government'.[91] An orange labelled 'no popery' was hurled at the viceroy and landed on the stage. An apple, the blade of a watchman's rattle and finally, an empty bottle were thrown at the viceregal box where Wellesley stood calmly, receiving the applause of some of the audience until the demonstration was over.

Subsequently, Plunkett attempted to prosecute three Orangemen arrested on charges of riot and conspiring to assault.[92] As Sheriff Thorpe, who would normally have selected the grand jury, was an Orangeman, the attorney-general insisted that Thorpe collaborate with Sheriff Cooper in drawing up the jury panel. Cooper, however, seems to have been content to give a verbal approval to the list submitted by Thorpe, and an Orange grand jury cleared one of the accused and dropped the conspiracy charge against the other two, leaving the two men charged with riot only. Plunkett would not accept this and filed *ex officio* information against the accused men.[93] Brownlow, the parliamentary Orangeman, brought the matter before the house of commons, declaring Plunkett's action to be unconstitutional. Plunkett answered him in the commons stating, 'It was proved [at the trial] that a plan had been concerted at an Orange lodge ... [The evidence] proved that five persons ... had arranged the outrage against the lord lieutenant. They had determined to give a proof of the unpopularity of his administration at the first opportunity ... It was proved ... that the [loyal] Mr Forbes [had] packed the audience ... and the rioteers were to act under his directions'. Plunkett went on to say, 'He had reason not only for impeaching the decision of the Grand Jury, but also the manner in which it was empanelled. He had reason to know that the Sheriff was related to two of the traversers in the close affinity of first cousin. He also had it upon oath that the Sheriff had declared that the traversers need

---

[91] T. Wright, *History of Ireland*, p. 465; O'Connell, *Select speeches*, ii. 181; Sir Harcourt Lees, *An address to the Orangemen of Ireland relative to the late riot at the Theatre Royal*, pp. 3–8.
[92] *Hansard 2*, viii. 996–9.   [93] Ibid.

Orangeism in Ireland, 1803–25

not be afraid of the result as he had a list of Orangemen for the jury in his pocket'.[94]

Brownlow had made a mistake in bringing the matter before parliament, as it was the Orange lodges, not Plunkett, which came under attack. Lord Milton declared:

> There were to be found in Ireland honourable men ... so shackled by the oaths and obligations of Orange Societies that they dared not act or decide according to the law of the land ... What could be expected from a government so divided ... where a Lord O'Neil, the professed head of the Orange faction, held a high official situation ... Why was it that a right hon. baronet [Sir George Hill] who was known to be a supporter of Orange principles, retained a high official appointment in Ireland?[95]

Demands were made by Brougham and Goulbourn for an enquiry into the conduct of Sheriff Thorpe. On April 22 when the matter was mentioned again in parliament, it was objected that it was irregular to put persons on trial as Orangemen who, though members of the lodges, had acted as individuals.[96] In May the enquiry was held. Members of the jury were questioned, but they gave vague and non-committal answers. One known Orangeman claimed that the sheriff had no reason to believe him an Orangeman. The foreman of the jury, Sir George Whiteford, said he had heard that Thorpe had an Orange panel, but on questioning Thorpe prior to the trial, Whiteford said Thorpe had denied it.[97] Nothing definite could be established. Yet it was clearly a case of a secret society using influence to protect its obviously guilty members from a well earned punishment. On a small scale, this had been a common occurrence in Irish courts whenever Orangemen, Defenders, Ribbonmen or any other secret society enjoyed the ascendancy. The Orangemen escaped punishment as did Sheriff Thorpe,[98] but the lodges lost more prestige by this evasion of law than they would had their members suffered punishment.

The first effect of an attack from enemies always stimulated the movement, and it does not appear that Orangemen resigned from the lodges as a result of Sheriff Thorpe's behaviour. If anything, it increased the confidence of the ordinary Orangeman in the power of his society. The lodges, however, were

[94] *Hansard 2*, viii. 994–6.　[95] Ibid., pp. 1003–04.
[96] *Hansard 2*, viii. 1161.　[97] Ibid., ix. 105–6.　[98] Ibid., p. 538.

vulnerable to legal action, and such abuses increased the determination of their enemies to crush them, while leaving their friends less willing to come to their defence. In February 1823 Joseph Hume, who was henceforth to become a tireless enemy of the lodges, demanded that appropriations for the yeomanry be cut and that their services be dispensed with at the earliest possible moment. The yeomanry, he maintained, consisted generally of Orangemen, and that they were responsible for the disturbances in the north.[99] He was challenged by Vesey Fitzgerald who said that nine out of ten yeomen in the south were catholics. Another member of parliament pointed out that of the 30,000 yeomen, 20,000 were from Ulster where few but Orangemen enlisted. On March 5 the Orange outrages were mentioned and Orange magistrates criticized, but more for past than current offences, Lord Gosford's remarks of 1795 being recounted. Goulburn defended the lodges while other speakers credited Orangemen with the suppression of the 1798 rebellion, although this was contradicted by Maurice Fitzgerald, the knight of Kerry, who declared that the rebellion was suppressed by a combination of loyal men. Finally, a motion to investigate Irish secret societies was withdrawn.[1] Again on March 10 Hume criticized the yeomanry, asserting that none but Orangemen were admitted to the ranks and that yeomen had recently displayed partisan zeal by burning the attorney-general in effigy.[2] These attacks prepared the way for the April debates on Plunkett's actions, which were so damaging to the reputation of the lodges.

4. O'CONNELL AND THE CATHOLIC ASSOCIATION

Attacks came also from another quarter. In the spring of 1823 O'Connell founded the Catholic Association.[3] It was designed to organize the catholic peasantry into a huge political association which, though rejecting physical force in theory, would, in fact, have the power to commence civil war at will.[4] The organization of such a movement would hardly have been

[99] *Hansard 2*, viii. 93.   [1] Ibid., pp. 443–90.   [2] Ibid., pp. 523–4.
[3] Curtis, *Hist. of Ireland*, p. 358.
[4] General George Warburton to the lord lieutenant, 26 Jan. 1825 (*Report on the state of Ireland, report from the select committee with minutes of evidence*, H.L. 1825 [181], ix. 24–5).

attempted with Saurin as attorney-general, and even under Plunkett and Wellesley, it was in danger of being crushed in its initial stages by Orange terrorism. O'Connell therefore spared no effort to take advantage of the rift between Orangemen and the Castle. The Orangemen were denounced by O'Connell with great violence on 25 April 1823 at a Dublin public meeting under the chairmanship of Lord Killeen. Another meeting, sponsored by the anti-Orange journalist, Lawless, was addressed by O'Connell in Belfast. On May 10 O'Connell was again in Dublin preparing an address to the king against Orangeism. He partly discredited himself by being careless of his facts when making accusations against the lodges, and he did not hesitate to repeat current rumours that Orangemen quoted passages from the Old Testament to justify the massacre of catholics in Ireland.[5] It appears O'Connell's campaign against the Orangemen at this time was less a reaction against the conduct of the Orangemen than an effort to rout them from their positions of influence at the Castle, in the yeomanry and in local government.

Of incidents involving Orangemen, however, there was an abundance. On 12 June 1823 a riot broke out at a fair at Maghera in county Derry,[6] which followed the pattern of previous quarrels. Yeomen, twelve of them Orangemen, were driven into the local barracks where they found arms and fired on their pursuers, wounding a score and killing several.[7] Against such violence on the part of the Orangemen must be balanced the great violence rampant in Munster, and the numerous small acts of revenge committed by Ribbonmen.

Leading Orangemen were worried about the increasing frequency of parliamentary attacks on their movement, and used what authority they had to restrain the unruly. In March 1823 the grand lodge of Armagh, at a meeting attended by county grand masters, district masters and representatives of 340 lodges, issued a statement which read:

We feel not less surprised than grieved that Orange associations should be accused of illegal interference in the state, or branded as an

[5] Evidence of O'Connell, ibid., pp. 169–70; see also *Morning Chronicle*, London, 28 Feb. 1825.
[6] Evidence of General C. Egerton, *Report on the state of Ireland, report from the select committee with minutes of evidence*, H.L. 1825 [181], ix. 354
[7] Evidence of Rev. Henry Cooke, ibid., p. 269.

intolerant and persecuting faction ... Where in this land have the laws been so well enforced and so cheerfully obeyed as in those districts where the Orange Association has more power and influence? ... and we call on them to show in all the outrages and rebellious insults which have disgraced the very name of Ireland, where had the true Orangemen been found who was not ranged on the side of these laws?[8]

That the Orange lodges were decidedly on the defensive may be inferred from the cautious attitude they took towards the July 12 parades in 1823. The Dublin district grand lodge asked all Orangemen to use their influence against efforts of protestants to celebrate the twelfth.[9] As a consequence, there was no celebration in Dublin while in Belfast and Derry orderly parades were held. Only in Armagh county was there trouble. There Ribbonmen attacked Orange parades at Keady, Crossgrove and Cram.[10] At Cram Orangemen fired on their attackers, killing one man,[11] and an Orangeman was charged with manslaughter at the next spring assizes.

The movement's leaders proved too late and ineffectual in their efforts to restrain members. They had too many enemies in parliament, and while attacking Orangemen involved little danger, defending them was a risky business. On 19 July 1823 the unlawful oaths bill was passed, directed against all secret societies including the Orangemen. Fearing they had been placed outside the law, the members of the grand lodge of Ireland informed the district masters:

The Bill for the prevention of Unlawful Oaths in Ireland, having now passed into law, you are requested to make known the same to all lodges in your vicinity, in order to prevent any of them from inadvertently subjecting themselves to its operations and penalties. It is now illegal to administer an oath on any person becoming a member of the lodge, or to extend or permit any declaration or test tantamount thereto.[12]

[8] Declaration of the meeting of 340 lodges at Armagh, 11 Mar. 1823 (ibid., supplement p. 356).
[9] Grand lodge address, 23 June 1823, in Sibbett, *Orangeism*, ii. 220.
[10] Ibid., p. 225.
[11] *Morning Chronicle*, London, 28 Feb. 1825.
[12] Grand lodge circular, 23 July 1823, in *Morning Chronicle*, 25 Feb. 1825.

The Orange order was, in effect, dissolved and reconstituted on a new basis. Although this device for evading the new law was successful and kept the lodges together under modified regulations, it caused great inconvenience and weakened the confidence of ordinary Orangemen in the powers of their influential members to protect them from the law. On August 4 a new system of rules and regulations was drafted, similar to those in force in the British lodges. Under the new system the lodge administered no oath, but members were admitted only after presenting evidence that they had taken at some time the oath of allegiance, of supremacy and of abjuration before a qualified magistrate.[13] It was further stated, 'This is, exclusively, a Protestant association, yet, detesting an intolerant spirit, it admits no persons into its brotherhood, who are not well known to be incapable of persecuting, injuring, or upbraiding anyone on account of his religious opinions'.[14]

No sooner had this new system been adopted than doubts were raised as to its legality. The autumn and winter of 1823-4 were spent, therefore, in efforts to place the lodges definitely within the law. Local lodges continued to function, but without the protection and direction of an effective grand lodge. It was not until March 1824 that the grand lodge was again in a position to offer leadership. On March 3 of that year it issued an order prepared at its half-yearly meeting in February that read:

Although the peculiar and trying circumstances under which the institution was placed for some time back were of sufficient notoriety in themselves to satisfy the minds of its members throughout the country of the unavoidable nature of the delay which has taken place in carrying on its affairs, the G.L. conceive it their duty to acquaint you that the chief cause of that delay was their anxious desire to have the institution placed upon the surest possible footing of security in regard to the law.[15]

The new system, as revised, is remarkable principally for its first two rules which read, 'Whereas the original Orange Institution was, by the proper authorities dissolved, it is

[13] *Report on the state of Ireland, report from the select committee with minutes of evidence*, H.L. 1825 [181], ix. 348.
[14] Ibid.
[15] Grand lodge declaration, 7 Feb. 1824 (ibid., supplement p. 353).

expedient that a new Association be formed, on similar principles', and 'that every member of the late Orange Institution, who is desirous of becoming a member of the new Association, shall undergo a new election as soon as possible and again, at any future period, when ever the Grand Lodge shall think it expedient'.[16]

Warrants were renewed for the fourth time, the other times being 1799, 1814 and 1823. These changes of rules and regulations had comparatively little effect on the composition of the leadership. One addition was the appointment of another member of the Verner family, James Verner, the son of James Verner of Diamond days, as deputy grand master. There was, it appears, some dissatisfaction among the Ulstermen with the restraints imposed on them by the grand lodge of Dublin. Colonel William Verner went so far as to suggest that a provincial grand lodge be permitted to meet in Armagh, but on being opposed by another prominent Ulster Orangeman—Colonel Blacker—this proposal was rejected. At the time the revised system was adopted, Earl O'Neill was grand master, Colonel Pratt, grand treasurer, and James Verner, deputy grand master.

There seemed no limit to which Orange leaders were willing to go to retain their legality. In the spring of 1824 they made a further sacrifice—that of banning all July 12 demonstrations.[17] By such a move the grand lodge seriously endangered its authority over the local branches, for too much restraint might drive the militant protestants out of the official Orange lodges, causing them to return to secret societies on the Peep O'Day Boy model, unconnected with and uncontrolled by the gentry and Dublin lawyers. In spite of this risk, James Verner appealed to all Orangemen, 'To act in the most strict conformity with an order which tends so strongly to shew how much the members of the Orange Association are willing to sacrifice to the feelings, and even prejudices, of their fellow subjects and how desirous they are that no excuses should be left for ascribing any of the disorders that afflict Ireland to their conduct or example'.[18]

Complete conformity to these instructions was not forth-

---

[16] *Report on the state of Ireland, report from the select committee with minutes of evidence*, H.L. 1825 [181], ix. 348.

[17] Grand lodge resolution, 21 May 1824 (ibid., p. 353).   [18] Ibid.

coming, but, on the whole, they were obeyed. Among the poor protestants in country districts, a few processions took place, while in Belfast some Orangemen raised an arch which was removed by the magistrates. The *Dublin Patriot*, a Castle organ, commented, 'We hoped this shocking system is on the wane ... we are not mistaken. The Lord-Lieutenant, at the risk of his life, gave it its first fatal shock, and Ireland is justly grateful to His Excellency.'[19] The twelfth in 1824 was orderly, but not, as the *Patriot* implied, because the Orangemen lacked power to create violence. This the Orangemen proved by becoming involved in a riot at Newry. The military was called out, but several soldiers took sides in the riot and fifteen were court-martialled. The court-martialled men were of both denominations. Other signs of life in the movement were the various dinners and indoor celebrations held by Orangemen throughout Ireland.

The Orangemen were faced, however, with an insoluble problem. The July 12 demonstrations were essential to the morale of the movement, as ordinary Orangemen regarded them as traditional demonstrations of loyalty and could not understand why their leaders should ban them, or even believe that the government really looked upon them with hostility. Yet the Orange grand lodge realized that the parades meant violence, and violence provoked legal action against the movement. In the conflict between the two points of view, the lodges were neutralized as a political force. They thus were unable to offer any effective opposition to the growing power of O'Connell's movement in 1824.

O'Connell's success may be accounted for, in no small measure, by the force of his personality and his genius as an organizer. Yet there were numerous factors in his favour, not the least of which was the inability of the Orange lodges to act against him. During 1824 the disorders in the countryside were brought under control.[20] Troops were used, but the constabulary showed a remarkable efficiency.[21] The success of the

[19] *Patriot*, 13 July 1824.
[20] Wellesley to Liverpool, 22 Nov. 1824 (C.P. Yonge, *Life of Liverpool*, iii. 312–3).
[21] Maj. Willcocks to Wellesley, 30 Dec. 1824 (*Report on the state of Ireland, report from the select committee with minutes of evidence*, H.L. 1825 [181], ix. 17.

governmental forces in putting down disorders lent considerable strength to O'Connell's argument that the methods of the secret society were hopeless. Less important, but of consequence, was the fact that the catholic hierarchy was worried by the progress of the Kildare Place Society schools at which the Bible was read without comment.[22] It was annoyed also at the distribution of Bibles carried out by the British and Foreign Bible society.[23] The catholic church, which probably would have felt compelled to support O'Connell in any case, thus had additional motives for encouraging political action by catholics.[24]

The Catholic Association was organized on two levels—partly as a gentleman's club with subscriptions of a guinea a year, and partly as an association of peasants who subscribed a penny a month. The gentleman's club, which was first organized, was comparatively small, but after the introduction of the penny-a-month subscription, the association soon gained the adherence of the overwhelming majority of Irish catholics. For the moment, the peasantry abandoned violence and, although the insurrection act was renewed in 1825, there were only a few places where disturbances continued.[25] O'Connell claimed full credit for having brought tranquillity to the countryside.[26] But this was of small comfort to the viceroy who had no intention of permitting a private association to substitute its authority for his own. Nor were O'Connell's methods such as to inspire the confidence of the government. In an address to the people of Ireland, O'Connell appealed, 'In the name, then, of common sense, which forbids you to seek foolish resources, by the hate you bear the Orangemen, who are your natural enemies, by the confidence you repose in the Catholic Association, who are your natural and zealous friends... we adjure you to abstain from all secret and illegal societies, and White Boy disturbances and outrage'.[27]

Copies of this address were sent to every parish in Ireland and

[22] Evidence of Rev. D. Murray, archbishop of Dublin (ibid., p. 263).
[23] Ibid., p. 395.
[24] F. Blackburn to chief secretary, 14 Jan. 1825 (ibid., pp. 20–3).
[25] Correspondence of police inspectors to government, Jan. 1825 (ibid., pp. 17–32).
[26] General G. Warburton to Wellesley, 26 Jan. 1825 (ibid., pp. 24–5).
[27] *Morning Chronicle*, 11 Feb. 1825.

read by priests. As the peasantry, especially in the south, were inclined to confuse Orangemen with protestants generally, it was obvious that a tranquillity inspired by such arguments had many qualities of an armed truce. Wellesley wrote to Lord Liverpool that the general prosperity of the country was disturbed by 'the noisy fury of the Catholic Association'.[28]

It is not likely that O'Connell could have organized this association had Saurin been left as attorney-general and the Orangemen given a free hand. If Orange yeomen had been sent to the south and O'Connell's organization dissolved as it had been in 1811 and was to be again in 1825, the peasantry would have had no choice but to continue its old secret society methods of resistance. Violence certainly would have continued, but the unarmed catholic population was unable to oppose the combination of forces at the disposal of the Castle. By appointing a liberal viceroy and denying itself the services of the Orangemen, who were forced to dissolve and reconstitute their organization in 1823,[29] the government cleared the way for O'Connell.

While O'Connell's association was gaining strength in Ireland, the bad impression made by the Orangemen continued to influence parliamentary opinion, but there was an increased coolness towards the catholics. Plunkett, who had little fondness for the lodges, felt compelled to point out, '... it could be no excuse for the Ribbonmen to say they combined for an illegal purpose because they were exposed to the violence and insults of [the Orange association]'.[30] He was challenged by Lord Althorp who read a letter from R. N. Bennett, a lawyer for the Ribbonmen, who claimed that the Ribbonmen were a wholly 'defensive society against the Orange party'.[31] In the house of lords, the prime minister's motion for an enquiry into the state of affairs in Ireland provoked Lord King to remark, 'Such an enquiry is not easily obtained. The learned lord of the woolsack [Lord Eldon] would resist any interference with one party. He would say, "these are my Orangemen, the only true Protestants".'[32]

Orangemen were mentioned again in parliament when a

---

[28] Wellesley to Liverpool, 22 Nov. 1824 (Yonge, *Life of Liverpool*, iii. 312–3).
[29] See above p. 209. [30] *Hansard 2*, x. 893.
[31] Ibid., p. 894. [32] Ibid., xi. 755.

petition from the Free Masons was presented asking that they be exempt from the laws against secret societies. The Masons made a point of emphasizing their abhorrence of Orange processions. In this debate, Brownlow, who was both a Free Mason and an Orangeman, expressed his agreement that the July 12 parades should be 'put down since as long as they continued, no man's life was worth a pin point and no man's property worth a year's purchase in Ireland'.[33] These remarks were regarded as desertion and treason by Orange farmers in Armagh, but the grand lodge let the matter pass.

The renewal of activity by the grand lodge in the spring of 1824 brought new petitions against the Orangemen on May 4. The petitioners—farmers and labourers of Westmeath—protested that since the late law against secret societies, the Orange lodges had increased and that wherever an Orange lodge was introduced, a Ribbon lodge was also formed.[34] This might have been true in Westmeath, but certainly was not general throughout Ireland. A few days later petitions were presented in parliament objecting to the activities of the Orangemen in the Cavan election. It was asserted that the notice of the approaching election was given on a placard headed by an effigy of King William wearing Orange colours, and an inscription to the 'glorious memory'.[35] The petition claimed that on the day of the election all avenues to the courthouse were packed with Orangemen and difficulties were placed in the way of the gentleman nominating the opposition candidate.

Henry Maxwell, an Orange member of parliament, declared that the sheriff had denied that the proclamation was headed with anything but the royal arms.[36] Goulburn said his advice to the Orangemen was to abandon a system which caused so much disquiet. While the former Orange grand master, General Archdall, said the terms 'Orangeman' and 'protestant' were synonymous, and for personal safety it was necessary for Orangemen to unite. Lords Althorp and Milton were agreed that the government should act against both the Ribbon and Orange societies.[37] Sir Francis Burdett maintained that Orangemen were driving industry and talent from the country.

[33] *Hansard 2*, xi. 17.   [34] Ibid., p. 446.   [35] Ibid., p. 652.
[36] Ibid., p. 654.   [37] Ibid., pp. 662, 690.

Brownlow gained the distinction of being the first man to avow himself an Orangeman in parliament. This he did when presenting petitions against O'Connell's association; on being attacked by Plunkett, he announced himself ready to supply all information desired on the lodges.[38] This was, no doubt, in conformity with the new policy of the grand lodge adopted in February. In a parliamentary battle, however, the Orangemen were no match for their opponents. New petitions were presented by Brougham on May 31 demanding redress for the alleged outrages committed in the north and south by Orangemen, and asking for equal justice between catholic and protestant under the insurrection act.[39] A fortnight later, in the debate on the insurrection act, it was asserted that Orange magistrates in Fermanagh connived at the release of fourteen Orangemen arrested for riot[40] while O'Connell's friend, John Lawless, again petitioned for an end to religious processions.[41] In all the debates the tone of government spokesmen, normally friendly to the lodges, was one of regret that Orange actions were provoking disorders. Only the Orange parliamentarians such as Brownlow and Archdall actually defended the lodges. The general opinion was that political secret societies, as such, were responsible for the unrest in Ireland.

By the opening of the 1825 session all other Irish problems were dwarfed by the rise of O'Connell's Catholic Association. It was mentioned in the king's speech on February 3, and a bill banning unlawful associations—directed against O'Connell's organization—was introduced. It was impossible to discuss this measure without raising the question whether the Orange lodges would be included. Once the friends of the catholics, such as Brougham, despaired of saving the Catholic Association, they made a point of insisting that the Orange lodges be included in the repressive measure. In this, they were joined by others who desired to demonstrate their impartiality by banning both organizations. Speakers gave long accounts, not necessarily accurate, of the past history of the lodges, some in their defence, but most otherwise. The question of the long-abandoned conditional oath was discussed, outrages cited, and the evil effects of the Orangemen in the yeomanry and the partiality

[38] *Hansard 2*, xi. 947. [39] Ibid., pp. 954–6.
[40] Ibid., p. 1326. [41] Ibid., p. 1434.

of Orange magistrates described. All this had, in one form or another, been discussed before.

A case was cited of a private in the 25th Regiment persuading several catholics to take an oath for the extermination of protestants and Orangemen for 'the purpose of betraying'.[42] Colonel Davies said that if the government wanted to show its disapproval of Orangemen, it had only to ban them from office. Hume cited as an example of the government's partiality the fact that in the Irish customs department there were 226 protestants and only twelve catholics. In the excise there were 365 protestants and only six catholics.[43] Grattan's son, who was now in the house of commons, continued the tradition of his father by asserting that the government's act was a declaration of war on the catholics of Ireland, while C. Hutchinson declared, 'The government was risking the safety of the Empire by putting down the Association. It was an association backed by the affection of the people, and to gratify not the Orange faction, but the rump of the Orange faction, Wellesley had permitted himself to be influenced to put down the Association.'[44]

Towards the end of the debates, Peel made it clear that the unlawful societies act would include the Orange lodges. When Brownlow, in an effort to obtain a further hearing for the lodges, presented petitions from the Orangemen calling for an enquiry into the movement, he stated, 'Orangemen were most anxious to clear themselves from a malignant libel [but] he did not apprehend that the Orange Societies would continue in Ireland after the Bill had passed'.[45] Peel took advantage of this remark to comment:

He was very happy to hear there would be an end of the Orange Societies in Ireland. He joined in the exhortation that the Societies would yield to the repeated sense of Parliament and obey what soon would be the law. It was unworthy of their loyalty to maintain a conflict with parliament by prolonging their existence. With regard to certain members of the Orange Lodges, he was able to assert that although in public they had continued to belong to the lodges for the purpose of exercising an influence over them, they were now bound to dissolve all connection.[46]

[42] *Morning Chronicle*, 11 Feb. 1825.
[43] Ibid., 22 Feb. 1825.
[44] *Morning Chronicle*, 11 Feb. 1825.
[45] Ibid., 4 Mar. 1825.
[46] Ibid.

When the bill became law, the Orangemen were compelled once more to dissolve their organization. They had, however, the consolation of appearing before a 'Committee of the House of Lords on the State of Ireland'. Colonel William Verner and Reverend Holt Waring took advantage of this to give an account of the organization.[47] Their testimony cleared the movement of many of the more ridiculous charges against it, but no effort was made during the enquiry to ask embarrassing questions.

The grand lodge held a final meeting in Dublin on 18 March 1825 with Colonel Pratt in the chair. A statement was drawn up and sent to all lodges which read, 'At no period was the Institution in a more flourishing condition, or more highly respectable in the numbers added to its ranks. Notwithstanding which, the Parliament of the United Kingdom have considered it necessary that all political societies should be dissolved. Of course, our society is included. It therefore becomes our duty to inform you that any lodge meeting after this day commits a breach of the law'.[48] The grand lodge of Ireland was at an end, and so was a phase of Orange history.

[47] *Report on the state of Ireland, report from the select committee with minutes of evidence*, H.L. 1825 [181], ix. 326–58.

[48] Declaration of the grand lodge, 18 Mar. 1825 (*Report on the state of Ireland, report from the select committee with minutes of evidence*, H.L. 1825 [181], ix. 354.

IX

ORANGE RESISTANCE TO CATHOLIC EMANCIPATION 1825-9

THE THREAT OF CATHOLIC EMANCIPATION being carried as a measure of the United Kingdom parliament had disturbed Orangemen of all classes at least since the act of union, but the defences against this eventuality were formidable. Cobbett wrote in 1823 that 'the Orangemen have for allies all the unconquerable prejudices of ninety-nine hundredths of the people of England'.[1] Although this sentiment was weaker in the house of commons where feeling on the catholic question was about equally divided, there remained an imposing array of 'protestant peers', headed by the dukes of York and Cumberland. As no measure of catholic relief was likely to be popular in Britain or viewed with favour by the king, the 'protestant' or ultra tory peers and their Orange allies could hope to defeat parliamentary efforts on behalf of the catholics by an 'appeal to the people', combined with pressure on the king by way of the royal dukes. Although the British lodges were undoubtedly a useful auxiliary to 'protestant' strength in Britain, the personal influence of ultra peers was sufficient to raise the 'no popery' cry without the aid of the Orangemen.[2] In Ireland, however,

[1] *Political Register*, London, 5 Apr. 1823, xlvi. 57.
[2] Keith Feiling, *The second tory party 1714-1832*, pp. 256-7.

the lodges provided an effective link between the popular protestantism of the Ulster peasants and the 'protestants' among the political classes. With the dissolution of the grand lodge of Ireland, this link was broken, and between the years 1825 and 1828, when many of the ultra peers were drawing closer to the British lodges and O'Connell revived his Catholic Association,[3] there was no parallel revival of the Irish Orange movement.

After the lords rejected the catholic emancipation bill of 1825, O'Connell took advantage of technicalities in the law to reconstitute the Catholic Association, and in the general election of 1826 he offered a demonstration of his power by organizing catholic forty-shilling freeholders in the great protestant strongholds in Waterford, Louth, Westmeath, and Cavan to vote against the candidates favoured by their landlords.[4] As this defeat was imposed on the great family interests with past Orange associations like the Beresfords and the Fosters, it is, at first glance, surprising that they accepted humiliation at the hands of O'Connell without, in the manner of 1798, playing the Orange card. Perhaps the best chance they had of defeating the Catholic Association was by organizing their protestant retainers into Orange societies, and employing them to create sufficient violence to bring about martial law and new repressive legislation.

However, in 1798 the yeomanry had provided a convenient means whereby Orange retainers could be armed and their activities given a cloak of legality. Moreover, the Camden administration was confronted by the danger of an armed uprising and French invasion at a time when it had doubts about the reliability of its armed forces. None of these conditions was present in 1826. The constabulary, organized by Peel in 1814 and improved by Wellesley, had supplanted the yeomanry as rural police. Although this force, which was selected by magistrates, included former Orangemen in the northern counties, its discipline prevented open displays of Orange sympathies[5] and outside Ulster it was recruited largely among the catholic population. O'Connell, unlike the men of

[3] P. S. O'Hegarty, *A history of Ireland under the union 1801–1922*, p. 34.
[4] P.R.O.N.I., Anglesey MSS 619/1/1–2; O'Hegarty, *Hist. Ire. under the union 1801–1922*, pp. 35–6.
[5] Evidence of Stovin, *Rep. on Orange lodges I*, H.C. 1835 [377], xv. 321.

'98, was determined to keep his followers from offering a direct challenge to the authority of the state, while Peel and the vice-regal administration were firm in rejecting all collaboration with the Orangemen. Moreover, O'Connell's initial success appears to have taken the Orange gentry, like the Fosters and the Beresfords, by surprise. The great reservoir of Orange strength in the border counties of Ulster could not be organized from below without a threat of physical force directed against Ulster. O'Connell posed no such immediate threat and the Orange gentry was kept, by the watchful eye of Peel, from making a serious effort to reorganize the movement from above. Peel's brother-in-law, Colonel Dawson, had provoked a sharp rebuke from the home secretary when he wrote in January 1826 that 'the feeling in the North of Ireland on the Catholic question is stronger than ever, and it appeared to me that the great majority of the Protestants only wanted an assurance of support to express their own feelings in the most unequivocal manner. I was therefore tempted, on the anniversary of the shutting of the gates of Derry, to give vent to my own sentiments, and to cheer up the Protestant spirit in as warm a manner as I could'.[6]

Without an Irish grand lodge or an immediate threat from O'Connell, the Ulster Orangemen were so feeble and divided in the summer of 1826 that there was really no Orange card to play. Fragments of the movement remained, meeting under warrants issued by the British grand lodge or the defunct Irish grand lodge. Sir Harcourt Lees, a clergyman of the established church who had been involved in the attacks on Wellesley and was considered by some to be a violent Orangeman, attempted to organize Irish Orangemen in a benevolent society on the model of the British lodges. Yet this experiment in moderation did not meet the needs of rural Ulster and achieved very little. The Loyal and Benevolent Orange Institution of Ireland was founded in 1825[7] with the earl of Aldborough as grand master and Viscount Montmorris as deputy grand master, but without the support of Verner, Blacker, Archdall, and others who had been active in the original movement. The declaration of the new society read, 'This association is formed by persons desirous of

---

[6] Dawson to Peel, 14 Jan. 1826 (Peel, *Private papers*, i. 391).
[7] Evidence of Blacker, *Rep. on Orange lodges I*, H.C. 1835 [377], xv. 109; Sibbett, *Orangeism*, ii. 287.

supporting the principles and practices of the Christian religion, to support and relieve distressed members of the Institution, and to offer assistance to such other religious and charitable purposes. We associate ourselves in honour of King William III, Prince of Orange, whose name we bear, and whose immortal memory we hold in reverence'.[8]

It was further stated that the organization was an exclusively Christian one, detesting 'every species of intolerance and excluding persons not well known to be incapable of upbraiding people on account of religious practices'. One of the objects of the new society was to aid in the efforts of the 'new reformation' —a belated attempt by evangelists and others to spread protestantism in Ireland, in which the Orangemen showed little interest. No oaths, signs or passwords were permitted, but Orangemen continued to meet together with their old banners and insignia. This society functioned until 1828 when it merged with the reconstituted Orange order, but at no time included all the supporters of the old movement. While the respectability of its sponsors made some impression upon the Orangemen, the latter had little enthusiasm for an organization so obviously designed to keep them on a tight leash.

In Waterford where the Catholic Association won its most complete victory, the protestant population was small and there was virtually no Orange tradition. It was in Dublin that John Claudius Beresford, the great Orangeman of 1798, had been active; yet it was a measure of the prestige of the movement when this once terrible leader of the yeomen was treated with mock servility as he walked amid the contemptuous but orderly crowds of the Catholic Association.[9] O'Connell's victories in the north were less complete, but in many respects more humiliating to Orangemen. Leslie Foster, who represented his family interest in Louth, wrote Peel, 'I entered upon the contest with upwards of five-sixths of the votes promised to me, and my opponent was the person in the county most unacceptable to the gentry', but Foster maintained, 'very many Protestants were forced to vote against me by threats of assassination or

[8] Printed address of Benevolent and Religious Orange Institution of Ireland, 12 June 1826 (N.L.I., Brunswick Club MSS 5017).
[9] Thomas Wyse, *An historical sketch of the late Catholic Association of Ireland*, i. 288.

having their houses burnt'.[10] He claimed that his voters were waylaid and beaten, and that Lord Oriel's tenantry, who voted for him, required a military escort. The Orange Lord Roden, whose interest was 250 votes which 'he gave to me heartily' brought Foster only ten. Although Foster's 'unacceptable' rival headed the poll, Foster himself retained his seat.[11]

While Foster's opposition had come from O'Connell's association, the defeats of other Orange candidates in Ulster merely reflected divisions among protestants. Colonel Forde, another Orangeman, was defeated by the family interest of Downshire and Londonderry. In Armagh, Colonel William Verner was defeated by Caulfeild, a brother of the earl of Charlemont, who was supported by Lord Gosford and Sir Capel Molyneux. These interests also supported the former Orangeman, William Brownlow,[12] referred to as 'Judas Brownlow' by Verner's supporters. In the course of the four day election, Verner's slogan 'Verner Forever' was satirized by a cartoon of a ragged peasant shouting 'Vermin Forever', under which was written 'One of Colonel V... voters'. On the last day of polling, Verner's followers matched the violence in Louth, described by Foster, by capturing after a stiff battle the tally returns of Brownlow before troops and police restored order.[13]

Immediately after O'Connell's victory, many of the gentry thought in terms of renewing their alliance with plebeian protestants. Foster wrote, 'The landlords will no doubt be driven to refuse freehold leases to Roman Catholics, and to encourage by all artificial means a Protestant population', but added that he feared a crisis of some kind would develop before this could be done.[14] Another landlord of Orange sympathies wrote, 'We have endeavoured to restrain the Protestants from processing on the twelfth of this month, but I am not sanguine of a general obedience to our counsel ... The present state of things cannot be endured. The Romans are united as one man,

[10] Foster to Peel, 8 July 1826 (Peel, *Private papers*, i. 410).
[11] Ibid.
[12] Evidence of Lord Gosford, *Rep. on Orange lodges I*, H.C. 1835 [377], xv. 263.
[13] Lord F. Leveson-Gower to Anglesey, 15 Aug. 1828 (P.R.O.N.I., Anglesey MSS 619/X/125); Sibbett, *Orangeism*, ii. 291.
[14] Foster to Peel, 8 July 1826 (Peel, *Private papers*, i. 412).

and common safety will justify counter-association against the chance or dread of commotion'.[15]

Although alarmed by the election and worried by the severing of the bond between landlord and tenant, neither Peel nor any member of the Castle administration considered for a moment encouraging the Orangemen as a counter-weight to O'Connell.[16] 'I have never had but one opinion,' Peel wrote to Hill, 'that it is true policy for the Protestant minority in Ireland to forebear, above all to refrain from demonstrations'.[17] In his replies to Hill and Foster, Peel suggested that the power of the priest and the Catholic Association would be temporary, and that time would bring about a reaction to clerical influence from which the landlords would benefit. Goulburn, the chief secretary, declared candidly, 'We are obliged to prevent an Orange procession, because we believe it may tend to riot or to exasperation; we cannot interfere with the Catholic Association, because there is doubt as to the possibility of doing so with effect'.[18] The chief secretary further stated that he considered that the protestants were subject to economic discrimination and other provocations which the catholics carried on within the limits of the law. He feared the 'two bodies coming into conflict', but that O'Connell wished to avoid such a clash and that he was 'complete master of the Roman Catholic clergy and they are complete master of the people'.[19]

Later in the year Hill reported 'lively active opposition to the popish claims has considerably abated. But, with a few exceptions in the North, those claims are more dreaded and abhorred than ever.' He accounted for the apathy by the growing conviction among protestants that the government intended to recognize catholic claims.[20] Immediately after the election, Peel expressed satisfaction with the work of the constabulary, and throughout the crisis neither he nor Goulburn anticipated an uprising. They discussed the state of the garrison and found it adequate, although Goulburn was disturbed by the removal

[15] Sir George Hill to Peel, 6 July 1826 (ibid.).
[16] Peel to Foster, 16 July 1826 (Peel, *Private papers*, i. 413).
[17] Peel to Sir George Hill, 16 July 1826 (ibid., p. 412).
[18] Goulburn to Peel, 25 July 1826 (ibid., p. 416).
[19] Ibid.
[20] Hill to Peel, 2 Nov. 1826 (ibid., p. 424).

of troops to Portugal towards the end of the year.[21] In considering possible legal action against the Catholic Association, Goulburn wrote, 'The main objection to forbearance which the law officers have urged is the imputation of dealing unfairly by the Orange societies, which the Act [of 1825] has effectually suppressed, while the Catholic Association has continued in full force. I do not give much weight to this objection, because I have never considered the suppression of the different societies as resting at all upon the same grounds.' He could see no grounds for putting down the Catholic Association which had not existed in January 1826 and was of the opinion that the societies were losing influence. Suppression could not, he believed, curtail the influence of the priesthood which he considered to be the most dangerous aspect of the current crisis. He added that the viceroy and attorney-general were equally opposed to prosecution.[22]

In the new year Orangemen derived some satisfaction from the defeat of the new catholic relief bill in the house of commons and by the duke of Cumberland consenting to become grand master of the British movement. The office had been left vacant after the duke of York had been forced to resign in 1821, and it was offered to Cumberland on his elder brother's death. However, the coming of the Canning administration and the continued quiet of the Orangemen induced O'Connell to write to the knight of Kerry that 'the Orange faction is already powerless from mere apprehension of losing office',[23] and insisted that if Lamb, afterwards Lord Melbourne, the new chief secretary, would cooperate, he could make the 'Orange faction in the Dublin Corporation crumble like a rope of sand'.[24] The new ministry, however, continued the practice of maintaining the balance between 'protestant' and 'catholic' in office. Joy, a protestant, was made attorney-general and two Orangemen—Gregory and Manners—were permitted to retain office. The Orangemen

---

[21] Peel to Wellesley, 1 July 1826 (ibid., p. 414); Peel to Goulburn, 20 Oct. 1826 (ibid., p. 420); Goulburn to Peel, 31 Oct. 1826 (ibid., p. 421); Goulburn to Peel, 11 Dec. 1826 (ibid., p. 427).

[22] Goulburn to Peel, 17 Dec. 1826 (Peel, *Private papers*, i. 429).

[23] O'Connell to knight of Kerry, 16 May 1827 (O'Connell, *Correspondence*, ii. 141).

[24] O'Connell to knight of Kerry, 28 May, 24 June 1827 (ibid., ii. 143).

had little to fear from such an arrangement and, with the return of Wellington and Peel to office early in 1828, might well have considered the government in safe hands.[25]

In effect, however, the equilibrium on which the policy of postponing the catholic question was based had been destroyed. With the continual shifts in the cabinet, the government lacked the stability of the Liverpool administration and the act of 1825, by effectively suppressing the Orange lodges, had removed the only possible counter-weight to O'Connell's agitation. As the act was to expire in 1828, the new viceroy, Anglesey, Lamb, the new chief secretary, and Peel considered the possibility of a new act to suppress the Catholic Association.[26] Lamb thought it best to let the act expire 'leaving the Roman Catholic Association, Orange Lodges, &c., &c., to the ordinary course of the law'.[27] This view was accepted by Anglesey[28] and concurred in by Peel.[29] It meant, in practice, that the government would accept the risk of allowing the Orangemen to reconstruct the grand lodge.

This decision had barely been reached when the precarious protestant majority was lost as a new catholic relief bill passed the commons. Although it was evident that the lords would reject the bill, a pro-catholic majority in the commons placed new obstacles in the way of repressive legislation in Ireland. In April the resignation of Lamb, Huskisson, and several others further weakened the government, and the selection of Vesey Fitzgerald as the president of the board of trade made necessary a by-election in county Clare which provided O'Connell with the occasion for a decisive demonstration of his power. There is some evidence that even without the stimulus of the Clare election an Orange revival was under way. In April petitions signed by protestants of Cavan were presented to parliament by the Orange member, Henry Maxwell.[30] In March Anglesey mentioned a projected visit of Sir Harcourt Lees to the Orange-

---

[25] *Annual Register*, London, 1828, lxx. 144.
[26] Peel memorandum 31 Mar. 1828 (Peel, *Memoirs*, i. 29); Lamb to Peel, 29 Mar. 1828 (ibid., pp. 24-5).
[27] Lamb to Peel, 29 Mar. 1828 (ibid., i. 28).
[28] Anglesey to Peel, 12 Apr. 1828 (ibid., i. 40-4).
[29] Peel to Anglesey, 1 May 1828 (ibid., i. 54).
[30] *Hansard 2*, xviii. 1520.

men in the north, and on the eve of the election he wrote, 'The Orangemen in the North are getting violent; Sir H. Lees has promised to keep them quiet'.[31] However, the Clare election was undoubtedly the principal cause of an Orange revival which continued, as far as Ireland was concerned, well after the granting of catholic emancipation in 1829.

Although O'Connell had clearly demonstrated his strength in 1826, his victory in 1828 appears to have taken both the Castle and the Clare gentry off guard. It is unlikely that there were many Orangemen in the area, and if there were, Fitzgerald, who counted heavily on his record as a friend of the catholics, would hardly have tolerated the slightest demonstration of Orange feeling. O'Connell, on his part, sensed the weakness of the Wellington government and did not look upon Lord Anglesey as a determined enemy or seriously consider the possibility that government would accept an alliance with the Orangemen.[32] There can be little doubt that the Clare election made the existing system of government impossible. 'I have polled all the gentry and all the fifty-pound freeholders—the gentry to a man,' wrote Vesey Fitzgerald, 'all the great interests broke down, and the desertion has been universal'.[33] Peel and most members of the government understood that no protestant candidate was likely to contest another southern election under more favourable circumstances than Vesey Fitzgerald. The cabinet believed that the 'catholic' majority in the commons excluded the possibility of disenfranchising the forty-shilling freeholders without granting catholic relief. There were even doubts in the minds of Anglesey and Peel about the stability of the Irish garrison which had so many catholics in its ranks.[34] In face of these circumstances, the viceroy and Peel were driven by degrees to the conclusion that catholic emancipation had to be accepted.

The Orangemen's one hope was to make an impressive

---

[31] Anglesey to Peel, 31 Mar. 1828 (Peel, *Memoirs*, i. 34); Anglesey to Peel, 21 June 1828 (*Hansard 2*, xxi. 994).

[32] Grenville to Buckingham, 25 Feb. 1828 (Lord Buckingham, *Memoirs of the court of George IV*, ii. 368); Greville, *Memoirs*, i. 157; P.R.O.N.I., Anglesey MSS 619/I/2.

[33] Vesey Fitzgerald to Peel, 5 July 1828 (Peel, *Memoirs*, i. 113).

[34] Anglesey to Peel, 26 July 1828 (ibid., i. 164).

demonstration of force while this decision was still in the balance. A protestant reaction was expected at the Castle where July 12 was anticipated with some anxiety.[35] Gregory, the undersecretary wrote, 'I fear nothing will prevent the Orangemen of the North from walking in procession on the 12th of July. The persons of rank who formerly had influence over them have lost it, and they are in the hands of inferior men, who are as violent as the lowest of their order'.[36] In spite of what was at stake, July 12 passed with comparatively little violence. There were demonstrations in the north and some clashes, while in Dublin the Castle guard turned out with Orange lilies which were promptly confiscated.[37] The absence of more general outburst on 12 July 1828 can, perhaps, be explained by the fact that the Clare election did not, in the manner of the Defenders of 1795, pose a direct threat to the protestant peasants in the border counties. Although they were disturbed by O'Connell's success, they were prepared to await the initiative of the gentry and placemen whose interests were more immediately threatened. The gentlemen Orangemen, on their part, had to create an organization which would unite the widest possible protestant sentiment and which was sufficiently respectable to avoid being suppressed as a secret society. This required time, and it was not until the middle of August that the protestant reaction which Anglesey had anticipated got under way.[38]

The agencies created by the Orangemen, called Brunswick clubs, were modelled on the Liberal clubs established by O'Connell prior to the Clare election. They were recruited from among former Orangemen, and listed among their patrons a substantial number of Orange peers, headed by the earl of Enniskillen. The local Brunswick clubs were drawn mostly from the lower classes, but dominated by parliamentarians, lawyers, and clergy of the established church. At the founding

---

[35] Anglesey to Peel, 30 June 1828 (Peel, *Memoirs*, i. 136-7).

[36] Gregory to Peel, 27 June 1828 (ibid., i. 110).

[37] Lord F. Leveson-Gower to Anglesey, 16 July 1838 (P.R.O.N.I., Anglesey MSS 619/X/112); Memo of conversation between O'Connell and Anglesey, 28 July 1828 (ibid., 619/I/2); Anglesey to Peel, 20 July 1828 (Peel, *Memoirs*, i. 158).

[38] Memo of conversation between O'Connell and Anglesey, 28 July 1828 (P.R.O.N.I., Anglesey MSS 619/I/2); see also *Hansard 2*, xxi. 997-8.

banquet, attended by 400, which was held on August 14 in honour of the Dublin member of parliament, George Moore, the usual Orange toasts were offered and the health of the duke of Cumberland pledged, but not in his capacity of Orange grand master.[39] There were, however, no oaths, signs or passwords, no atmosphere of mystery to appeal to the imagination, and no association was claimed with the Diamond system. It had little attraction for the peasantry, and like the Benevolent Society was regarded with suspicion by the older Orangemen among the Armagh gentry. Blacker remarked that 'the old political game of ins and outs was played too glaringly. Attempts were made to organize Brunswick Clubs throughout the country, but the people like myself, being satisfied with the Orange Institution, did not enter into the views of those great ones who never joined it, and now, as it appears, were endeavouring to supersede it'.[40]

In imitation of O'Connell's association, the Brunswick clubs collected protestant rent, and considered but never put into effect measures to counteract the catholic tenants' refusal to take leases under Orange landlords.[41] However, the objective of the clubs was to impress the British government with the hazards of granting catholic emancipation, and the principal activity of the Brunswickers was to prepare petitions and hold public meetings. The movement spread rapidly through Ulster in the autumn in a manner which recalls the initial growth of the volunteers in 1778 and the raising of the yeomanry in 1796, 108 clubs being founded in twelve weeks.[42] In November 1828 Leslie Foster wrote that among the protestants of Ireland 'almost all the peasantry, the farmers, and mechanics belong, or are on the eve of belonging, to the Brunswickers. The majority of the upper and middle ranks do not belong to them, but wish them all success.'[43]

[39] Brunswick Club MSS 5017 in N.L.I., see press clipping notice of the founding of the Brunswick Constitution Club, 15 Aug. 1828; see also Sibbett, *Orangeism*, ii. 306.
[40] A.M., Blacker MSS vi. 229.
[41] Evidence of Lord Gosford, *Rep. on Orange lodges I*, H.C. 1835 [377], xv. 285; Evidence of W. Blacker, ibid., [476], xvi. 220; Greville, *Memoirs*, i. 148.
[42] N.L.I., Brunswick Club MSS 5017, see press clippings; Sibbett, *Orangeism*, ii. 307.
[43] Foster to Vesey Fitzgerald, 14 Nov. 1828 (Peel, *Memoirs*, i. 266).

Yet in spite of this remarkable growth, the efforts of the Brunswick clubs to adopt O'Connell's methods could only be effective in the hands of a majority. 'It is only', wrote Anglesey, 'in that part of the country where, from their numbers, they are in no danger from the machinations of the Catholics, that the Protestants unite for mutual protection'.[44] He further expressed fears that the Brunswickers' power in the north would provoke reprisals against protestants in the south. Although neither the viceroy nor Peel was inclined to give the Brunswick clubs equal weight with the Catholic Association, O'Connell was worried about their influence in government circles. 'The Orange faction', he wrote, 'is endeavouring to beard the government. Their ostentatious display of peerage in the Brunswick Clubs is made in order to terrify the government of Lord Anglesey. It would be idle to conceal from ourselves that the great enemy of the people of Ireland is his Majesty; the Saurins and Lefroys are struggling to give their friends in the ministry and the men near the Throne a notion that their party is strong enough in Ireland to continue misgovernment with impunity'.[45]

O'Connell felt the necessity of demonstrating the weakness of the Brunswick movement by adopting a project that was ideally designed to bring out in full force the most powerful and irreconcilable element of Orangeism—the Ulster peasantry, and at the same time drive the government towards the repressive policies from which he had most to fear. He had created a semi-military order along masonic lines—known as the 'Liberators'—to protect tenants from landlord reprisals. Although not organized as an armed body, many Liberators had weapons and were clearly an agency through which O'Connell's Association could be converted into an instrument of physical force. O'Connell commissioned the Belfast journalist, John Lawless, an old foe of Orangeism, to lead his legions into the northern counties in what was represented as a non-violent pilgrimage in which thousands of disciplined catholics from the south would parade through Ulster, holding political meetings attended by the catholic minority. O'Connell wrote, 'The mission of Mr Lawless is one of the greatest importance. Lawless may be arrested, but the compensation would outweigh

[44] Anglesey to Peel, 2 Oct. 1828 (Peel, *Memoirs*, i. 234).
[45] O'Connell, *Correspondence*, ii. 164.

the insolence offered. He will organize the collection of Catholic rent in as many parishes as possible; abolish secret societies, and soothe and allay irritation caused by the orgies of the Orangemen'.[46]

It is obvious O'Connell, in adopting this project which was to place his movement in jeopardy, had no comprehension of the latent strength of Orangeism. The viceroy wrote Peel:

It seems agreed on all sides that public feeling was never at so high a pitch... The organization of the Catholics is complete. They carry banners. They march by word of command in good order, but they commit no outrage, and I discourage interference or any display both of the military and the constabulary... The Brunswickers are rivalling the Association in violence and in rent... I use the term 'Brunswickers' and 'agitators' as the common designation of the two extreme opposing parties... the 'Brunswicker' establishment is not very flattering to the king, his ministers, or to the army, since it deems it necessary to take the whole under its especial protection... The catholics are persuaded that the Brunswickers will bring on collision.[47]

As O'Connell's forces approached Ulster, the Orangemen gathered in armed bands. Lawless tried to frighten them by claiming a following of tens of thousands,[48] but he could hardly have assembled a force much stronger than 10,000 in one place. At Drogheda, his carriage was drawn through the town in triumph, but once in Orange territory his efforts collapsed. Outside Ballybay, two of his followers were killed, and the concentration of armed Orangemen under the direction of innkeeper Sam Gray dissuaded him from marching into town.[49] Yet he managed to evade serious trouble until September 30 when he attempted to march into the city of Armagh. As soon as his intention became known, Orangemen, armed with yeomanry muskets, gathered in the vicinity of the city while the military commander, General Thornton, stood by, helpless to intervene. 'There was no adequate military force at hand',

[46] O'Connell to Edward Dwyer, 22 Aug. 1828 (O'Connell, *Correspondence*, ii. 162).

[47] Anglesey to Peel, 8 Sept. 1828 (*Hansard 2*, xxi. 998–9).

[48] Wellington to Anglesey, 28 Sept. 1828 (P.R.O.N.I., Anglesey MSS 619/II/16).

[49] *Annual Register*, London, 1828, lxx. 138; see also Evidence of Captain Duff, *Rep. on Orange lodges III*, H.C. 1835 [476], xvi. 145.

Orange Resistance to Catholic Emancipation, 1825–9

General Thornton wrote to the chief secretary on September 28. 'Its total amount at the three posts of Armagh, Monaghan and Clones... only amounted to about one hundred rank and file'.[50] Peel lamented General Thornton's predicament 'as an officer of the King's troops being called to enter into negotiations with a body of armed men on one hand and a mischievous demagogue on the other'.[51] On October 2 the viceroy wrote, 'If the leaders of the Brunswickers would be prevailed on to set their faces against the assembling and the organization of Protestants... if they would trust to the power of the government... instead of attempting to dictate to all, then this unhappy country might hope for comparative peace'.[52]

The initiative behind the gathering of the Orange bands came from below, and it may be doubted that any of the Orange gentry could have prevailed upon innkeepers like Sam Gray to restrain their followers to the extent of permitting Lawless to march unopposed through Ulster. Nor, in view of the weakness of the local military, had the Orangemen any reason to put confidence in the government. There was a general reaction against the Catholic Association in Ulster, and even Lord Gosford presided over a meeting of Armagh magistrates who passed a resolution declaring Lawless a menace to peace. Wellington urged Anglesey to arrest Lawless or hold him to bail. 'I hope the government will have the means of proving to all that they are watching over the public peace', Wellington wrote, 'and that their power is too strong for those who make audacious attempts to intimidate on the one hand and to disturb the public peace on the other'.[53] The opposition of the Orangemen at Armagh put an end to the enterprise of Lawless. O'Connell had no desire to risk a passage of arms with Orange bands, who were simply yeomen out of uniform. His numerous but inadequately armed and undisciplined army would have suffered the fate of the United Irish in '98. Public opinion in Britain would have forced a Castle intervention which would have destroyed the patient work of the Catholic Association.

[50] Thornton to chief secretary, 28 Sept. 1828 (*Hansard* 2, xx. 189).
[51] Peel to Anglesey, 27 Sept. 1828 (P.R.O.N.I., Anglesey MSS 619/V/45).
[52] Anglesey to Peel, 2 Oct. 1828 (*Hansard* 2, xxi. 999).
[53] Wellington to Anglesey, 28 Sept. 1828 (P.R.O.N.I., Anglesey MSS 619/II/16); see also 619/II/201 and 619/II/17.

In fact, the indignation in Great Britain against O'Connell[54] gave the Orangemen an unique opportunity to show their influence. Even Wellington commented, 'I am not surprised at the Protestants of Ireland associating in defence of their lives and property'.[55] Had the Orangemen at this point found a demagogue of genius it is possible that the strength of their own revival in combination with the alarm that Lawless caused in Britain might have been used to force a wavering government to suppress the Catholic Association without granting emancipation. Yet no such leader arose from their own ranks or could be found in the ultra tory camp, and when O'Connell grasped the danger of the situation and prudently called off the campaign, the opportunity passed, and with it the only chance of the Irish Orangemen forcing Wellington and Peel to fall back on a policy of repression.

Yet if the fight in Ireland had been lost, the British Orangemen were still determined to use their influence in the lords and with the British public to persuade the king to resist the advice of his ministers. The minutes of a meeting[56] held at the residence of Lord Kenyon in June 1828, with the duke of Cumberland in the chair, gives an indication of the state of the British movement. The marquess of Chandos, the son of the duke of Buckingham, and Ogle Moore, a member of parliament, were initiated as Orangemen; four new warrants were issued, one member suspended, and a resolution of thanks tendered to Lord Kenyon. Cumberland's patronage of the movement was, undoubtedly, an attraction, and it is probable that the lodges attracted some members on their merits as social clubs and benevolent societies. However, the number of British lodges at no time exceeded 300,[57] of which about thirty were military. The minimum number of men in a lodge meeting under a warrant was five and the maximum seldom exceeded thirty.[58] It is, therefore, unlikely there were more than 6,000 Orangemen in the 270 civilian lodges meeting in public houses in London,

[54] *Hansard 2*, xxi. 999.
[55] Wellington to Anglesey, 30 Sept. 1828 (P.R.O.N.I., Anglesey MSS 619/II/18).
[56] *Rep. on Orange lodges IV*, H.C. 1835 [605], xvii. app. 15, 117.
[57] Evidence of Fairman, *Rep. on Orange lodges IV*, H.C. 1835 [605], xvii. 23; Evidence of Chetwoode, ibid., xvii. 9; see also ibid., app. 20, p. 145.
[58] See app. B. and C, v, vi, vii.

the Midlands and the North.[59] As the London lodges numbered about fifteen,[60] there were probably less than 500 Orangemen in the capital. However, by an unintentional collusion between Orangemen, anxious to magnify their strength, and their enemies interested in presenting them as a menace, a figure of 150,000 was agreed upon,[61] and generally accepted in contemporary debates and the press as the actual strength of the movement at this time. It is evident that these workingmen's clubs, scattered about urban and industrial areas of Britain, provided indifferent material for the creation of a national protestant movement to meet the threat posed by the Clare election. The Orange tradition had a limited appeal in Britain, and the elaborate procedure necessary to make an Orangeman did not lend itself to hasty expansion.

As in Ireland, Brunswick clubs were formed as a means of gathering the widest possible protestant support, but there were not enough Orangemen in Britain to provide a firm base for the Brunswick movement. While it is possible that in London, Lancashire, and Manchester, where lodges were well established, Orangemen helped to organize Brunswick clubs, the creation of such societies in Britain was largely the work of Orange peers such as Lord Kenyon, the marquess of Chandos, the earl of Winchelsea, and their ultra tory allies. Great meetings were held throughout the country, of which one, reported to have numbered 20,000[62] was held 6 September 1828 at Newton Abbey, Kent, attended by the earl of Winchelsea, Sir E. Knatchbull, Sir John Brundes, a member of parliament, Lord Teynham, Colonel Wingfield-Stratford and Lord Bexley. None of these prominent tories was, at the time, a member of the grand lodge, and there does not seem to have been an Orange movement in Kent. Large Brunswick club meetings were also held in Buckinghamshire on the initiative of the recently-created Orangeman, the marquess of Chandos.

Kenyon, it appears, intended the clubs to be the nucleus of a new party to which the ultras could give their whole support. This party, as he envisaged it, would not merely oppose further concessions to catholics, but would, in effect, repeal the Irish catholic relief act of 1793. In a letter to the Brunswick clubs he

[59] See app. C, vi-vii. [60] Ibid.
[61] *Hansard 3*, xxxi. 783. [62] *Annual Register*, London, 1828, lxx. 144.

declared, 'Looking at Ireland and reflecting back to what has passed since 1793, and calling to mind especially the last general election, and the late election for Clare, it is quite evident that the grant of the elective franchise to the Papists is the cause of all the mischievous influence which the Catholic Association and Papist priests possess over the minds of the Papists'. Kenyon went on, 'I cannot but be well aware that disturbances may be produced by so strong an act. Still, I venture to call on the Protestants of the empire to petition, that the threatening Papist millions in Ireland be deprived of a franchise which is not possessed by the quiet, the loyal Papists of Great Britain'.[63] Similar but more cautiously worded sentiments were expressed by Leslie Foster.[64]

However, Kenyon's hope of founding a new party or rallying tories around the Orange leaders had a limited attraction when the government appeared to be in 'safe' hands.[65] Brunswickers could not convincingly present themselves as agents of Wellington or Peel, or alternatively, denounce the Hero of Waterloo and Orange Peel as enemies of the protestant establishment. Although they were uneasy about the government attitude, they had no proof of the decisions taken after the Clare election, while Cumberland hesitated to accept the fact of Wellington's conversion until told by the duke himself.[66] Peel's brother-in-law, George Dawson, had outraged 'protestant' sentiment by referring during the celebration of the siege of Derry to the 'gallant foe outside the gates',[67] and Anglesey had irritated the duke of Cumberland by granting O'Connell an interview.[68] More alarming was the use O'Connell made of a non-committal letter Wellington had written to the catholic primate of Ireland.[69] In December, however, when the viceroy, commenting on Wellington's letter, expressed his conviction that catholic

---

[63] Sibbett, *Orangeism*, ii. 310.
[64] Foster to Vesey Fitzgerald, 14 Nov. 1828 (Peel, *Memoirs*, i. 265).
[65] *Annual Register*, London, 1828, lxx. 144.
[66] Willis, *Ernest Augustus*, pp. 175–8.
[67] Aspinall, *Correspondence of George IV*, iii. 437–8; see also Buckingham, *Memoirs of the court of George IV*, ii. 380; A.M., Blacker MSS vi. 229.
[68] Aspinall, *Correspondence of George IV*, iii. 453.
[69] Cumberland to the king, 10 Jan. 1829 (Aspinall, *Correspondence of George IV*, iii. 451).

Orange Resistance to Catholic Emancipation, 1825-9

emancipation was desirable,[70] he was dismissed and replaced by the duke of Northumberland.[71] This seemed reassuring to the ultras and Orangemen who were reluctant to attack Wellington. Actually, there were considerable differences between the viceroy and the duke of Wellington[72] as to how the catholic question should be handled, but Anglesey's dismissal had been made as a concession to the king, and the shades of difference among Peel, Anglesey, and Wellington were of less importance than their acceptance of the necessity of granting emancipation. The problem of the ministers was to win over the king, and the most forceful argument that could be used was the impossibility of finding an effective protestant leader to replace Peel in the commons. On the eve of the throne speech, the king gave way, and with the opening of the parliament of 1829, the Orangemen and ultras were confronted with the announcement of the ministers' intentions.

In face of this, the Orange peers undertook a desperate last-minute resistance, centred around the duke of Cumberland. 'The rage and despair of the Orangemen is very amusing',[73] Greville wrote after the throne speech, but they were not without resources. The king was still wavering on the subject, and if he could be persuaded to call a general election, they might appeal to the country. Although O'Connell could not be voted out of existence, nor an adequate protestant leader in the commons be voted into being, the apparent strength of protestant feeling in the country indicated a victory for Brunswick principles. Everything depended upon the king, and Wellington, fearing the influence of Cumberland, had endeavoured to keep him in Germany.[74] Cumberland returned, however, and was greeted by cheering crowds as he rode towards London.[75] Wellington, as the apostate from protestant principles and the man most likely to influence the king, became the principal target for ultra attacks. So insulting did Wellington consider

---

[70] Anglesey to Dr Curtis, 23 Dec. 1828 (*Annual Register*, London, 1828, lxx. 150).
[71] Wellington to Anglesey, 28 Dec. 1828 (*Hansard 2*, xxi. 1015).
[72] Same to same, 11 Nov. 1828 (P.R.O.N.I., Anglesey MSS 619/II/22).
[73] Greville, *Memoirs*, i. 167, entry 4 Feb. 1829.
[74] Wellington to Knighton, 26 Feb. 1829 (Aspinall, *Correspondence of George IV*, iii. 454).
[75] Willis, *Ernest Augustus*, p. 176.

remarks made by Lord Winchelsea that the matter was settled by a duel.[76] The work of plebeian Orangemen certainly contributed to the deluge of protestant petitions received by the government, but the only factor likely to move the king was the personal influence of the duke of Cumberland. Greville commented that the king 'gives the ministers uneasiness from time to time. The Duke of Cumberland has been tampering with him through the agency of Lord Farnham [an Orangeman]; great attempts have been made to induce him to throw obstacles in the way of the measure'.[77] During the debate in the lords, Cumberland attacked Wellington, but his speech was less pointed than Kenyon's, who asked the prime minister, why, in a question so important as this, he did not advise the king to hold an election. Although Lord Eldon continued to hope that the king would veto the bill, the influence of the ministers proved decisive and the measure became law in April.

[76] Wellington to Buckingham, 21 Apr. 1829 (Buckingham, *Memoirs of the court of George IV*, ii. 397).
[77] Greville, *Memoirs*, i. 182, entry 1 Mar. 1829.

X

REPEAL, PARLIAMENTARY REFORM, AND THE TITHE WAR, 1830-4

CATHOLIC EMANCIPATION, followed as it was by the return of the catholic peasantry to Defender methods, served as a spur to the Orange revival which began with the Clare election. Thrown back on their own resources, the Orangemen held July 12 processions amid violence that tried the patience of the Wellington government during its last period in office. However, with the advent of the Grey ministry, the seasonal and relatively minor disorders provoked by the Orangemen were overshadowed by the tithe war[1] and O'Connell's agitation for repeal.[2] For a time, Melbourne showed an inclination to tolerate the lodges,[3] but the Orangemen's collaboration with the tories in opposing the reform bill of 1832 and their more vigorous opposition to church disestablishment soon alienated the whig ministry. Although there were some defections from

---

[1] Rev. J. W. Stokes to Melbourne, 23 Apr. 1832 (P.R.O.N.I., Anglesey MSS 619/VI/51).

[2] Melbourne to Anglesey, 16 Dec. 1830 (ibid., 619/VI/6); see also ibid., 619/IV/1,80; *Hansard 3*, xv. 733.

[3] Melbourne to Anglesey, 22 Dec. 1830 (P.R.O.N.I., Anglesey MSS 619/VI/7); same to same, 29 Dec. 1830 (ibid., 619/VI/12).

the ranks on the question of repeal of the union[4] and parliamentary reform,[5] the Orange movement as a whole gained strength during this period.

While victory dissolved the alliance between catholic peasants and their upper and middle class co-religionists, defeat drove the plebeian and gentlemen Orangemen into closer association. The lapse of the act of 1825 enabled Orangemen to reconstitute the grand lodge of Ireland in the autumn of 1828. Eustace Chetwoode, the British grand secretary, visited Ireland, and at a meeting on September 15 gave the English signs and passwords to Irish Orangemen as an initial step towards formal revival of the old form of the Irish movement.[6] Accompanied by Reverend John Graham, Chetwoode then went north, travelling through Ulster and visiting the old Orange centres where the organization was revived, bringing into prominence again the Verners, Blackers, and Atkinsons who had regarded the Loyal and Benevolent Society and the Brunswick clubs with suspicion.[7] In November Chetwoode returned to Dublin to re-establish the grand lodge which was henceforth linked to the British grand lodge through the duke of Cumberland who, as head of both lodges, was given the title of imperial grand master. Sir Harcourt Lees protested against his society being superseded and complained that the movement was now divided.[8] However, as the earl of Enniskillen presided over the Dublin meeting and many of the prominent patrons of the Benevolent Society attended, it is evident that Lees had very little influence. Under the new system, the leadership of the Irish lodges was divided among three deputy grand masters—the earl of Enniskillen representing the aristocratic patrons of the movement, Colonel William Verner, the Armagh gentry, and Robert Hedges Eyre, of county Cork, who probably represented the Orangemen of the south. This division of the

---

[4] *Hansard 3*, i. 586; Melbourne to Anglesey, 16 Dec. 1830 (P.R.O.N.I., Anglesey MSS 619/VI/3); *Rep. on Orange lodges I*, H.C. 1835 [377], xv. app. 6, pp. 76–7.

[5] *Hansard 3*, iii. 825.

[6] Rules of the Orange society in *Rep. on Orange lodges I*, H.C. 1835 [377], xv. app. 3, pp. 20–4.

[7] A.M., Blacker MSS, vi. 229.

[8] P.R.O.N.I., Anglesey MSS 619/VIII/23.

office of deputy grand master had been fore-shadowed by Verner's demand in 1824 for a provincial grand lodge of Ulster, and seems to have reflected the reluctance of the Orangemen in the border counties to place themselves completely under the authority of the aristocratic and political Orangemen. However, the earl of Enniskillen, as confidant of the duke of Cumberland, could, if necessary, invoke the authority of the imperial grand master in cases of serious difference. The problem of the Brunswick clubs was settled by a decision that 'the secretaries of county, district, and primary lodges be directed to co-operate with officers of the different Brunswick Clubs to secure uniformity in the text of their petitions and resolutions against Roman Catholic emancipation'.[9] The restoration of the grand lodge of Ireland had, in most essentials, made the Brunswick clubs redundant, as they do not appear to have attracted many who were not willing to become Orangemen. But as long as catholic emancipation remained an issue, it was not expedient to let the clubs die.

In the grand committee of the new Irish grand lodge, fifteen of the twenty-five members were clergymen of the established church.[10] This was a new development in Orangeism, clearly the result of an anticipated attack on the tithe and church establishment. Since the days when Reverend Philip Johnson had organized Orange lodges on the estate of the marquess of Hertford, clergymen had taken part in the movement, but had never been so prominent on the grand committee. This raised again the problem of presbyterians and dissenters among the Orangemen. The address passed by the grand lodge declared that 'we associate... as supporters of the true religion by law established in this United Kingdom... to support by every lawful means, the religious and civil establishment', but added 'this is exclusively a Protestant Association, yet, detesting an intolerant spirit, it admits no persons into its brotherhood who are not well-known to be incapable of persecuting... any one on account of his religious opinions... We recognize no other exclusiveness; our Institution receives, nay, solicits, into its circles, every man whose religion and character can stand these

---

[9] Rules of the Orange society, 1828, in *Rep. on Orange lodges I*, H.C. 1835 [377], xv. app. 6, p. 73.

[10] Sibbett, *Orangeism*, ii. 329.

tests.'[11] This last sentence is clearly a recognition of the dissenters' contribution to the movement. However, in spite of the existence of dissenters' support of Orangeism, no dissenting clergy or dissenters of prominence appear in the grand lodge or in the leadership of the movement—the tithes could hardly have been popular with dissenters, nor for that matter, with episcopalian peasants.[12] Yet, the Orange peasants who evaded the tithe themselves, when they could, had every reason to fear the combination of catholics organized to oppose it, and appear to have accepted the necessity of giving formal support to all aspects of church establishment as a surviving symbol of protestant ascendancy.

In the eyes of plebeian Orangemen, however, the most important assertion of the ascendancy was by way of the July 12 processions. The triumph of catholic emancipation doubtless undermined the confidence of the Orange peasants in the power of resolutions and petitions or the influence of their leaders in the Brunswick clubs and the grand lodge, while the success of their opposition against Lawless had enhanced their self-confidence. It was natural that they should feel the necessity of making it clear to the catholics of Ulster that the act of 1829 had not broken the spirit of Orangeism. Moreover, the peasants, having neither government jobs nor the expectation of them, had little to risk by processions except the momentary displeasure of the authorities. Almost any year's processions can be taken as an index of the vitality of the movement,[13] as they were normally the occasion for attacks on the lodges in parliament and the press as well as physical assaults on the part of Ribbonmen. The Orange gentry in the border counties, such as the Blackers, Atkinsons, and Verners were convinced of the necessity of tolerating processions, but gave formal support to government efforts to put them down. However, their frequent but ineffectual remonstrances with the

[11] Rules of the Orange society in *Rep. on Orange lodges I*, H.C. 1835 [377] xv. app. 3, pp. 20-4.
[12] Melbourne to Anglesey, 16 Dec. 1830 (P.R.O.N.I., Anglesey MSS 619/VI/3).
[13] Dawson to Sir George Hill, 23 July 1829 (P.R.O.N.I., DOD 642/210); Evidence of Kernan, in *Rep. on Orange lodges III*, H.C. 1835 [476], xvi. 84-9, 98-9; Sibbett, *Orangeism*, ii. 344-9.

plebeian Orangemen on the subject of processions and violence appear to have had no other effect than relieving the Ulster leaders of legal responsibility for the acts of ordinary Orangemen.[14] On the other hand, aristocratic and political Orangemen who had much to lose by government disfavour were worried about the consequences of processions and violence generally. Nearly every government office that mattered was still filled by protestants—many of them Orangemen—or, in the view of the lodges, potential Orangemen. Disorders during processions, like the questionable legality of the Orange oath, had been advanced by O'Connell and the radicals as grounds for the dissolution of the Order and for the dismissal of Orangemen from public office. Moreover, the precedent of the forced resignation of the duke of York in 1821 must have suggested to the duke of Cumberland the possibility that he might be subjected to a similar humiliation if the lodges became involved in serious disorders. Orangemen in office had in the past evaded and defied government restrictions on Orange celebrations, but the failure of their demonstration against Wellesley seems to have made them cautious, and where they dominated the lodges, as in Dublin, there were no processions.

In the spring and summer of 1829 the full force of the grand master's influence was used to discourage processions on July 12. In May Cumberland wrote to the earl of Enniskillen, probably at his special request:

Caution and vigilance are at the present crisis specially requisite for the prosperity and safety of our cause, particularly in respect of our public processions which, I think, ought by all means to be avoided . . . as leading, or at least, being interpreted to lead, to an infraction of the law, and a breach of the public peace, which . . . would probably be followed up by some legislative measure ruinous to the Orange Institution. I assure you, I feel an intense anxiety on this subject.[15]

In spite of this appeal from Cumberland, which was undoubtedly supported by Enniskillen and probably by Orangemen in office generally, the lodges were content to issue an equivocal

---

[14] A.M., Blacker MSS vi. 365.
[15] Duke of Cumberland to Enniskillen, 12 May 1829 in *Rep. on Orange lodges IV*, H.C. 1835 [605], xvii. app. 2, p. 8.

statement that reflected the influence of the Verners and Blackers and the pressure of plebeian Orangemen. The statement read, 'Of the recommendation contained in the letter of our illustrious Grand Master, the Committee do not conceive it necessary to say much. They merely declare their opinion, that the utmost vigilance and caution are required to prevent the strength of Protestant Ireland from being broken and dispersed.' The statement went on, 'They conceive the same motive which induced the destruction of the Constitution of 1688, in the late Bill passed by Parliament, exists still in undiminished force, and will urge the enemies of Protestantism to avail themselves of events, likely to arise from the processions on the 12th of July, to crush the last supporters of Protestant loyalty in this country—the Orangemen'.[16] This counsel, signed by Enniskillen, Verner, and twenty others could not, as an Orange historian put it 'be interpreted as a command'.[17] It was evidently designed to relieve the grand lodge of responsibility for the processions without putting the Orangemen who marched on the twelfth in the position of defying its authority.

The northern Orangemen, on their part, were determined to show by vigorous celebrations of the Boyne that if catholic disabilities were no longer a matter of law, they were still to be a matter of fact. In their turn, the catholics appear to have feared that the assembly of large numbers of protestants would be accompanied by new outbreaks of 'wrecking', and hoped that the act of 1829 would result in the government and gentry taking their part in future encounters with the Orangemen. They consequently gathered in Defender-like bands at various points in the countryside amid rumours of impending Orange outrage, and announced their intention of putting down 'treasonable Orangemen'.[18] Over twenty Orange processions were held on Monday, 13 July 1829, in which possibly 50,000 Orangemen marched before crowds of several times that number. Of these, the largest were at Portadown, Ballybay, and Caledon, while the Belfast parade was relatively small, and there was no parade in Derry, probably as a result of the influence of George Dawson, the local member of parliament.

[16] Sibbett, *Orangeism*, ii. 337.   [17] Ibid., ii. 338.
[18] Peel to Wellington, 27 July 1829 (Peel, *Private papers*, ii. 117–8).

Disorders arising from the demonstrations were reported in Armagh, Newry, Belfast, and Strabane, which resulted in considerable bodily injury and a few deaths.[19] More serious violence, however, came about in the countryside when Orange parties, returning from the processions, encountered catholic bands assembled as Ribbonmen. In Tyrone an Orange lodge led by Waterloo veteran Sergeant Bartley, numbering fourteen armed yeomen and six civilians accompanied by some women and children, was confronted by a large Ribbon band near Glenoe. After some efforts at negotiating, Bartley's party took refuge in a stone house and was subject to a foolhardy Ribbon assault during which two Orangemen and possibly forty Ribbonmen were killed.[20] In Fermanagh on the estates of the earl of Enniskillen, several groups of Ribbonmen hovered in the hills near an indoor celebration of the Boyne. At great personal risk, the earl attempted to induce his catholic tenants to disperse, but they evaded his efforts and attacked the Orangemen on their way home, killing three. The catholic solicitor, Randall Kernan, testified that the encounter took place after drunken Orangemen had attacked the catholics with fixed bayonets, and it is possible that in this instance it was the protestants who were provoked into an ill-advised attack against superior forces.[21] This incident was followed by several days of tension during which Ribbon bands assembled in the hills while protestant volunteers were organized to aid crown forces.

As a test of strength, the processions and disorders of 1829 were indecisive. The Orangemen had demonstrated their power in the older Orange centres, but the ability of the catholics to assemble in large bands of Ribbonmen in the countryside constituted a formidable challenge. Yet the real challenge posed by the disorders was to the government, but Peel was hardly less annoyed by the Orange processions than by the catholic efforts at opposition. In a letter to Wellington, he advocated 'proving by severe example that the Roman Catholic party was not to

[19] Dawson to Sir George Hill, 23 July 1829 (P.R.O.N.I., Hill papers DOD 642/210); Evidence of Hancock, *Rep. on Orange lodges III*, H.C. 1835 [476], xvi. 119.
[20] Sibbett, *Orangeism*, ii. 340.
[21] Evidence of Kernan, *Rep. on Orange lodges III*, H.C. 1835 [476], xvi. 84-5, 98-9.

undertake the task of suppressing Orange processions'.[22] The duke of Northumberland issued a viceregal proclamation on July 18 condemning processions. He did not name Orangemen, but it was obviously directed against them. Although Peel held the duke of Cumberland responsible for the disorders, he was restrained from action by Wellington who wrote, 'I entertain no doubt that the Duke of Cumberland is doing all the mischief in Ireland he can. The difficulty will be to prove a case of which we can take notice ... If we are not prepared to proceed to extremities, I am inclined to think that we ought not to notice the Duke's conduct at all'.[23]

The attitude of Wellington and Peel towards Cumberland must be considered in the context of the irritation caused by his opposition to catholic emancipation, his efforts to influence the king against the ministry, and, not least, his practice of referring to the prime minister as 'King Arthur'.[24] Cumberland's letter to the Irish Orangemen can hardly be interpreted as an encouragement of processions, but an address to the Orangemen on any matter of policy, on the part of the duke, in the view of Wellington and Peel constituted an intervention in Irish affairs which usurped the powers of the ministers. Matters were further complicated the following July 12 as a result of Cumberland's signature appearing on recently-issued Orange warrants. When an Orange party was halted by police who read to them the duke of Northumberland's proclamation against processions, the Orangemen, with a real or pretended belief in the precedence of the king's brother over the king's servants, waved their Orange warrants bearing the grand master's signature and shouted that 'the Duke of Cumberland was a greater duke than the Duke of Northumberland'.[25]

Precautions taken against July 12 riots in 1830 seemed to make the position of the government clear. Viceregal proclamations prohibiting processions were posted on churches and public buildings, while special circulars were sent to all Ulster magistrates, but the police and local garrisons were not adequate to prevent demonstrations, and they received indifferent sup-

---

[22] Peel to Wellington, 27 July 1829 (Peel, *Private papers*, ii. 120).
[23] Wellington to Peel, 24 July 1829 (ibid., ii. 118).
[24] Greville, *Memoirs*, i. 227, entry 24 July 1829.
[25] Evidence of J. S. Crawford, *Rep. on Orange lodges I*, H.C. 1835 [377], xv. 305.

Repeal, Parliamentary Reform, Tithe War, 1830–4

port from the magistrates. Parades were held in the usual Orange centres in about the same proportion as the previous year, in the course of which there were several encounters with police who were henceforth denounced as 'papist'. A few Orangemen were arrested but none punished.[26] As in 1829, the more serious violence resulted from clashes between Orangemen and Ribbonmen in the countryside, and the incident or series of incidents that took place around Maghera[27] in Londonderry illustrates the limitations of government efforts even when local authorities with military assistance acted with reasonable energy. As a precaution against anticipated trouble, one company of the 64th regiment was stationed at Maghera and another at Dawson Castle. In the course of the day, the troops marched about alternatively dispersing parties of Orangemen and Ribbonmen. When magistrates attempted to act without troops, they were caught between the cross-fire of the warring bands. Towards evening the military interrupted an armed encounter during which several catholic houses had been burned, and troops disarmed and arrested twenty-six or so Orangemen. The Orangemen were 'rescued' the next day in a courtroom riot, during which police were instructed by the magistrates not to resist. The Orangemen later appeared with the rescuers and some Ribbonmen at the Derry assizes where a few were sentenced to from eighteen months to two years hard labour while the rest were acquitted.[28] The effectiveness of these sentences may be judged from an incident in Armagh in November of the same year. On this occasion a party of Orangemen were beaten and their drums broken by the catholics of Maghery when an informal and amiable concert was dissolved into a fight by the playing of party tunes. When the Orangemen returned in force to Maghery to seek redress, they were halted for a while by Colonel William Verner, but his authority was insufficient to prevent them from wrecking the village.[29] Yet, if he feared the consequences of their violence,

---

[26] Sibbett, *Orangeism* (2nd ed.), ii. 65.
[27] *Rep. on Orange lodges III*, H.C. 1835 [476], xvi. app. 90–3.
[28] *Rep. on Orange lodges I*, H.C. 1835 [377], xv. app. 246–52; Sibbett, *Orangeism* (2nd ed.), ii. 67–8.
[29] Evidence of W. Verner, *Rep. on Orange lodges III*, H.C. 1835 [476], xvi. 254–8; Evidence of W. J. Hancock, ibid., pp. 119–21.

Colonel Verner apparently sympathized with their grievance as he was unable to identify any of the offenders in court, and efforts at prosecution broke down.[30]

These less than effective efforts to control Orangemen are not so much a reflection upon the intentions of the government as upon the limitations of its resources. The police and troops could not be everywhere at once, while magistrates offered indifferent co-operation and the normal procedure of courts could be neutralized by the refusal of witnesses to testify. The annual July 12 disturbances and periodic incidents, such as the sacking of Maghery, could hardly justify the proclamation of martial law, and with the development of the tithe war in the south, violence in Ulster shrank to the proportion of a nuisance.

The tithe war marks a minor turning point in the fortunes of Orangeism as it directed the attention of a hostile whig government towards violence in the south, brought the yeomanry again into prominence, and induced the gentry in several counties to consider reviving the southern lodges. The 'war' itself was another effort of the Irish peasantry to redress by violence an inefficient and unjust system of landholding of which the tithe was the most obvious but hardly the most oppressive feature. Like Defenderism in 1793, resistance to the tithe sapped the vitality of the landlord-magistrate system. Yet concessions in regard to the tithe would be interpreted as an attack on church establishment, and would confront the whig government in Britain with an issue which it wished to evade at that time. Stanley, a firm upholder of church establishment, was made Irish secretary, but his views on the necessity of using coercion were hardly stronger than those of Melbourne, who had become home secretary. Melbourne (William Lamb), no doubt influenced by the state of affairs in 1828 when he had been Irish secretary, was inclined to blame O'Connell for the tithe war. He wrote Anglesey, whom the whigs had returned to the office of viceroy, 'O'Connell wields the most decided influence over the whole physical force of the country'.[31] Yet the relapse of the peasantry into secret society methods can easily be attributed to the failure of O'Connell to interest them in his

[30] Evidence of W. J. Hancock, ibid., p. 180.
[31] Melbourne to Anglesey, 16 Dec. 1830 (P.R.O.N.I., Anglesey MSS 619/VI/6).

agitation for repeal. The nature of the land problem made a complacent peasantry inconceivable, and the only real alternative to perpetual agitation was secret society violence and rule by coercion. Since the police force, as it stood, could not by itself make coercion effective, a measure reviving the yeomanry, which Peel had carefully avoided during the days of the Catholic Association, was adopted by the whigs as the most economical means of supplementing the power of the military and police.[32] 'If this really becomes serious', Melbourne wrote, 'remember there is no body in Ireland like the Protestant yeomanry in the North ... They must be won to the support of the government, if possible. Nothing would have so much effect in doing this as the calling them out and showing a disposition to encourage them'.[33] Melbourne's concern for the northern protestants was, no doubt, increased by the efforts O'Connell was making to appeal to the spirit of 1782[34] and to win Orange support for his campaign against the union.

The ministry decided to re-equip the yeomanry with more modern weapons so that it could be called out on active service. This meant that regulars in the north could be relieved for service in the southern provinces, and that small corps of yeomanry would operate as auxiliaries to crown forces in the south. This gave some measure of relief to the government, but it meant that Orange yeomen could be employed to collect tithes and provided a means by which the lodges could be revived in the south. In the border counties, the re-arming of the yeomanry would, as a matter of course, be interpreted as a government gesture towards Orangemen, and as such gave them a moral victory over the local catholic population. It would increase the difficulties of the police in Ulster who were already called 'papist' by Orangemen,[35] and in general expand the means by which the lodges could assert their influence in matters where whig policies clashed with Orange convictions.

The most serious consequence of re-arming the yeomanry

---

[32] Melbourne to Anglesey, 29 Dec. 1830 (P.R.O.N.I., Anglesey MSS 619/VI/12).
[33] Same to same, 22 Dec. 1830 (ibid., 619/VI/7).
[34] Same to same, 16 Jan. 1833 (ibid., 619/VI/78).
[35] Evidence of Captain David Duff, *Rep. on Orange lodges III*, H.C. 1835 [476], xvi. 141–2.

came about in Newtownbarry in Cavan on 18 June 1831 when yeomen were called out by magistrates to seize cattle for non-payment of the tithe. A crowd of over 1,000 stoned the yeomen who ultimately fired on the crowd, killing seventeen and wounding another twenty.[36] This brought about demands in parliament for disbanding the yeomanry, and made the prospect of further violence on July 12 particularly alarming to the Orange grand lodge. A special appeal was prepared which read, 'The undersigned friends of the yeomanry consider it absolutely essential to sustain the representation made by them in parliament for the forebearance of that party, and their disposition to observe the law, they will join no procession of the Orangemen on the 12th July'.[37] At the same time, the police sent their annual circular to the magistrates instructing them to prevent processions likely to prove dangerous. Yet, from the Orangemen's viewpoint, a failure to march on July 12 meant a surrender of prestige that could cancel out the advantage gained by the re-arming of the yeomanry. There was, however, comparatively little violence when the twelfth arrived; two yeomanry officers were dismissed for participating in a procession, but police reported that there were few yeomen recognized in the processions and none of the recently-issued yeomanry arms was displayed. A scuffle between Orangemen and catholic colliers occurred near Dungannon,[38] while another encounter took place near Banbridge and in the south the Wexford yeomanry, known as the Ogle True Blues, displayed Orange colours. In August, O'Connell again protested in parliament against processions,[39] but no action was recommended until the spring of 1832 when a bill forbidding processions was again considered. By this time relations between the Orangemen and whigs had cooled because of opposition to parliamentary reform, but the anti-procession bill was not passed. Yet, the mere raising of the question alarmed the Orange peers who again attempted to use Cumberland's prestige to restrain the Orangemen. In an open letter to the lodges, the duke wrote, 'With regret, therefore, but with a full conviction of the wisdom of

---

[36] *Hansard 3*, iv. 296; ibid., v. 1183; ibid., vi. 644–68.
[37] Evidence of S. Blacker, *Rep. on Orange lodges I*, H.C. 1835 [377], xv. 137.
[38] Evidence of Capt. D. Duff, ibid., III. [476], xvi. 108.
[39] *Hansard 3*, iv. 1412–22.

my advice, I call upon you, one and all, to make the sacrifice of declining this year to attend the Orange processions on the glorious 12th'.[40] County grand masters, like Grier of Tyrone, openly opposed Lord Caledon, lord lieutenant of the county, on the question of processions,[41] and were prepared to defy the authority of the peers in the grand lodge. However, it was not expedient to defy the duke of Cumberland whose name lent so much prestige to the movement, and some exertions were made to conceal the duke's command from ordinary Orangemen. On July 2 the county grand masters of Ulster passed a resolution declaring it to be inexpedient to circulate the duke's address as 'he had written it under the impression that parliament was about to declare processions illegal'.[42] The police reported that the July 12 processions were well attended, and although there was comparatively little violence, it was because of these parades that parliament passed an anti-procession act in August 1832. The effect of this act was noticed the following year when police, who were still powerless to prevent parades, noted that the numbers involved had fallen off considerably.

The anti-procession act placed the Orange gentry between the dual pressure of the Castle and the plebeian Orangemen. Colonel Blacker, who had joined the movement as a youth in 1795, was confronted with an Orange procession at his doorstep. As a magistrate, he could follow no course but to advise them to disperse, but to indicate his sympathy with the movement he had the ladies of his household stand behind him wearing Orange lilies.[43] Although this compromise was applauded by the Orangemen, it proved unacceptable to the Castle, and Blacker was deprived of his commission of the peace. His neighbour, Colonel William Verner, took up the matter with the viceroy, but on receiving no satisfaction, he resigned his own commission as magistrate. However, the embarrassment of the Orange magistrates was more than redressed by the frustration of the efforts of John Hancock, a magistrate employed

---

[40] Duke of Cumberland to Orangemen, 21 June 1832 (*Rep. on Orange lodges I*, H.C. 1835 [377], xv. 137).

[41] *Hansard 3*, xiii. 1223.

[42] Evidence of Lord Caledon, *Rep. on Orange lodges I*, H.C. 1835 [377], xv. 372; Evidence of S. Blacker, ibid., p. 126.

[43] A.M., Blacker MSS vi. 365.

on the Brownlow estate to take measures against the Orangemen. Hancock had already provoked the Orangemen by securing the dismissal of a yeomanry sergeant[44] and by his efforts to organize a yeomanry corps along non-denominational lines. On 21 July 1833 Hancock appeared as a witness against fourteen Orangemen who had taken part in a procession at Armagh. Holmes, the defence attorney, turned the proceedings into a farce, and the case was dismissed.[45] The acquittal was celebrated by the ringing of bells and parades of Orangemen about the town, ending with an attack on Hancock's residence.[46]

At the spring assizes in 1834 the Castle sought to discourage further demonstrations by the prosecution of nearly five hundred Orangemen, accused of marching in the July 12 processions the previous year. The fines imposed were nominal, but this gesture appears to have impressed the Ulster leaders to the point where even district lodge masters supported the annual plea of the grand lodge to refrain from outdoor demonstrations on the twelfth. Although the Orange historian, Sibbett, claims that demonstrations were few in 1834,[47] police reports suggest that at least 15,000 took part in parades in the more important Orange centres in Ulster.[48] It would seem that the processions had become so much a part of the tradition of rural Ulster that it was beyond the power of the police, the grand lodge, or the gentry to effect their suppression. The parades were still a formidable demonstration of power, and perhaps from the point of view of more plebeian Orangemen, an adequate assertion of the protestant ascendancy. Moreover, the police and magistrates who had taken measures against the Orangemen were subject to insults, boycott, and an occasional physical assault. Captain Duff, the chief constable in Dungannon, was called 'Papist Duff', while John Hancock was threatened in his home, and on one occasion shots were fired

[44] Evidence of W. J. Hancock, *Rep. on Orange lodges III*, H.C. 1835 [476], xvi. 187.
[45] A.M., Blacker MSS vi. 366; see also Sibbett, *Orangeism* (2nd ed.) ii. 194.
[46] W. J. Hancock to Sir Wm. Gosset, 24 July 1833 (*Rep. on Orange lodges III*, H.C. 1835 [476], xvi. 192–3).
[47] Sibbett, *Orangeism*, (2nd ed.), ii. 115.
[48] *Rep. on Orange lodges III*, H.C. 1835 [476], xvi. 130–7.

at the residence of Sir Frederick Stovin, the inspector of police. These actions of ordinary Orangemen put Orange peers and parliamentarians in an awkward position from time to time, but they sought compensation for this embarrassment by efforts to turn the Orange spirit against the repeal movement, parliamentary reform, and attacks on church establishment. On his part, O'Connell, recognizing the force of the Orange tradition, tried to win over the Orangemen by appealing to the spirit of 1782. The repealers for a time wore orange and green sashes, and O'Connell on one occasion drank a toast with a glass of Boyne water. The duke of Northumberland, whose efforts to control the July 12 processions had incurred the enmity of the Orangemen, was denounced by O'Connell as odious to all parties. In Dublin where the union had never been popular, a former sheriff was expelled from the movement for entertaining O'Connell.

In Ulster, too, O'Connell's appeal resulted in some minor defections. The grand lodge was informed that Orangemen had met with catholics in November 1830 on a hill between Portadown and Lurgan where 'Orange and Green' flags had flown side by side,[49] while reports from Sligo stated that Orangemen were about to unite with catholics. Five Orangemen were expelled from the grand lodge of Ireland on December 30, and during the year it was thought necessary to pass resolutions against Orangemen 'uniting with papists'.[50] O'Connell's main bid for Orange support was made in January 1831 when Counsellor Costello was sent north to win Ulster for repeal. While Costello's mission was unquestionably a failure, Orangemen showed more restraint than they had during the days of Lawless. Costello, who was well known in Cookstown, county Tyrone, attempted to raise the standard of repeal there on a market day. This provoked a small riot in which he suffered nothing more than broken coach windows. He reached Dungannon under constabulary protection but made no effort to address the hostile crowds of Orangemen; nor did he think it expedient to address a repeal meeting during a subsequent visit to Armagh. In Belfast, Costello was greeted by an Orange proclamation, signed by district master Thomas White, which

---

[49] *Rep. on Orange lodges I*, H.C. 1835 [377], xv. app. 6, p. 75.
[50] Ibid., p. 76.

called upon Orangemen to hold themselves in readiness to aid the magistracy in case of disturbance, and he left the city after an address to a small indoor meeting.[51]

Had it not been for the recent memories of Lawless and an atmosphere of tension created by clashes with the Ribbonmen, O'Connell's appeal to the Orangemen might have made a more powerful impression. However, since 1798 the vague fear of domination by the catholic majority appears to have exercised greater influence on protestant opinion in Ulster than any momentary irritation with the British government or the desire to form part of an Irish state. Moreover, a cautious reference to repealers as enemies of the state on the part of any prominent Orangeman would mark the repealers out for attack by the more restless elements among the lodges, and once violence of any kind had started, it tended to arouse old enmities and to end in the traditional divisions along denominational lines. The creation of 'protestant associations' at the end of 1831, organized along the lines of the Brunswick clubs, was a reaction to O'Connell's efforts to win over the Orangemen, but even if O'Connell had confined his appeal to catholics, the organization of this kind of society was looked upon by men of local importance as a means of demonstrating their usefulness to the British government and the Castle. However, as O'Connell's repeal movement never achieved the force of the Catholic Association, the protestant associations faded away without reaching the proportion of the Brunswick clubs.

While the question of repeal was an Irish issue, and as such the concern of Orangemen, the question of parliamentary reform was clearly a party issue, and it showed the Irish Orangemen to be indifferent allies of the tories. Stewart Blacker, an Orangeman testifying in 1835, declared, 'A great number of Orangemen were stanch and consistent Reformers themselves, only they did not take precisely the same sweeping views of reform as the managers of the Bill'.[52] There were, however, Orangemen prepared to support the bill as it stood, despite a grand lodge resolution against reform and a circular sent to all districts encouraging the preparation of addresses

---

[51] Sibbett, *Orangeism*, (2nd ed.), ii. 77–9; see also Evidence of Captain Duff, *Rep. on Orange lodges III*, H.C. 1835 [476], xvi. 125–6, 144–5.

[52] Evidence of S. Blacker, *Rep. on Orange lodges I*, H.C. 1835 [377], xv. 124.

against the bill.[53] Some petitions were forwarded to parliament,[54] but there was no anti-reform enthusiasm among the Orangemen. The strength of reform sentiment within the lodges can be measured by the disciplinary action taken against Orange reformers. For supporting the bill John Hitton was expelled in June and Major Brownrigg in September.[55] Two clergymen were expelled from the grand lodge,[56] and it was ordered that Dublin district lodges 'remove from the list of officers of the Grand Lodge the name of any person supporting the Reform Bill, who voted for the Reform candidate at the last election'.[57] At this time circulars were issued recommending support of the protestant conservative fund and the Brunswick fund.[58] In conjunction with this effort to support tory policy, Lord Roden requested petitions against the national education system which permitted catholics religious instruction in state-supported schools.[59]

These efforts to tie Orangeism to tory politics and even to long-term policies like opposition to catholic education in state schools evoked an indifferent response from ordinary Orangemen. They were not so much tories, as allies of the tories whose support could not be taken for granted on matters such as parliamentary reform or even repeal of the union. On the other hand, the question of church disestablishment appears to have brought the Orangemen closer to the tories. This can be explained partly by the fact that any measure of disestablishment would have the appearance of a victory for the catholic secret societies engaged in the tithe war, and partly by the activities of the episcopalian clergy who, in this period, made an effort to revive the Orange movement in the south. Orangeism in the south had never been strong outside of Dublin and Bandon in Cork, although there was a lodge in Wexford and small groups of Orangemen meeting occasionally in most counties. With the rise of O'Connell's Catholic Association, the landlords had pursued a policy of conciliation, but with the

---

[53] Ibid., see also app. 6, p. 76.   [54] *Hansard 3*, iii. 825.
[55] Evidence of S. Blacker, *Rep. on Orange lodges I*, H.C. 1835 [377], xv. 124; see also ibid., app. 6, p. 76.
[56] Ibid., p. 124.   [57] *Hansard 3*, xxx. 71.   [58] Ibid., p. 70.
[59] Resolution of grand lodge of Tyrone, 27 Apr. 1832, in *Rep. on Orange lodges III*, H.C. 1835 [476], xvi. 123.

Repeal, Parliamentary Reform, Tithe War, 1830–4

spread of the tithe war, the landlords of Cork, Sligo, and Wexford counties, apparently under the influence of the clergy, again organized some of their protestant tenants into Orange lodges. It is difficult to estimate the strength of this southern revival, but in Bandon which had a strong Orange tradition, a public meeting of 5000 Orangemen was held in 1834.[60] The revival certainly did not involve all the elements that had been organized to put down the Whiteboys in the previous century, and there is no evidence of Orange strength in the most disturbed counties—Clare, Rosscommon, Galway, and Tipperary.

The interests and sentiments opposed to church disestablishment both in Ulster and the southern counties were brought into focus by the election following the fall of the Melbourne government in November 1834. The Orangemen drew up petitions to the king thanking him for deferring to his subjects' wishes in using his prerogative to dismiss the ministry.[61] In the election campaign itself, Orangemen circulated placards calling voters to rally to the crown. In Tyrone one of these read:

Protestants of Tyrone will you desert your King? No; you will die first. The King, as becomes a son of George the Third, has spurned from his council the men who would have overturned the most valued institutions of your country, and would have led your monarch to a violation of his coronation oath. Your Sovereign has done his duty, will you abandon yours? If you will not; if you will support your King as honestly as your King has supported you; if you will maintain the liberties for which your fathers fought with their blood, you will be found at the great Protestant meeting to be held in Dungannon on Friday[62] November 12, 1834.

Orangemen and tories met together at this meeting which was one of many held that day. Present were Lords Caledon, Belmore, Abercorn, Hamilton, and Alexander, and of these only Lord Caledon, the lord lieutenant of the county, objected to the presence of Orangemen who claimed that 75,000 attended this meeting, that 30,000 met at Cavan, 5,000 at Bandon, and 3,000 in Dublin.[63]

These election meetings were, to some degree, demonstrations

---

[60] *Rep. on Orange lodges I*, H.C. 1835 [377], xv. app. 6, p. 77.
[61] *Hansard 3*, xxvi. 537.
[62] Evidence of Stovin, *Rep. on Orange lodges I*, H.C. 1835 [377], xv. 323.
[63] Ibid., app. 6, p. 77.

of physical force, for many Orangemen came armed, and some marched in formation carrying Orange insignia. They mark the peak of Orange strength in the period between catholic emancipation and the second dissolution of the grand lodge in 1836. During these years the lodges had continued the revival which began at the time of Lawless's march on Ulster in 1828. Their hold on the protestant population had been tightened by the tithe war, and their power in relation to the catholic population had been strengthened by the decision to re-arm the yeomanry. The power of Ulster Orangemen to hold processions on July 12 in defiance of the authorities and even of their own leaders was asserted, but in the southern counties the lodges were generally content to hold indoor celebrations on the twelfth. While the Orangemen had wavered a little on the question of repeal and parliamentary reform, they remained allies of the tories and put their full strength behind Peel's government in 1834. The Irish movement was in 1835, to all appearances, as strong as it had been in 1825 at the time of the first dissolution of the grand lodge. Although the whigs were undoubtedly irritated by the Orange processions and the Orange connection with tory politics, they were also annoyed with O'Connell and inclined to accept the lodges as an established element in Irish politics. It is doubtful that the second Melbourne government would have taken special measures against the Irish movement had it not been for the peculiar activities of the British lodges which came to a rather sensational climax in the summer of 1835.

XI

ORANGE CONSPIRACY
1831–6

WITH THE PASSAGE of the catholic emancipation act, the British Orange movement suffered the demoralization which normally accompanies defeat. Local lodges were indifferently attended, and the grand lodge apparently did not meet between 15 June 1829 and February 1831. A meeting planned for November 1830 was postponed because the duke of Cumberland could not attend.[1] Cumberland himself was less formidable now, as he had little influence with the new king.[2] Yet that fact in itself, combined with his concern over the reform agitation, may explain the attention he devoted to the Orange movement after 1831.

Many ultra tories believed the country to be on the verge of revolution and were inclined to experiment with popular agitation in order to counteract the influence of the political unions. Although the Carlton Club was founded in 1831, it was not yet evident that the weakened tories were to be re-organized as a conservative party under Sir Robert Peel. It is not surprising, then, that Cumberland, Kenyon and the Orange peers attempted to rally the scattered forces of toryism under their own leadership through the agency of the Orange lodges. It is,

---

[1] Proceedings of the grand lodge 1828–31, in *Rep. on Orange lodges IV*, H.C. 1835 [605], xvii. app. 2, p. 8.
[2] Willis, *Ernest Augustus*, p. 203; Greville, *Memoirs*, ii. 5, entry 6 July 1830.

however, curious that they entrusted this project to a political adventurer whose record and general manner should have made them cautious.

William Blennerhasset Fairman had been commissioned in the 18th or Royal Irish Infantry, achieved the rank of captain and had been given the colonial rank of lieutenant colonel in the 4th Ceylon Foot.³ Apart from the fact that he joined the London Orange lodge in 1814, little is known of his early career. In a letter to the duke of Cumberland, he claimed to have exposed a plot against the house of Brunswick in 1809 and to have rendered special services to the duke of York.⁴ It is evident from a suit brought against him for debt in 1822 that his financial affairs were precarious. Fairman apparently had some talent as a courtier and showed considerable skill in cultivating the aquaintance of prominent Orange peers and winning their confidence. It is possible that his extravagant prose, flamboyant oratory and abundant energy recommended him as a man ideally suited to effect the desired liaison between the tory peers and the lower classes.

By 1831 he had, in some manner, come to share with Chetwoode the office of deputy grand secretary of the London Orangemen. A year previously, during the last days of George IV, he wrote to the duke of Cumberland suggesting there was a plot afoot on the part of the duke of Wellington to make himself first regent for the Princess Victoria and ultimately lord protector in the manner of Cromwell.⁵ If the expected death of George IV was followed shortly by that of his brother, the duke of Clarence, the heir to the throne would be Princess Victoria. It was desired by many that special provision be made to exclude the possibility of Cumberland becoming regent. As Fairman refers to a previous unanswered communication, this letter appears to be the second he addressed to Cumberland and there is no reason to believe it received any more attention than did the first. About the same time and with as little success, Fairman attempted to get a letter to the same effect published in the *Morning Post*.⁶

³ *Orange Conspiracy*, p. 197.
⁴ Fairman to ——, n.d. (ibid., pp. 201–2).
⁵ Fairman to Sir Chas. Cockburn, 14 July 1831 (ibid., pp. 203–4).
⁶ Sydney Taylor to Fairman, 6 Apr. 1830 (ibid., p. 203).

After the failure of his direct approach, the colonel secured an interview with Cumberland by way of Lord Kenyon. A series of interviews followed during which Fairman seems to have made a favourable impression on the duke. The nature of the discussion remains obscure. However, it is possible to infer from Fairman's other correspondence that he denounced the duke of Wellington and suggested that Cumberland re-organize the Orange lodges along more militant lines[7] to protect the state against Wellington's ambition.

Prior to his conversations with the Orange grand master, Fairman had written Sir Charles Cockburn claiming there were over 175,000 Orangemen and though 'in regard to numbers we are infinitely less on this side of the water ... my own fine fellows who compose the lodges in the capital and its environs, none of whom are Reformers, for upon this vital point I sounded them out, are staunch to the backbone... At my summons they would assemble, and under my command they would place themselves for putting their principles to the test.'[8] His own fine fellows numbered less than 500 as there were fifteen lodges in the London area, and the lodges seldom exceeded thirty in membership.[9] This letter ended with a denunciation of 'one of whom it would ill become me to speak except in terms of reverence, but has nevertheless been weak enough to ape the coarseness of a Cromwell'.[10] What Kenyon and the duke of Cumberland thought of Fairman at this time is difficult to say, but in their letters to him he was addressed with confidence and respect and they decided to employ him to re-organize the Orange movement.

The attendance of Colonel William Verner and a number of Irish parliamentarians at the Imperial Grand Lodge meetings in 1832 indicates that the Irish members of parliament in London were giving support to the British movement, while some of the peers who had supported the Brunswick clubs in 1828 were again rallying to the duke of Cumberland. At the February meeting, the marquess of Thomond, Colonel Perceval, a mem-

[7] *Orange Conspiracy*, pp. 201–23).
[8] Fairman to Sir Chas. Cockburn, 14 July 1831 (ibid., pp. 203–4).
[9] See app. C vi–vii.
[10] Fairman to Sir Chas. Cockburn, 14 July 1831 (*Orange Conspiracy*, pp. 203–4).

ber of parliament, and Colonel Wingfield Stratford were initiated as Orangemen.[11] At the second meeting in April 1832 the duke of Cumberland nominated Fairman for the office of deputy grand secretary from which Chetwoode had been removed.[12] The motion was seconded by Lord Kenyon and supported by the duke of Gordon.

Throughout the spring of 1832 plans were made to send the new deputy grand secretary on a tour of the Midlands, the North and Scotland.[13] Similar action had been taken when Chetwoode had been sent to Ireland to revive the movement there in 1828. The new tour, however, was more ambitious and Cumberland provided Fairman with an itinerant warrant empowering him to found lodges where he saw fit.[14] He was paid a guinea a day by way of expenses and a circular was sent to all lodge masters announcing his visit.[15]

Fairman's tour appears to have been an attempt to rally a substantial section of the nobility, gentry and conservative-minded middle class to the British Orange movement in the manner that a section of the Irish gentry rallied to Orangeism in 1797. Many peers in the grand lodge may have imagined that there was a parallel between the reform agitation and the activities of the United Irishmen. The difficulty was that the landed classes in Britain had no equivalent of the Armagh peasantry anxious to press upon them the leadership of the Orange societies. Moreover, as the landlords themselves were not threatened with anything like a Defender movement, they felt no immediate need to organize their tenants in Orange lodges. Even if such rural lodges had been created, it is difficult to see what they could have done to counteract the urban reform agitation.

The existing Orange strength was in the cities and here it is conceivable that the movement might have been useful to the tories. A skilful agent of the grand lodge might have aroused among the Orangemen a suspicion of the reformers and held out the flattering and exciting invitation to come forward and save the country. Yet the Orangemen, as urban dwellers, had

---

[11] Proceedings of the grand lodge, 16 Feb. 1832, in *Rep. on Orange lodges IV*, H.C. 1835 [605], xvii. app. 2, p. 18.
[12] Ibid., app. 16, p. 119.   [13] Evidence of Fairman, ibid., p. 17.
[14] Ibid., report p. ix.   [15] Ibid., app. 3, p. 41.

no material interest in opposing reform, and many influential local Orangemen were reformers. And if Cumberland and Kenyon judged Fairman a man likely to make an effective impression on the lower classes, they were proved mistaken.

Fairman apparently continued his practice of 'sounding out' Orangemen on reform,[16] but now in the role of personal representative of the duke of Cumberland. If the testimony of Joseph Haywood, the district master of Sheffield in 1832, can be trusted, the colonel told Orangemen that they must make a stand. He asked them if they would rally to the duke of Cumberland 'if any row took place'. Haywood further accused Fairman of declaring that 'his majesty had no right to sanction the revolutionary measures of the government in passing the Reform Bill [of 1832] and that a row was expected to take place'.[17] From the tone of Fairman's correspondence, the accusation seems plausible, but there is no evidence that he spoke with the knowledge and approval of the duke of Cumberland. There is, however, a good deal of evidence that he took a different view of his mission than did Kenyon and the Orange peers.

During the summer Kenyon wrote, 'If any of the heads of the Dissenters (I mean Christian Dissenters) could be brought to assist us, we should do well almost everywhere, and I am sure ours is the cause of all friends to Christianity'.[18] In November, while Fairman was in the Midlands, Lord Wynford, the deputy speaker of the house of lords, wrote Fairman that conservatives should improve, as well as defend, their country's institutions and 'above all things, attend to the correction of vices and improving the conditions of the poor'.[19]

In contrast to the above, there are passages in Fairman's correspondence which suggest preparation for civil war. To Lord Londonderry he declared, 'We have the military with us as far as they are likely to avow their principles and sentiments'.[20] On another occasion he wrote the duke of Gordon, 'By our next general meeting, we shall be assuming, I think, an

---

[16] See above p. 256.   [17] *Orange Conspiracy*, p. 190.
[18] Lord Kenyon to Fairman, 5 Aug. 1832 (ibid., p. 211).
[19] Lord Wynford to Fairman, 6 Nov. 1832 (ibid., p. 213).
[20] Fairman to Londonderry, 30 July 1832 (*Rep. on Orange lodges IV*, H.C. 1835 [605] xvii. app. 21, p. 182.

attitude of boldness as will strike the foe with awe, but we inculcate the doctrine of passive obedience and non-resistance too religiously by far'.[21] Again to Londonderry he wrote, 'What the Catholics and Unions have achieved by agitation in a factious cause, we might achieve in a righteous one ... If we prove not too strong for the present government, such a government will prove too strong for us.'[22] In the same letter he complained that the British gentry had not come forward to support the Orange lodges in the same manner the Irish gentry had.

We have lodges at Newcastle, Shields, Darlington, and round about, but these are mere trunks without heads. Unless men of staunch influence and consideration step forward as county grand masters (I speak advisedly) it is of no means or use for the classes in humbler walks of life to assemble for such a purpose. The field is now open to your Lordship. The opportunity is exclusively yours.

Fairman's Quixotic letters, like his conversations with local Orangemen, were probably intended as a means of sounding the peers out on the question of a coup d'etat. The colonel perhaps hoped that if he could acquire sufficient evidence of popular support among the peers and the people, he could interest the duke of Cumberland in the project. It is possible that he sounded out the duke himself at least to the extent of assuring him that the country would look to him as a man of action in any future crisis. It remains a puzzle why Kenyon failed to perceive that Fairman's indiscretions would ultimately give the radicals grounds for launching a new effort to have the movement declared illegal. Kenyon and the Orange peers certainly gave Fairman no encouragement for his 'project', and the worse that can be said is that they read his letters and still employed him.

As a means of turning the Orangemen into an effective auxiliary of toryism, Fairman's tour met with indifferent success. The minutes of the grand lodge meeting in June show that Orangemen had joined Attwood's Birmingham Political Union and that a lodge in Ripponden had turned radical.[23]

---

[21] Fairman to the duke of Gordon, 11 Aug. 1832 (ibid., p. 183).
[22] Fairman to Londonderry, 29 July 1832 (ibid., p. 182).
[23] *Rep. on Orange lodges IV*, H.C. 1835 [605] xvii. app. 2, p. 27.

This may have happened before Fairman's arrival, but even during the elections of 1834 the grand lodge proved unable to guarantee the Orange vote, and as late as 1835 the grand lodge was reprimanding Orangemen for 'imbibing false notions of reform'.[24]

In February 1833 Fairman was recalled to London briefly for the meeting of the grand lodge and then he proceeded to Scotland. Although there was no Scottish grand lodge, the duke of Gordon had accepted the title of deputy grand master of Scotland. The duke, however, had no connection with the existing Scottish Orange lodges which numbered forty-five, with twelve in Glasgow, ten in Ayr and the others in Edinburgh, Dumfries, Elland and Stranraer.[25] Like the Orangemen in the Midlands, the Scottish members were drawn from the lower classes and were useful to Fairman as evidence of Orange influence among the people, but they were unruly and wanting in spontaneous enthusiasm for the 'tory' cause. Yet they welcomed Fairman's visit and appreciated his talent for showmanship. He was greeted with parades which, in the opinion of the authorities, increased local disorders.[26] The immigrant Irish catholics had formed Ribbon societies and riots between them and Orangemen were common.[27] After one parade in his honour, Fairman addressed the Orangemen from the window of the lodge hall, tossing coins to the crowd and offering free wine to those who cared to drink the health of the duke of Cumberland.[28]

During his Scottish tour, Fairman stayed with the duke of Gordon and was able to use the prestige of the duke's name to found a gentlemen's lodge called the Royal Gordon.[29] This lodge was probably intended to stand in the same relation to the Scottish Orangemen as did the Dublin lodge to the Irish and the London lodge to the English movement. Fairman hoped, perhaps, that the Scottish gentry, or at least the tory leaders, would join the Royal Gordon lodge and make it the nucleus of the grand lodge of Scotland. The results proved disappointing.

---

[24] Ibid., p. 60.   [25] See app. C vi-vii.
[26] Evidence of Cosmo Innes, in *Rep. on Orange lodges IV*, H. C.1835 [605], xvii. 141-7.
[27] Evidence of Motherwell, ibid., pp. 166-7.   [28] Ibid., p. 94.
[29] Evidence of Motherwell, ibid., p. 161.

Where the London lodge was able to attract a number of ultra tory peers, the Gordon lodge attracted two journalists—Craigie and Motherwell, the latter the editor of the *Glasgow Courier*. Craigie, who was the more enthusiastic promoter of the lodge, appears to have been excited by the prospect of using the social prestige attached to the dukes—especially royal dukes—to create a political organization.[30]

Fairman left Scotland after promising the Orangemen a visit from the duke of Cumberland. He proceeded to Yorkshire where he used the same method with equal success. A friend of the duke of Cumberland was a welcome guest among the gentry, and the promise of a visit from the duke was sufficient inducement for 'gentlemen of substance' to found at Barnsley the Royal Cumberland lodge.[31] Fairman wrote, 'If he [the duke of Cumberland] would but make a tour into these parts, for which I have prepared the way, he would be idolized'.[32] A hint of the duke's attitude towards such an undertaking is given in a letter written previously by Kenyon who wished 'his royal highness would, without neglecting the prime consideration, namely, the fitness of anything proposed, attend, in addition to that, to what is popular. Our enemies attend to that alone, which is base; we seem to disregard it too much, which is foolish'.[33]

When Fairman returned to London, the question of Irish church revenues had displaced reform, and new political alignments were taking shape. Cumberland appears to have counted more on his personal influence than on the power of the Orange movement to protect church interests, as he decided in July 1833 that the grand lodge would hold no meeting while the Irish bill was being debated. Colonel Fairman, who had by now, no doubt, renounced his more ambitious schemes, was occupied with a variety of minor projects among which was the distribution of anti-catholic books to a number of peers.[34]

At this time Kenyon was considering a new project for influ-

---

[30] Correspondence between Craigie and Fairman, Apr. to July 1833, (ibid., app. 22, 189–92).
[31] Fairman to Kenyon, n.d. (ibid., app. 13, p. 113).
[32] Same to same, 12 Feb. 1833 (ibid., p. 112).
[33] Kenyon to Fairman, 28 Dec. 1832 (*Orange Conspiracy* pp. 214–5).
[34] Same to same, 10 July 1833 (ibid., pp. 218–9).

encing the press. Kenyon had made previous efforts in this direction. As early as 1820, when the grand lodge was still in Manchester, he had attempted to arouse enthusiasm for an Orange press and had recommended the grand lodge to recognize two newspapers—the *Hibernian Journal* and the *True Briton*—for their stand against catholic emancipation. In 1823 thanks were voted to three other publications, *John Bull*, the *Edinburgh Evening Post* and the *Glasgow Courier*.[35] On another occasion, the *Saunders News-Letter* and the *Antidote* received Orange support by way of advertisements. Yet these publications were not owned by the Orange Order and their principal service was to write exaggerated accounts of Orange activities. As Kenyon's earlier press ventures had proved expensive and unsatisfactory, he was no longer willing to finance new efforts himself. However, he considered that the *Age*—a newspaper indulging in violent abuse of radical-whig leaders—should have Orange support and suggested that the Carlton Club purchase a newspaper.[36]

In the autumn of 1833, Fairman again went north but his second tour yielded few results. His request to the grand lodge in October for power to expel unruly members indicated trouble with ordinary Orangemen. He also reported a rebuff from higher quarters—that no support was forthcoming from the duke of Buccleugh.[37] November was spent by the colonel as guest of the duke of Gordon whom he persuaded to become official patron of the Royal Gordon Lodge.[38] This appears to have been the only achievement of his somewhat expensive tour.

Shortly thereafter, the grand lodge was troubled by legal and financial matters. The conviction of six labourers of Tolpuddle, Dorset, in March 1834, on charges of administering illegal oaths alarmed Orangemen lest it be used as a precedent for taking measures against the lodges. The question was discussed at the June meeting of the grand lodge, but the Orangemen believed they were on reasonably safe ground as their society administered no oath as such but merely insisted that all members take an oath of allegiance and supremacy before a magistrate.

[35] *Rep. on Orange lodges IV*, H.C. 1835 [605], xvii. report p. xix.
[36] A. Aspinall, *Politics and the press*, pp. 341–9.
[37] *Orange Conspiracy* p. 220.
[38] Evidence of Fairman, in *Rep. on Orange lodges IV*, H.C. 1835 [605], xvii. 44; see also report p. xxiv.

Nevertheless, they took the precaution of ordering a new edition of the rules to be printed in which minor alterations were made to better secure their legality.[39]

Apart from these legal questions, the lodges were faced with a minor financial crisis as a result of Fairman's tour. In theory the lodges paid a shilling for each member to the grand lodge. These dues were so far in arrears that Cumberland signed an appeal to Orangemen to pay their dues. A special collection amounting to £74 had to be taken among members of the grand lodge to help meet Fairman's tour expenses. Of this amount Cumberland paid £50 and Kenyon £3.[40] Meanwhile, the question of Irish church revenues had again given Cumberland hope of influence at court. In a speech to the grand lodge in June 1834, he praised his brother, the king, and a resolution was passed approving the 'heart-inspiring declaration of His Majesty in defence of the Established Church'.[41]

Shortly after this meeting, Fairman, who probably had nothing to do and was seeking a new project, attempted to interest the Carlton Club in Orangeism. In this enterprise, he sought the assistance of Randall E. Plunkett,[42] the Irish deputy grand master and member of parliament for county Meath, as well as J. F. Staveley, a member of the British grand committee. He submitted to them a draft of a circular he intended to send to the Carlton Club, but the Orange tories were so horrified at his style that they endeavoured to dissuade the colonel from his purpose. Staveley tactfully advised moderate wording and he particularly objected to the reference to the 'wretched remains of our Constitution'.[43] Plunkett wrote, 'The utmost we can offer is ... rational advice. Where advice takes the form of censure, or is clothed in severity of language, it must defeat its object wherever there is room for a difference of opinion.'[44] He suggested that instead of having Fairman write a circular, they should have Edmund Swift, the keeper of the crown jewels, write a pamphlet. Plunkett declared, 'Conservatism is inferior to Orangeism, as it is solely, and almost selfishly,

---

[39] Ibid., app. 2, pp. 58–61.   [40] Ibid., app. 2, p. 59.
[41] Ibid.
[42] Plunkett to Fairman, 8 June 1834 (ibid., app. 14, p. 113).
[43] Stavely to Fairman, 29 June 1834 (ibid., app. 14, p. 114).
[44] Plunkett to Fairman, 5 July 1834 (ibid., app. 14, p. 115).

political. I cannot consent to lose your valuable exertions by identifying you with the politics of the Carlton Club. I should fly at a higher game and endeavour to make members of the Carlton Club Orangemen... who, when they engraft our solemn and venerable institution upon their more worldly views, will have attained to all that can be desired.'[45]

In spite of this advice, Fairman persisted, and a revised version of his original draft was sent to members of the Carlton Club informing them, 'This society [the Orange Order] is useful for the purposes of intercourse between the higher and lower orders... for correspondence with bodies or individuals, and is capable of being rendered eminently available in elections, whenever it is desirable to return representatives whose principles are the protection of the Protestant Establishment'.[46]

It was also mentioned that the lodges were useful for presenting petitions and loyal addresses, and he hinted that they would be happy to supply physical force against radicals if the occasion should arise. There is no doubt that this appeal went unheeded. Peel had no particular desire for close cooperation with the ultras,[47] much less the Orangemen, and the grand lodge would hardly find it necessary to appeal to the ultras through the medium of the Carlton Club. If a tory squire, after reading the circular, had come to the grand lodge asking for Orange assistance, Fairman could have done no more than invite him to form a lodge among his tenants. Moreover, in urban areas where the lodges were relatively numerous, it was far from certain that Carlton Club members could depend upon their assistance in an election. Not only were many Orangemen inclined towards parliamentary reform but in the elections of 1834, when the Orange leaders were doing their best to rally protestant support against the threat to the Irish church establishment, they exercised an indifferent control over the votes of their own members. In Rochdale, where Orangemen were numerous, a sizable minority of the members including a lodge master voted against the tory candidate in spite of the efforts of the district masters on behalf

---

[45] Ibid.
[46] Address to the Carlton Club, 13 June 1834 (ibid., app. 14, p. 114).
[47] Peel to Goulburn, 3 Jan. 1833 (Peel, *Private papers*, ii. 213); Croker to Lord Hertford, 19 Apr. 1831 (ibid., ii. 181).

of the tories.⁴⁸ The grand lodge was furious, but decided against large-scale expulsions. Only two were expelled, one of whom was an innkeeper, James Whittles, who later testified that he joined the movement to promote the trade of his establishment.⁴⁹

As nearly all lodges met in taverns of some kind, innkeepers played an important role in the organization. Rules had been made from time to time forbidding publicans from holding office, but do not appear to have been well enforced. The Orange leaders were annoyed continually by requests from members to secure them licenses to establish public houses, but it is impossible to say how many of these got results. Although the expectation of patronage attracted some to the movement, the benefits appear to have been meagre. Fairman recommended several men for the police force, but it is clear that his recommendations were not of much assistance.⁵⁰ Being a known Orangeman was, in fact, more likely to be grounds for exclusion from government employment as the movement's enemies were more powerful than its friends at this time.

British Orangemen could not expect the immunity from the law which their Irish brethren enjoyed. Orange magistrates were few. Apart from the sums expended on legal aid to members arrested for the 'cause', the lodges provided little protection to the members in Britain. Some individual lodges were organized as benefit societies, but the financial arrangements they made were entirely independent of the grand lodge.⁵¹ The yearly revenue of the movement was about £200, which was collected from a variety of sources such as the issue of new warrants, dues from local lodges, and special contributions from prominent Orangemen.⁵² Kenyon wrote in January 1833 that he had spent, on behalf of the 'cause', 'nearer £20,000 than £10,000 in the last two years',⁵³ but by the 'cause', he probably meant a number of conservative enterprises in which he was involved, particularly the newspapers.

Members of the grand lodge were unpaid and, apart from

---

[48] Evidence of Whittles, *Rep. on Orange lodges IV*, H.C. 1835 [605], xvii. 158.
[49] Ibid., p. 159.
[50] Evidence of Colonel C. Rowan, ibid., pp. 157–8.
[51] Kenyon to Fairman, 7 Jan. 1833 (*Orange Conspiracy* p. 215).
[52] *Rep. on Orange lodges IV*, H.C. 1835 [605], xvii. app. 2, pp. 4–44.
[53] Kenyon to Fairman, 7 Jan. 1833 (*Orange Conspiracy* p. 215).

the deputy grand secretary, did little work. Fairman drew on organizational funds for travelling purposes. Kenyon's franking privileges were used to avoid postal charges, and his home at Portland Square was a meeting place. From references to financial irregularities among the leaders of the local lodges, it is evident that small sums of money were misappropriated. Chetwoode, who for ten years had been deputy grand secretary, appears to have been discharged for not providing receipts for money sent to the grand lodge, but no action was taken against him.[54] When Fairman complained of his financial straits to Kenyon in September 1834, he received the rather cool reply, 'I am very sorry to hear of your taking up money from the money-lenders'.[55]

By the autumn of 1834 Fairman seems to have been losing the confidence of the duke of Cumberland and Kenyon, and he resigned as deputy grand secretary although he retained the office of district grand master for London. After the unexpected death of Craigie, the Royal Gordon lodge in Scotland collapsed, leaving the Scottish movement very much as it had been before Fairman's tour.[56] The Rochdale vote weakened Fairman's prestige, and Plunkett's letter indicated that his circular to the Carlton Club had provoked ridicule among parliamentary Orangemen. One of his last efforts was, however, the least creditable of his career. He issued a circular addressed to government pensioners telling them, 'It is the bounden duty of such, . . . to enlist under the banners of a loyal association, instead of repairing to factious unions . . . at the imminent risk of incurring a just forfeiture of their hard-earned remunerations, of which a scrupulous government would not hesitate to deprive them. Of this intelligible hint the half-pay of the army and navy might do well to profit.'[57]

At the opening of 1835 the lodges were counting very much on the king. In the spring of the previous year, the withdrawal of Althorp to the house of lords led Melbourne to doubt his

---

[54] Proceedings of the grand lodge, 4 June 1832 (*Rep. on Orange lodges IV*, H.C. 1835 [605], xvii. app. 2, pp. 27-8).

[55] Kenyon to Fairman, 13 Sept. 1834 (*Orange Conspiracy* p. 222).

[56] Evidence of Motherwell, *Rep. on Orange lodges IV*, H.C. 1835 [605], xvii. p. 163.

[57] *Orange Conspiracy* p. 200.

ability to carry on without a leader in the commons. He explained the situation to the king, offering to resign and pointing out that the alternative was to have Russell as leader in the commons. Distrust of Russell led the king to accept Melbourne's resignation. The result was a tory government and new elections during which the efforts of the Orangemen to become the acknowledged allies of the Carlton Club failed. The elections, which were not greatly affected by the Orange vote, reduced the whig majority, but the whigs lost more to the radicals than to the tories. Peel thus became prime minister, governing without a majority in parliament. With the election over, the British Orangemen directed their efforts to encouraging Peel to remain in office in opposition to the whig majority. Cumberland visited the king and Peel, but with little effect. Kenyon wrote Peel in March expressing his conviction that if the cabinet resigned 'the House of Lords ... will pass every measure, however infamous', and appealed to him 'not to quit our Sailor ... King'.[58] Peel, however, was defeated six times in six weeks and resigned.

Although the new Melbourne government was little disposed to make an issue of Orangeism, the absence of a whig majority in the house made it sensitive to pressure from the radicals and Irish members. Demands for a parliamentary investigation of Orangeism had been made as early as 1813. When Hume and Finn brought the question up again in the spring of 1835, the demand was granted.[59] The select committee appointed to enquire into Orangeism was composed at first of twenty-seven members including eight Orangemen and twelve hostile to Orangeism. The committee submitted four reports to parliament. These were printed in three volumes amounting to 4,500 pages. Of the first three reports—dealing exclusively with the Irish Orange lodges[60]—two were presented on July 20 and the other on 6 August 1835.[61] The final report of the committee dealt with the English Orange lodges[62] and was presented on 7 September. The Irish reports were presented without a summary or conclusions while the committee on the lodges in Great Britain

---

[58] Kenyon to Peel, 26 Mar. 1835 (Peel, *Private papers*, ii. 295).
[59] *Hansard 3*, xxvii. 135.
[60] *Rep. on Orange lodges I*, H.C. 1835 [377], xv.
[61] Ibid., [475-6], xvi.   [62] Ibid., [605], xvii.

under the direction of Hume presented a summary of the material arranged to suggest that the lodges were a dangerous society.[63]

These reports established beyond doubt what had been general knowledge in Ireland since 1795—that is—that the Orangemen controlled the Irish yeomanry, had lodges in the army, enjoyed a certain immunity from justice in Ulster and were frequently engaged in civil disturbances. The fact that the duke of Cumberland was head of a society which had lodges in the army was sufficient to force government action. The military lodges were—from the point of view of legality—the Achilles' heel of Orangeism. On 4 August 1835 Hume moved eleven resolutions declaring Orangeism illegal and placing emphasis on its existence in the army. He proposed an address to the king calling attention to the duke of Cumberland's position as a field marshal in the army and Orange grand master.[64] Russell asked that the debate be postponed until 11 August in the hope that the duke would resign as grand master. The next day Cumberland wrote to the select committee declaring his ignorance of the lodges in the army 'as the warrants which he signed were given to him in batches'.[65] Hume moved his resolutions again on August 11, modified so that Cumberland could not be charged with deliberately signing warrants for military lodges, and a few days later the king promised vigour in suppressing secret societies in the army.[66] A week later the Orange grand lodge declared all military warrants null and void.[67] Meanwhile, Fairman again came into prominence. Hume reported on August 19 that the colonel, who had been called to testify before the select committee, refused to produce a letter-book dealing with the military lodges. Even though urged by Orangemen to co-operate, Fairman persisted in refusing, and when an order was sent out for his arrest he could not be found.[68]

[63] Ibid., [605], xvii. see report pp. i–xxvii.
[64] *Hansard 3*, xxx. 58–79.
[65] Cumberland to John Patten, 5 Aug. 1835 (*Rep. on Orange lodges II*, H.C. 1835 [475], xvi. 4).
[66] *Hansard 3*, xxx. 559.
[67] Cumberland to Orangemen, 27 Aug. 1835 (*Rep. on Orange lodges IV*, H.C. 1835 [605], xvii. report p. iii.
[68] *Hansard 3*, xxx. 803.

Orange Conspiracy, 1831-6

By September 1835 all the reports on the lodges had been presented, but the duke of Cumberland made no move to resign as grand master or to dissolve the order. In October, Hume and Sir William Molesworth, the editor of the Benthamite *London and Westminster Review*, acquired new evidence which they used to represent the lodges as a dangerous conspiracy. Haywood, the district master of Sheffield, who had been expelled from the society in June 1835 on charges of being a trouble-maker,[69] wrote to Kenyon accusing Fairman of sounding out Orangemen in 1832 on the question of a coup d'etat.[70] A faint hint of Haywood's character is given in a letter he wrote to the grand lodge in 1832 complaining of people 'who had joined the lodges for sordid and unworthy motives'.[71] Molesworth described him as an excitable but honest man. Fairman took legal action against Haywood, and Hume came to the latter's defence. The evidence, however, was not to be tested in court as Haywood burst a blood vessel and died while awaiting trial.

About the same time, Hume somehow acquired a number of Fairman's letters including those written by and to him during his tours. Armed with this evidence, Hume and Molesworth renewed their attack on the Orangemen when parliament met again in 1836.[72] They presented their evidence in a manner designed to leave the impression that Cumberland contemplated a coup d'etat through the agency of the Orange lodges. Molesworth even suggested that the Orange peers be tried on the same charges as the Dorsetshire labourers who had been transported to the South Seas for belonging to an illegal society.

Many were prepared to credit the case presented by Hume and Molesworth. Cumberland's opposition to catholic emancipation and parliamentary reform had made him a sinister figure in the eyes of radicals and whigs, and the information in the select committee reports could easily be used to give the impression that the Orange lodges in Britain were a formidable

---

[69] Proceedings of the grand lodge, 4 June 1835 (*Rep. on Orange lodges IV*, H.C. 1835 [605], xvii. app. 2, p. 73).

[70] *Annual Register*, London, 1837, lxxvii. 11-2.

[71] Proceedings of the grand lodge, 19 Apr. 1832 (*Rep. on Orange lodges IV*, H.C. 1835 [605], xvii. app. 2, p. 21).

[72] *Hansard 3*, xxxi. 779-870.

force capable of putting a coup d'etat into effect. Hume created this illusion by accepting the wholly unreliable statements of various Orangemen that the total strength of the movement in the United Kingdom was 300,000.[73] He allowed 100,000 for Britain and hinted that it might even be as high as 150,000 with 40,000 in London. As shown previously,[74] the British movement could hardly have exceeded 6,000. One Orange witness, when questioned closely, doubted that more than 2,000 London Orangemen could be assembled in one place[75] and it is questionable whether even 500 could be assembled.[76] The figure of 300,000, however, if considered with the existence of military lodges and Fairman's rash letters, was at least circumstantial evidence of a serious conspiracy. Hume and Molesworth may have believed that such a conspiracy had been considered, but apart from this, they were anxious to see the societies dissolved and were delighted at the opportunity to embarrass the tories. They were, moreover, interested in discrediting all efforts of the conservatives to organize popular movements and warned that the Orange lodges would be reorganized as conservative societies.[77]

The story of an Orange conspiracy, however, has been credited by reputable historians. Halévy, who was prepared to accept the radical point of view, wrote, 'Nor did the Ultra Tories shrink from contemplating wilder projects. Incredible though it may seem, there can be little doubt that their leader, the Duke of Cumberland, the King's brother, believed it possible to set aside by a military coup d'etat his little niece, the Princess Victoria, who was a devoted whig, and seize the succession of William IV'.[78] Halévy based his opinion largely upon the article in Molesworth's *London and Westminster Review*[79] and upon Miss Claire Jerrold's *The Early Court of Queen Victoria*, in which she presents a conversation between the duke of

[73] Ibid., p. 783.   [74] See above p. 230.
[75] Evidence of Fox Cooper, *Rep. on Orange lodges IV*, H.C. 1835 [605], xvii, 67–8; see also list of London lodges in 1830, ibid., app. 15, p. 118.
[76] See above p. 256.
[77] *Orange Conspiracy* p. 201.
[78] Elie Halévy, *A history of the English people in the nineteenth century*, iii. 191; see also E. L. Woodward, *The age of reform 1815–1870*, p. 96.
[79] Halévy, *Hist. of the English people in the nineteenth century*, p. 162, see footnote.

Orange Conspiracy, 1831–6

Cumberland and his aide-de-camp, but gives no source for her information.[80]

If a conspiracy existed, its military aspects were not in evidence. Among the civilian lodges, there were no signs of the kind of preparation that normally precedes a coup d'etat—no gathering of arms as there had been prior to Emmet's rebellion, nor any efforts to create an underground army such as the United Irish had prior to 1798. The most that 6,000 or so Orangemen could have done was to serve as special constables or stand by and cheer the duke as he rode through the streets. However, a number of cheering crowds might be a very effective auxiliary to a British Caesar if he were supported by a substantial section of the military. But any military support which Cumberland received would have to come from the Orange lodges in the army. It is inconceivable that he would have received support from the Peninsular veterans who made up the bulk of its senior and field officers. The numerous colonels in the Orange movement were, like Fairman, on half pay and not in a position to influence any body of troops in Britain. There remains, then, the Orange movement within the army.

The military lodges were a legacy of the rebellion of 1798 which the grand lodges of Britain and Ireland had permitted to survive, but had not done much to encourage or justify. If the commanding officers objected to a particular lodge, it was dissolved, but many officers were disposed to tolerate the lodges. As the military lodges—or warrants—included no officers, it was quite possible for lodges to function unknown to the officer commanding. Orders from Horse Guards in 1813, 1822, 1828 and 1835[81] to dissolve the military lodges and the numerous questions asked in parliament about them had not put an end to their existence. Doubtless, the Orange leaders kept the military lodges alive partly out of inertia and their reluctance to discourage Orange enthusiasts and perhaps in the hope that they might prove useful in the future. It does not appear, however, from either their numbers or location that the military lodges could have been at any time the means of staging a coup d'etat. One or two military representatives attended grand lodge meetings after Fairman became grand

[80] Claire Jerrold, *The early court of Queen Victoria*, p. 114.
[81] *Rep. on Orange lodges IV*, H.C. 1835 [605], xvii. report p. xxvi.

secretary but, if the minutes of the meetings can be relied upon, the military representatives remained silent at the meetings. Correspondence between Orange secretaries and soldiers discussed only dues, initiations and troubles with commanding officers.

In 1830 there were thirty-one military warrants under the British grand lodge.[82] There is no evidence of a substantial increase in the years which followed. Military lodges, as a rule, consisted of a sergeant and a dozen or so men who, like civilian Orangemen, met in public houses. No lodges existed in the Guards regiments which formed the main strength of the London garrison. The number of military Orangemen was, then, perhaps 500 in Britain, distributed about in groups of from five to thirty in different military units in a severely-disciplined army led by Wellington's officers. Not even a Colonel Despard or Robert Emmet would have attempted a coup d'etat with such a scattered and unreliable band.

Yet, if the Orange movement, as it stood, was incapable of serious revolutionary action, Colonel Fairman had certainly given the matter thought. Among his many projects was a 'military' one, the nature of which is not revealed in his letters. He wrote of 'the military being with us'[83] and there are references in his letters to Wellington playing the role of Cromwell. Fairman was undoubtedly an intriguer, but his manoeuvres seemed designed primarily towards winning the confidence of influential noblemen. His incautious talk of violence was, without doubt, evidence of earnest reflections on the subject, but nothing more. In practice he followed the less exciting plan of attempting to found lodges among the middle class and gentry by offering the patronage of great peers and promising visits from the duke of Cumberland. His refusal to produce the letter-book for the parliamentary committee and his sudden disappearance may have been designed to conceal evidence damaging to himself, or possibly to convince prominent Orangemen that he was protecting them. In an undated letter, Fairman wrote to 'D—— C——, Esq.', asking him to return 'the Palladiums, with a small packet of letters from kings and princes I left for your perusal, you will oblige me very much. As circumstances will at length compel me to seek

[82] See app. B v.   [83] See above p. 258.

a compensation from royalty, for my services and surrenders in their service... should not an appeal to their justice... be productive of the desired end,... I shall enforce my claims through the medium of the press.'[84] This letter and others used by Hume as evidence of an Orange conspiracy were published by Molesworth in the April 1836 issue of the *London and Westminster Review*. It is unlikely that Hume secured the letters from Haywood who was not in the inner circles of Orangeism. The letters may have been stolen from Fairman, but the letter quoted above suggests an alternative. It is possible that Fairman was driven, by a combination of financial need and resentment against his colleagues, to sell the letters either directly or indirectly to Hume.

Although the charges of Orange conspiracy may have been wanting in substance, they provided a dramatic end to the first phase of Orange history. On 23 February 1836 Hume moved an address to the king requesting the dismissal of all Orangemen from civil and military office but Russell, with Hume's approval, softened this by asking the king to take measures against secret societies.[85] The royal reply on February 25 made it clear that measures would be taken against Orangeism,[86] and the duke of Cumberland thereupon dissolved the lodges.[87]

[84] *Orange Conspiracy* p. 223.
[85] *Hansard 3*, xxxi. 820–33.
[86] Ibid., p. 870.
[87] Ibid., p. 946.

XII

IN RETROSPECT

~~~~~~~~~~~~~~~~~~

THE FOUNDING OF THE ORANGE LODGES in 1795 by peasants of the border counties of Ulster was designed to defend the privileges of the poorer protestants who formed a kind of plebeian aristocracy in Ireland. By reviving the Orange tradition, which had declined during the middle decades of the century, they hoped to find allies among the governing classes who had shared with them the advantages of what was called the 'protestant ascendancy'. To placemen, the ascendancy meant a protestant monopoly of government office; to the gentry and clergy, security from attack on rents and tithes from catholic secret societies; and to the peasant, the right to use violence against the economic competition of the catholics, and above all, the exclusive right of a protestant to possess firearms. Of all classes benefiting by the 'ascendancy', it was the protestant peasantry that most feared any rise in the status of catholics and was most inclined toward independent action.

During the sixties and seventies of the eighteenth century, the Ulster peasantry organized secret societies known as Oakboys and Steelboys, which protested against the leasing of land to catholics, but directed their energies primarily against the landlords, as did the contemporary catholic secret society in Munster known as the Whiteboys. In both provinces, the landlord-magistrate system of justice was paralysed by secret society terrorism. In Munster, however, landlords organized

In Retrospect

bands of protestant retainers to suppress Whiteboys by extra-legal terrorism, while the Ulster disturbances were, apart from ineffectual gestures by the military, permitted to run their course. A generation later new disturbances broke out in Ulster when the protestant peasantry began daybreak raids to disarm catholic peasants who had acquired arms from the disbanded volunteers. The degree to which these arms had fallen into the hands of the lower classes generally gave seasonal collisions of mobs at fairs and cockfights a serious character. The half-organized gangs taking part in such disturbances were not necessarily formed along denominational lines, and special efforts were made by dissenting clergymen and middle class radicals to prevent the growth of distinct protestant or catholic bands. However, the presence of armed catholics in bands of any kind was disturbing to the protestant peasantry, and rival factions soon broke into denominational groups—the catholic bands taking the name 'Defenders'. The disorders arising out of the raids and clashes between Defender and protestant bands induced Charlemont to reconstitute special protestant volunteer units which secured a temporary tranquillity at the expense of the catholics.

In the face of superior protestant strength, the Defenders grew into a federated society which, by 1791, had branches in the southern counties where their attacks were directed against the landlords in the manner of the Whiteboys. The position of the catholics was strengthened greatly by the catholic relief act of 1793, the disbanding of Charlemont's new volunteers, and the organization of a predominantly catholic militia. As the Defenders set up cells in the militia, disarmed protestant peasants, and made rent collection in the south difficult without effective measures being taken against them by the Castle, a section of the gentry began to think in terms of independent action, while scattered bands of Ulster peasants called Peep O'Day Boys continued their raids and considered organizing a protestant federation along the lines of the Defenders. The early efforts of the gentry to organize a society to put down the Defenders were suppressed by the viceroy who feared that such an organization would lead to another volunteer movement. Yet the government resources were insufficient to prevent the growth of protestant bands which were now being formed by the more respectable elements of the protestant peasantry who were in contact with that section of the gentry most sympathetic to the Orange tradition. It was against this background that the Defenders took advantage of their superior organization to concentrate several thousands of their number in county Armagh in September 1795, thus bringing about the clash at the Diamond.

The organization of the Orange movement which followed this encounter was carried out with virtually no aid from the gentry, and the attacks on catholic dwellings in Armagh during the autumn and winter of 1795–6 were to keep the landlords away from the lodges for a year. These attacks, however, had the effect of convincing the catholics they had nothing to hope for from the government and gentry, and drove them into the camp of the republican United Irishmen whose overtures they had hitherto ignored. The merging of the republican and catholic organizations transformed the Defenders from an agrarian secret society with limited objectives into a revolutionary movement, and provided the middle-class republicans with what soon became an underground army. As the growing strength of republican forces paralysed the landlord-magistrate system of local government, and it soon became apparent that the under-disciplined forces of the crown were inadequate, the leading landlords demanded the right to raise yeomanry corps for local protection. In the autumn of 1796 the Castle, in spite of its distrust of independent action on the part of the gentry, felt compelled to yield. As the new yeomanry force was at first boycotted by republicans and liberals, its ranks were filled largely by Orangemen. The gentry thus found themselves in command of corps of armed Orangemen whose services were indispensable in the face of the revolutionary threat, and felt they must accept the invitation held out to them by the Orange leaders to put themselves at the head of the lodges. A gentlemen's lodge was formed in Dublin which provided the nucleus for the grand lodge of Ireland and placed itself at the head of the Ulster Orangemen while encouraging landlords in the south to form lodges among their protestant tenants.

By the end of 1797 the movement included a substantial section of all the elements benefiting from the 'ascendancy'— the protestant peasantry, the placemen, and the gentry.

In Retrospect

Moreover, lodges were organized among protestants serving in the militia and even in regular and fencible regiments. As the movement grew in strength and respectability, efforts were made to disassociate it from the raids of the early protestant bands and the attacks on catholic dwellings that followed the battle of the Diamond. The leaders of the lodges repudiated violence, making insults to catholics grounds for expulsion from the movement, and there followed some formal exchanges of good wishes between loyal catholics and Orangemen in several parishes in Ulster. Yet in the disarming of the provinces carried out by the military and yeomanry, it was the catholic population that suffered most and they held the Orangemen responsible for the severity of the repressive measures. As a result of this, rumour, fanned by agitation, exaggerated the extent of Orange 'terror' in Ulster to the point where the appearance of Orange badges in the south was accepted by the peasantry as evidence of an impending massacre of catholics. The rebellion that broke out in May 1798 therefore took on more and more the character of a religious war, even though its nominal leaders were, for the most part, men of protestant background influenced by the enlightenment. During the series of incidents that made up the rebellion of '98 there were only token risings in Ulster, the original centre of the United Irish movement, while the character of the rising in Wexford and the natural tendency to rally to the winning side drove many former republicans into the Orange camp.

During the rebellion the Castle not only tolerated Orange lodges in the armed forces but accepted the necessity of arming small bodies of Orangemen organized as such. However, the greatest contribution of the lodges to the Castle was the arousing among all classes of protestants, by an appeal to the tradition of 1690, an Orange spirit which matched, and indeed often exceeded, in zeal and ferocity, the revolutionary spirit to which it was opposed. This spirit carried through the organizing of the yeomanry and revived the morale of poorly-disciplined armed forces whose efficiency had been seriously undermined by United Irish and Defender propaganda and infiltration. Yet however useful the Orange spirit had been during the uprising, it had also played its part in driving the catholic population to revolt; and once the rebellion was broken, it became an em-

In Retrospect

barrassment to the government. The task of disentangling the Castle from its alliance with the Orangemen and arresting the spirit of vengeance unleashed against the rebellious population fell to the Cornwallis administration. Although the viceroy, at the cost of his popularity, managed to check the worst excesses, the Orangemen had become so much involved in the government service that their influence could not be eliminated without dismissing the greater part of the placemen and disbanding the yeomanry and militia. Meanwhile, the Orange grand lodge made further efforts to keep plebeian Orangemen from discrediting the movement by dismissing unruly members and regularizing its constitution and by-laws.

While the movement was thus preparing to entrench itself in the position gained during the rebellion, the lodges were faced with the question of the union. Here they showed themselves to be the heirs of the volunteers as well as the Peep O'Day Boys, for an influential section of Orangemen under the pressure of the Dublin corporation and the gentry opposed union. Although the threat of mass resignations from the yeomanry, posed by Saurin, and resolutions passed by various lodges, aroused the apprehension of the government, the influence exercised by the Castle through the Orange placemen and the absence of strong anti-union sentiment among the Ulster peasantry proved decisive, and the Orangemen, after several futile protests, accepted union. With the passage of union the Orange lodges were reorganized under the titular leadership of peers and parliamentarians who set the tone of the grand lodge and forced into the background the plebeian founders of the movement and the Ulster gentry. Had it not been for Emmet's rebellion and the renewal of war after the brief peace of Amiens, the movement would probably have lost most of the influence it had acquired during the 1798 rebellion. Orangemen were received coldly by the Hardwicke administration, and the disbanding of the militia and yeomanry would have deprived the movement of its greatest source of patronage and prestige. However, the shock of Emmet's rebellion and the renewal of war gave these military formations another fourteen years of vigour in the course of which Orangemen frequently asserted the protestant character of the state by periodic demonstrations that normally included insults to the catholic population. This was tolerated

In Retrospect

by every viceregal administration except that of Bedford from 1805 to 1807, whose ineffectual efforts to break Orange influence only served to underline its strength. At the end of the war, the apparent security of the protestant establishment, with Peel as Irish secretary and Saurin as attorney-general, sapped the vitality of Orangeism. While the grand lodge was virtually dormant, the plebeian lodges in Ulster continued forming Black lodges or inner circles in defiance of grand lodge policy.

In 1819 agrarian disturbances led to a renewed employment of the yeomanry and consequent revival of Orangeism in the course of which the question of Black lodges was settled by a compromise. While Orange leaders were engaged in reorganizing their resurgent movement, the Wellesley administration undertook reforms designed to curtail the protestant ascendancy. As these reforms involved the dismissal of influential Orangemen from government service, it is not surprising that it was the Dublin placemen who took the initiative by staging a violent demonstration against the viceroy in a Dublin theatre. This demonstration was merely the most dramatic episode in a campaign designed to indicate the will of protestant Ireland to resist further concessions to catholics. Although the resolution of the viceroy to exclude Orange influence from the Castle was strengthened by such protests, the emotions they aroused lent force to the Orange revival. However, the viceroy had struck a mortal blow at Orange influence; liberals were given preference over Orangemen at the Castle; the government was openly hostile to Orange demonstrations, and catholics were given greater preference than before. Still more damaging to Orange interests was the re-organization of the constabulary which created a police that displaced the yeomanry as the principal agency for keeping the peace in the countryside. Yet Orange influence survived in local government in Ulster as it did in the Dublin corporation, and could not be eliminated completely even in the Castle administration.

The hostility between the Orangemen and Castle during the Wellesley administration virtually excluded the possibility of government collaboration with the lodges against the rising tide of O'Connell's Catholic Association in the early twenties. However, such collaboration was unnecessary as the existence of a powerful and spirited Orange movement served in some degree to balance the as yet untried strength of O'Connell. Yet neither Wellington, Peel, nor the viceroy considered the lodges as useful allies and in 1825 repudiated their support by consenting to the dissolution of the Orange organization at the same time that they dissolved O'Connell's association. This unequivocal hostility of the government broke the unity and, for a time, the spirit of the movement to the point where the reconstitution of the Catholic Association failed to evoke a parallel revival of Orangeism. Many Orangemen, like Brownlow, considered the movement dead and sought to come to terms with the catholics. Such defections further demoralized the Orangemen and excluded the possibility of effective resistance to O'Connell during the elections of 1826.

Had the lawyers, placemen, and political Orangemen been capable of independent action, these elections might have been followed by a major Orange revival, but the movement was still illegal and the political Orangemen could not act in defiance of the Castle and British government. The passivity of the Orangemen in the face of his election triumphs led O'Connell to assume that Orangeism was a spent force, and he hoped to demonstrate this to the new viceroy, Lord Anglesey, and the British cabinet by having his agent Lawless parade through the border counties of Ulster at the head of the semi-military organization of the Catholic Association called the Liberators. This ill-advised expedition was admirably designed to re-animate the Orange spirit of the Ulster gentry and peasantry which had been dormant only from want of leadership from above or a direct threat from O'Connell. The expedition, which in some respects resembled the movement of the Defenders towards the Diamond in 1795, provided the Ulster protestants with an opportunity to demonstrate their capacity for spontaneous action and created a favourable occasion for another Orange revival. O'Connell was forced to abandon his Ulster project and in the wake of his defeat, the political Orangemen, with support from the ultra tories in Britain, organized the Brunswick clubs. These societies were designed to rally all classes of protestants against catholic emancipation, and by the end of the summer of 1828 included nearly all those attached to the Orange tradition. Although the Brunswick clubs demonstrated the vitality of Orangeism, they were unsatisfactory to ordinary

In Retrospect

Orangemen because they provided neither a means of defeating catholic emancipation nor the attractions of membership in a secret society. Therefore, with the expiration of the act which had dissolved the Irish lodges, the movement was reconstituted in its traditional form in 1828.

The Orange revival that began with the march of Lawless on Ulster continued in force after catholic emancipation. Although the state was no longer committed to the protestant ascendancy, the Ulster Orangemen hoped to enforce an unofficial ascendancy through their own strength, and sought to demonstrate their power in July 12 processions. In their turn, the catholics asserted their right to oppose the 'unlawful' demonstrations of Orangemen by force. Fearing that the July 12 parades would jeopardize the legality of the movement, the Orange peers, headed by the duke of Cumberland who had become titular grand master in 1827, used their influence in the interests of moderation, but they were powerless to restrain the Ulster Orangemen. Although anti-processions acts were passed in the years immediately after catholic emancipation, the authorities were unable to prevent either Orange processions on July 12 or the counter demonstrations of Ribbonmen and the subsequent clashes between the two groups. By 1831, however, the petty incidents that resulted from these processions were overshadowed by the tithe war. In the face of this threat, Melbourne, who was also irritated by O'Connell's repeal movement, undertook to re-arm the yeomanry. The revival of this force was understood by catholic and protestant peasants in Ulster as a government gesture towards the Orangemen and so raised the prestige of the movement that there was a partial revival of Orangeism in a few centres in the south. During this period the lodges were further strengthened by the adherence of a considerable number of episcopalian clergy who saw in them a means of resisting church dis-establishment. After the re-arming of the yeomanry, the Orange grand lodge made more serious efforts to curtail the July 12 processions, but it was only when an Orange magistrate was deprived of his commission of the peace that the Ulster gentry made efforts to disassociate itself from these demonstrations. Yet plebeian Orangemen continued to march on the twelfth and did not hesitate to abuse as 'papists' all police and magistrates who attempted to interfere.

In Retrospect

Apart from processions, the Orangemen irritated the whigs by efforts to oppose the reform bill of 1832 and by their support of Peel's minority government in 1834. However, this was largely the work of the British Orangemen who had gained an influence among a section of tory peers immediately prior to catholic emancipation. Orangeism had taken root in Britain as a result of military lodges formed in British militia regiments and the migration of Irish to the Midlands. It was a purely urban movement organized as a benevolent society and, apart from Lord Kenyon, Bishop Nixon, and a few Midland magistrates, enjoyed no patronage from the upper classes. Kenyon's early efforts to establish an effective gentlemen's lodge in Britain aroused some sympathy among the Orange peers, but was defeated by the storm raised by the radicals in parliament. Although no measures were taken to suppress the Orangemen, the debates in parliament were sufficient to raise doubts about the legality of the movement, and forced the resignation of the duke of York from the office of grand master in 1821. However, on the eve of catholic emancipation, the duke of Cumberland was induced to become grand master and a substantial section of British peers were made Orangemen. At this time the Irish grand lodge had been dissolved and the British leaders were able to offer some degree of moral support to fragments of the scattered Irish movement. The principal effort of Orange peers at this time was the organization of the Brunswick clubs, but in organizing these clubs the Orange tories appear to have made little use of the Orange lodges already established in Britain.

After the passage of the catholic emancipation act, Kenyon and perhaps the duke of Cumberland hoped that the Orange lodges might provide the nucleus for a new party based on ultra-tory principles. Towards this end a half-pay officer, Lieutenant-Colonel Fairman, was employed to re-organize the British movement. Fairman was sent on a special mission which, it was hoped, would induce the tory gentry to take the leadership of the British movement as the gentry in Ireland had done on the eve of the 1798 rebellion. However, while Fairman publicly invited the gentry to come forward and lead the plebeian Orangemen, he found it difficult to assert his own authority over them, and soon concluded that it was not feasible to bring the existing lodges into contact with the gentry. His only solid

In Retrospect

achievement was the establishment of two gentlemen's lodges, one in Glasgow where he attracted members by his association with the duke of Gordon, and one in Yorkshire where he promised a visit from the duke of Cumberland.

During his travels Fairman corresponded with a number of peers interested in Orangeism to whom he made a number of extravagant statements that suggested he considered revolution imminent, and was prepared to take drastic counter measures if he received adequate support. Although he received courteous replies and some expressions of personal sympathy from these tory peers, there is no evidence they showed interest in his projected counter revolutionary measures. It is likely that in addressing plebeian Orangemen he was far less discreet in his language and gave some of them grounds for believing that he was actively engaged in a conspiracy to establish a regency under the duke of Cumberland. These speeches were reported to Hume and Molesworth by disaffected Orangemen some years after Fairman's tour, and Hume seems to have been convinced that there actually was a conspiracy involving the duke of Cumberland and other tory peers. Apart from the evidence he collected against Fairman, Hume had the fact that Orange lodges had existed in various units of the army since the rebellion of 1798. Although such clubs were illegal, there is no evidence that they had any political importance or that they could have contributed much substance to a real conspiracy.

The question raised by the radicals brought about a select committee investigation of the lodges which the Orangemen accepted as a means of clearing themselves of the charges against them. Much of the evidence submitted to the select committee was damaging to the Orangemen, and an air of mystery was created by Fairman's disappearance during the investigation, but no tangible evidence of a conspiracy was presented. The subsequent publication of Fairman's correspondence by Molesworth indicated that the colonel was in need of money, while the possibility that Fairman himself sold some of his letters to Molesworth is not to be excluded. Fairman was a political adventurer with an active imagination and a flamboyant manner of speech who perhaps dreamed and talked of a coup d'etat. It does not appear that he was employed to arrange a conspiracy, but it is a reflection on the judgment of

Kenyon that he was employed at all. Yet the existence of lodges in the army and their obviously illegal character made proof of a conspiracy unnecessary. When it became obvious that parliament was not prepared to let the issue subside, the duke of Cumberland had no choice but to announce the dissolution of the grand lodge. Thus an organization founded by Irish peasants and first headed by an innkeeper was dissolved two generations later by a royal duke.

The Orange lodges in both Great Britain and Ireland were, in theory, organizations of the well-affected dedicated to the preservation of the existing order. In Ireland, where the well-affected among the peasantry felt they had something to defend, they were able to co-operate with the more privileged orders. In Britain the Orange lodges were merely a series of miscellaneous clubs calling themselves loyalists, and hostile to the catholics. No government, whig or tory, regarded Orangeism with anything but suspicion. The tories, in spite of their distrust of popular movements, were inclined to tolerate the Orangemen because they disliked suppressing professed loyalists. The whigs were inclined towards suppression, but until 1836 felt that it was inexpedient. There can be little doubt that the services which the Orangemen pressed on the Castle in 1798 were useful, and that the Orangemen, by the mere existence of their organization, offered the government a last resort should its other resources become exhausted. Yet the Orangemen represented a distinct interest of their own which made them actively oppose any government measures designed to conciliate the catholic majority in Ireland. They were thus both a barrier to revolution and an obstacle to compromise.

BIBLIOGRAPHY

Synopsis

INTRODUCTION	*page* 285
A. ORIGINAL SOURCES	290
I. Manuscript material	290
II. Printed material	291
1. Parliamentary proceedings	291
2. Parliamentary papers	291
3. Letters, speeches, diaries, memoirs and histories	291
4. Newspapers and other periodicals	294
5. Pamphlets	295
B. SECONDARY SOURCES	296

INTRODUCTION

The major manuscript sources for the history of the Orange lodges are to be found in the unpublished Rebellion papers and Westmorland papers in the Irish Public Record Office, the Lake manuscripts and Brunswick Club papers in the National Library of Ireland, the Pelham manuscripts in the British Museum, and the Downshire manuscripts and Anglesey papers in the Public Record Office of Northern Ireland.

The Rebellion papers contain reports sent to Dublin Castle by magistrates in areas affected by the rise of Orangeism, and the instructions from Dublin Castle to the magistrates. They also contain correspondence between various members of the gentry and the Castle, in which the Orangemen are discussed. In the Pelham manuscripts is to be found the correspondence of Chief Secretary Pelham with the military commanders in the north during the years immediately preceding the rebellion of 1798. These manuscripts also contain correspondence between the Castle and the British government, revealing the misgivings and helplessness with which the Irish government

Bibliography

regarded the rise of Orangeism. The Pelham manuscripts are in the British Museum, but typed copies are in the Belfast Public Record Office.

The Downshire manuscripts include correspondence between the influential Ulster nobleman, Lord Downshire, and his estate manager, as well as correspondence with members of the Irish gentry and the Castle. These letters throw particular light on the manner in which the yeomanry was raised during 1796 and 1797. The Westmorland papers (Fane collection) include the correspondence of the viceroy, Lord Westmorland, with members of the British and Irish governments at the time of the formation of the 'protestant party' in 1792–3.

The Lake manuscripts provide a supplement to the Pelham correspondence. They are a collection of 180 letters from General Lake, the military commander in Ulster during the early days of Orangeism, to Brigadier-General Knox, Pelham, and others. They relate principally to the disarming of Ulster, and reveal the attitude of the military and some magistrates towards Orangeism.

The Anglesey papers throw light on the relations between O'Connell and the Castle and show the attitude of the vice-regal administration towards Orangeism and O'Connell's movement from 1828 to 1833. The Brunswick Club papers offer an abundance of newspaper clippings, circulars and proclamations of the Brunswick Clubs during the period immediately preceding catholic emancipation. Additional information on this period is presented in the Hill papers which include the correspondence of Sir George Hill, a parliamentary Orangeman.

In tracing the history of the British Orange lodges and military lodges, the Home Office and War Office papers in the London Public Record Office provide scraps of information on the activities of individual Orangemen. In a special category are the Blacker manuscripts in the Armagh Museum which were written some time after 1840 by Colonel William Blacker, an active participant in early Orangeism. Even when allowance is made for his Orange sympathies and vagaries of memory, Blacker's lengthy narrative offers a rough guide to events at the time of the battle of the Diamond and provides an interesting supplement to his testimony before the parliamentary select committee. The Stowe manuscripts in the Royal Irish Academy provide information on the origin of the Defenders and Peep O'Day Boys, most of which appears to have been taken from Edward Byrne's *An impartial account of the late disturbances in county Armagh 1784–1791*.

Of the printed sources examined, by far the most important are the United Kingdom parliamentary debates and the reports of the parliamentary select committee on Orange lodges in 1835. The Irish parliamentary debates, although carelessly reported, reveal the fluctuating attitude of the gentry on the 'catholic question', and the efforts of Grattan and others to use the 'Orange bogey' as a means of embarrassing the government. The debates also contain a record of the numerous speeches of such prominent Orangemen as Ogle and Duigenan. The United Kingdom parliamentary debates provide an excellent index of the prominence which the Orangemen enjoyed from 1800 to 1836. In some cases, the parliamentary

Bibliography

debates have been supplemented by the more complete reports of parliamentary proceedings offered in London newspapers. As a rule, British newspaper accounts of Orangeism go little beyond a report of the parliamentary proceedings. The speeches in parliament reveal the stand taken by members and cabinet ministers towards the Orange movement, but they contain contradictory and misleading information on the movement itself. This is especially true with regard to statements concerning the size and organization of the movement, as both Orangemen and those demanding suppression of the movement were anxious to exaggerate its strength.

The four select committee reports on the Orange lodges together form the most important single source for the history of the movement after 1800. In the appendices of the reports are copies of the minutes of meetings, financial statements, membership lists, correspondence of officials of the movement, and various rules, regulations, oaths and other material relevant to the history of the lodges. Three of the reports deal with the Irish movement and the fourth with the British and military lodges. The first two are taken up mainly with the testimony of Orangemen, including Colonels William Verner and William Blacker and others prominent in the lodges. They were examined on the nature of the movement, its early history and various incidents involving outrages charged to the Orangemen. As the more important witnesses were called to testify at least twice, their answers to and evasions of very pointed questions are revealing. The third report deals principally with the testimony of men hostile to Orangeism—a captain of police, a physician, a substantial presbyterian farmer who had served on juries, a solicitor of the established church, a catholic barrister, and the estate manager of member of parliament Charles Brownlow—all of whom had long been residents in areas affected by Orangeism, and most were eye-witnesses to incidents involving Orangemen. No conclusion or summary of evidence is offered in the Irish reports, possibly because of differences of opinon among committee members.

In the fourth report dealing with the British and military lodges, a summary is provided which is designed to suggest that the Orangemen were engaged in a dangerous conspiracy. Although the summary does not give a balanced appraisal of the material, the report itself is of great value. Its appendix presents minutes of British grand lodge meetings during the last three years of the movement's existence, as well as correspondence covering the entire period of British Orangeism and the testimony of Lord Kenyon, Colonel Fairman, C. E. Chetwoode and others concerned with British Orangeism. With the reports of 1835 should be considered the 1825 report of the house of lords committee on the state of Ireland. This committee called Colonel William Verner and O'Connell—both at their own request— to give information concerning the Orangemen. Most, but not all, the evidence in this report was repeated in the 1835 reports.

The *Charlemont MSS*, published by the Historical Manuscripts Commission, contain much material relating to the rise of Orangeism of which the most interesting are the letters to Charlemont from Jephson in Armagh and Haliday in Belfast. The *Fortescue MSS*, also published by the Historical Manuscripts Commission, contain the correspondence of Grenville with

Bibliography

Buckingham and others, revealing the whig attitude towards the activities of Orangemen during the Cornwallis administration. The later correspondence of Grenville with Bedford and Grey indicates the whig reaction to the association of the royal dukes with Orangeism.

The letters published in the *Beresford correspondence* have been selected so cautiously that they throw little light on the history of Orangeism. Of other published correspondence, the *Auckland papers*, the *Cornwallis correspondence* and the *Castlereagh correspondence*, if read together, contain nearly all the essential correspondence of the viceroys and chief secretaries with influential Irishmen and Englishmen—both in and out of government—who were most concerned with British policy in Ireland during the 1795–1801 period. This correspondence should logically be supplemented by that of Lord Clare, the chancellor, but unfortunately he chose to have his papers destroyed.

There is an abundance of pamphlet material available on the 1795–1836 period of Irish politics. Most of it is of a polemical nature, and although it sometimes offers useful information about individuals concerned with Orangeism, it too often gives a misleading impression of the strength and influence of the Orange movement. Newspaper accounts of Orange activities are untrustworthy and difficult to evaluate, and require confirmation from independent sources. A contemporary magazine article entitled 'Orange Conspiracy' in the *London and Westminster Review* is of considerable value as it contains Colonel Fairman's letters, but the text of the article itself is interesting only as an example of Molesworth's somewhat sensational journalism.

R. M. Sibbett's *Orangeism in Ireland and throughout the empire* might be called an official history of Orangeism as it was written by an Orangeman and approved by members of the grand lodge. It first appeared in serial form in the *Belfast Weekly News* during the 'Home Rule' agitation prior to the first world war and was published in book form in 1915. The first edition of the two-volume work carries the history of the movement to 1830 while the second edition, published in 1939, was revised by an anonymous 'member of the Order', and includes the later period of Orangeism. Sibbett was in contact with people in possession of old grand lodge resolutions and correspondence relative to the internal history of Orangeism, not to be found elsewhere. He is also the only source on some aspects of the very early history of British Orangeism and it has been assumed that the information he offers on such matters as the numbers held by military lodges and the times and places of founding of lodges is accurate. The same assumption has been made about the information he offers on the subject of the Black lodges and documents relating to the internal history of Orangeism during the 1815–30 period. Most of the material he quotes appears to have been drawn from the select committee reports, and as this has been faithfully reproduced, it is reasonable to assume that similar documents drawn from other sources are authentic. However, Sibbett's history is a rambling narrative in which interesting folklore and excerpts from original documents are mixed with general history of questionable relevance, with little serious attempt at organization. Although Sibbett would hardly trouble to invent

Bibliography

facts or documents, he indulged liberally in 'out of context' quotation and omitted inconvenient evidence. His particular failing is the desire to conceal differences among Irish protestants. For example, a reader having no other source might be left with the impression that Charlemont and Gosford were vaguely sympathetic to Orangeism.

Sibbett acknowledges his debt to early Orange historians and his history incorporates much of their research. Of these, Ogle R. Gowan, the Wexford Orangeman who fostered the early Canadian movement, requires special attention. His *Annals and defense of the Loyal Orange Institution of Ireland*, written in 1825, is also official history, but it is better organized and written closer to the events considered. His later work, *Orangeism: its origin and history*, provides material about Wexford Orangemen during the rebellion. Gowan is an intelligent, if partisan, observer. There is little offered in the works of other Orange historians writing after 1860 that cannot be found in Gowan or Sibbett.

Sir Richard Musgrave, the Orange historian of the 1798 rebellion, was involved in Irish politics during the decade which preceded union. His work has thus the merits and shortcomings of a partisan eye-witness. Another work concerning early Orangeism signed M.P. was probably published about 1829. While it offers a moderately hostile but interesting discussion of the movement, many of the author's observations may be confirmed by independent evidence. The author presents what purports to be an eye-witness account of the battle of the Diamond and although this account fits into the general outline of events in Armagh at the time of the Diamond, it leaves the impression that the initial gathering of the Defenders in September 1795 was defensive, but as indicated in chapter one, there is considerable evidence to the contrary.

Reverend H. W. Cleary's *The Orange Order* was published in 1899. Father Cleary, a catholic, was primarily concerned with the history of Orangeism in Australia and New Zealand and the section of his book dealing with the Irish background of the movement is drawn largely from sources hostile to Orangeism. Cleary was influenced in some instances by the English catholic historian, Francis Plowden. Plowden's voluminous works are a kind of anthology of charges made against Orangemen and collected without much discrimination. Although Plowden was a contemporary of early Orangemen, he did not have a first hand knowledge of Irish politics. His abundant footnotes are often merely personal comments and the authorities cited dubious witnesses, but the appendices in his works are useful and some of his charges can be sustained by independent evidence.

Froude and Lecky discussed Orangeism in their histories of eighteenth century Ireland. Froude reproached the government for not offering the Orangemen whole-hearted support while Lecky entered into a discussion of the Orangemen's relations with the Castle during the rebellion period, but did not attempt to trace the details of the origin of the movement or its internal history.

Bibliography

A. ORIGINAL SOURCES

I. MANUSCRIPT MATERIAL

LONDON

  British Museum
    Pelham correspondence: Add. MSS 33101–13.

  Public Record Office
    Home Office papers: H/O 40/1–2; 50/413; 51/171.
    War Office papers: W/O 3/284; 43/67; 3/126.

DUBLIN

  Public Record Office
    Frazer MSS.
    Higgins letters 620/18/12.
    Rebellion papers (normally kept in the State Paper Office, Dublin Castle).
    State of the country papers 408, 458, 615.
    Westmorland papers, Fane collection (normally kept in the State Paper Office).

  National Library of Ireland
    Brunswick Club papers (MSS 5017).
    Lake correspondence (MS 56).

  Royal Irish Academy
    Stowe MS.

BELFAST

  Public Record Office of Northern Ireland
    Anglesey papers and books (DOD 619).
    Downshire MSS.
    Drennan letters (typescript).
    Hill papers (DOD 642).
    Groves documents (T 808).
    Macartney letters (DOD 572).
    McCance collection (DOD 272).
    Verner papers (T 1023).

ARMAGH

  Armagh Museum
    Blacker MSS (seven volumes).
    Paterson collection.
    Minute-books of Churchill Orange Lodge 162, July 1797–1803, 1802–17.

Bibliography

II. PRINTED MATERIAL

[Place of publication London except where otherwise stated]

1. *Parliamentary proceedings*

The parliamentary register of the history of the proceedings and debates of the house of commons of Ireland, vols vii–xvii, Dublin, 1793–7.

Cobbett's parliamentary history, vols x–xxvi, 1808–13.

Hansard's parliamentary debates, vols xxix–xli, 1814–20; vols i–xxv (new series), 1820–30; vols i–xxxii (third series), 1830–6.

Hansard's parliamentary history of England from the earliest period to the year 1803, vol. xxxvi, 1801–3.

A report on the debate in the house of commons of Ireland, Tuesday and Wednesday, the 22nd and 23rd of January, 1799, on the subject of an union. Dublin, 1799.

2. *Parliamentary papers*

Report from the select committee of the house of lords appointed to enquire into the state of Ireland; more particularly with reference to the circumstances which may have led to disturbances in that part of the United Kingdom, H.L. 1825 [181], ix.

Report from the select committee appointed to enquire into the nature, character, extent and tendency of Orange lodges, associations or societies in Ireland, with the minutes of evidence and appendix, H.C. 1835 [377], xv.

Second report from the select committee appointed to enquire into the nature, character, extent and tendency of Orange lodges, associations, or societies in Ireland, with the minutes of evidence and appendix, H.C. 1835 [475], xvi.

Third report from the select committee appointed to enquire into the nature, character, extent and tendency of Orange lodges, associations or societies in Ireland, with the minutes of evidence and appendix, H.C. 1835 [476], xvi.

Report from the select committee appointed to enquire into the origin, nature, extent and tendency of Orange institutions in Great Britain and the colonies, with the minutes of evidence, appendix and index, H.C. 1835 [605], xvii.

3. *Letters, speeches, diaries, memoirs, and histories*

Auckland, Lord William, *Journal and correspondence*, 4 vols, London, 1861.

Barrington, Sir Jonah, *Historic anecdotes of the legislative union*, London, 1809.

Barrington, Sir Jonah, *Historic memoirs of Ireland*, Dublin, 1833.

Barrington, Sir Jonah, *Personal sketches of his own times*, New York, 1856.

Barrington, Sir Jonah, *The rise and fall of the Irish nation*, Paris, 1833.

Bibliography

Beresford, John, *Correspondence, illustrative of the thirty years of the Irish parliament, selected from his original papers*, ed. William Beresford, 2 vols, London, 1854.
Buckingham, Duke of, *Memoirs of the court and cabinets of George III, from original family documents*, 4 vols, London, 1855.
Burke, Edmund, *Correspondence*, ed. Earl Fitzwilliam, 4 vols, London, 1844.
Byrne, John, *An impartial account of the late disturbances in the county Armagh 1784–1791*, c. 1798.
Castlereagh, Viscount, *Memoirs and correspondence*, ed. Marquess of Londonderry, 8 vols, London, 1848.
Charlemont, Lord, *Manuscripts and correspondence*, 2 vols, Historical Manuscripts Commission, 1891–4.
Cornwallis, Marquess, *Correspondence*, ed. Charles Ross, 3 vols, London, 1859.
Drennan letters, being a selection from the correspondence between W. Drennan and his brother-in-law and sister, Samuel and Martha McTier, during the years 1776–1819, ed. D.A. Chart, Belfast, 1931.
Edgeworth, Maria, *Chosen letters, printed from memoirs of Maria Edgeworth*, London, 1867.
Ellenborough, Lord, *Diary*, ed. Lord Colchester, 2 vols, London, 1881.
Fitzgibbon, John, *Some Fitzgibbon letters, from the Sneyd Muniments in the John Rylands library*, ed. R. B. McDowell, Manchester, 1952.
Fortescue MSS preserved at Dropmore, vol. ix. Historical Manuscripts Commission, 1915.
Fox, Charles J., *Memorials and correspondence*, ed. Lord John Russell, 4 vols, London, 1853.
King George IV, *Letters*, ed. A. Aspinall, 3 vols, Cambridge, 1938.
Gowan, Ogle R., *Annals and defence of the Loyal Orange Institution of Ireland*, Dublin, 1825.
Gowan, Ogle R., *Orangeism: its origin and history*, Toronto, 1859.
Granville, Lord, *Private correspondence between 1782 and 1821*, ed. Lady Granville, 2 vols, London, 1916.
Grattan, Henry, *Memoirs of the life and times*, 5 vols, London, 1839–46.
Grattan, Henry, *Selected speeches to which is added his letter on the union, with a commentary on his career and character*, ed. Daniel Owen Madden, London, 1845.
Greville, Charles F., *Greville memoirs: a journal of the reigns of King George IV and King William IV*, 3 vols, London, 1874.
Hardy, Francis, *Memoirs of the private life of James Caulfeild, earl of Charlemont*, London, 1810.

Bibliography

Hay, Edward, *History of the Irish insurrection of 1798, giving an authentic account of the various battles fought between the insurgents and the king's army, and a genuine history of the transactions preceding that event*, Dublin, 1803.

Latocnaye, M. de, *A Frenchman's walk through Ireland 1796–7*, translated from the French by John Stevenson, Belfast, 1917.

MacNeven, W. J., *Pieces of Irish history, illustrative of the condition of the Catholics of Ireland, and of the origin and progress of the political system of the United Irishmen and of their transactions with the government*, New York, 1807.

Martin, J. C., *Report of a speech delivered at the first general meeting of the Brunswick Constitutional Club of Ireland, 1828*, 1829.

McDonagh, Michael, *The viceroy's post-bag: correspondence hitherto unpublished of the earl of Hardwicke, first lord lieutenant of Ireland after the union*, London, 1904.

McKenzie, W., *History of the Orange Society*, Dublin, 1809.

Melbourne, Viscount William, *Memoirs*, ed. W. M. Torrens, 2 vols, London, 1878.

Moore, Sir John, *Diary*, ed. Major-General Sir J. R. Maurice, 2 vols, London, 1904.

M.P., *The history of Orangeism, its origin, its rise and its decline*, Dublin, c. 1829.

Musgrave, Sir Richard, *Memoirs of the different rebellions in Ireland*, Dublin, 1802.

O'Connell, Daniel, *Correspondence of the liberator*, ed. W. J. Fitzpatrick, 2 vols, London, 1888.

O'Connell, Daniel, *Select speeches*, 2 vols, Dublin, 1868.

Peel, Sir Robert, *Memoirs*, ed. Earl Stanhope and E. Cardwell, 3 vols, London, 1857.

Peel, Sir Robert, *Private papers*, ed. C. S. Parker, 3 vols, London, 1891.

Peel, Sir Robert, *Private papers*, ed. George Peel, London, 1920.

Plowden, Francis, *The history of Ireland from its invasion under Henry II to its union with Great Britain*, 5 vols, London, 1805–6.

Plowden, Francis, *The history of Ireland from its union with Great Britain, in January 1801, to October 1810*, 3 vols, Dublin, 1811.

Report of the trials of Messrs. Hanbridge, Graham, etc. for an alleged conspiracy against the Marquis Wellesley, lord lieutenant of Ireland, 1823.

Richardson, W., *History of the origin of the Irish yeomanry*, Dublin, 1801.

Russell, Lord John, *Early correspondence 1805–40*, ed. Rollo Russell, 2 vols, London, 1913.

Sheil, Richard L., *The speeches of Richard Lalor Sheil, with a memoir by Thomas MacNevin*, Dublin, N.D.

Bibliography

Stanhope, Earl, *Miscellanies*, London, 1863.
Stanhope, Earl, *Life of Pitt*, 3 vols, London, 1854.
Stuart, James, *Historical memoirs of the city of Armagh for a period of 1373 years, comprising a considerable portion of the general history of Ireland*, Newry, 1819.
Taylor, Sir Herbert, *The Taylor papers, being a record of certain reminiscences, letters, and journals in the life of Lieut.-General Sir Herbert Taylor, who at various stages in his career had acted as private secretary to King George III, to Queen Charlotte, and to King William IV*, ed. Ernest Taylor, London, 1913.
Teeling, Charles, *The history of the Irish rebellion of 1798: a personal narrative*, Dublin, 1828.
Tone, T. Wolfe, *Autobiography*, ed. Sean O'Faolain, London, 1937.
Tone, T. Wolfe, *Letters*, ed. Bulmer Hobson, Dublin, 1920.
Tone, T. Wolfe, *Life, written by himself and completed by his son, together with extracts from his political writings*, ed. Bulmer Hobson, Dublin, 1921.
Tone, T. Wolfe, *Life, written by himself and continued by his son, with his political writings....*, 2 vols, Washington, 1826.
Wakefield, Edward, *An account of Ireland*, 2 vols, London, 1812.
Wellesley, Marquis, *Wellesley papers*, 2 vols, London, 1914.
Wellington, Duke of, *Speeches in parliament*, London, 1854.
Wellington, Duke of, *Civil correspondence and memoranda, Ireland from 20 Mar. 1807 to 2 Apr. 1809*, ed. his son, London, 1860.
Wellington, Duke of, *Despatches, correspondence, and memoranda, 1819–32*, ed. his son, 8 vols, London, 1867–80.
Windham, William, *Windham letters*, London, 1916.
Wyse, Thomas, *Historical sketch of the late Catholic association of Ireland*, 2 vols, London, 1829.
Young, Arthur, *Tour in Ireland*, London, 1892.

4. *Newspapers and other periodicals*

Annual Register, vol. lxx. London, 1828, vol. lxxviii. 1837.
Armagh Guardian, 22, 26 Jan. 5, 12 Feb. 1926.
Belfast News-Letter.
British Volunteer, Manchester.
Dublin Evening Post.
Dublin Patriot.
Edinburgh Review, vol. 62. 1835–6.
Faulkner's Dublin Journal.
Hibernian Journal, Dublin.
London and Westminster Review, vol. iii–xxv. April–July 1836.
Morning Chronicle, London.

Bibliography

North Star, Belfast.
Political Register, vol. xlvi. London, 1825.
Protestant Watchman, vol. 1. Dublin, 1848.
The Public Register or Freeman's Journal, Dublin.
The Times, London.
Wheeler Manchester Chronicle.

5. Pamphlets

An address to the duke of Sussex, London, 1813.
Bull, C. P., *The Orange Institution of Ireland*, Dublin, 1830.
Cooke, Edward, *An address for and against an union between Great Britain and Ireland by a friend to Ireland*, Dublin, 1798.
Cupples, S., *The duties of an Orangeman deduced from the nature and principles of their association: a discourse delivered before the Orange Societies of the districts of Lisburn and Belfast, 12 July 1804*, Belfast, 1804.
Doyle, Wesley, *Considerations vitally connected with the present state of Ireland, particularly in reference to the Roman Catholic question and the Orange system*, Scarborough, 1824.
Duigenan, Patrick, *An answer to the address of the Right Honourable Henry Grattan*, Dublin, 1798.
Fitzgibbon, John, *The lord chancellor's speech, 19 Feb. 1798, on the Catholic claims on a motion made by the earl of Moira*, Dublin, 1798.
Giffard, John, *A short address to the members of the loyal associations on the present state of public affairs*, Dublin, 1798.
Knox, Alexander, *Essays on the political circumstances of Ireland written during the administration of the Earl Camden by a gentleman of the North of Ireland*, Dublin, 1798.
Lees, Sir Harcourt, *An address to the Orangemen of Ireland, relative to the late riot at the Theatre Royal*, Dublin, 1823.
An Orangeman's letter to Theobald Mackenzie, Esq., the Catholic Advocate, in reply to calumnies against the Orange Institution, 1799.
Plowden, Francis, *A plain statement of facts*, Reprint Lisburn, 1905.
Recent scenes and occurrences in Ireland: one year of the administration of Marquess Wellesley, in a letter to a friend, London, 1823.
Scrope, G. Poulett, *How is Ireland to be governed? A question addressed to the new administration of Lord Melbourne*, London, 1834.
Stock, Joseph, *A narrative of what passed at Killalla in the County of Mayo and the parts adjacent during the French invasion in the summer of 1798 by an eye-witness*, Dublin, 1800.
Wilson, Richard, *A narrative of various murders and robberies, committed in the neighborhood of the relater, upon the Roman Catholics by a banditti describing themselves as Orangemen*, Dublin, 1808.

Bibliography

B. SECONDARY SOURCES

Aspinall, A., *Politics and the press*, London, 1949.
Bagwell, Richard, *Ireland under the Tudors*, 3 vols, London, 1899.
Bagwell, Richard, *Ireland under the Stuarts and the Interregnum*, 3 vols, London, 1909.
Banks, William, *The Orange Institution of Ireland*, Toronto, 1898.
Benn, G., *A history of the town of Belfast, from earliest times to the close of the eighteenth century*, 2 vols, London, 1877.
Cleary, H. W., *History of the Orange Society*, London, 1899.
Crone, J. S., *Concise dictionary of Irish biography*, Dublin, 1928.
Curtis, E., *A history of Ireland*, London, 1945.
Cusack, Thomas, *Orangeism: its principles, its purposes, and its relation to society, defined and defended*, Belfast, 1875.
Dictionary of national biography, 24 vols, London, 1908–27.
Dunlop, Robert, *A history of Ireland*, Oxford, 1922.
Falkiner, C. Litton, *Studies in Irish history and biography, mainly of the eighteenth century*, London, 1902.
Fawcett, Mrs. L., *Life of Sir William Molesworth*, London, 1901.
Feiling, Keith, *The second tory party 1714–1832*, London, 1938.
Fitzpatrick, W. J., *The Secret service under Pitt*, London, 1892.
Fortescue, Sir J. W., *British army 1783–1802*, London, 1905.
Froude, James A., *The English in Ireland in the eighteenth century*, 3 vols, London, 1872.
Halevy, Elie, *A history of the English people in the nineteenth century: The liberal awakening*, London, 1950.
Inglis, Brian, *Freedom of the press in Ireland 1784–1841*, London, 1954.
Jerrold, Claire, *The early court of Queen Victoria*, London, 1912.
Lecky, W. E. H., *History of Ireland in the eighteenth century*, 5 vols, London, 1892.
Lecky, W. E. H., *History of England in the eighteenth century*, 8 vols, London, 1882.
Leslie, Lt.-Col. J. H., 'The Loyal and Friendly Society of the Orange and the Blew', *Journal of the Society of Army Historical Research*, vi, no. 26, Oct. 1927.
MacAnally, Sir Henry, *The Irish militia 1793–1810*, London, 1949.
McDowell, R. B., *Irish public opinion 1750–1800*, London, 1943.
McDowell, R. B., *Public opinion and government policy in Ireland 1801–46*, London, 1952.
MacDermot, Frank, *Theobald Wolfe Tone, a biographical study*, London, 1939.
MacNevin, Thomas, *History of the volunteers of 1782*, Dublin, 1845.
Madden, Richard R., *The United Irishmen—their lives and times*, 4 vols. Dublin, 1857–60.

Bibliography

Madsen, A., *The Loyal Orange Association—facts and fables: a rejoinder to the Reverend Father Cleary's book 'The Orange Society'*, Melbourne, 1898.

Maxwell, W. R., *History of the Irish rebellion in 1798*, London, 1891.

Morris, W. O'Connor, *Ireland from 1798 to 1898*, London, 1898.

O'Callaghan, J. C., *The Irish in the English army and navy*, Dublin, 1843.

O'Callaghan, J. C., *History of the Irish brigade*, Dublin, 1854.

O'Hegarty, P. S., *History of Ireland under the union 1801–1922*, London, 1952.

O'Brien, R. B. (ed.), *Two centuries of Irish history*, London, 1888.

Rogers, Edward, *The revolution of 1688 and a history of the Orange Association of England and Ireland*, Belfast, 1881.

Rogers, Patrick, *The Irish volunteers and Catholic emancipation 1778–1793*, London, 1934.

Sibbett, R. M., *Orangeism in Ireland and throughout the empire*, 2 vols, Belfast, 1914–5; 2nd ed., London, 1939.

Simms, J. G., *The Williamite confiscation in Ireland 1690–1703*, London, 1956.

Twiss, Horace, *The public and private life of Lord Chancellor Eldon, and selections from his correspondence*, 3 vols, London, 1844.

Walpole, C. G., *A short history of the kingdom of Ireland, from the earliest times to the union with Great Britain*, London, 1882.

Western, J. R., 'Formation of the Scottish militia', *Scottish Historical Review*, xxxiv, Apr. 1955.

Wolsey, W. H., *Orangeism in Portadown district*, Portadown, 1935.

Yonge, C. D., *Life of Robert Banks Jenkinson, second earl of Liverpool*, 2 vols, London, 1868.

APPENDIX A

RULES OF THE ORANGE SOCIETY, 1798

The following are excerpts from the rules of the Orange society revised by the grand lodge of Ireland on 20 Nov. 1798, and cited in *Report on the Orange lodge I*, H.C. 1835 [377], xv. 2:

1. *General declaration of the objects of the Orange Institution*

We associate to the utmost of our power to support and defend His Majesty, George III, the constitution, and laws of this country, and the succession to the throne in His Majesty's illustrious House, being Protestant; for the defence of our persons and properties, and to maintain the peace of our country; and for these purposes, we will be at all times ready to assist the civil and military powers, in the just and lawful discharge of their duty. We also associate in honour of King William III, Prince of Orange, whose name we bear, as supporters of his glorious memory, and the true religion by him completely established; and in order to prove our gratitude and affection for his name, we will annually celebrate the victory over James at the Boyne on the 1st day of July [O.S.] in every year, which day shall be our grand day for ever.

We further declare, that we are exclusively a Protestant association, yet detesting as we do any intolerant spirit, we solemnly pledge ourselves to each other, that we will not persecute or upbraid any person on account of his religious opinion, but that we will, on the contrary, be aiding and assisting to every loyal subject of every religious description.

Appendix A

2. Qualifications requisite for an Orangeman

He should have a sincere love and veneration for his Almighty Maker, productive of those lively and happy fruits, righteousness and obedience to his commands; a firm and steady faith in the Saviour of the world, convinced that He is the only mediator between a sinful creature and an offended Creator. Without those he can be no Christian—of an humane and compassionate disposition, and a courteous and affable behaviour. He should be an enemy to savage brutality and unchristian cruelty; a lover of society and improving company; and have a laudable regard for the Protestant religion, and a sincere regard to propagate its precepts; zealous in promoting the honour of his King and country; heartily desirous of victory and success in those pursuits, yet convinced and assured that God alone can grant them; he should have an hatred of cursing and swearing, and taking the name of God in vain (a shameful practice); he should use all opportunities of discouraging it among his brethren; wisdom and prudence should guide his actions, honesty and integrity direct his conduct, and honour and glory be the motives of his endeavours. Lastly, he should pay the strictest attention to a religious observance of the Sabbath, and also of temperance and sobriety.

3. Obligation of an Orangeman

I . . . do solemnly and sincerely swear of my own free will and accord, that I will, to the utmost of my power, support and defend the present King, George III, and all the heirs of the Crown, so long as he or they support the Protestant ascendancy, the constitution, and laws of these kingdoms; and I do further swear that I am not, nor was ever a Roman Catholic or papist; that I was not, am not, nor ever will be, an United Irishman, and that I never took an oath of secrecy to that society; and I do further swear in the presence of Almighty God that I will always conceal, and never reveal, either part or parts of this that I am about now to receive, neither write it, nor stamp, stain, nor engrave it, now cause it to be done, on paper, parchment, leaf, bark, brick, stone, or anything so that it might be known; and that I am now become an Orangeman, without fear, bribery, or corruption.

Appendix A

4. Marksman obligation

I ... of my own free will and accord, in the presence of Almighty God, do hereby most solemnly and sincerely swear, that I will always conceal, and never reveal, either part or parts of this which I am about to receive, and that I will bear true allegiance to His Majesty, George III, and all the heirs of the Crown, as long as they maintain the Protestant ascendancy, the laws and constitution of these kingdoms; and that I will keep this part of a Marksman from that of an Orangeman, as well as from the ignorant, and so will not make a man until I become Master of a body nor after I am broke; and that I will not make a man or be present at the making of a man, on the road, or behind hedges, and that I will be aiding and assisting to all true Orange honest Marksmen, as far as it is in my power, knowing him or them to be such, and that I will not wrong a brother Marksman, nor know him to be wronged of anything of value worth apprehending, but I will warn and apprize him of it if in my power it lies. All this I swear with a firm and stedfast resolution, so help me God, and keep me stedfast in this, my Marksman obligation.

5. Secret articles of the lodges

i. That we will bear true allegiance to His Majesty, George III, and his successors so long as he or they support the Protestant ascendancy, and we will faithfully support and maintain the laws and constitution of this kingdom.

ii. That we will be true to all Orangemen in all just actions, neither wronging nor seeing him wronged to our knowledge without acquainting him thereof.

iii. That we are not to see a brother offended for six pence or one shilling, or more, if convenient, which must be returned next meeting, if possible.

iv. We must not give the first assault to any person whatever, that may bring a brother into trouble.

v. We are not to carry away money, goods, or anything from any person whatever, except arms and ammunition, and those only from the enemy.

vi. We are to appear in ten hours' warning, or whatever time is required; if possible, but provided it is not hurtful to

Appendix A

ourselves and family, and that we are served with a lawful summons from the master, otherwise we are fined as the company may think fit.

vii. No man may be made an Orangeman without the unanimous approbation of the body.

viii. An Orangeman is to keep a brother's secret as his own, unless in case of murder, treason or perjury, and that of his own free will.

ix. No Roman Catholic can be admitted on any account.

x. Any Orangeman who acts contrary to these rules shall be expelled, and the same reported to all Lodges in this Kingdom and elsewhere.

APPENDIX B

ARMY REGIMENTS HOLDING ORANGE WARRANTS
IN 1830

The following is a list of army regiments holding Orange warrants in 1830, cited in *Report on Orange lodges IV Report from select committee ... in Great Britain*, H.C. 1835 [605], xvii. p. xii.

Warrant No. 30—13th Light Dragoons
,, 31—Royal Sappers and Miners
,, 33—24th Regiment of Foot
,, 58—95th or Rifle Brigade
,, 64—35th Regiment
,, 65—Royal Artillery Drivers
,, 66—43rd Regiment
,, 67—Royal Artillery
,, 77—Royal Horse Artillery
,, 84—42nd Foot (Highlanders)
,, 87—59th Foot
,, 94—Rifle Brigade 2nd Battalion
,, 104—Rifle Brigade
,, 114—21st Foot
,, 125—7th Dragoons
,, 131—16th Light Dragoons
,, 165—51st Light Infantry
,, 181—6th Foot
,, 190—6th Dragoon Guards
,, 204—5th Dragoon Guards
,, 205—Royal Artillery 4th Battalion
,, 232—Royal Artillery 7th Battalion

Appendix B

Warrant No.	238—67th Foot
,,	241—29th Foot
,,	243—Royal Sappers and Miners
,,	248—Royal Artillery 5th Battalion
,,	254—Royal Artillery 6th Battalion
,,	258—94th Foot
,,	260—17th Foot
,,	269—1st Royal Dragoons
,,	207—6th Dragoon Guards

APPENDIX C

ORANGE DISTRICTS AND MEMBERSHIP IN GREAT BRITAIN IN 1830

The following is a list of the Orange districts in Great Britain in 1830, the number of lodges in each district, and the membership, as cited in *Report on Orange lodges IV Report from the select committee... in Great Britain*, H.C. 1835 [605], xvii. app. 20, p. 145.

District	Number of lodges in district	Membership in district
Ayr	10	113
Ashton-under-Lyne	4	
Bury	10	
Bolton	7	
Blackburn	5	95
Barnsley	8	
Bristol	6	
Birmingham	6	
Burnley	5	104
Bradford	18	444
Bilston	3	
Carlisle	4	
Chowbent	8	101
Cambridge	3	
Congleton	3	
Cardiff		
Dumfries	2	16
Edinburgh	5	

Appendix C

District	Number of lodges in district	Membership in district
Elland	3	120
Glossop	6	323
Glasgow	12	
Gloucester	3	
Halifax	8	208
Huddersfield	5	79
Haslingden	6	144
Kidderminster	2	
Kilmarnock		
London	15	
Liverpool	13	
Leicester	4	
Leeds	14	257
Manchester	14	
Middleton	5	
Newcastle-on-Tyne	16	
Norwich	3	
Oldham	6	
Plymouth & Portsmouth Docks	10	
Rochdale	12	339
Ripponden		
Stockport	2	25
Sheffield	4	25
Tredegar	6	
Unattached	93	
Wigan	9	
Woolwich	9	
Winchester	2	
Wilsonstown	2	

INDEX

Abbot, Charles, 141
Abbott, Richard, 15
Abercromby, Ralph, 84–9, 95–6, 110, 198
Age, 262
Aldborough, 3rd earl of, 218
Alexander, Alderman, 179
Altamount, Lord, 30
Althorp, John Charles Spencer, viscount, 211–12, 266
Ancient Britons, 72–3, 77, 151
Ancient Order of Hibernians, 8
Anglesey, Henry William Paget, 1st marquess, 223–5, 227, 229, 232–3, 244, 280
Annesley, Francis Charles, 1st earl of, 146
Antidote, 262
Anti-Defender associations, 76
Anti-procession bills, 246–7, 281
Archdall, General, 198, 212–13, 218
Argyle fencibles, 153
Armstrong, John, 96, 102
Ashton-under-Lyne, 151
Atkinson, Joseph, 17–20, 30, 35
Atkinson, William, 113
Atkinson, Wolsey, 90, 92
Auckland, William Eden, 1st baron, 89, 103, 141
Auriol, Lieutenant Colonel, 183

Ballybay, 228, 240
Bandon, 182–3, 251–2
Bandon, Lord, 182–3

Barclay, Alexander, 11–12
Barnsley, 261
Barrington, Jonah, 2, 76, 124
Bartley, Sergeant, 241
Battle of the Boyne, 2, 102
Battle of the Diamond, 16–18, 29, 30, 35, 40, 61, 113, 116, 153, 277
Bedford, 6th duke of, 178–9, 197, 279
Belfast, 48, 60, 64, 71–3, 77, 83, 86, 97, 99, 100, 134, 146, 183
Belfast News-Letter, 40, 62, 68, 142
Bell, Alexander, 186
Benburb, 11, 14
Bennett, R. N., 211
Beresford family, 23, 28, 35, 60, 76, 85, 90, 93, 103, 109, 122, 217–18
Beresford, John, 128
Beresford, John Claudius, 86, 89, 91, 107, 124, 130, 133, 143, 146, 161, 196, 219
Bexley, Nicholas Vansittart, baron, 231
Blacker, Stewart, 20, 92, 250
Blacker, William, 30, 31, 39, 43, 58, 66, 90, 91, 103, 113, 186, 208, 218, 226, 236, 240, 247
Blayney, Andrew Thomas, 11th baron, 75, 79
Boycott, 9, 248
British Volunteer, 152
Brownlow, William, 20, 38–9, 202–3, 211, 213–14, 220, 280

Index

Brougham, Henry Peter, Baron Brougham and Vaux, 203, 213
Brundes, John, 231
Brunswick clubs, 225–33, 236–8, 250–51, 256, 280, 282
Buccleugh, duke of, 262
Buckinghamshire, John Hobart, 2nd earl of, 89, 109–10, 197, 230
Burdett, Francis, 212
Burke, Edmund, 5, 27
Burke, Richard, 27
Bury, 151
Bushe, Charles, 124

Caledon, 240
Caledon, Lord, 252
Camden, John Jeffreys Pratt, 2nd earl of, 1st marquess, 29, 31, 35, 45, 48–9, 60, 62–3, 65, 84–6, 89, 93, 108, 110, 180, 217
Canning, George, 170–1, 189, 222
Caravats, 181
Carhampton, Henry Lawes Luttrell, 2nd earl of, 15, 31, 35, 46, 68, 84, 110
Carlton Club, 254, 262–4, 266–7
Castle clique, 23–4, 85–6, 89, 109
Castlereagh, Robert Stewart, viscount, 2nd marquess of Londonderry, 99, 103, 108, 113, 120, 124–5, 127, 131–2, 137, 140–1, 145, 170–1, 174, 189
Catholics, in armed services, 106; Association, 140, 204, 210–14, 217, 219, 221–3, 228–30, 251, 279, 280; attacks on processions, 11; attacks on property, 8, 29–30, 36, 38, 48, 73, 79–80, 113–15, 186, 243, 276; Board, 190, 195; Committee, 7, 27–8, 52–4, 58, 178, 189; conventions, 27; hierarchy, 83, 140, 145, 210; loyal addresses, 90, 99, 106, 205; march through Ulster in 1828, 227–9; peasantry, 29, 48, 51–2, 62, 81–2, 107, 110, 138–40, 188, 200, 204, 235; relief, 166, 194, 216, 222–3; relief bill of 1792,

24; relief act of 1793, 24, 76, 118–19, 143, 179, 231, 275; rent, 94, 228; restrictions on, 23
Cavan elections, 212
Chandos, marquess of, 2nd duke of Buckingham and Chandos, 230–1
Charlemont, James Caulfeild, earl of, 7, 10–11, 19, 33, 38, 45–6, 48, 59–60, 72, 83, 94, 112, 132, 220
Chetwoode, C. Eustace, 154, 157, 172–3, 175, 236, 255, 257, 266
Church, established, 13–4, 18, 25, 40, 52, 235, 237, 244, 249, 251, 261–4, 281
Clarence, duke of, 255
Clare, John Fitzgibbon, 1st earl of, 22–3, 28, 52, 60, 85, 89, 108–9, 119–20, 138, 140–1, 143, 146–7, 165, 180
Clare, election in 1828, 223–5, 231–2
Cockburn, Charles, 256
Coercion bills, 138
Committee for Reform in Scotland, 26
Connor, Captain, 183
Constabulary, 147, 188, 200, 209, 217, 221, 242–3, 245, 247, 249, 279
Cooke, Edward, 16, 41–2, 44–5, 47, 72, 82, 86, 94, 98, 108, 120–4, 131, 140–1
Cope, Archibald, 17–19
Cope, Richard, 131
Cornwallis, Charles, 1st marquess, 108–9, 114, 120, 123–5, 128–9, 131–2, 135–7, 140, 145, 278
Costello, Counsellor, 249
Coup d'état, 259, 269–71, 273
Craigie, Laurence, 261, 266
Cromwell, Oliver, 255–6, 272
Cumberland, duke of, 159, 164–6, 179–80, 197, 216, 222, 226, 230–47, 254–9, 261, 263, 266–73, 281–4

Index

Dalrymple, William, 31, 37-9, 43, 85
Darley, Alderman, 196
Dawson, George, 218, 232, 240
Defenders, 8-16, 23-4, 29, 32, 34, 40, 43, 46-9, 52-3, 83, 142, 156, 181, 203, 225, 235, 275-6, 277; convicted, 35; in militia, 7, 13, 56; unite with United Irishmen, 51, 81
Diamond, 14, 16, 29, 146, 280
Dian, 14, 18, 20, 35
Dissenters, 25-6, 48-9, 68, 145
Donegal, Lord, 92, 147
Downshire, Arthur Hill, 2nd marquess of, 36-7, 46, 57, 59-60, 65, 97, 99, 132, 135-7
Dragooning of Ulster, 64, 90, 96, 100
Drennan, William, 126
Dublin, corporation, 24, 165, 177-8, 189, 278; *Evening Post*, 40; *Patriot*, 209
Duff, David, 248
Duigenan, Patrick, 23, 76, 94, 109, 115, 119, 125-6, 130, 140, 143-4, 164, 178, 180, 190-1, 198
Dundas, Henry, 160-1
Dungannon, 20, 31, 59, 66, 74, 79, 246, 249; plan, 41-2, 45

Edinburgh Evening Post, 262
Eldon, John Scott, 1st earl of, 211, 234
Ely, Lord, 121
Emmet, Thomas Addis, 52, 148-9; rebellion, 148-50, 271, 278; appeal to Orangemen, 149
Enniskillen, earl of, 225, 236-7, 239-40; his encounter with Orangemen and Ribbonmen, 241
Eyre, Robert Hedges, 236

Fairman, William Blennerhasset, 255-73, 282-3; address to Carlton Club, 264; circular to pensioners, 266

Fant, 5
Farnham, 2nd earl of, 5th baron, 234
Faulkner's Journal, 58, 62, 121
Fay fencibles, 74
Fife fencibles, 104
Finn, W. F., 267
Fitzgerald, Edward, baron, 25, 52, 82, 96
Fitzgerald, Maurice, 194, 204, 222
Fitzgerald, Vesey, 204, 223-4
Fitzgibbon, John, see Clare, earl of
Fitzwilliam, William Wentworth, 2nd earl of, 28-9, 45, 86, 89, 108, 178, 197
Fletcher, Colonel, 154-8, 171
Forde, Colonel, 220
Forkhill, 11-12, 72
Foster, John, 23-4, 119, 122, 128, 131, 135, 137, 164, 178, 180, 217—8
Foster, Leslie, 219-20, 226, 232
Freeman's Journal, 162
French invasions, 62, 84, 102, 110-12, 217
Friends of Civil and Constitutional Liberty, society of, 167

George III, 41, 118, 141, 143, 164, 168, 172, 179
George IV, prince of Wales, 3, 62, 165-7, 195-6, 216, 230, 233, 254-5, 263, 266-7
Giffard, Harding, 92, 115, 130
Giffard, John, 62-3, 72-3, 178-80, 191, 198
Glasgow Courier, 262
Gordon, Colonel, 160-1
Gordon, duke of, 257-8, 260, 262, 283
Gosford, Lord, 32-8, 42, 94, 131, 220, 229; his address on persecution of catholics, 33
Goulburn, Henry, 198, 212, 221-2
Gowan, John Hunter, 97
Gowan, Ogle, 97
Graham, John, 236

Index

Grattan, Henry, 6, 27–8, 34, 45, 60–2, 76, 118, 126, 132, 137, 140, 145, 166, 178–80, 188, 194
Gray, Samuel, 228–9
Gregory, William, 222, 225
Grenville, William Wyndham, baron, 109, 110, 166, 197
Greville, Charles, 233–4
Grey, Charles, 2nd earl of, 166, 235

Halévy, Elie, 270
Haliday, Edward, 46, 77
Hancock, John, 247–8
Hardwicke, Philip Yorke, 3rd earl of, 141, 144–5, 177–9, 278
Harvey, Bagenal, 98
Hay, Edward, 98
Haywood, Joseph, 258, 269, 273
Hearts of Oak, Oakboys, 4, 5, 7, 9, 274
Hearts of Steel, Steelboys, 5, 7–10, 274
Hertford, 3rd marquess of, Viscount Yarmouth, 46–7, 157, 165–7, 170, 237
Hibernian Journal, 262
Higgins, Francis, 62–3, 131
Hill, George, 79, 125, 180, 203, 221
Hompesch regiment, 106
Horse Guards, 160, 271
Hudson, Edward, 11–12, 48, 72, 83, 112–3
Hume, Joseph, 188, 204, 214, 267–70, 273, 283
Huntly, marquess of, 5th duke of Gordon, 166

Imhoff, Charles, 164
Informers, 63, 71, 82, 95–6, 102, 157
Insurrection acts, 194, 200, 210
Irish garrison, 187, 195, 221, 224, 242

Jacobinism, 167; club, 26; principles, 110
Jackson, Richard, 11
Jebb, Richard, 124

Jerrold, Claire, 270
John Bull, 262
Johnson, Philip, 46–7, 58, 68, 134, 165, 237
Joy, Henry, 222
Kemmis, Thomas, 43
Kent, duke of, 167
Kenyon, Lord, 155, 165–7, 170–5, 230–4, 254–69, 282, 284
Keogh, Joseph, 27, 60, 189
Kernan, Randall, 241
Kildare Place Society schools, 210
Killalla, 110
King, Alderman, 179
Knatchbull, Edward, 231
Knife, J. F., 114
Knights of Malta, 199
Knox, General, 64–9, 72, 75–6, 88, 97, 100
Knox, Thomas, 37, 41–6, 59, 66, 68

Lake, General, 64–7, 71, 73, 76–7, 83, 85–8, 96–7, 103, 108, 110
Lamb, William, see Melbourne
Lane, Thomas, 36, 97
Latouche, David, 23
Lawless, John, 205, 213, 227–30, 238, 249–50, 280–1
Lees, Harcourt, 218, 223–4, 236
Lens, Serjeant, 173
Lever, John, 158
Liberators, 227, 280
Lisburn, 134, 146
Lisnagade, 12
Littlehales, Edward, 184
Liverpool, R. B. Jenkinson, 2nd earl of, 160, 162–3, 191–2, 210
Lofty, William, 186
London and Westminster Review, 269–70, 273
Londonderry, 1st marquess of, 258–9
Loughgall, 9, 16
Loyal associations, 31, 37, 42, 45–6, 76
Luddites, 156–7, 167
Lurgan, 20, 38–9, 77–8, 114, 134, 249

Index

Magistrate system, 9, 15, 34-5, 41, 49, 64, 96, 147; catholic, 201, 217, 246; stipendiary, 200
Maitland, General, 158
Manners, Thomas Manners-Sutton, 1st baron, 222
Markethill, 7
Martial law, 70, 96
Masonic Orange lodge, 3; system, 12, 14, 43, 77, 160, 169, 227; Masons clash with Orangemen, 147
Maxwell, Henry, 212, 223
Maxwell, J. W., 79
Melbourne, William Lamb, 2nd viscount, 222-3, 235, 244-5, 266-7, 281
Methodists, 40
Michel, Major-General, 183
Military incidents, 77-8
Militia, 41, 45-6, 49, 53, 56, 62, 71, 84, 97, 100, 107, 111, 123, 130, 145-8, 278; Armagh, 72, 102; catholic, 55, 102, 275; Cavan, 65, 72, 102; Clare, 184; disbanded, 194; Downshire, 55, 57; Dublin, 73, 97; English, 151-2; Fermanagh, 72, 102; First West York, 160; Irish, 13, 53-5, 111, 149, 151, 184; Kerry, 78; Kilkenny, 111; King's County, 183; Lancashire, 135, 151; Limerick, 55; Longford, 74, 111; loyalty of, 101-2; Monaghan, 71-2, 104, North Cork, 98; Northumberland, 163; officers of, 87-8, 102; protestant 56; Queen's County, 41, 57; Wiltshire, 163
Milton, viscount, 5th earl of Fitzwilliam, 212
Moira, 2nd earl of, 84, 86, 89
Molesworth, William, 269-70, 283
Molyneux, Capel, 118, 220
Monaghan, 79
Montmorris, Viscount, 218
Moore, George, 226

Moore, John, 55, 86-9, 102, 105, 108
Moore, Ogle, 230
Morning Post, 255
Motherwell, William, 261
Murphy, John, 98
Musgrave, Richard, 56, 92, 143-4, 164, 179, 198
McClellan, Baron, 186
McCracken, Henry Joy, 100
McKean, James, 133
McKey, James, 99
MacNeven, William James, 52, 55
McTier, Martha, 126

Nappach fleet, 7, 8, 10
Neilson, Samuel, 123
Newport, John, 174, 192-3
Newry, 72, 77
Nixon, Ralph, 152-9, 162-71, 282
Northern Star, 32, 36, 39, 47, 59, 64-6, 71
Northland, Viscount, 20, 31, 66
Northumberland, 3rd duke of, 233, 242, 249
Nugent, General, 47, 64, 97, 100

Oaths, 64, 70, 77; of allegiance, 103, 105, 171, 175, 207, 262; conditional, 193, 213; extermination of protestants, 214; illegal, 44, 160, 262; Orange, 2, 21, 39, 78; unlawful oaths bill of 1823, 206; United Irish, 68, 70
O'Beirne, Captain, 74
O'Connell, Daniel, 188-9, 196-200, 204-5, 209-11, 217-18, 221-33, 244-5, 249, 253, 280; approves action against Ribbonmen, 201; opposed union, 189, 245
O'Connor, Arthur, 52, 82
Ogle, George, 23, 32, 36, 122, 128, 133, 143, 164, 198
O'Neill, Charles Henry St. John, 1st earl of, 46, 203
O'Neill, Constantine, 186

Index

Orange, addresses to catholics, 90, 106; Antrim lodges, 113, 134, 148; Aldermen of Skinners' Alley, 2, 125; Apprentice Boys, 2; Armagh lodges, 133; attempts to influence press, 262; Black Knights, 199; Black lodges, 79, 115, 141, 195, 279; bogey, 48, 101, 205; Boyne Club, 42; Boys, 14, 20, 34, 38–9, 41, 46, 74, 87; British grand lodge, 153–9, 163, 165–7, 172, 174; clergymen, established church, 218, 237, 281; convictions, 35, 43, 79, 147, 243; Diamond system, 198, 226; lodges disclaim anti-catholic sentiments, 114, 207, 219, 237; dissenters in lodges, 49, 69, 79, 237–8, 258; dissolution of lodges, 208, 215–6, 239, 253, 280; Down lodges, 134, Dublin lodges, 41, 63, 75–6, 82, 90, 109, 122, 133, 200, 276; early clubs, 2; early meetings, 20, 43, 68; established church, members of in lodges, 18, 61, 69–70, 76; expulsions from lodges, 262, 265; extermination oath, 47, 80, 82, 94, 106, 115; fencibles, 111; financial difficulties, 263, 266; gentry support of order, 19, 37, 44, 50–1, 75, 92, 94, 119, 123, 225, 236, 276; Glorious Order of the Boyne, 2; government hostility to lodges, 45, 279; government support of lodges, 34, 40, 45, 51, 74, 76, 81, 112, 159; grand lodge of Ireland, 91, 114–16, 127, 132, 142, 157, 168, 190, 195, 198–9, 207, 209, 212, 215, 237, 246, 276, 281; grand lodge of Ulster, 77–8, 90, 237; grand lodge reconstituted, 236, 281; higher orders, 78–9, 195, 198; hostility to administration, 200; jury, 203; control of justice, 185; immunity from justice, 115, 142, 185–6, 265, 268; legality of lodges, 159, 161–2, 168, 170, 173–5, 192, 195, 208, 239, 268, 282; Loyal and Benevolent Institution, 218, 226, 236; Loyal Order of the Orange and Blew, 3, 36, 154, 167; magistrates, 36, 47, 70, 157, 177, 179, 181, 186, 193, 204, 213–4, 243–4, 281; Middlesex and Surrey lodges, 153, 161; military lodges, 101, 159–60, 193, 268, 270–2, 282; Marksmen, 78; lodges in militia regiments, 57, 71, 87–8, 90–2, 101, 144–5, 148, 163; oath, 21, 168–70, 173, 175, 192, 207, 239; opposition to concessions to catholics, 140, 143; opposition to reform bill of 1832, 235, 249, 258, 282; opposition to union, 123–5, 130, 133, 180, 278; origin of lodges, 1, 16, 17; outrages, 29–30, 34, 36, 44, 49, 66, 73–4, 79–80, 84, 98, 105, 107, 113, 147, 204; parades, 184, 190, 196, 201, 206, 209, 240, 278; Peep O'Day Boys in lodges, 19, 20; petitions, 42, 186, 214, 238, 252; petitions against Orangemen, 212; presbyterians in lodges, 40, 112, 237; principles and rules, 18, 44, 68, 79, 92, 114, 148, 153, 155, 162, 167–70, 190, 192–3, 195, 198, 206, 263–4; Purple order, 78–9, 116, 195, 198; support of repeal, 249, 251, 253; reformers, 250–1, 253, 256, 258, 260, 264; resolutions, 68–70, 92, 113, 127, 133, 148, 153–4, 173, 238; revival in south, 251–2; revival after 1829, 235, 280–1; riots, 146, 152–3, 185, 200, 209, 213, 243; riot in Kilkeel, 185; Maghera riot of 1823, 205; Maghera riot of 1830, 243; Maghery riots of 1830, 243–4; Royal Arch Purple lodges, 195; Royal Cumberland lodge, 261; Royal Gordon lodge, 260–62, 266; Royal Boyne Society, 2,

182; rules forged, 114–15; Scarlet lodges, 195; Scottish lodges, 260; strength, 79, 83, 90, 102, 236, 248, 252; strength in Britain, 230–1, 256, 270; strength exaggerated, 82, 230–1, 256; strength in south, 82; terror, 80–1, 100, 277; Trinity College students, 40–1; twelfth celebrations, 6, 38–9, 51, 77, 145, 152, 183, 199, 206, 208–9, 212, 220–1, 225, 235, 238–53, 281; warrants, 20, 57, 72, 151, 155, 163, 175, 208, 218, 230, 242, 257, 268, 272; yeomanry, 57–8, 67–8, 70, 72, 74, 79, 90, 97–8, 101, 112, 123, 145, 182–4, 188, 213, 229, 245

Orangeism, decline of, 199, 254, 268; growth of in Britain, 151, 153, 159, 259; origin in Britain, 151–2; attacks on by Ministry of All Talents, 178; parliamentary committees on, 215, 267, 283; parliamentary attacks on, 61, 79, 168–9, 171, 174, 192–3, 203–5, 213, 238, 269; in Wexford, 97–8, 251

Orangemen, armed, 69, 95, 98, 103, 113, 150, 276; auxiliaries to regular forces, 81, 95, 101, 103; join Birmingham Political Union, 259; have no influence in yeomanry or with gentry in Britain, 158, 259, 282; in constabulary, 157–8; defended in parliament, 169, 191, 193, 204, 213; Irish members attend Imperial Grand Lodge in London, 256; meet in public houses, 19, 265, 272; in Liverpool, 153, 171; in London, 153–6, 159, 161, 172, 231, 255–6, 260, 270; number of, 39–41, 43, 51, 77, 79, 93, 162, 231, 240, 270; in Oldham, 151; in O'Neiland East, 134; refuse to serve with papists, 59, 182; evade Cumberland's injunction against processions, 239, 247; disclaim responsibility for acts of violence, 114–5, 142

Outrages, 35–6, 52–3, 55, 61, 72, 139; military, 81, 106

Paine, Thomas, 144
Parliamentary protestants, 24
Parnell, Henry, 46, 171, 192–4
Parnell, John, 119, 122
Patriot party, 6
Peel, Robert, 180, 190–4, 198, 214, 217–42, 254, 264, 267, 279–80
Peep O'Day Boys, 7–9, 12–18, 32, 35, 40, 43, 47, 275, 278; presbyterians among, 10
Pelham, Thomas, 34, 41, 46, 49, 59, 64–8, 73, 82, 85–6, 99, 108
Penal code, 4, 9, 189
Perceval, Colonel, 256
Perceval, Lord, 180, 190–1
Peterloo massacre, 157, 171
Petitions, 5, 24, 158, 164–5, 178, 192–3, 196, 212–3, 223, 226, 232–3
Placemen, 23, 62, 75, 109, 119–20, 150, 179, 225, 274–9
Pitt, William, 24, 28–9, 60, 63, 89, 118, 120, 140–1, 145, 178
Plowden, Francis, 47, 164, 188
Plunkett, Randal, 263, 266
Plunkett, William Conyngham, 198, 201–5, 211
Pole, Wellesley, 189
Ponsonby, family, 25, 28, 135
Ponsonby, William, 127, 131–2, 137
Portadown, 39, 240
Portland, William Henry Cavendish-Bentinck, 3rd duke of, 28, 35, 48–9, 60, 63, 73, 92–4, 125, 164, 180
Protestant ascendancy, 4, 69, 113, 150, 168, 178, 180, 191, 198, 200, 238, 248, 274, 279, 281
Protestant associations, 250
Protestant party, 76

Index

Reform agitation, 257
Repeal agitation, 189, 235, 249, 281
Regiments, British, 9th Dragoons, 56; 13th Dragoons, 162; 24th Dragoons, 78; 95th Rifles, 163; Royal Artillery, 104, 145; King William's Regiment, Fourth of Foot, 3
Resolutions, loyal, 77
Revolution, of 1782, 6, 118; society, 26
Ribbonmen, 181–2, 188, 198, 200, 203, 205, 211, 238, 241, 250, 260, 281
Richmond, Charles Lennox, 9th duke of, 180, 186, 189–90, 194
Riot, state of, 9, 158
Rochdale, 151, 264, 266
Rochford, Lieutenant-Colonel, 91
Rockites, 195
Roden, Lord, 220, 251
Rowan, Hamilton, 52, 123
Royal Irish Artillery, 56
Russell, Thomas, 148
Russell, John, 1st earl of, 267–8, 273

Saunders News-Letter, 262
Saurin, William, 122, 126–7, 180–1, 189, 191, 198, 205, 211, 278–9
Scottish fencibles, 53, 56, 66
Scullabogue, 99
Seaver, Thomas, 195, 198
Shannon, 3rd earl of, 121, 127
Shaunavests, 181
Sheares brothers, 96
Sibbett, R. M., 35, 155, 248
Sirr, Charles Henry, 63, 76, 145, 149, 179
Sidmouth, Henry Addington, 1st viscount, 172
Sling, Henry, 195, 198
Sloan, James, 19–20, 31, 35, 68, 90, 142
Stanley, Colonel, 151
Stanley, Edward Geoffrey Smith, 14th earl of Derby, 244

Stanton, Henry, 153–4, 161–2
Staveley, J. F., 263
Stockdale, J. J., 167, 171, 173
Stockport, 151
Stovin, Frederick, 247
Sussex, duke of, 167
Swift, Edmund, 118, 166–7, 191, 263

Tandy, Napper, 6, 52, 111
Taylor, Colonel, 154–7, 166–7, 171–3
Teynham, Lord, 231
Theatre riot, 201–2, 279
Thomond, marquess of, 256
Thorpe, Sheriff, 201–3
Thornton, General, 228–9
Threshers, 181
Times, 166
Tithes, 13, 52, 94, 195, 245, 279; commutation of, 140, 200; war, 181, 235, 237–8, 244, 251, 253
Tone, Theobald Wolfe, 26–8, 52, 107, 109, 111, 126, 138, 141, 144, 189
Trimble, William, 37
Troy, John, 99
True Briton, 262
Ultra-tories, 150, 155, 159, 164, 216–7, 230, 233, 254, 261, 270, 280, 282
Union, 177; catholic attitude towards, 120, 129; legal profession's attitude towards, 121–2; petitions against, 132, 135; presbyterians' attitude towards, 121, 126, 129; repeal of, 139
United Irishmen, 21–85, 93–110, 116, 129, 138–9, 144, 147–9, 156, 175, 257, 271, 276–7; in armed forces, 66, 68; masons, 77; in militia, 56–7, 71, 88, 96; join Orangemen, 77, 83, 99, 104, 130; outrages, 99, 107; number of, 52–3, 80; in south, 83, 95, 100, 107

Index

Verner, James, 17–20, 30, 32–3, 35, 43, 51, 58, 61, 67–8, 73, 75, 92, 131, 187
Verner, John, 154
Verner, Thomas, 17, 76, 91–2, 130, 143, 146–7
Verner, William, 78, 102, 104, 208, 215, 218, 220, 236, 240, 243, 247, 256
Victoria, Princess, 255, 270
Vinegar Hill, 98, 100
Volunteers, 6, 7, 10–12, 22, 24, 33, 50, 65, 103, 130, 147, 149, 193, 275; Orange character of, 6

Waddell, James, 38, 44
Waring, Holt, 37, 39, 43–4, 59, 215
Wellesley, Lord, 197, 200–1, 205, 211, 214, 217–18, 239, 279
Wellington, Arthur Wellesley, 1st duke of, 173–4, 180, 190, 197, 223–4, 229–35, 241–2, 256, 272, 280
Westmorland, John Fane, 10th earl of, 24, 141
Wexford, 101, 190
Whigs, Irish, 25; clubs, 26, 60
Whitbread, Samuel, 169
Whiteboys, 4–5, 9, 12–13, 23–4, 53, 83, 139, 181, 188, 210, 252, 274–5; act, 30, 36, 39
Whiteford, George, 203
Whitworth, Charles, Viscount, 194
Wigan, 151
Wilbraham, Bootle, 158
William Henry, Prince, 3
William of Orange, 2, 41, 160, 212, 219
Wilson, James, 14, 18, 35
Wilson, Richard, 187
Winchelsea, 9th earl of, 231, 234
Wingfield-Stratford, Colonel, 231, 257
Winter, Daniel, 14–9, 31
Wolfe, John, 2nd Viscount Kilwarden, 35, 150
Woodburne, W. A., 155, 173
Worthey, Stewart, 169
Wrecking, 36, 38, 42–3, 47, 240
Wynford, 1st baron, 258
Wynn, Charles Williams, 168–70
Wynne, Watkin Williams, 151

Yeomanry, 45–6, 49, 53, 58, 61, 65, 72–3, 77, 84, 90, 95, 97, 101, 103, 126, 130–2, 135–7, 146–50, 177, 181, 184, 200, 205, 217, 244, 268, 276–81; Armagh, 184; attacks on during tithe war, 246; Bann, 183; Belfast, 104; Dublin, 76, 146; excesses, 65; Mourne, 185; numbers, 60; Omagh, 183; parliamentary attacks on, 204; re-equipped, 245; Scarva, 183
York, duke of, 3, 36, 159, 164–7, 172–5, 180, 197, 216, 222, 239, 255, 282

For Product Safety Concerns and Information please contact our EU representative GPSR@taylorandfrancis.com
Taylor & Francis Verlag GmbH, Kaufingerstraße 24, 80331 München, Germany

www.ingramcontent.com/pod-product-compliance
Lightning Source LLC
Chambersburg PA
CBHW061427300426
44114CB00014B/1581